IMMIGRATION AND OPPORTUNITY

IMMIGRATION AND OPPORTUNITY

Race, Ethnicity, and Employment in the United States

Frank D. Bean
and
Stephanie Bell-Rose
Editors

Russell Sage Foundation
New York

The Russell Sage Foundation

Library of Congress Cataloging-in-Publication Data

Immigration and opportunity: race, ethnicity, and employment in the United States / Frank D. Bean and Stephanie Bell-Rose, editors.

    p. cm.

    Includes bibliographical references and index.

    ISBN 0-87154-123-8 (cloth)   ISBN 0-8715-151-3 (paper)

    1. United States—Emigration and immigration—Economic aspects.

    2. Alien labor—United States.

    3. Afro-Americans—Employment.

    I. Bean, Frank D. II. Bell-Rose, Stephanie.

JV6471.I443 1999

331.'0973–dc21   9-37689

                                          CIP

RUSSELL SAGE FOUNDATION
112 East 64th Street, New York, New York 10021
10 9 8 7 6 5 4 3 2 1

CONTENTS

CONTRIBUTORS

FRANK D. BEAN is professor of sociology and director of the Immigration Policy Research Project at the University of California, Irvine.

STEPHANIE BELL-ROSE was formerly legal counsel and program officer at the Andrew W. Mellon Foundation.

RICHARD D. ALBA is professor of sociology and public policy at the University of Albany.

BARRY EDMONSTON is director of the Population Research Center and professor of urban studies and planning at Portland State University.

WALTER C. FARRELL JR. is professor of social work and associate director of the Urban Investment Strategies Center at the University of North Carolina at Chapel Hill.

MARK A. FOSSETT is professor of sociology at Texas A & M University.

WILLIAM H. FREY is professor of sociology with the Center for Social and Demographic Analysis, State University of New York at Albany, and senior fellow at the Milken Institute, Santa Monica, California.

JENNIFER E. GLICK is assistant professor (research) of sociology and a research associate of the Population Studies and Training Center at Brown University. She will join the faculty of the Department of Sociology at Arizona State University in 2000.

JAMES H. JOHNSON JR. is William Rand Kenan Jr. Distinguished Professor and director of the Urban Investment Strategies Center at the University of North Carolina at Chapel Hill.

KAREN D. JOHNSON-WEBB is a doctoral candidate in the Department of Geography at the University of North Carolina at Chapel Hill.

JOHN R. LOGAN is professor of sociology and public policy and director of the Lewis Mumford Center for Comparative Urban and Regional Research at the University of Albany.

JEFFREY S. PASSEL is principal research associate in the Population Studies Center at the Urban Institute, Washington, D.C.

ALEJANDRO PORTES is professor of sociology and faculty associate of the Woodrow Wilson School of Public Affairs at Princeton University.

MICHAEL J. ROSENFELD is doctoral candidate in the Sociology Department at the University of Chicago.

MARTA TIENDA is Maurice P. During Professor in Demographic Studies and professor of sociology and public affairs at Princeton University, where she also serves as director of the Office of Population Research.

JENNIFER VAN HOOK is assistant professor of sociology at Bowling Green State University.

ROGER WALDINGER is professor of sociology at the University of California, Los Angeles.

MARY C. WATERS is Harvard College Professor of Sociology at Harvard University.

MICHAEL J. WHITE is professor and chair of the Department of Sociology at Brown University. He is also a faculty affiliate of the Brown University Population Studies and Training Center.

FRANKLIN D. WILSON is professor of Afro-American studies and sociology at the University of Wisconsin, Madison.

MIN ZHOU is associate professor of sociology at the University of California, Los Angeles.

ACKNOWLEDGMENTS

Any project that involves the commissioning of numerous research papers and their preparation for publication cannot be completed without the help and support of many individuals and institutions. The present study on the implications of immigration for African Americans and other racial and ethnic minorities in the United States is no exception. We are grateful to have the opportunity here to express what is surely an inadequate measure of thanks to those who contributed in ways large and small to the completion of this endeavor. In particular, we are infinitely grateful for the interest and support of the Andrew W. Mellon Foundation in policy-relevant immigration research in general and in the subject of this inquiry in particular. Without the financial support of the Mellon Foundation, the many strands of research reported in this volume would not have been possible. This book builds on an earlier, related study, also supported by the Mellon Foundation that examined the economic implications of immigration for African Americans. The earlier study became *Help or Hindrance? The Economic Implications of Immigration for African Americans*, edited by Daniel S. Hamermesh and Frank D. Bean.

We have benefited in numerous ways from collaboration with the Urban Institute in Washington, D.C., in the planning and completion of both this and the earlier study. This collaboration involved most especially the advice and counsel of Michael Fix at numerous points in the evolution of both projects, as well as the institute having generously made available its space for project conferences and workshops. The Lyndon B. Johnson School of Public Affairs and the Population Research Center at the University of Texas at Austin provided support of many kinds, including space for workshops and library, computer, and administrative support. The American Academy in Berlin provided an intellectually stimulating environment during portions of the fall and spring semesters of the academic year from 1998 to 1999 for Frank D. Bean to write and lecture on some of the material included in the book.

In addition to institutions, numerous individuals contributed enormously to the betterment and completion of the study. At the Mellon Foundation, Tina Lee, Trecia Canty, and Stephanie Creaturo provided administrative and research assistance. At the University of Texas at Austin, Cecilia Dean, Eve Kleinman, Jenny Frary, and Randy Capps lent valuable administrative and research assistance. Other persons contributed editorial and substantive advice on the introduction to this volume, including Bernard Watson and Cynthia Gibson. At a workshop at the University of Texas, Susan Gonzalez Baker, John Butler, Yanyi Djamba, Christopher Ellison, Rogelio Saenz, Myron Gutmann, Angela James, Art Sakamoto, David Spener, Bryan Roberts, and the contributors to this book supplied extremely useful comments on early drafts of the papers and suggestions for their revision. Also, two anonymous reviewers at the Russell Sage Foundation were very helpful in making comments for revisions. Finally, each of our spouses, Carolyn Boyd and Christopher Rose provided the kind of support and encouragement without which projects like this would falter.

INTRODUCTION

Immigration and Its Relation to Race and Ethnicity in the United States

Frank D. Bean and Stephanie Bell-Rose

This book examines the intersection of immigration and race or ethnicity in the United States in the latter part of the twentieth century. We devote attention primarily to the implications of post–World War II immigration for labor-market and demographic outcomes in the African American population, although some of the book's theoretical and empirical analyses scrutinize these factors for other racial or ethnic minorities, as well. The volume is intended to complement an earlier book that studies the more general economic implications of immigration for African Americans (Hamermesh and Bean 1998). That study found that somewhat lower levels of education and much lower levels of wealth and asset accumulation among African Americans prevent blacks to a considerable extent from deriving the same degree of economic gain from immigration that accrues to majority whites. The findings of still other research document the decline in black employment that has occurred over the past thirty years, even as average black wages have increased (Jaynes 1990). Taken together, these research results raise questions about the nature and extent of the immigration's influence both on black labor-market outcomes, especially employment, and on the size and composition of both the black and the total U.S. populations.

The findings of the research endeavors reported here not only shed light on the degree to which recent immigration has affected African American labor-market and employment outcomes; they also help clarify ongoing debates concerning the current economic status of the black population in the United States, how much it has improved in recent decades, and what factors have affected it. Based on analyses of social science data, some observers, such as Andrew Hacker (1995), have been decidedly pessimistic about the degree of improvement in African American economic status; others, like Abigail and Stephen Thernstrom (1997), have argued that the historical record, at least during most of the twentieth century, justifies

1

more positive and optimistic conclusions. Still other analysts argue that the evidence supports a more dualistic picture, one that involves increasing social and economic bifurcation in the black population generally (Farley 1996), especially in such high-immigration cities as Los Angeles (Grant, Oliver, and James 1996). The present set of studies about immigration and race or ethnicity—which involve research endeavors carried out by some of the country's leading sociologists and demographers on how immigration has affected black employment, occupation, labor-market outcomes, employment niches, self-employment, interpersonal hiring networks, migration patterns, residential segregation, and relative population composition—indicate that immigration and the greater racial or ethnic diversity that it has generated contribute in multiple ways to both positive and negative changes in the employment and demographic situations of African Americans. This research thus supports the idea that the economic well-being of blacks, at least as influenced by immigration, involves mixed results that reflect the dualistic portrait of African American economic progress at the end of the twentieth century.

The new immigration also holds implications for the dynamics of racial and ethnic relations and for public policy in the United States. It is not yet clear, however, whether the increasing racial and ethnic diversity deriving mostly from recent immigration trends will ultimately prove to operate as a cohesive or a divisive force in American society (Suro 1998). It is thus especially important that the country formulate and nurture policies that will help ensure that increasingly sharp racial and ethnic fault lines do not develop as a result of immigration. Analysts must determine the extent to which the economic and humanitarian benefits associated with the country's relatively generous immigration policies over the past thirty years or so are generating a growing need to foster greater socioeconomic opportunities for economically vulnerable individuals least likely to partake of the economic benefits derived from immigration. At least in part because immigration's economic benefits are unevenly distributed throughout the general population, immigration calls attention to those members of American society whose economic status is most precarious, and immigration's composition (now largely Latino and Asian) highlights the importance of addressing the policy domains of immigration and race or ethnicity jointly rather than separately. In this context, careful analysis of public policies designed to improve prospects for socioeconomic mobility is essential.

THE INTERSECTION OF IMMIGRATION
AND RACE OR ETHNICITY

To explore the implications of immigration for racial and ethnic groups in the United States, we must first clarify what we mean by the terms, race and ethnicity. Following the thinking of George M. Frederickson (1988, 3), we define race as a "consciousness of status and identity based on ancestry and color." Dropping the color criterion from this phraseology gives a useful definition of the term ethnicity. Frederickson's definition of race can be fruitfully used to refer to the black population in the United States; but in the cases of the new Latino and Asian immigrant groups, neither the term "race" nor "ethnicity" seems by itself to provide a totally suitable label because it is not clear that "color" is (or is becoming) an attribute that society ascribes to immigrants from Latin America and Asia, at least on a consistent basis. For example, some Latinos view themselves and are seen by others as white, some as brown, and some as black. We thus deliberately use the somewhat imprecise term "race or ethnicity" in the following discussion to refer to groups that distinguish themselves on the basis of ancestry or color (or both).

In thinking about immigration and race or ethnicity, and in particular about how immigration affects the dynamics of racial and ethnic identity in the United States, which in turn may influence racial and ethnic relations, it is important to recall that immigration and race sometimes seem to represent features of the American experience that are very nearly polar opposites, at least as they have been characterized in the postwar period. Few phenomena have so captured the American imagination as immigration, and none has so contradicted American ideals as race (Cose 1992). The image of the successful immigrant enshrined in the Emma Lazarus poem at the base of the Statue of Liberty epitomizes not only the fulfillment of the American dream of equal opportunity and unlimited social mobility but also the capacity of the American nation to offer the oppressed of the world the possibility of both freedom and prosperity. Indeed, the United States is often described as a nation of immigrants, an idea Oscar Handlin elevates to near mythological status by noting that the history of America is synonymous with the history of immigration (Handlin 1973). Numerous books about immigration have incorporated into their titles some variation of the phrase "the golden door," words suggesting the possibility that newcomers and their descendants can achieve a better life in America than the one they left behind (see, for example, Reimers 1985; Waldinger 1996). This essentially optimistic and inclusionary view of immigration still resonates strongly in American culture, even as it is challenged by new concerns that competition for resources and environmental strains might place limits on the country's capacity to absorb new immigrants. The resulting tensions have created ambivalent attitudes about immigration in the 1980s and 1990s, contributing to the development of sometimes seemingly contradictory positions toward immigration, such as adamant opposition to unauthorized migration but support for the continuation of current levels of legal immigration (Bean and Fix 1992).

The matter of race, and more specifically relations between whites and African Americans, falls into a different category, however. If immigration has often symbolized the hopeful and uplifting side of the American experience, the practice of slavery in many of the colonies and subsequent states for the first two and a half centuries after European settlement has constituted a more negative and exclusionary part of the historical picture (Tocqueville 1945). Whereas the incorporation of many strands of immigration into the U.S. economic mainstream represents the success of the American experience, the lack of such full incorporation in the case of the African American population almost one and one-half centuries after the end of the Civil War represents for many observers the country's most conspicuous failure and an indication of the residual power of racial discrimination throughout American society (Fredrickson 1988; Rose 1997). Although social and economic progress among blacks has occurred, the questions of how much, when, how fast, and why are still the subjects of much debate and little consensus (Hacker 1995; Thernstrom and Thernstrom 1997). Even some of the most optimistic observers of the past three decades has not been able to conclude that blacks have reached economic parity with whites or that the prospects of social and cultural integration seem close at hand (see, for example, Glazer 1997). The establishment by President Bill Clinton of the Presidential Initiative on Race and the call for a renewed national dialogue on the topic, focusing primarily on relations between black and white Americans, is merely the most recent manifestation that American achievements fall short of American ideals in this area.

African Americans, of course, were involuntary immigrants to the United States. During the eighteenth century, they were the single largest immigrant group arriving in the country (Berlin 1998). Despite this, their experience cannot be understood as analogous to that of other immigrant groups. Most blacks came to the United States under chattel slavery that bound not only them but also their children to their owners for life (Morgan 1998). The modes of entry and the reception in America of immigrants from Africa were thus especially harsh and debilitating compared with the experience of immigrants from other countries and generally make it impossible to address the experience of blacks in this country as just another chapter in the story of immigration. Nor is it any less an oversimplification to view the difficulties of recent immigrants as just another chapter in the history of racism in the United States.

Although it is misleading to treat the dynamics of immigration and race as essentially similar, neither is it satisfactory to treat race and immigration as completely separate phenomena. Perhaps because slavery has been such a blight on the national historical landscape, it has sometimes been easier to examine race in relatively compartmentalized terms. Thus, David Brion Davis notes that until recently, American historians have tended to study slavery largely in geographically limited ways—as part of the history of the South, for example (Davis 1998). In general, scholars' treatments of immigration have been conspicuous for the omission of any discussion of black perspectives or experience concerning immigration (note Glazer's [1997] observations on this point). Whatever the reasons for such compartmentalization, examples of the tendency to think that immigration and race can be treated as largely separate issues continue even today. Thus, a recent National Academy of Science report argues that immigration to the United States over the past thirty years held few implications for African Americans because most blacks live in different parts of the country from those areas receiving most of the immigrants (Smith and Edmonston 1997). However, when the states of the Deep South are excluded, the geographic distribution of immigrants and blacks does not support the idea that the two groups live largely in different parts of the country and thus are likely to have affected one another.

Part of the tendency to view immigration and race as separate issues in the postwar period may derive from a desire to forget that the two have often been historically conflated, often in ways that do not flatter the recollection. For example, the Chinese Exclusion Act of 1882 forbade the entry of Chinese largely for expressly racist reasons (Reimers 1998). Much has been written recently about the considerable extent to which the immigrants of the nineteenth and early twentieth centuries were often treated as if they were black (Ignatiev 1995; Jacobson 1998). Indeed, a virulent racism has often seemed to provide a handy device to be employed in the service of excluding immigrants when it seemed desirable to do so (Higham 1963). Perhaps the optimism borne of the U.S. victory in World War II and of the strong economy of the 1950s encouraged the idea that immigration and race issues could be approached as separate matters in the latter part of the twentieth century.

If addressing immigration and race issues separately ever made analytical sense, however, it certainly does not in the case of the post-World War II period, during which when the two phenomena have been intertwined in often subtle ways. During those years, American conceptions about immigration and race appear to have been mutually reinforcing, sometimes optimistically and sometimes pessimistically, in a continuing reflection of the country's basic mythological orientation toward each. This mutual interplay also serves as a reminder that popular responses to immigration and racial and ethnic relations, as well as reactions to the public policies that have been contrived to address immigration and racial and ethnic issues, can and do influence one another, sometimes for the better, sometimes for the worse. For example, the participation of blacks in the armed forces of the United States during World War II set the stage for the Civil Rights movement of the 1960s and for the eventual removal of legal barriers to the participation of African Americans in the institutions of American society (Morris 1984; Higham 1997). To a considerable extent the same forces that sought to maximize equal opportunity for blacks through changes in the legal system contributed to the removal in 1965 of the discriminatory provisions of the National Origins Quota Act of 1924 and their replacement with family reunification criteria as the primary basis for the granting of entry visas to immigrants (Reimers 1985).

In similar fashion, the national mythology about the historic experiences of previous immigrants in overcoming hardship and discrimination and in fulfilling the American dream has often seemed to suggest that African Americans might also achieve integration and economic progress if only legal barriers to equal opportunity were eliminated (Glazer 1975). However, although progress has been made, the task of quickly achieving parity between the black and white populations has proved more difficult than the initially optimistic foresaw. Just as popular ideas about the historical experience of immigration raised hopes for black success as a result of the passage of civil rights legislation in Congress during the 1960s, so the slow progress made bridging the divide between black and white has perhaps contributed to the emergence of a more pessimistic assessment about the benefits of immigration for America in the late twentieth century. Moreover, if the optimistic outlook borne of the country's experience with the successful incorporation of earlier immigrants has served to reinforce the hopeful idea that lingering discriminatory barriers to black achievement could be overcome by antidiscrimination policies, then so too did the de facto and de jure expansion of affirmative action policies to millions of recently arrived immigrants contribute to the disillusionment of many Americans with such policies (Fuchs 1995, 1997; Suro 1998).

THE DEMOGRAPHIC AND GEOGRAPHIC ASPECTS OF IMMIGRATION AND RACE

It is in the context of national issues about the extent to which the black population has become fully incorporated into American society that questions about the degree of immigration's recent impact on African Americans hold special resonance. The expectation that immigrants might influence the country in general and blacks in particular derives, in part, from the sheer magnitude of recent immigration. Its volume has not only increased since the end of World War II but has also gained momentum, reaching numbers in the 1990s, when both legal and unauthorized migrants are counted, that are comparable to the previous all-time highs occurring during the first two decades of the twentieth century. The national origins of U.S. immigrants have also changed sharply over the past fifty years. Before 1960, the vast majority came from European countries or Canada (often more than 90 percent when calculated on a per decade basis). Even as late as the 1950s, more than two-thirds (67.7 percent) of all arrivals were from these countries. During the 1960s, however, when family reunification criteria rather than national origin quotas became the basis for allocating entry visas, the composition changed rapidly. By the 1980s, only 12 percent of legal immigrants had originated in Europe or Canada, whereas nearly 85 percent reported origins in Asia, Latin America, or the Caribbean (U.S. Immigration and Naturalization Service 1998; Bean et al. 1997).

These relatively recent changes in the national origins of immigrants have converted the United States from a largely biracial society consisting of a sizable white majority and a small black minority (together with a very small Native American minority of less than 1 percent) into a multiracial, multiethnic society consisting of several racial and ethnic groups. This trend became discernible in the 1950s but began to accelerate in the 1960s. By 1998, more than a quarter of the U.S. population designated itself as either black, Latino, or Asian. The speed with which the Latino and Asian groups have been growing has meant that the proportion of African Americans in the racial and ethnic minority population has been declining. By 1990, blacks were no longer a majority of this population, making up only 48 percent of racial and ethnic minorities. By 1998, their share had fallen to 43 percent.

How much difference immigration per se has made to changing the racial and ethnic mix of the U.S. population and to its overall growth during the twentieth century can be ascertained by examining the contribution of immigration since 1900 to population growth for the major racial and ethnic groups (as distinct from the amount of growth that resulted from any excess of births over deaths among the pre-1900 entrants and native-born members of each of the groups). Barry Edmonston and Jeffrey Passel (1994) find that post-1900 immigration has accounted for about 30 percent of the growth of the total U.S. population since 1900. Even more significant, they find that immigration's contribution to the growth of the various major racial and ethnic subgroups has varied enormously, accounting for nearly all of the growth among Latinos and Asians (85.7 percent and 97.3 percent, respectively) but virtually none of the overall twentieth-century growth among blacks. Interestingly, since 1980 an increasing amount of black immigration from Africa and the Caribbean has begun to change this equation. According to Yanyi Djamba and Frank D. Bean (1998), black immigration accounted for almost a quarter of the population growth among blacks during the 1980s. Immigration during the twentieth century has thus contributed to a decline in the relative size of the black population as a part of the overall racial and ethnic minority population in the United States, although recent increases in black immigration have begun to reverse this trend.

Although the number of new entrants to the United States has risen appreciably over the past thirty years (Bean et al. 1997), raising the percentage of the U.S. population that is foreign born to almost 10 percent by 1998 (U.S. Bureau of the Census 1999), the consequences of immigration depend on, among other things, how the foreign-born population is distributed geographically. The foreign-born population is not evenly dispersed throughout the country. California, New York, Florida, Texas, Illinois, and New Jersey (in that order) receive disproportionately large shares of newcomers—about 70 percent of all foreign-born persons in the United States lived in these states in 1998 (ibid.). Because the African American population is concentrated in the South (in 1997, about 55 percent of blacks resided in the states the Census Bureau calls the South), a region of the country containing relatively few immigrants except in Texas and Florida, it is sometimes thought that immigration exerts little impact on blacks. However, when one tallies Texas and Florida (states containing lots of immigrants) with other states outside the South, the majority of African Americans (about 57 percent) live in parts of the country containing substantial numbers of immigrants.

Further disaggregation reinforces this point. An investigation of the implications of immigration for African Americans must especially examine the structure and process of black employment. Given that blacks continue to be disproportionately concentrated in semiskilled and unskilled jobs (Farley 1996), the large numbers of new immigrants with low levels of education and work skills are particularly salient for African American labor-market outcomes.[1] In the case of immigration's impact on unskilled workers, especially, such impacts are thought to exert their influence through local labor-market dynamics, usually represented in U.S. research studies by variables calculated for metropolitan areas. What does the evidence show about the extent to which blacks and immigrants reside in separate local labor markets? At first glance, the answer seems to be that, to a modest degree, blacks and immigrants do indeed live in different places. Correlating the percentage of blacks in 1990 with the percentage of foreign born across the 175 largest metropolitan areas in 1990 yields a figure of -0.12. However, this figure proves to be entirely a function of including in the set of the metropolitan areas examined cities in the Deep South (Alabama, Georgia, Louisiana, North Carolina, and South Carolina), places containing large black but very small foreign-born populations. With these Deep South cities removed, the correlation is 0.10, indicating just the opposite. In other words, during the 1970s and 1980s, there existed some tendency for immigrants and blacks to concentrate in the same, not in different, places, except in the Deep South. It would thus seem premature to conclude on the basis of the geographic distributions of immigrants and blacks, whether by state or by city, that immigration has few implications for African Americans on account of the geographic distribution of immigrants.

IMMIGRATION AND THE ECONOMIC WELL-BEING AMONG AFRICAN AMERICANS

What can be said about how immigration has affected economic status among African Americans in the postwar period? How and to what degree has immigration directly influenced economic well-being among blacks? How has economic status been affected by affirmative action? To answer these questions, it is necessary to examine connections among immigration, economic trends among blacks, and affirmative action policies. Accordingly, we explore trends in black economic status over the past four or five decades, the role that affirmative action has played in contributing to these trends, and the role that immigration has directly played in contributing to these trends.

Trends in Black Economic Status

Research evidence compiled on wage trends starting in the early 1960s indicates an appreciable narrowing of the gap between black and white wages from 1963 through 1975, with little change occurring in this gap from that point on. In 1994, black mean weekly earnings remained about 12 percent below those of whites, thus representing considerable progress when compared with the gap of more than 43 percent that existed in 1963. However, a stagnation that has occurred since 1975 indicates that progress toward wage parity has been at a standstill. Because blacks and other minorities are less likely to be employed on a stable basis during any given year (Tienda and Hsueh 1996), many blacks have not been able to convert the gains in hourly wages that have taken place into equivalent gains in annual income. Moreover, the probability of employment among blacks has been declining since the early 1970s, especially among black males with a high-school education or less, and the drops have been of substantial magnitude (Jaynes 1990). In 1970, black male employment rates were almost the same as those for white males. By 1985, the employment rate of college-educated black males was 12 percentage points below that of whites (80 percent versus 92 percent), and the employment rate of blacks with less than a high-school education was 23 percentage points lower (53 percent versus 76 percent) (ibid.).

These trends are of even greater concern given that the gap between blacks and whites in the percentage of high-school graduates from eighteen to twenty-four years of age has been growing from near parity in the mid-1970s to as much as 10 percentage points in the mid-1990s (Farley 1996). If this trend continues, progress as measured by increasing ratios of black to white wage rates would be offset by declines in employment, especially among the less educated, the relative numbers of whom may be increasing compared with whites. Stated differently, the economic prosperity of the 1980s and the 1990s has disproportionately benefited those with higher levels of education (Gottshalk 1997), and it is whites who increasingly are located in that category.

Affirmative Action and Black Economic Progress

Given the gains in economic status among African Americans made in the 1960s and early 1970s and the stagnation of further gains thereafter, it is important to ask what role government action played in shaping this trend. The 1964 Civil Rights Act established the Equal Employment Opportunity Commission (EEOC), and employers with at least one hundred workers were required to report the numbers of minorities and women in all classifications of jobs. President Lyndon Baines Johnson in 1965 and President Richard Nixon in 1974, through executive orders, instructed federal contractors "to take affirmative action to ensure that applicants are employed without regard to their race, color, religion, sex, or national origin" [3 C.F.R. 169 202(1)(1974)]. Programs pursuing affirmative action goals have ranged from government procurement regulations that set aside contracts for competitive bidding limited to minority-owned businesses to private-sector efforts such as preferential admissions to colleges and universities and aggressive recruitment efforts to build a more diverse corporate workforce. These efforts complement and extend civil rights statutes enacted by various government bodies to eradicate discrimination.

Government policies contributed significantly to black progress from 1940 through 1973—a period during which there was a clear record of improving average material status of blacks relative to whites. In their seminal work, *A Common Destiny: Blacks and American Society*, Gerald Jaynes and Robin Williams (1989) expound that "purposeful" actions and policies by governments and private actors over several decades made a large difference in the opportunities and conditions of black Americans. Many blacks attained middle-class status because government and private programs enabled them to achieve better education and jobs, both through affirmative action employment and education programs and through enforcement of equal employment opportunity laws (Leonard 1990; Jaynes and Williams 1989). For example, significant improvement in black educational attainment occurred after the passage of the Civil Rights Act of 1964. Among blacks who were the parents of babyboomers—that is, among black people born from the mid-1920s through the mid-1930s—only 45 percent completed high school, whereas 72 percent of whites of the same age did. By contrast, among those blacks born in the decade just after 1964, 75 percent completed high school, narrowing the gap with whites to about 10 percentage points (Farley 1996, 209). Growth in enrollment and completion rates of blacks in colleges and universities in the past three decades is partially attributable to governmental affirmative action policies encouraging institutions of higher education to seek out these individuals and institutional policies designed to increase diversity, as well as the improved preparation of black students and women that came about through enforcement of civil rights laws and school desegregation (U.S. Council of Economic Advisers 1998).

Other evidence also supports the hypothesis that antidiscrimination policies have had positive effects on African Americans (ibid.). One important factor contributing to minority students' economic gains in elementary- and secondary-school performance as measured by the National Assessment of Education Progress from 1970 to 1990 is the quadruple increase in numbers of black parents with college degrees or college experience over this period, reaching 25 percent in the 1990s. After enactment of the Civil Rights Act of 1964, improvement in relative wages was most substantial in the South, where state fair-employment laws were weakest, institutional discrimination greatest, and federal antidiscrimination efforts most focused. Although it appears that there had been some progress in relative earnings of blacks before 1964, the U.S. Council of Economic Advisers (1998) cites evidence that progress accelerated substantially from 1964 to 1973 and that federal attacks on racial exclusion in the South were critical to the acceleration. Blacks moved into several southern industries from which they had previously been excluded, notably textiles.

Increased black employment during the late 1970s in the contracting industry was related to enforcement by the Office of Federal Contract Compliance programs of its requirement that large contractors develop affirmative action programs to remedy underutilization of minorities and women. Affirmative action programs instituted by the Federal Communications Commission (FCC) have encouraged a marked increase in the percentage of minority-owned broadcast and cable television systems. In 1978, 0.5 percent of all licenses were minority owned; by the late 1990s, through the FCC's tax certificate program, nearly 3 percent were (Edley 1996). More generally, affirmative action programs in contract procurement (such as set-aside and sheltered-competition programs) resulted in the number of contracts awarded to minority-owned firms (including, of course, those owned by blacks) increasing by more than 125 percent between 1982 and 1991 (ibid.).

The Economic Impact of Immigration on Blacks

If affirmative action has worked to improve the economic status of blacks, what can be said about the role immigration has played in affecting the economic situations of African Americans? Assessing the economic consequences of immigration for African Americans requires first examining the economic impact of immigration on the entire country. By economic impact, we mean the overall combination of effects resulting from such factors as immigration's impact on jobs and wages and its impact on the prices people pay for goods and services. At this general level, the most authoritative assessment of immigration's economic consequences has been carried out by the National Research Council (NRC) of the National Academy of Sciences (Smith and Edmonston 1997). The council reached two major conclusions: Immigration exerts a positive effect on the U.S. economy overall but only a small adverse impact on the wage and employment opportunities of competing native groups; and immigration benefits high-skilled workers and the owners of capital but not low-skilled workers or those who do not own capital. The report did not delve deeply into the question of the economic implications of immigration for blacks. Fortunately, a recent series of research projects commissioned to examine this question provides relevant evidence (Hamermesh and Bean 1998). When the results of the several studies from this set are taken together, they indicate that recent immigration to the United States appears to have exerted negative effects on the economic situations of African Americans. The impact uncovered by each individual research project was small: If viewed in isolation, none of the individual projects would be thought to constitute strong evidence that immigration generates adverse economic effects on African Americans. As a set, however, the studies provide compelling documentation that the overall positive economic effects of immigration emphasized by the NRC in the country as a whole do not extend to African Americans. This is perhaps not surprising given that the NRC study also found that such benefits were concentrated among the highly skilled and the owners of capital, both of which groups include disproportionately fewer African Americans than whites.

Conclusion

The record with respect to improvements in the economic status of blacks in the United States over the past four decades or so is thus a mixed one. Gains occurred in the late 1960s and early 1970s when civil rights laws and antidiscrimination policies in the form of affirmative action directives helped to lend a positive boost to the economic situations of blacks. Since then, progress has stalled. Without question, much of this stagnation derives from the negative effects of economic restructuring on persons with no more than a high-school education (Smith 1998), a group that includes disproportionate numbers of African Americans. Some of it may also derive from the fact that immigration has, on average, worked against the economic interests of the black community, although the extent to which such a trend may have coincided with the effects of restructuring remains unknown. Whatever the case, researchers now conclude on the basis of the most recent evidence that one of the major forces for the improvements that have occurred in black economic status over the past forty years has been affirmative action (see, for example, Smith 1998).

In general, the economic implications of immigration for African Americans appear less than benign. The fact that gains in black economic status ceased during the high-immigration 1980s and 1990s, after notable gains following passage of antidiscrimination laws and adoption of affirmative action policies in the 1960s and 1970s, encourages the idea that immigration has done little to generate opportunities for economic advancement for native blacks. Moreover, this conclusion is buttressed by the compilation of research evidence indicating that immigration appears to worsen slightly the already precarious economic positions of African Americans, especially those with a high-school education or less. Thus, the racial and ethnic diversification of the Untied States population over the past three decades brought about by immigration, a trend some analysts might have thought would bring advantages to nonwhite minorities, including blacks, seems, at least at this point in time, not to have improved the economic status of African Americans overall; and given recent political and legal developments limiting affirmative action (Bowen and Bok 1998), its current prospects for improving black economic status may be even less than in the past. Analysts should evaluate the many humanitarian, social, and economic benefits of immigration within a context that includes both the arguably small economic price paid by blacks and the appropriate role of policies that promote economic opportunity for vulnerable segments of our society.

THE CHAPTERS IN THIS BOOK

There is no reason to think that blacks are less likely than the members of the general population to experience the impacts of immigration uniformly. Just as persons in the total population with greater access to capital and with higher levels of education are more likely to benefit economically from immigration, so, too, are blacks likely to experience divergent effects depending on their levels of education and capital accumulation. In short, socioeconomic status seems to operate to condition the implications of immigration. Immigration may have worsened the economic situations of those in the population with lower socioeconomic status, including many African Americans. By contrast, immigration seems likely to have fostered economic gain, and perhaps social integration as well, for those with higher socioeconomic status. For example, the increased racial and ethnic intermarriage that has occurred in the United States in recent years (Bean et al. 1997; Berg 1995; Hacker 1995), a trend that may plausibly derive at least in some measure from the increased racial and ethnic diversification of American society, appears more pronounced among minorities with higher levels of education (Qian 1995, 1997; Kalmijn 1993; McLanahan and Casper 1995).

The focus of the present volume is on the employment status and labor-market implications of immigration for racial and ethnic minorities, especially African Americans, a topic that takes on added resonance given the deterioration in employment that has occurred among blacks over the past two decades. That many of the implications of immigration seem to be conditioned by socioeconomic status also suggests that other social-structural and interactional contingencies besides socioeconomic position may be involved in mediating the impact of immigration on African American employment status and structure. The research reported in this book involves a search for such conditions, focusing predominantly on factors operating at the level of the labor market and on the role such factors play in generating both positive and negative immigration consequences among blacks. Thus, we ask; Does increased immigration work to help or hurt the employment situations of native blacks, and, if so, under what conditions? Are there instances where immigrants provide points of comparison in employment outcomes with blacks that seem to suggest that immigration contributes to or ameliorates African American disadvantage? These are the broad kinds of questions addressed by the chapters in this volume.

The first chapter, by Frank D. Bean, Jennifer Van Hook, and Mark Fossett, addresses the question of how social- and spatial-structural conditions in American cities operate to cushion or enhance competitive and complementary relationships between immigrants and native blacks. Drawing upon urban ecological theory, the authors hypothesize that the absence of overlap in social and spatial structures fosters symbiotic working relationships in urban economies between immigrants and native blacks and makes complementary relationships (that is, positive labor-market outcomes of immigration) more likely. Arguing that, in the case of native blacks, an examination of employment is more likely to reveal labor-market effects than are measures of earnings and wages or measures of unemployment, the authors estimate fixed-effects models of the impact of immigration to isolate the influence of what they term "residential autonomy" on the probability of employment of black males. Their results show that the social- and spatial-structural features of cities matter for studying immigration effects in general and that increasing spatial-structural autonomy raises the likelihood that immigration will be associated with rising black employment.

Michael Rosenfeld and Marta Tienda examine the process of immigrant succession into the occupational niches African Americans once dominated and whether this trend enhances or detracts from displaced workers' occupational mobility. Focusing on Mexican immigrants (highly concentrated, geographically, and the largest group of contemporary immigrants) and U.S.-born blacks in three cities—Los Angeles, Chicago, and Atlanta—they find support for both views of the impact of immigration: Immigrants take low-skill jobs away from natives but also help push natives upward in the occupational stratification system. By examining several occupational niches—ranging from those with heavy immigrant influence to those with a total absence of foreign-born workers—Rosenfeld and Tienda discover that occupational niches are undergoing ethnoracial succession, from native control to domination by one or more immigrant groups. Yet even among these niches, by 1990 few showed complete turnover to immigrant control.

At the same time, the researchers find, these transitions, caused by increases in immigration of the unskilled, generally help to improve the occupational mobility of domestic workers. From 1970 to 1990, for example, black employment grew in administrative and managerial, as well as professional and technical occupations, in all locations. The public sector has been largely resistant to labor-market pressure from immigrants, primarily because these jobs exclude noncitizens and require a civil service exam. During the same period, black representation among postal clerks rose in Los Angeles and Chicago, and the number of black women elementary-school teachers doubled in all three cities. As the authors note, "Immigration has been the driving force behind the expansion of school systems in two of the three cities . . . and the important job of teaching these children falls almost exclusively to black and white natives." This suggests that rather than creating a tax burden by requiring more education and services, immigrants not only expand job opportunities for natives but also propel them up the occupational ladder.

Franklin Wilson examines whether employment in ethnic niches enhances labor-market opportunities for urban workers and whether the immigrant share of the workforce of an employment sector is associated with joblessness, low occupational attainment, and low hourly wages. After reviewing 1980 and 1990 data for thirty-two major industry categories and seven occupational categories, stratified within metropolitan areas by ethnicity, Wilson finds that employment in industry- and occupation-based niches of coethnics constitutes a substantial share of the workforce of urban minority workers. At least one in four African American, Asian, and Latino workers are employed in niches dominated by coethnics, with the majority of African Americans located in industries and occupations in which no other group has a niche. Between 1980 and 1990, however, all groups except African Americans experienced an increase in the number of industry- and occupation-based niches; in fact, blacks experienced a decline in the number of niches they occupied.

Unlike other studies, Wilson's finds that a high immigrant share of the workforce in an employment sector in 1980 was associated with joblessness for African Americans and Latinos and with lower occupational status and wages for all groups. Changes in the level of immigration between 1980 and 1990 were associated with greater joblessness for African Americans and lower joblessness for Latinos, lower occupational attainment for blacks and Latinos, and lower hourly wages for members of all groups. Overall, Wilson finds little support for the hypothesis that niche employment offers advantages; in fact, high joblessness, low occupational status, and low wages are associated with employment in niches, with immigrants faring worse than nonimmigrants.

Self-employment has long been touted as a vehicle for enhancing individual and collective economic mobility among ethnic minorities. Previous studies have found that a high self-employment rate for an ethnic or racial group is strongly associated with a high average income for that group. Furthermore, the self-employed earn more on average that wage and salary workers. Compared with other ethnic groups, blacks traditionally have had lower levels of self-employment, the reasons for which continue to be debated. Low levels of self-employment among blacks have been particularly troubling because self-employment has historically been viewed as a route of economic advancement for disadvantaged groups. John Logan and Richard Alba examine whether racial and ethnic groups in two cities—New York and Los Angeles—have been organized into enclaves or niches and the impact these have had on the socioeconomic success of the groups. They show that although whites maintained predominant ownership in many sectors, their ownership has weakened, and that other groups has grown selectively. Mexicans in Los Angeles and Puerto Ricans in New York City, for example, have low levels of self-employment because they are concentrated in certain niches (the public sector for Puerto Ricans and the private sector for Mexicans). However, new immigrant groups—Koreans and Chinese—have established and expanded enclave economies, providing employment to a large share of their group members. New sectoral concentrations have been established by some groups with low levels of ownership, including blacks, who are shifting toward self-employment in sectors where they were already concentrated as workers.

Logan and Alba assert that the payoff from self-employment varies among entrepreneurial groups. Although Koreans, for example, have been most successful, establishing large enclaves and entrepreneurial niches, ultimately they earn less money. Neither blacks nor Mexicans have reaped special rewards from a more entrepreneurial strategy. In light of mixed returns to self-employment and sectoral specialization, these authors assert, it would seem unlikely to offer a solution for those groups, like Mexicans, who find themselves at the bottom of the economic hierarchy. Of all the options they describe, public employment may be the best option, because it has proved so beneficial for blacks and Puerto Ricans.

Alejandro Portes and Min Zhou analyze which factors contribute to self-employment within specific ethnic groups, as well as the effect of immigrant enclaves on African Americans' earnings and their propensity for self-employment. In reviewing census data, the researchers find that self-employed workers have higher average earnings than salaried coethnics. Even when individual characteristics, which can account for a substantial proportion of the variance, are taken into account, they fail to eliminate the positive and significant effect of self-employment. Being married exerts one of the strongest effects on probability of self-employment, except for African Americans—the only group in which married men stand no better chance of becoming entrepreneurs than single men. The presence of children also has a positive net effect for all immigrant groups, except for native whites and blacks. Thus, for African American men, marriage and other family variables bring no measurable returns to entrepreneurship, placing this group at a relative disadvantage. Portes and Zhou also find that immigrants with high levels of human capital are attracted to entrepreneurship in areas of ethnic concentration where opportunities and resources for business creation exist. They argue that these enclaves, however, do not usurp African Americans' economic opportunities but may actually support African American entrepreneurship. Among cities with the largest immigrant enclaves, self-employed African American surpass the average earnings of their salaried counterparts in virtually every case, which suggests that the effects of immigrant business concentration are not deleterious to the economic returns of African Americans.

In addition to ethnic niches and enclaves, immigrants also have established strong networks, which provide them with opportunities to learn about and secure employment in certain industries or sectors. Roger Waldinger argues that such networks are beneficial to immigrants but are often exclusionary to African Americans and others outside the group. To illustrate the dual nature of networks, Waldinger conducted a series of in-depth interviews (in 1993 and 1994) with managers and owners in 230 establishments in Los Angeles and found that such persons rely heavily on network-driven referrals from the Mexican and Central American workforce, especially for entry-level jobs. When hiring for more-skilled jobs, however, businesses tend to use more formalized procedures such as interviews, reference and background checks, and tests. Such formalized screening involves multiple steps, reducing the advantages enjoyed by members of a referral network and severely curtailing its influence. Waldinger asserts that civil service requirements and procedures make government an effective institutional barrier to competition from most immigrants, which is why the same procedures that keep immigrants out of bottom-level public-sector jobs affect less-skilled African Americans similarly. He concludes that immigrants' rich networks can help newcomers, but the repeated action of network hiring favors those with ties to insiders—an outcome that those lacking similar connections, including African Americans, are likely to view as unfair. Bureaucracy, in contrast, may open doors to African Americans that networks close because of an insistence on more formal, objective, screening processes. Still, Waldinger acknowledges, no matter how formalized the process, selection always involves a personal element and may introduce bias, which would unfavorably affect African Americans. Ultimately, network and bureaucracy can both be seen as systems of social exclusion—and their victims are most likely to be black.

In a case study of how immigrant networks can adversely affect African Americans, Mary Waters analyzes the interpersonal and workplace dynamics of a large corporate cafeteria where the workforce was once dominated by African Americans but is now primarily West

Indian. West Indians have a higher labor-force participation rate than African Americans—a trend that has been attributed to both individual factors (West Indians' work ethic or values) and structural elements (selectivity of immigration, structural consequences of immigration, and institutional bias). Waters finds a combination of these factors at play in the company she studied, including network hiring, which gave West Indians greater access to jobs; West Indians' tendency to assess the value of the jobs differently from natives; and white managers' preference for hiring West Indians over African Americans. Immigrants' perceptions of African Americans mirrored those of their white bosses, which contributed to workplace tensions among native-born and immigrant workers. These results, she argues, demonstrate that despite empirical evidence suggesting that immigration does not necessarily take jobs from African Americans or detract from their occupational mobility, explanations for workplace changes that continue to dominate the day-to-day interactions among workers and managers are cultural rather than structural. The danger is that these kinds of perceptions and explanations are often those that find their way into policy debates about immigration, affirmative action, and other issues.

Most discussions of immigration-induced migration emphasize the economic "pushes" and "pulls" of declining Rust Belt and Northeast metropolitan areas, coupled with strong job-generating engines that have evolved in "New South" metropolitan areas such as Atlanta. Somewhat less attention has been given to the impact of immigration on out-migration patterns of African Americans, especially those with low skills, from immigrant-heavy areas outside of the South. This dynamic not only will shape the distribution patterns for blacks, but also hold important implications for the racial and ethnic makeup of these "gateway" regions, which are becoming demographically distinct from other parts of the country. William Frey asserts that the areas experiencing the heaviest immigration flows are also experiencing a selective out-migration of natives, especially African Americans, to other parts of the country where fewer immigrants reside. Using 1990 census data and post-1990 estimates, Frey finds that both blacks and whites tend to out-migrate in response to immigration inflows in high-immigration areas (HIAs). Although the magnitude of the response to immigration is stronger for whites than blacks, the socioeconomic patterns are similar: That is, out-migration patterns are most pronounced among the least educated segments of the population for both whites and blacks from high-immigration states. Also, both poor whites and blacks are more "push-oriented" in their out-migration patterns, moving away from the high-immigration states and toward more diffuse destinations that differ from conventional long-distance migration destinations. The greatest impact of immigration-influenced black out-migration is in regional differences emerging in metropolitan areas and states. Both whites and blacks out-migrating from HIAs and high-immigration states are headed toward mostly white, mostly black, or largely white and black metropolitan destinations. Therefore, sharper divisions may emerge between regions receiving large numbers of nonblack immigrant minorities and large stretches of the country that remain largely white or white and black.

Underscoring Frey's assertion that areas with high levels of immigration are experiencing considerable changes, James Johnson, Karen Johnson-Webb, and Walter Farrell review what happens when Latino immigrants move beyond traditional port-of-entry communities into states and communities with little or no experience with Latino immigration. In examining census data, they find no overlap between the states that from 1980 to 1994 had Latino population growth in excess of the national average—Arkansas, Georgia, Iowa, Maryland, Minnesota, Nebraska, Nevada, and Tennessee—and the seven traditional port-of-entry states: California, Arizona, New Mexico, New York, Florida, Texas, and New Jersey. The eight states with the highest rates of increases in the Latino population also had sizable increases in black and Asian populations from 1980 to 1994 but experienced relatively slow white population growth. The authors find that reactions to the Latino newcomers have been mixed: Business leaders are excited about the role immigrants play in local economies and about the emerging market opportunities afforded by their presence. Local citizens, however, have concerns about their effects on the social fabric of communities, and this has led to ethnic tensions and conflicts over schools, jobs, housing, and the like. The researchers suggest that more vigilant action on the part of state and local officials be taken to stem the tide of antagonism and to prevent what has occurred in other cities, such as Los Angeles.

Some believe that recent immigration to metropolitan areas polarizes residential patterns between blacks and whites. Others assert that immigration results in more cross-racial intermingling. Michael White and Jennifer Glick examine the impact of immigration on residential segregation, particularly segregation between blacks and whites, by studying the distribution of thirty-nine major ethnic groups located in 285 metropolitan areas. They find that, generally, the longer a group has been in the United States, the less segregated are its immigrant members and their descendants. However, there are many exceptions to this, especially among African Americans, who are far more segregated than their vintage would indicate. White and Glick also analyze whether the presence of ethnic groups of more recent vintage has exacerbated African Americans' segregation. Using a key social indicator of race relations from 1980 to 1990, they discover that metropolitan areas experiencing a growth in immigrants show lower levels of segregation between blacks and whites. Thus, they find no evidence to suggest that immigration is driving the United States to become a more segregated society.

This trend toward a more multiracial and multiethnic society is likely to continue well into the future, according to demographers Barry Edmonston and Jeffrey Passel. They predict that by the year 2010, Latinos will become the largest ethnic minority group in the nation, and non-Hispanic whites will become less numerous. Blacks will increase substantially in number, but their proportion of the total pouplation will remain the same. Predicting the proportions of ethnic and racial groups in society is complicated by intermarriage and the way in which descendants of intergroup marriages identify themselves. By 2050, for example, the number of Latinos could range between 67 million and 147 million, depending on the self-identification of Latinos with mixed ancestry. The black population could be as large as 55 million by 2040 if mixed-ancestry blacks choose to identify themselves as black. The researchers point out that such blurring of ethnic and racial lines means that definitions and ideas about race may change in the near future, challenging the idea that the assimilation capacity of new immigrants is less than that of earlier waves of immigrants.

THE IMPLICATIONS FOR RACIAL AND ETHNIC RELATIONS AND POLICY

The findings reported in the chapters in this book thus indicate that the increasing racial and ethnic diversity of the population of the United States resulting from immigration is contributing to the emergence of a more complex system of stratification in the country than the one existing in the recent past (since the end of World War II). The presence of so many immigrants adds another dimension of complexity to that system of stratification, one that may operate independently of race and ethnicity. That is, to the degree that immigrants, because of their limited proficiency in English and other characteristics, are channeled into certain sectors of employment, labor-market segmentation along nativity lines, as well as along racial and ethnic lines, may be increasing. Undoubtedly, these two kinds of segmentation overlap to a considerable degree, but the substantially increasing diversity introduced by immigration multiplies the possible dimensions along which segmentation can occur. The findings of the research reported here indicate that it is not yet clear how to conceptualize these structural arrangements. They also indicate that some of these arrangements appear to operate in ways that have positive implications for African American employment (ethnic enclaves and patterns of residential autonomy, for example), whereas others seem to operate in ways that have negative employment implications (such as concentrations of ethnic- and immigrant-specific network hiring). An important challenge for future research is to conceptualize these new structural arrangements and to develop theories about their determinants and consequences that clarify the ways through which new immigration affects not only native racial and ethnic minorities but also previous immigrants already in the country.

Theory building also needs to focus on how the new and increased diversity deriving from immigration ultimately operates to affect racial and ethnic identity in the United States. David Reimers (1998) attributes much of the U.S. turn against immigration in the early 1990s to concerns that American identity is becoming fragmented and less Europe oriented. In writing about the implications of Latino immigration for the United States, Roberto Suro (1998) has noted that "identity has once again become a problem for the United States, and as before, the crisis or reinvention will create a new identity that embraces the nation's new constituents. The presence of so many Latinos ensures that matters of race and language, of poverty and opportunity, of immigration policy and nationality will be central issues in the process" (321). One possible outcome of the process of identity reformation may be that racial or ethnic status will simply become less relevant as a basis for workplace and occupational stratification as well as other forms of social organization in the United States. Increasing rates of racial and ethnic intermarriage over the past two decades provides an example of trends consistent with this possibility (Bean et al. 1997). Such phenomena as the emergence of an interracial political leadership group in Queens, New York, an area of extremely high racial and ethnic diversity during the 1980s and 1990s (Sanjek 1998), and the formation of collaborative organizations such as National Voices for an Inclusive Twenty-First Century show that high levels of diversity may work to foster cooperation and solidarity rather than divisiveness and contention.[2] Ascertaining the conditions under which racial and ethnic diversity is more likely to lead to positive as opposed to negative outcomes thus constitutes a significant topic for further research, one whose findings will have substantial implications for public policy.

Another possibility is that increased diversity will reduce the salience of some dimensions of racial and ethnic stratification but leave others intact, or perhaps even enhanced. In that event, an important question involves the nature of the major racial and ethnic fault lines in American society that will persist or be enhanced. The degree to which such fault lines delineate racial and ethnic divides between whites and nonwhites or between blacks and nonblacks will be especially consequential. The posture the country adopts toward policies designed to enhance opportunity among the disadvantaged may be especially likely to influence the degree to which racial fault lines retain their salient character. Further closures of the gap in socio-economic attainment between African Americans and whites may be slowing or ceasing altogether, particularly with respect to education and perhaps especially in regard to higher education. Some of this change may derive from demographic shifts triggered by immigration, some to the erosion of support for affirmative action. Recent research by Caroline Hoxby (1998) shows that immigration creates "crowding effects" in the use of preferences in granting admission and financial aid in private upper-tier institutions of higher education, thus perhaps diminishing opportunities for native-born African Americans to gain access to prestigious schools and the pathways to status and high income such schools often provide (Bowen and Bok 1998). Elimination of scholarship programs targeting blacks, such as the recent challenge to the Benjamin Banneker scholarship program at the University of Maryland, may lead to diminished opportunities. Several other legal challenges presently working their way through the courts may constrict black educational opportunities further in the future.

Some observers have speculated that part of the political backlash against both immigration and affirmative action results from resentment about the benefits that immigrants have sometimes received from affirmative action policies originally intended to provide support primarily for groups like native-born African Americans (Fuchs 1995). If immigration has contributed to this kind of backlash, it introduces a special element of irony into analyses of the implications of immigration for African Americans. On balance, immigration appears often to have rendered the economic situations of African Americans a bit worse than they otherwise might have been, although the research results reported in this book suggest that the extent to which this occurs varies with social-structural circumstances. Analysts should then consider whether a slowing of black economic progress as a result of immigration may intensify the need for special programs. To the degree that immigration presents blacks with somewhat more difficult circumstances to overcome to improve their economic circumstances, raises at least a couple of questions. Do the generally widespread economic and humanitarian benefits derived from immigration and enjoyed by the larger society provide a rationale for maintaining policies that promote black economic gains in the future? Should generous immigration policies that operate to fulfill societal goals and that provide opportunities for newcomers to pursue the American dream be accompanied by equally forward-looking opportunity enhancement policies designed to improve the chances of economic success among historically disadvantaged groups and others for whom the playing field needs leveling? Careful consideration of these questions, together with the development and implementation of policies designed to increase further economic opportunities among the disadvantaged, might help to bolster a positive national mythology both about immigration and about race and ethnicity as the United States moves into the twenty-first century.

NOTES

1. In fact, the educational distribution among recent immigrants is bifurcated, with relatively high proportions of both high- and low-skilled immigrants (see chapter 1 in this volume).

2. National Voices is a coalition involving the National Conference for Community and Justice, the Anti-Defamation League, Leadership Education for Asian Pacifics, the National Council of La Raza, and the National Urban League.

REFERENCES

Bean, Frank D., Robert G. Cushing, Charles Haynes, and Jennifer V. W. Van Hook. 1997. "Immigration and the Social Contract." *Social Science Quarterly* 78(2): 249–68.

Bean, Frank D., and Michael Fix. 1992. "The Significance of Recent Immigration Policy Reforms in the United States." In *Nations of Immigrants: Australia and the United States in a Changing World*, edited by Gary P. Freeman and James Jupp. New York: Oxford University Press.

Berg, Ruth. 1995. *Low Fertility Among Intermarried Mexican Americans: An Assessment of Three Hypotheses*. Ph.D. diss., University of Texas, Austin.

Berlin, Ira. 1998. *Many Thousands Gone: The First Two Centuries of Slavery in North America*. Cambridge: Harvard University Press, Belknap Press.

Bowen, William G., and Derek Bok. 1998. *The Shape of the River: Long-Term Consequences of Considering Race in College and University Admissions*. Princeton: Princeton University Press.

Cose, Ellis. 1992. *A Nation of Strangers: Prejudice, Politics, and the Populating of America*. New York: Morrow Press.

Davis, David B. 1998. "A Big Business." *New York Review of Books* 45(10): 50–53.

Djamba, Yanyi K., and Frank D. Bean. 1998. "African Americans, African Immigrants, and Black Immigrants from Countries South of the United States: Toward an Afro-Labor Queue." University of Texas, Austin, Population Research Center. Unpublished paper.

Edley, Christopher F. 1996. *Not All Black and White: Affirmative Action, Race, and American Values*. New York: Hill and Wang.

Edmonston, Barry, and Jeffrey S. Passel, eds. 1994. *Immigration and Ethnicity: The Integration of America's Newest Arrivals*. Washington, D.C.: Urban Institute Press.

Farley, Reynolds. 1996. *The New American Reality: Who We Are, How We Got Here, Where We Are Going*. New York: Russell Sage Foundation.

Fredrickson, George M. 1988. *The Arrogance of Race: Historical Perspectives on Slavery, Racism, and Social Inequality*. Connecticut: Wesleyan University Press.

Fuchs, Lawrence H. 1995. "A Negative Impact of Affirmative Action: Including Immigrants in Such Programs Flies in the Face of Civil Rights." *Washington Post*, Feb. 25–26, national weekly edition.

———. 1997. "The Changing Meaning of Civil Rights, 1954–1994." In *Civil Rights and Social Wrongs: Black-White Relations Since World War II*, edited by John Higham. University Park: Pennsylvania State University Press.

Glazer, Nathan. 1975. *Affirmative Discrimination: Ethnic Inequality and Public Policy*. New York: Basic Books.

———. 1997. *We Are All Multiculturalists Now*. Cambridge: Harvard University Press.

Gottshalk, Peter. 1997. "Inequality, Income Growth, and Mobility: The Basic Facts." *Journal of Economic Perspectives* 11(2): 21–40.

Grant, David M., Melvin L. Oliver, and Angela D. James. 1996. "African Americans: Social and Economic Bifurcation." In *Ethnic Los Angeles*, edited by Roger Waldinger and Mehdi Bozorgmehr. New York: Russell Sage Foundation.

Hacker, Andrew. 1995. *Two Nations: Black and White, Separate, Hostile, and Unequal*. New York: Ballantine Books.

Hamermesh, Daniel, and Frank D. Bean, eds. 1998. *Help or Hindrance?: The Economic Implications of Immigration for African Americans.* New York: Russell Sage Foundation.

Handlin, Oscar. 1973. *The Uprooted.* Boston: Little, Brown.

Higham, John. 1963. *Strangers in the Land.* New Brunswick: Rutgers University Press.

———. 1997. *Civil Rights and Social Wrongs: Black-White Relations Since World War II.* University Park: Pennsylvania State University Press.

Hoxby, Caroline M. 1998. "All School Finance Equalizations Are Not Created Equal." Working paper series, National Bureau of Economic Research, Cambridge, Mass.

Ignatiev, Noel. 1995. *How the Irish Became White.* New York: Routledge.

Jacobson, Matthew Freye. 1998. *Whiteness of a Different Color: European Immigrants and the Alchemy of Race.* Cambridge: Harvard University Press.

Jaynes, Gerald D. 1990. "The Labor Market Status of Black Americans: 1939–1985." *Journal of Economic Perspectives* 4(4): 9–24.

Jaynes, Gerald D., and Robin M. Williams Jr., eds. 1989. *A Common Destiny: Blacks and American Society.* Washington, D.C.: National Academy Press.

Kalmijn, Matthijs. 1993. "Trends in Black/White Intermarriage." *Social Forces* 72(1): 119–46.

Leonard, Jonathan S. 1990. "The Impact of Affirmative Action Regulation and Equal Employment Law on Black Employment." *Journal of Economic Perspectives* 4(4): 47–64.

McLanahan, Sara, and Lynne Casper. 1995. "Growing Diversity and Inequality in the American Family." In *State of the Union: America in the 1990s,* edited by Reynolds Farley. Vol. 2, *Social Trends.* New York: Russell Sage Foundation.

Morgan, Phillips. 1998. *Slave Counterpoint: Black Culture in the Eighteenth-Century Chesapeake and Lowcountry.* Chapel Hill: University of North Carolina Press.

Morris, Aldon D. 1984. *The Origins of the Civil Rights Movement.* New York: Free Press.

Qian, Zhenchao. 1995. "Changes in American Marriage, 1970–1990: Forces of Attraction, Assortive Mating and Interracial Marriage." Dissertation, University of Pennsylvania. *Dissertation Abstracts International, A: The Humanities and Social Sciences* 55(9): 3002–A.

———. 1997. "Breaking the Racial Barriers: Variations in Interracial Marriage between 1980 and 1990." *Demography* 34(2): 263–76.

Reimers, David M. 1985. *Still the Golden Door: The Third World Comes to America.* New York: Columbia University Press.

————. 1998. *Unwelcome Strangers: American Identity and the Turn Against Immigration*. New York: Columbia University Press.

Rose, Peter I. 1997. *Tempest-Tost: Race, Immigration, and the Dilemmas of Diversity*. New York: Oxford University Press.

Sanjek, Roger. 1998. *The Future of Us All: Race and Neighborhood Politics*. Ithaca: Cornell University Press.

Smith, James P. 1998. "Race and Ethnicity in the Labor Market: Trends over the Short and Long Run." Paper presented at the National Academy of Sciences' Research Conference on Racial Trends in the United States. Oct. 15–16, Washington, D.C.

Smith, James P., and Barry Edmonston, eds. 1997. *The New Americans: Economic, Demographic, and Fiscal Effects on Immigration*. Washington, D.C.: National Academy Press.

Suro, Roberto. 1998. *Strangers Among Us: How Latino Immigration Is Transforming America*. New York: Alfred A. Knopf.

Thernstrom, Stephan, and Abigail Thernstrom. 1997. *America in Black and White: One Nation, Indivisible*. New York: Simon & Schuster.

Tienda, Marta, and Sheri Hsueh. 1996. "Gender, Ethnicity, and Labor-Force Instability." *Social Science Research* 25(1): 73–94.

Tocqueville, Alexis de. 1945. *Democracy in America*. New York: Alfred A. Knopf.

U.S. Bureau of the Census. 1999. *Current Population Survey, 1998: Annual Demographic Files*. CD-ROM data file (CD-CPS98-03 + INPOV). April 21, Atlanta, Ga.

U.S. Council of Economic Advisers. 1998. *Economic Report of the President*. Washington, D.C.: U.S. Government Printing Office.

U.S. Immigration and Naturalization Service. 1998. *1997 Statistical Yearbook of the Immigration and Naturalization Service*. Washington, D.C.: U.S. Government Printing Office.

Waldinger, Roger. 1996. *Still the Promised City?: African Americans and New Immigrants in Postindustrial New York*. Cambridge: Harvard University Press.

PART I

Spatial and Occupational
Structure and Labor Markets

CHAPTER 1

Immigration, Spatial and Economic Change, and African American Employment

Frank D. Bean, Jennifer Van Hook, and Mark A. Fossett

Few issues occupy as prominent a place in the ongoing debate about the impact of immigration in the United States as the question of the degree to which immigration affects the labor-market experiences of native minorities. Interest in this issue arises in part because postwar levels of U.S. immigration have risen substantially over the past thirty years or so, after a long lull during the early to middle part of the century. With the passage of the National Origins Quota Act in 1924, the occurrence of the Great Depression during the 1930s, and the emergence of an unfavorable immigration climate during World War II, immigration to the United States dropped sharply, decreasing from more than seven hundred thousand per year during the first two decades of the twentieth century to less than seventy thousand per year from 1925 through 1945. Since World War II, however, immigration has steadily increased, reaching levels by the late 1980s and early 1990s approaching the all-time highs set in the early part of the century. When the numbers of unauthorized migrants legalized as a result of the 1986 Immigration Reform and Control Act (IRCA) are included in the totals, the levels for 1990 and 1991 exceed all previously recorded highs (U.S. Immigration and Naturalization Service 1996, 25, 34, tables 1 and 4).

Interest in the labor-market consequences of immigration further derives from the fact that many recent immigrants have little education. Although the educational distribution among immigrants shows the same relative concentration of highly educated persons as that among natives, it also reveals a higher proportion of persons with low educational attainment. In 1995, for example, 20.4 percent of both immigrants and natives reported sixteen or more years of schooling; however, 41.2 percent of immigrants, in contrast with 61.5 percent of natives, reported twelve to fifteen years of schooling, and 38.4 percent of immigrants, compared with 18.2 percent of natives, reported fewer than twelve years. Given that African Americans and most native minorities continue to exhibit lower (even if converging) levels of schooling compared with white natives (Farley 1996), research examining the labor-market impacts of immigration on native minorities has special resonance for scholars interested in immigration consequences.

Interest in the impact of immigration on the labor market is also driven by changes in economic conditions that have occurred over the past twenty-five years. Beginning in the early 1970s in the United States, growth in real wages began to level off (Levy 1987, 1995, 1997), unemployment began to rise (Reischauer 1989; Farley 1996), and calls for immigration reform began to emerge (Bean, Telles, and Lowell 1987). From 1970 to 1980, African American unemployment rose from 6.9 to 13.2 percent, compared with an increase from 4.5 to 7.1 percent in the overall population. During the 1980s, when unemployment decreased, it remained high among blacks, at 11.3 percent in 1990 in comparison to 5.5 percent in the entire population (U.S. Department of Labor 1971, 1981, 1991). Given Richard Freeman's (1991) finding that unskilled black workers benefit from relatively tight labor-market conditions, it is not unreasonable to hypothesize that the labor-market effects of immigration on African Americans might depend on the overall vitality and structure of the labor markets within which both immigrants and African Americans seek employment. This possibility is reinforced by the historical observation that black economic opportunities in and migration to northern industrial cities increased during the 1920s and 1950s, when cheap immigrant labor was scarce (Simon 1989; Kuznets 1977).

According to the early empirical research literature, however, the labor-market effects of immigration on African Americans, as with other racial and ethnic minority groups, appear to have been small (Muller and Espenshade 1985; Borjas 1986a; Stewart and Hyclak 1986; Bean, Lowell, and Taylor 1988; Borjas 1987; DeFreitas 1988, 1991; Taylor et al. 1988; Altonji and Card 1991; Lalonde and Topel 1991). But as real wages of less-skilled American workers continued to stagnate and even to decline during the 1980s and early 1990s (Levy 1995; Kosters 1991), and as income inequality has further increased (Juhn, Murphy, and Pierce 1991; Karoly 1992; Levy 1997), a renewed research interest in immigration's effects on the labor market has emerged. Recent analyses of the aggregate economic effects of immigration show that immigration works to benefit those who possess capital and higher skills but extracts an economic cost from those with lower skills, including African Americans (Smith and Edmonston 1997; Borjas 1998). Thus, some researchers find that immigration has contributed to an increase in the earnings gap over the past fifteen to twenty years between low-skilled and high-skilled American workers (Borjas, Freeman, and Katz 1992, 1996), and others find that wage inequality has recently increased by larger amounts in those regions of the country experiencing the greatest immigration (Topel 1994). All of this suggests that the effects of immigration may be more complex than the earlier studies might have indicated.

CONSIDERATIONS INVOLVING RESEARCH APPROACHES

Research that has sought to assess the labor-market effects of immigration has largely relied on the examination of variation in the concentration of immigrants in geographic areas to uncover any impacts. Typically, areas with greater relative numbers of immigrants (or changes therein) are compared with those with lesser concentrations (or changes) to ascertain whether labor-market outcomes (employment, unemployment, hourly wage, weeks worked, or annual earnings) differ (or change) accordingly. The comparisons often involve introducing sophisticated statistical methodologies to try to unravel the degree to which any labor-market differences observed may be effects of other factors (including immigrants' being drawn to areas that pay high wages). Despite the use of a variety of approaches to isolate immigration impacts, some researchers have grown skeptical that area-based approaches can yield satisfactory indications of immigration effects, largely for two substantive reasons. First, any natives adversely affected (in fact or potentially) may move away from (or avoid moving into) impacted areas, thus "arbitraging" any negative effects stemming from immigration (Borjas 1994). Second, over the past couple of decades, immigrants have continued to locate predominantly in areas where previous immigrants reside. Because those areas of the United States with higher income growth in the 1970s tended to exhibit lower growth in the 1980s, relationships between immigration and such labor-market outcomes as income could appear positive in one time period and negative in the other. As George Borjas, Richard Freeman, and Lawrence Katz (1997) argue, "Our finding that the pattern of regional wage changes has shifted drastically over time—while the same regions keep receiving immigrants—suggests that unobserved factors are driving the evolution of the regional wage structure, that these factors have little to do with immigration, and that these factors dominate the data" (19).

Such results drive home the point that area-based studies, to reach their maximum potential, must give particular care to model specification to control for factors that may confound results. For example, previous studies might be inconclusive because they did not adequately take into account the dynamics of local race relations. The sociological and demographic literature repeatedly finds that relative racial-group size affects the degree of social and economic competition between minority and majority groups (Blalock 1967; Frisbie and Niedert 1976; Tienda and Li 1988; Olzak 1992; Beggs, Villemez, and Arnold 1997). The greater the relative size of the African American population in a city, the greater the sense of group threat and racial prejudice on the part of whites (Fossett and Kiecolt 1989; Quillian 1996) and the more likely African Americans are to experience unfavorable labor-market outcomes (for example, lower earnings and higher unemployment). Because recent immigrants have tended to concentrate in cities in the Southwest and in coastal cities that contain relatively smaller numbers of African Americans but relatively larger numbers of Hispanics, the relative sizes of the foreign-born and the African American populations are inversely related across cities in the United States depending on the set of cities examined, as noted previously. Given this, if the effect of relatively larger numbers of foreign-born persons were to worsen (or enhance) African American labor-market outcomes, then the effects of the relative concentrations of African Americans and immigrants would tend to offset one another (or to overlap) and be confounded in research that does not systematically include both variables in statistical models.

Another reason previous studies might be inconclusive is that often they have not adequately taken into account the effects of selective out-migration of native populations. Theory and research show that discouraged and unemployed workers are likely to migrate to areas that offer better labor-market opportunities (see, for example, Ritchey 1975; Borjas 1989). In metropolitan areas characterized by declining opportunities, indicators of job opportunities for a local labor market, such as the unemployment rate, might remain constant or even show improvement if sufficient numbers of unemployed workers moved out of the area. If large influxes of immigrants into local labor markets reduced labor-market opportunities for African Americans and large numbers of consequently unemployed and discouraged African American workers migrated out of areas in response to the reduced opportunities, then statistical models that are designed to measure the labor-market impact of immigration, but do not include controls for out-migration of African Americans, could fail to detect negative impacts of immigration on African American employment experiences.

THEORETICAL CONSIDERATIONS

Economic and Sociological Theory

The impact of immigration on any native group, including African Americans, is viewed by economics and sociology as working in different ways. Economic theories provide a framework within which to analyze the consequences of immigration, but they do not predict whether increasing immigration will have positive or negative impacts (Borjas 1984, 1989, 1990). For economists, ascertaining labor-market effects is thus an empirical matter that requires determination of the extent to which immigrants are either substitutes or complements in the process of production. Immigrants may either compete with native-born workers (that is, substitute for natives) or enhance the productivity of natives (that is, complement natives) (Borjas 1990). Various empirical approaches have been employed to estimate substitution and complementarity effects on labor-market outcomes (Borjas 1990; King, Lowell, and Bean 1986). Within the framework of these approaches, the labor-market outcomes of one labor-input group (such as native African Americans) are generally viewed as a function of the relative concentration and change in size of other labor-input groups (such as immigrants). Findings of negative effects on the labor-market outcomes of such groups as African Americans associated with increasing immigration indicate substitutability, whereas positive effects indicate complementarity.

Unlike economic theory, sociological theory provides more in the way of theoretical bases for predicting positive or negative immigration effects. As outlined classically in the work of human ecologists like Robert Park and Ernest Burgess (1921) and Amos Hawley (1945, 1950), and more recently and explicitly in the work of Fredrik Barth (1956, 1969), Blau (1994), Hawley (1970, 1986) and Susan Olzak (1992),[1] the key theoretical proposition is that complementarity among social groups is enhanced when such groups occupy separate social-structural locations and niches. Because scarce resources often lead to group competition—that is, because two or more racial or ethnic groups may "try to acquire the same valued resources, such as jobs, housing, or marriage partners" (Olzak 1992, 28)—social-structural variables that foster complementarity and mitigate competition are of particular theoretical significance. Complementarity represents what Hawley (1986) terms "symbiosis," and competition what he terms "commensalism." Other things being equal, most especially differences in economic status among groups, the tendency for the division of labor to evolve in the direction of specialization operates to enhance productivity. Competition among socially differentiated groups for scarce resources, however, may override this tendency to the extent that competing groups occupy the same social and spatial structures. Such competition is minimized when groups show little overlap in social- and spatial-structural positions. Symbiosis or commensalism is also more or less likely depending on the extent to which scarce resources (jobs, in the present case) are rendered more or less plentiful and the relative sizes of one of the groups pursuing such scarce resources become relatively larger or smaller.

In the case of immigrants, one way in which a group might function as a complementary source of labor is illustrated by the case of unauthorized migrants. Because of their willingness to fill low-paying, often temporary, jobs at the base of the social hierarchy (Piore 1979; King, Lowell, and Bean 1986), undocumented migrants may play an economic role that is otherwise difficult to fulfill. Their ready availability and flexibility may enhance economic expansion and cushion the shocks of cyclical changes (DeFreitas 1988). Although the wages undocumented workers receive have been found to be a function of their education, experience, and duration of job-specific training (Massey 1987), it is the economic niches they occupy and the employment conditions they are often willing to accept (as compared with those that are acceptable to legal immigrants or natives), as well as the potential increases in demand and productivity that may accompany these, that lead to the possibility that such workers may complement native workers, at least under certain conditions.

Demand in the Local Labor Market

The focus of the present research is on processes of labor-market complementarity and competition and how these are affected not only by the injection of immigrants into local labor markets but also by certain social- and spatial-structural features of the urban locales that are destinations for immigrants. We argue that the degree of complementarity and competition in urban areas are variables rather than constants, and we postulate that the degree of labor-market competition is affected by social- and spatial-structural factors whose level and change may be hypothesized to increase (or decrease) the intensity of group efforts to acquire scarce resources and the tendency of groups to occupy non-overlapping social structures. This approach has much in common with work in sociology that sees social processes (including immigration processes) as affected by social capital and neighborhood effects (Coleman 1990; Portes 1995; Wilson 1987).

Thus, we theorize in the first instance that the strength and vitality of urban labor markets as reflected in the local demand for labor affects the intensity of labor-market competition between immigrants and natives. Specifically, we suggest that the tightness of the local labor market influences the direction and magnitude of immigration effects by affecting competition for scarce resources (jobs or higher wages). To state the matter in economic terms, we note that the fundamental law of factor demand "divides the labor demand elasticity into substitution and scale effects" (Hamermesh 1993, 24). Thus, to the extent that immigrants constitute an exogenous input of labor to a local labor market (and the research literature suggests that this is essentially true [Filer 1992; Bartel 1989]), and to the degree that employers are constantly inclined to substitute less expensive for more expensive labor (which also tends to be true [Hamermesh 1993]), then new immigrants exert two possibly offsetting effects on the wages and employment of other workers. Their arrival increases aggregate demand (the scale effect) and thus the price of labor. At the same time, their arrival increases the possibility of substitution and thus may drive down the price of labor. We hypothesize that the propensity to substitute is constant but that the role of the scale effect varies depending on the tightness of local labor markets. In short, the tighter the labor market, the greater the complementarity. We also hypothesize that complementarity depends on certain social- and spatial-structural features of local labor markets.

Contingencies of Social and Spatial Structures

What are these structural features? During the 1970s and 1980s, the United States shifted from a manufacturing-based to a more information- and services-based economy, with these changes affecting some cities more than others (Sassen 1990). It is well documented that these shifts have been particularly hard on African Americans, especially in the Northeast and Midwest (Holzer and Vroman 1991; Wilson 1987). Moreover, regions and cities vary considerably, not only in their pattern of restructuring (Kasarda 1985, 1989, 1995) but also in the extent to which they receive immigrants (Waldinger 1989). That cities like New York and Chicago during the 1980s experienced both net out-migration and the influx of large numbers of immigrants (Fix and Passel 1991) suggests that no single perspective on structure or change is likely to encapsulate fully the labor-market dynamics affecting the employment and earnings prospects of different racial and ethnic groups in urban areas.

Theories about spatial and skills mismatches, industrial and occupational restructuring, and job queuing point to factors affecting the likelihood that complementarity or competition will occur in the labor market. Originally formulated as an explanation of structural unemployment (Holzer and Vroman 1991), the spatial mismatch hypothesis has also been invoked to explain the emergence of underclass areas in inner cities (Wilson 1987, 1996; Kasarda 1989). The hypothesis links the development of urban poverty and the growth of such areas both to the decline of manufacturing jobs and to their movement to the suburbs (Wilson 1996). Inner-city African Americans with low levels of education, because they lack the resources to relocate to the suburbs or to travel to jobs located there, suffer a "mismatch" between the location of employment and residential opportunities that impairs their economic well-being. All else being equal, the greater the infusion of low-skilled immigrants into cities, the greater any negative effects associated with mismatch. Conversely, any negative effects of low-skilled immigration on native African Americans can be expected to be most severe in areas of greater mismatch.

Although the spatial-mismatch hypothesis points to some of the structural circumstances under which job competition and displacement between less-skilled immigrants and natives might be exacerbated, mismatch notions by themselves do not provide satisfactory explanations of urban population and economic change because they provide little basis for understanding why large numbers of immigrants have moved into cities that have also experienced manufacturing declines. Urban economic-restructuring perspectives, with their emphases on the globalization of the economy and the growth of the service sector (Sassen 1988, 1989, 1990), provide more in the way of an answer. Some cities that have experienced declines in manufacturing have also witnessed substantial increases in service jobs. Large postindustrial cities with substantial financial and business service sectors have generated large numbers of both new high-status, high-paying jobs and new low-status, low-paying jobs (Waldinger 1986, 1989, 1996). In short, an economic-restructuring perspective, by focusing on the growth of services in their most advanced form, emphasizes increased demand for both high- and low-skilled labor. Because less-skilled immigrants have been willing to fill low-level and often unstable jobs, the economic-restructuring hypothesis is better suited to explain both the decline in black manufacturing employment and the increase in immigrant employment, at least as these have occurred together in certain kinds of cities.

When manufacturing jobs held by African Americans disappear and such workers must look elsewhere for employment, do low-skilled African Americans compete with low-skilled immigrants for expanding low-level service jobs, or is there sufficient growth in the demand for such employment to accommodate the needs of both groups? One view, which has been termed the job-queuing hypothesis following the work of Stanley Lieberson (1980), postulates that ethnic groups are arranged in a hiring preference queue. All else being equal, employers do not move down the queue until all members of higher-ranked groups have been hired; rather, they exhaust preferred labor-force pools before moving to less-favored groups. Thus, when demographic change causes the size of the preferred white group at the top of the queue to shrink, a vacancy chain is set in motion that results in nonwhites moving up as replacements for whites. As the supply of white replacement labor diminishes, opportunities for immigrants and for blacks who have lost manufacturing jobs increase. More generally, the overall labor-market impact of low-skilled immigrants on native blacks and Hispanics in a given city may depend on the change in the number of low-skill manufacturing jobs, the degree of movement of low-skill manufacturing jobs to the suburbs, the growth in high-level services, and the change in the supply of low-skill jobs resulting from declines in the size of preferred groups standing higher in the job hierarchy. These factors vary across local labor markets. In some, their relative balance is such that immigrants and low-skilled minorities can be absorbed more easily as replacement labor and as holders of new jobs in the service sector. In others, their relative balance is such that competition and displacement are more likely to result.

We also hypothesize that more successful and sizable ethnic economies provide, ceteris paribus, relatively more employment opportunities for the members of the same racial or ethnic group and thus reduce the competitive effects of social-structural overlap and increase the possibility of complementarity. Samuel Cohn and Mark Fossett (n.d.). have found that, net of other factors, blacks experience better employment opportunities in neighborhoods where they are residentially concentrated, especially in larger cities. However, areas of black residential concentration are also likely to be within larger areas of high segregation, and such areas have historically evolved in ways that have served to isolate and limit economic opportunities for African Americans in the larger society (Massey and Denton 1993). To a substantial degree, the residential segregation of African Americans represents a spatial-structural mechanism of discrimination and is related to worse rather than better labor-market outcomes for African Americans (ibid.). This tendency has been so strong that in most instances it undoubtedly overwhelms any positive tendency for blacks to benefit from residential concentration and from spatial-structural separation. To distinguish these alternative consequences of residential separation of blacks and whites, we use the term "residential segregation" in speaking of the (overwhelmingly larger) negative consequences and "residential autonomy" in speaking of possible positive consequences. All else being equal, we suggest, black autonomy is a factor related to minimal niche overlap between immigrants and African Americans. We hypothesize that, as a result, black and Hispanic residential autonomy operates, other things being held constant, to lessen the competitive labor-market effects of immigration.

In sum, we suggest that complementarity (or symbiosis) between immigrants and African Americans is enhanced:

1. the tighter the local labor market

2. the lesser the city's manufacturing decline

3. the greater the city's growth in high-level services (which we proxy with an index of socioeconomic status)

4. the greater the size of the immigrant group's coethnic economy (because it indicates less social-structural overlap)

5. the larger the African American economy (because, other things being equal, larger size indicates increased African American employment opportunities and less structural overlap)

6. the smaller the size of the majority population (because a shrinking majority population will reduce the scarcity of African American employment opportunities

7. the greater the immigrant and African American residential autonomy (because the concentration of minority employment opportunities in minority areas, other things being held constant, will operate to minimize immigrant and African American social-structural overlap in such cases)

DATA AND METHODOLOGICAL APPROACH

In an attempt to shed light on the extent to which the direction and magnitude of labor-market effects of immigration on African Americans depend on variation in local labor-market tightness and socio-demographic structure, we use census data for 187 U.S. metropolitan statistical areas (MSAs) in 1980 and 1990 to examine the degree to which measures of general employment opportunities and socio-demographic structure in MSAs condition the effects of immigrant concentration on African American labor-force participation and unemployment rates. We use data from the Public Use Microdata Sample (PUMS), based on the long-form questionnaire, which is filled out by about one in six of all households answering the decennial Census. Demographers use the PUMS because it includes detailed questions regarding the characteristics of individuals and households, including demographics, family structure, education, labor force participation and income (U.S. Bureau of the Census 1990).

We focus on areas with at least five hundred African American men in the labor force in each of the years 1980 and 1990, excluding areas with fewer than five hundred to improve reliability of the measures of unemployment and labor-force participation, which are based on sample data.[2] To maximize the sample sizes on which our measures of MSA characteristics are based, we do not use measures from the smaller public use microdata samples; rather, we obtain data from the 1980 and 1990 volumes published by the U.S. Bureau of the Census. The measures available in the published volumes are based on samples that include between 18 and 100 percent of the U.S. population, depending on the specific item. Except for estimates of population growth, the MSA characteristics for 1980 and 1990 are estimated from populations residing in the MSA as the area was defined geographically in 1980 and 1990, respectively. To minimize the amount of change in MSA characteristics observed between 1980 and 1990 that derives from change in the geographic boundaries of the MSA rather than change in the population, we exclude areas whose population changed more than 15 percent as a result of adjustments in the area's geographic boundaries. In some cases, two or more 1980 MSAs were consolidated by the Census Bureau into a single MSA in 1990. For these cases, we combined the constituent MSAs in 1980 into a single case to match the 1990 MSA definition. In other cases, a new MSA was formed in 1990 where one had not existed in 1980; these MSAs are excluded from the analysis.

We examine the impact of immigrant concentration on the unemployment and labor-force participation and unemployment rates among African American men. Ideally, it would be best to examine the labor-market experiences of native-born African American men, but our data sources do not provide measures of labor-force participation and unemployment broken down by sex, race, and nativity. Nevertheless, exclusion of the foreign born from the measures would probably not lead to significant changes in the results because only a small percentage of African Americans (4.9 percent) were foreign born in 1990 (U.S. Bureau of the Census 1993). Because the unemployment rate does not necessarily or always capture the extent to which persons may become discouraged and drop out of the labor force, we focus first and primarily on the impact of immigration on the labor-force participation rate among African American men. Also, we do not examine wages or earnings, because relative to that of whites, black income has not deteriorated as much over the past twenty-five years, as has black labor-force participation (Jargowsky 1996, 127–29). The participation rate of the black labor force is measured as the percentage of civilian, noninstitutionalized black males age sixteen and older in the black civilian labor force. The unemployment rate for African American men is measured by the percentage of unemployed males age sixteen and older in the civilian labor force.

The independent variable of central interest is the percentage of the metropolitan-area population that is foreign born and originated in North and South America (during the 1980s, 95.7 percent of the Western Hemisphere foreign born originated in South or Central America, Mexico, or the Caribbean). In comparison with immigrants of other national origins, this population is more recent in origin and is composed of economic migrants with relatively low skills, a group that seems especially likely to compete directly with African Americans for jobs. We assess the tightness of local labor markets by examining the unemployment rate for non-Hispanic white men, a variable that measures (albeit imperfectly) the strength of labor demand in the local labor market. Thus, the effects of the measures of the foreign-born population on African American unemployment and labor-force participation rates are estimated both net of and conditional on the general demand for labor.

Several variables are included either as controls or in models in which the interactions between immigration and these variables are presented. Population growth over the previous decade—measured by expressing the interdecade change in population from 1970 to 1980 and from 1980 to 1990 as a percentage of the 1970 or 1980 population, respectively—is included as a control for longer-term metropolitan economic vitality.[3] Total current population size in 1980 or 1990 is included as a measure of the size of the labor market. The percentages of African Americans and native-born Hispanics in the area's population are included as controls for competition between majority and minority groups, based on the consistent finding that relative outcomes for blacks on socioeconomic matters are inversely associated with the relative size of the black population (Blalock 1967; Dowdall 1974; Farley 1987). The percentage of native-born Hispanics is included based on the finding that interethnic competition is further heightened by the presence of multiple minorities (Frisbie and Niedert 1976). Out-migration among African Americans is included as a control for differential selective out-migration. Out-migration is measured as the number of African Americans age twenty and older who moved out of the area during the previous five years as a percentage of the original African American population (for example, for 1990, out-migration is measured as the number who had moved out of the area since 1985 as a percentage of the 1985 population). Other controls are the welfare benefit rate (measured by using the natural log transformation of the average monthly family benefit for Aid to Families with Dependent Children), the percentage of the labor force in durable-goods manufacturing, the percentage of union membership of the state nonagricultural labor force, and the mean socioeconomic status (SES) of occupations in the local area, based on Nam-Powers socioeconomic status scores (Nam and Terrie 1986).[4]

We use the index of dissimilarity (D) to measure residential segregation between African Americans and non-Hispanic whites and between Hispanics and non-Hispanic whites. The most commonly used measure of the spatial distribution of different groups, the index indicates "the proportion of minority members that would have to change their area of residence to achieve even distribution" (Massey and Denton 1988, 284; Duncan and Duncan 1955). We utilize dissimilarity measures that were originally compiled by Roderick Harrison and Daniel Weinberg (1992) on the basis of census tract data. We also employed a number of other measures of spatial distribution, including exposure (for example, p-star), concentration, centralization, and clustering, but because these other measures were so highly correlated with dissimilarity, the results were largely unaffected by which measure we used.

Descriptive statistics for the variables included in the analyses are shown in table 1.1. The average African American male labor-force rate is 70.0 percent for 1980 and 70.5 percent for 1990. The average African American unemployment rate is 12.6 percent for 1980 and 14.6 percent for 1990. It is noteworthy that the percentage in the metropolitan areas of native-born Hispanics and Western Hemisphere foreign born are low, and the latter variable has a somewhat small

Table 1.1   Models of Labor-Force Participation of African American Men, Description of Variables

Variable	Mean		Standard Deviation	
	1980	1990	1980	1990
Labor-force participation				
African American men (%)	70.0	70.5	5.4	6.1
Non-Hispanic white men (%)	77.5	76.1	4.2	4.0
Unemployment				
African American men (%)	12.6	14.6	4.8	4.5
Non-Hispanic white men (%)	5.6	5.3	2.1	1.5
Foreign born, Western Hemisphere (%)	1.6	1.9	3.0	3.9
Increase in proportion of foreign born[a] (%)	1.0	0.2	1.6	1.2
Current population (logged)	12.9	13.0	1.0	1.0
African American (%)	11.0	11.7	9.6	9.8
Native-born Hispanic (%)	4.2	5.7	7.4	8.3
Non-Hispanic white (%)	82.2	79.2	12.3	13.7
African American out-migraton[b] (%)	15.2	17.2	12.4	10.1
Union membership[c] (%)	22.3	14.4	8.6	6.4
Labor force in durable-goods manufacturing (%)	14.7	11.1	8.3	5.8
Welfare benefit[d]	5.4	5.7	0.4	0.5
Socioeconomic status[e]	50.2	52.5	2.5	2.3
Residential segregation[f]				
Between African American and white	63.9	59.2	12.8	12.4
Between Hispanic and white	37.3	37.3	13.7	13.2

Notes: Based on a sample set of 187 U.S. metropolitan statistical areas.
[a]Over previous decade.
[b]Over previous five years.
[c]Of state nonagricultural labor force
[d]Logarithm of average state AFDC monthly benefit per family.
[e]Mean Nam-Powers SES for total employment civilian labor force.
[f]Index of dissimilarity measure.

standard deviation. The restricted range of variation in this variable increases the difficulty of finding reliable estimates of its influence on African American labor-force participation rates.

One of the problems that plague cross-city research on immigration's impact on labor-market outcomes is that both variables may be affected by unmeasured attributes of the cities under examination. As noted above, immigrants have continued to locate in the same destinations even when the economic attractions of those places have varied. This suggests the possibility that certain enduring attributes of cities across time continue to draw immigrants. These attributes could include geographic location, past histories of immigration and racial or ethnic discrimination, cultural factors, and so on. To try to control for these sorts of influence, we consider the following models at two points in time:

(1.1) $LMO_{i1} = \alpha_1 + X_{i1} \beta_1 + Z_i \gamma_1 + \varepsilon_{i1}$, and
(1.2) $LMO_{i2} = \alpha_2 + X_{i2} \beta_2 + Z_i \gamma_2 + \varepsilon_{i2}$,

where

$i = 1, 2, \ldots n,$

X and Z are vectors of independent variables, and β and γ are vectors of parameters. The vector X represents variables that influence labor-market outcomes (LMO) and differ across cities and from time 1 to time 2, whereas Z represents enduring attributes that differ across cities but are the same for city i from time 1 to time 2 ($Z_{i1} = Z_{i2} = Z_i$). The parameters of these models can be estimated if measurements are available for both X and Z and if ε_1 and ε_2 are random disturbances and uncorrelated with X and Z.

If measures of Z are not available, however, estimates of β_1 and β_2 will be biased. One solution, sometimes called a "first-difference" model (Allison 1990; Firebaugh and Beck 1994) or "fixed-effects" model (Jargowsky 1996), is to subtract equation (1.1) from equation (1.2) to obtain

$$LMO_{i2} - LMO_{i1} = \alpha^* + (X_{i2} - X_{i1}) \beta_2 + (\beta_2 - \beta_1) X_{i1} + \varepsilon_i^*,$$

where

$\alpha^* = \alpha_2 - \alpha_1,$
$\varepsilon_i = \varepsilon_{i2} - \varepsilon_{i1}$, and
$\gamma_1 = \gamma_2.$

Based on a model of this type, the effects of X can be estimated "free" of the effects of Z. Changes in labor-market outcomes are thus viewed as a function of changes in the independent variables and of the initial levels of X. In what follows, we estimate both cross-sectional models for 1980 and 1990 data and the fixed-effects change models. Because changes in the labor-market outcome variables may be a function of their initial values, we also include LMO_{i1} as a predictor in the fixed-effect equations. To test the degree to which the factors hypothesized above modify the effects of immigration, we also include interaction terms between immigration and these factors, which, because of multicollinearity, are added to the models one at a time in order to gauge their effects.

FINDINGS

Table 1.2 displays estimates for models of African American labor-force participation. The table shows the results of three models (the table columns). The first and second are cross-sectional ordinary least squares (OLS) regression models pertaining to the 1980 and 1990 data, respectively. As already noted, cross-sectional models may produce biased estimates of the impact of immigrant concentration on African American labor-market outcomes if any uncontrolled MSA characteristics are correlated with both labor-market outcomes and immigrant concentration. In an attempt to control for unmeasured MSA characteristics, we also estimate a third model, a fixed-effects or first-difference model. The first-difference model estimates the change in labor-market outcomes as a function of changes in immigration concentration and other MSA characteristics. This model controls for all MSA characteristics that remain constant from 1980 to 1990 and therefore produces unbiased estimates as long as there exist no uncontrolled factors that affect both the change in African American labor-market opportunities and the relative size of the immigrant population (Schoeni 1996; Firebaugh and Beck 1994). Within each set of models, we include the percentage of Western Hemisphere foreign born, the various economic and social-structural variables, and other control variables; then we add a multiplicative interaction term between the percentage of Western Hemisphere foreign born and the various economic and social-structural variables, to test the degree to which the effects of immigration depend on the social- and spatial-structural factors predicted by the theoretical considerations introduced in the previous section.

We should note that one of the enduring attributes that may affect the results is a city's historical and institutional tendency to discriminate against blacks. Indeed, there is substantial reason to think that

Table 1.2   Models of Impact of Immigration on Labor-Force
Participation Among African American Men

Variable	Cross-sectional Model, 1980	Cross-sectional Model, 1990	Fixed-Effects Model
Intercept	46.810*	22.401*	18.522*
Baseline measures			
African American labor-force participation (%)			− 0.262*
Foreign born (%)			− 0.064
Measures of control variables[a]			
Current population (logged)	− 0.259	0.402	12.208*
African American (%)	− 0.155*	− 0.160*	0.111
Native Hispanic (%)	− 0.060	− 0.195*	− 0.088
African American out-migration[b] (%)	0.053 +	0.121*	− 0.002
Union membership[c]	− 0.020	− 0.159*	0.229*
Labor force in durable-goods manufacturing (%)	0.155*	0.176*	− 0.071
Welfare benefit[d]	1.419	2.312*	− 0.520
Socioeconomic status[e]	0.484*	0.857*	0.921*
Non-Hispanic white male unemployment	− 0.935*	− 1.509*	− 0.073
Residential segregation between African Americans and whites[f]	− 0.019	− 0.113*	0.169*
Foreign born, Western Hemisphere	0.235 +	0.258*	0.218
R-squared[g]	0.331	0.544	0.207

Notes: Based on a sample set of 187 U.S. metropolitan statistical areas.
[a]Stock measures in cross-sectional models, difference measures in fixed-effects model.
[b]Over previous five years.
[c]Of state nonagricultural labor force
[d]Logarithm of average state AFDC monthly benefit per family.
[e]Mean Nam-Powers SES for total employment civilian labor force.
[f]Index of dissimilarity measure.
[g]Adjusted.
*$p < .05$, + $p < .1$.

this tendency in large measure accounts for residential segregation
and the negative effects of segregation and the percentage of blacks on
labor-market outcome variables. This pattern, however, is so strong
that it is likely to swamp any tendency for immigration's effects to be
mediated by residential segregation measures. When the pattern is
removed in the fixed-effects models, the results should be more likely

to reveal the effects predicted by the urban ecological theoretical considerations noted earlier.

Turning to the findings for African American labor-force participation (table 1.2), we note first that the control variables generally behave as would be expected in 1980 and 1990. In particular, the higher the unemployment rate of non-Hispanic whites and the greater the percentage of African Americans in the metropolitan population, the lower the labor-force participation of African Americans. The controls for industrial structure and average socioeconomic status exhibit the expected relationships. Also, the greater the black out-migration, the higher the labor-force participation, and the greater the residential segregation, the lower the black labor-force participation. We also note that although we are not utilizing sample data in the usual sense of the term (that is, we are working with the universe of MSAs that contain sufficient numbers of blacks to allow analysis), these and some other variables generally show *t*-ratios greater than twice their standard errors. Turning to the immigration variable, we observe that the higher the percentage of Western Hemisphere foreign born, the higher the rate of black participation in the labor force.

The fixed-effects results shown in the third column of table 1.2 illustrate that controlling for enduring city attributes does change the results in certain important and predicted ways. Most especially, the effects for percentage of blacks, union membership, and residential segregation change from negative to positive, implying cross-city variation in unmeasured enduring attributes that bias the results. We hypothesized that one attribute affecting the change in these variables' effects is the city's historical and institutional tendency to discriminate against blacks. When this factor is removed, these variables, all of which can be argued to indicate lesser amounts of social-structural overlap between blacks and immigrants, net of discriminatory tendencies, become related to increases in black participation. When we examine the immigration variable, we see that it shows about the same effect in both the cross-sectional and fixed-effects models, although it is not statistically significant in the latter. Thus, increases in the population of Western Hemisphere foreign born, controlling for the immigration levels in 1980, are less likely to be related to increases in black participation in the fixed-effects model than in the cross-sectional models.

In general, then, greater concentrations of immigrants seem to indicate a complementary relationship with the labor-force participation of black males, although this relationship is not statistically significant when enduring city attributes are controlled. What happens to this relationship under conditions of varying social- and spatial-structural factors? That is, does complementarity increase under conditions of increasingly tight labor markets, increasing socioeconomic status, the absence of declines in manufacturing, larger racial or ethnic economies, and higher racial or ethnic residential autonomy? To answer these questions, we added interaction terms between immigration and the various social- and spatial-structural indicators to the fixed-effects model shown in the third column of table 1.2. The coefficients for the main and interaction terms are shown in table 1.3, along with their evaluations (at the twenty-fifth and seventy-fifth percentile points of the conditioning variable) of the equations' first derivatives with respect to the immigration variable. Seven of the eight interaction terms show the predicted direction of effect, the one exception being that for durable-goods manufacturing. Increases in immigration raise black labor-force participation in places with larger manufacturing declines rather than in places with lesser declines, just the opposite of what was predicted. But the other variables show effects in the predicted direction. For example, increases in immigration raise black participation in the labor force more in rising SES cities than in nonrising SES cities, as they do in cities with larger black populations and in cities with higher residential segregation between blacks and whites. Thus, the predictions of urban ecological theory concerning the likely complementarity or competitiveness of immigrants are generally borne out by the results, once enduring city attributes (fixed effects) are removed from the data.

Although we do not expect unemployment results to be as strong because unemployment does not always consistently decline with rising vitality of labor markets (sometimes it increases when aggregate demand rises because more job seekers are drawn into the labor force), we also present comparable results for black unemployment in tables 1.4 and 1.5. In general, as we expected, few effects are statistically significant, and about half as many operate in the predicted direction here as in the case of black labor-force participation. Nonetheless, it is noteworthy that in the case of the residential autonomy measures, especially, the findings parallel those for labor-force participation. In addition to the unemployment analyses, we also conducted additional analyses in the case of labor-force participation that examined second-difference effects. Thus, we tested for the effects of increasing growth in the number of immigrants on increasing or decreasing change in black labor-force participation. As in the previous analyses of labor-force participation, the results (not shown here for reasons of space) were in the predicted direction in six of the eight

Table 1.3   Models of the Impact of Immigration on Labor-Force Participation Among African American Men, as Conditioned by Urban Economic and Social-Structural Changes

Variable	Coefficient	Slope for Foreign Born[a]		Effect in Predicted Direction
		25th Percentile	75th Percentile	
Strength of economy and economic restructuring				
1a. White male unemployment (%)	−0.068			
1b. Foreign born (%)	0.257	0.549	0.112	yes
1c. (1a) × (1b)	−0.191			
2a. Socioeconomic status[b]	0.885*			
2b. Foreign born (%)	−0.007	0.199	0.322	yes
2c. (2a) × (2b)	0.115			
3a. Labor force in durable-goods manufacturing (%)	−0.083			
3b. Foreign born (%)	−0.152	0.439	−0.040	no
3c. (3a) × (3b)	−0.109			
Queuing and ethnic economy				
4a. Native-born Hispanic (%)	−0.032			
4b. Foreign born (%)	−0.193	−0.166	0.063	yes
4c. (4a) × (4b)	0.117			
5a. African American (%)	−0.039			
5b. Foreign born (%)	0.173	0.195	0.463	yes
5c. (5a) × (5b)	0.242			
6a. Non-Hispanic white (%)	−0.246			
6b. Foreign born (%)	−0.338	−0.196	−0.306	yes
6c. (6a) × (6b)	−0.035			
Ethnic separation versus overlap				
7a. Segregation between African Americans and whites[c]	0.154+			
7b. Foreign born (%)	1.044*	0.008	0.806	yes
7c. (7a) × (7b)	0.140*			
8a. Segregation between Hispanics and whites[c]	0.168*			
8b. Foreign born (%)	−0.322	−0.624	−0.120	yes
8c. (8a) × (8b)	0.112+			

Notes: Based on a sample set of 187 U.S. metropolitan statistical areas.
[a]Evaluated at the 25th and 75th percentiles of the conditional variable.
[b]Mean Nam-Powers SES for total employment civilian labor force.
[c]Index of dissimilarity measure.
*$p < .05$, + $p < .1$.

Table 1.4   Models of the Impact of Immigration on Unemployment Among African American Men

Variable	Cross-Sectional Model, 1980	Cross-Sectional Model, 1990	Fixed Effects Model
Intercept	0.447	8.295	7.072*
Baseline measures			
African American labor-force participation (%)			−0.383*
Foreign born (%)			0.074
Measures of control variables[a]			
Current population (logged)	−0.027	−0.668*	−5.194*
African American (%)	0.093*	0.074*	0.155
Native Hispanic (%)	0.080*	0.111*	−0.268
African American out-migration[b] (%)	0.029+	−0.015	0.051*
Union membership[c] (%)	0.095*	0.076	−0.180*
Labor force in durable-goods manufacturing (%)	0.031	0.127*	−0.202*
Welfare benefit[d]	0.557	−0.350	0.360
Socioeconomic status[e]	−0.156	−0.064	−0.605*
Non-Hispanic white male unemployment	1.463*	1.723*	1.439*
Residential segregation between African Americans and whites[f]	0.079*	0.130*	0.053
Foreign born, Western Hemisphere	−0.166*	−0.067	0.191
R-squared[g]	0.713	0.575	0.562

Notes: Based on a sample set of 187 U.S. metropolitan statistical areas.
[a]Stock measures in cross-sectional models, difference measures in fixed-effects model.
[b]Over previous five years.
[c]Of state nonagricultural labor force.
[d]Logarithm of average state AFDC monthly benefit per family.
[e]Mean Nam-Powers SES for total employment civilian labor force.
[f]Index of dissimilarity measure.
[g]Adjusted.
*$p < .05$, + $p < .1$.

tests, although several were not statistically significant. To note just one example, increasingly rapid growth in immigration from the 1970s to the 1980s reduced black participation more in cities in which overall SES is not rising than in cities in which SES is rising, as predicted by the hypothesis.

In sum, social- and spatial-structural separations appear related to

Table 1.5   Models of the Impact of Immigration on Unemployment Among African American Men, as Conditioned by Urban Economic and Social-Structural Changes

Variable	Coefficient	Slope for Foreign Born[a]		Effect in Predicted Direction
		25th Percentile	75th Percentile	
Strength of economy and economic restructuring				
1a. White male unemployment (%)	1.442*			
1b. Foreign born (%)	0.200	0.262	0.169	no
1c. (1a) × (1b)	−0.040			
2a. Socioeconomic status[b]	−0.697*			
2b. Foreign born (%)	−0.309	0.138	0.405	no
2c. (2a) × (2b)	0.250			
3a. Labor force in durable-goods manufacturing (%)	−0.192*			
3b. Foreign born (%)	0.504	0.001	0.409	no
3c. (3a) × (3b)	−0.093			
Queuing and ethnic economy				
4a. Native-born Hispanic (%)	−0.371			
4b. Foreign born (%)	0.943	0.894	0.472	yes
4c. (4a) × (4b)	−0.215			
5a. African American (%)	0.276			
5b. Foreign born (%)	0.219	0.203	−0.003	no
5c. (5a) × (5b)	−0.185			
6a. Non-Hispanic white (%)	−0.181			
6b. Foreign born (%)	0.765	0.330	0.668	yes
6c. (6a) × (6b)	0.107 +			
Ethnic separation versus overlap				
7a. Segregation between African Americans and whites[c]	0.056			
7b. Foreign born (%)	0.037	0.234	0.083	yes
7c. (7a) × (7b)	−0.027			
8a. Segregation between Hispanics and whites[c]	−0.070			
8b. Foreign born (%)	0.226	0.316	0.166	yes
8c. (8a) × (8b)	−0.033			

Notes: Based on a sample set of 187 U.S. metropolitan statistical areas.
[a] Evaluated at the 25th and 75th percentiles of the conditional variable.
[b] Mean Nam-Powers SES for total employment civilian labor force.
[c] Index of dissimilarity measure.
*$p < .05$, + $p < .1$.

greater complementarity between immigrants and the African American population. This pattern is particularly pronounced in the case of residential segregation between blacks and whites. Thus, once the overwhelmingly strong negative effects of high levels of residential segregation on male African American labor-market outcomes are taken out of the data by examining the change scores in only the fixed-effects models, the predictions of urban ecological theory that high residential autonomy between blacks and whites will be related to increased black labor-force participation is borne out. In other words, the greater the increase in immigration between 1980 and 1990, the greater the increase in black male labor-force participation in cities whose autonomy scores increased (or did not decline).

One mechanism through which such processes occurred is revealed by recalling that such cities were experiencing the least immigration. Places where the relative numbers of immigrants were few could not experience declines in segregation between blacks and whites on account of immigration; rather, they would show little change and would thus fall at one end of the residential segregation spectrum. Conversely, if immigrants tended to move into the same central-city areas occupied by many African Americans, and because of their Western Hemisphere origins, reported themselves as white in the census, then their movement into black areas would have the effect of lowering measures of residential segregation between blacks and whites, although perhaps at the same time increasing labor-market competition. In such cities, immigrants and blacks would be predicted to enter into the kinds of competitive relationships that lower black labor-force participation.

This mechanism may have been supplemented by selective migration of blacks out of or into autonomous areas. Residential autonomy between blacks and whites could have increased over time because blacks relocated from suburbs into central cities, or such autonomy might have declined because blacks moved from central cities to suburbs. The most adequate and precise test of such possibilities would involve the examination of data at the level of the census tract, which is a research undertaking of such magnitude and cost as to be beyond the scope of this book. But to obtain some tentative suggestion as to whether such processes might have occurred, we looked at migration between central cities and suburbs across cities grouped according to their level of change in residential autonomy between blacks and whites. The results are shown in table 1.6. As can be seen, in cities where the largest declines in residential autonomy occurred, net movement of blacks took place from the central city to the suburbs. In cities experiencing gains or little decline in residential autonomy

Table 1.6 Intra-City Migration Patterns Among the Black Population Age Twenty-Five and Older, by 1980 to 1990 Changes in Segregation Between Blacks and Whites and Educational Attainment

Type of City and Educational Attainment	Average Change in Segregation	Percent Who Moved Within City	Of Intra-city Movers, Percentage Who Moved from		Net Percent Migration to Suburb
			Central City to Suburb	Suburb to Central City	
Largest declines in segregation (bottom 25 cities)	−12.8				
Total black population age 25+		6.9	23.6	4.6	19.0
Less than high school		7.2	18.0	4.4	13.6
High school graduate		7.7	21.5	3.6	17.9
Some college		6.7	28.0	6.6	21.4
College graduate		5.1	34.5	3.5	31.0
Little change in segregation (middle cities)	−4.4				
Total black population age 25+		11.5	5.8	6.9	−1.1
Less than high school		10.1	2.8	6.4	−3.6
High school graduate		12.6	5.8	5.5	.3
Some college		12.7	7.6	7.4	.2
College graduate		10.5	9.2	10.0	−.8
Increases in segregation (top 25 cities)	1.7				
Total black population age 25+		5.5	4.2	9.8	−5.6
Less than high school		4.0	1.2	7.0	−5.8
High school graudate		6.1	4.7	9.2	−4.5
Some college		6.6	5.3	9.3	−4.0
College graduate		5.9	5.8	16.6	−10.8

Source: 1990 1 percent Public Use Microdata Sample.

during the 1980s, net gains in movement took place in the other direction, that is, from suburbs to central cities. In both of these cases, the migration was selective of more highly educated blacks, thus reinforcing the possibility of job creation in the case of cities becoming more autonomous and worsening it in the case of cities becoming less autonomous. In short, both immigration and selective migration may have contributed to the finding of less complementarity in less autonomous areas.

SUMMARY AND DISCUSSION

The study of the labor-market impacts of immigration, despite its rather clear significance for social science and social policy, has proved an almost intractable topic for investigation. Although there seem to exist rather straightforward reasons to think that immigration might, at least under some conditions, undermine the labor-market positions of natives, particularly those natives who are most vulnerable to economic shocks and dislocations, such as racial or ethnic minorities and workers with low levels of education, research results have not consistently shown the existence of such effects. There are many reasons why this might be the case, including the possibility that effects get "watered down" over time because of migration patterns; the possibility that models are incorrectly specified; and the possibility that research done in different decades yields different results because of varying rates of economic growth by region and decade. There is yet another possible reason: that previous research has not taken into account that cities vary in their social- and spatial-structural features and that these factors influence in the likelihood that social groups, including racial or ethnic and immigrant groups, will encounter circumstances that foster symbiotic (that is, complementary) or competitive labor-market relationships. In other words, the social-structural features of some cities are more conducive than others to complementary relations. The failure to take this into account in research design and model specification is likely to lead to research results that are inconsistent and seemingly contradictory

This chapter has focused on several social- and spatial-structural factors that urban ecological theory suggests might constitute important mediators of competitive and complementary relationships in urban labor markets. These include the local demand for labor, the size of racial or ethnic economies, the relative size of high-level business services, the decline in manufacturing, the relative size of job queues (groups, especially majority whites), and racial or ethnic residential autonomy. We argue that studying the effects of immigration on the labor-force participation of blacks is both strategic and important— strategic in that other labor-market outcomes are not as likely to reveal immigration's impacts as is labor-force participation, and important in that the study of employment in the case of African Americans holds special theoretical and practical significance because of the declines in black male employment that have occurred over the past twenty-five years. Our results indicate that black labor-force participation is in fact more sensitive to concentrations of immigrants than is unemployment. They also show that seven of the eight structural contingency variables examined condition the impact of immigration in the direction predicted by theory. That is to say, taking other contaminating sources of influence into account, factors that serve to minimize the amount of social- and spatial-structural overlap between these groups operate to increase the likelihood that immigrants and African Americans stand in complementary relationship to one another in the urban economy. This tendency emerged in particularly strong fashion in the case of the measures of residential autonomy.

We should emphasize at this point, in the strongest terms possible, that this does not mean that discriminatory racial or ethnic residential segregation can be viewed as possibly having a good side. The reader should not forget that we have sought to remove the influence of this dimension of variation across cities and to examine the effects of residual variation, which we term autonomy. This variation reflects the concentration of black population independent of the effects of discrimination, and because it has been shown to bear some positive relationship to the likelihood of black employment, it appears to provide a relative "cushion," as it were, from the competitive effects stemming from the influx of immigrants into the labor market.[5] Areas that show this tendency to the greatest degree have also enjoyed relatively greater movement back into the central city of highly educated blacks, whereas those that have experienced the greatest competition from immigrants have experienced the opposite—the movement of highly educated blacks from the central city to the suburbs.

Overall, then, the results imply that low-skilled immigrants in general are a source of complementarity for the African American population but that the beneficial impact of an immigrant presence for black employment is mitigated by factors that channel blacks and immigrants into similar places in the economy and workplace. Unfortunately, some of these factors themselves are associated with past and current practices of discrimination. Thus, the fact that more residentially autonomous blacks are buffered from competition to some extent is not entirely a positive story, because even the residual variation in segregation may be attributed to the influence of racial and ethnic stratification. That is, even if many blacks live with other blacks by choice, rather than by force of discriminatory housing practices, part of the reason they make such choices may be racial and ethnic stratification in the society. Because, other things being equal, current residential autonomy is related to a greater likelihood of employment among blacks that is separate from immigrant employment, the results from this research suggest that policies that provide the opportunity for the development of strong black employment niches offer the prospect of strengthening black economic prospects in an era of continuing high immigration.

NOTES

1. See Fossett and Cready (1998) for an overview of ecological approaches to the study of racial and ethnic differentiation and inequality.

2. Employment data in the census are based on a one-in-six sample. Restricting the sample to metropolitan areas with at least five hundred African American men in the labor force ensures that the unemployment rate for African American men is computed using a sample of at least eighty African American men. For an area with an unemployment rate of 10 percent, this implies a standard error for the estimated unemployment rate of about 3.3.

3. To restrict measures of population growth to growth resulting from real population change and not that arising from an MSA's annexation of counties, consistent MSA definitions were used to compute population growth (that is, for growth from 1980 to 1990, population estimates were obtained for the MSA as it was defined geographically in 1990).

4. Additional variables were also considered but are not included in the final analyses because their effects proved unimportant or because the variables are redundant with other variables already included in the model. A partial listing of these alternative controls includes the percentage of the labor force in construction (closely correlated with population growth), white-collar employment (closely correlated with the mean socioeconomic status of jobs), a dummy variable for location in the South (correlated with the percentages of blacks and AFDC recipients), and size of metropolitan area (no effect, net of controls for the unemployment rate for Anglo-American men).

5. There is more than a passing parallel here with Roger Waldinger's (1986, 1989) findings regarding the impact of minority concentration in ethnic employment "niches." Concentration in an industry niche can often be traced to discrimination and lack of opportunities outside the ethnic niche. Nevertheless, it can lead to "ethnic enclosure," which may serve as a buffer to competition from other ethnic groups. Just as all niches are not equally attractive, all neighborhood-based labor markets also are not equally attractive. Nevertheless, holding discrimination constant, ethnic enclosure of a limited geographic labor market may provide one resource to a group with restricted options.

REFERENCES

Allison, Paul D. 1990. "Change Scores as Dependent Variables in Regression Analysis." *Sociological Methodology* 20: 93–114.

Altonji, Joseph G., and David Card. 1991. "The Effects of Immigration on the Labor Market Outcomes of Less-Skilled Natives." In *Immigration, Trade, and the Labor Market*, edited by John M. Abowd and Richard B. Freeman. Chicago: University of Chicago Press.

Bartel, Ann. 1989. "Where Do the New U.S. Immigrants Live?" *Journal of Economics* 7(4): 371–91

Barth, Fredrik. 1956. "Ecological Relationships of Ethnic Groups in Swat, North Pakistan." *American Anthropologist* 58(6): 1079–89.

―――. ed. 1969. *Ethnic Groups and Boundaries*. Boston: Little, Brown.

Bean, Frank D., Lindsay Lowell, and Lowell Taylor. 1988. "Undocumented Mexican Immigrants and the Earnings of Other Groups in the United States." *Demography* 25(1): 35–52.

Bean, Frank D., Eduardo Telles, and Lindsay Lowell. 1987. "Undocumented Migration to the United States: Perceptions and Evidence." *Population and Development Review* 13(4): 671–90.

Beggs, John J., Wayne J. Villemez, and Ruth Arnold. 1997. "Black Population Concentration and Black-White Inequality: Expanding the Consideration of Place and Space Effects." *Social Forces* 76(1): 65–91.

Blalock, Hubert M., Jr. 1967. *Toward a Theory of Minority-Group Relations.* New York: John Wiley and Sons.

Blau, Peter M. 1994. *Structural Contexts of Opportunities*. Chicago: University of Chicago Press.

Borjas, George. 1984. "The Impact of Immigrants on the Earnings of the Native-Born." In *Immigration: Issues and Policies*, edited by V. M. Briggs Jr. and Marta Tienda. Salt Lake City, Utah: Olympus Publishing.

―――. 1986a. "The Demographic Determinants of the Demand for Black

Labor." In *The Black Youth Employment Crisis*, edited by Richard Freeman and Harry Holzer. Chicago: University of Chicago Press.

———. 1986b. "The Sensitivity of Labor Demand Functions to Choice of Dependent Variable." *Review of Economic Statistics* 68(1): 58–66.

———. 1987. "Immigrants, Minorities, and Labor Market Competition." *Industrial and Labor Relations Review* 40(3): 382–92.

———. 1989. "Economic Theory and International Migration." *International Migration Review* 23(3): 457–85.

———. 1990. *Friends or Strangers: The Impact of Immigrants on the U.S. Economy.* New York: Basic Books.

———. 1994. "The Economics of Immigration." *Journal of Economic Literature* 32(4): 1667–1717.

———. 1998. *The Economic Progress of Immigrants.* Cambridge, Mass.: National Bureau of Economic Research.

Borjas, George, Richard Freeman, and Lawrence Katz. 1992. "The Labor Market Effects of Immigration and Trade." In *Immigration and Trade*, edited by Richard Freeman and George Borjas. Chicago: University of Chicago Press.

———. 1996. "Searching for the Effect of Immigration on the Labor Market." *American Economic Review and Proceedings* 86(2): 246–51.

———. 1997. "How Much Do Immigration and Trade Affect Labor Market Outcomes?" Harvard University. Unpublished paper.

Cohn, Samuel, and Mark A. Fossett. n.d. "What Spatial Mismatch?: The Spatial Proximity of Blacks to Employment in Boston and Houston in 1980." *Social Forces.* Forthcoming.

Coleman, James S. 1990. *Foundations of Social Theory.* Cambridge: Harvard University Press.

DeFreitas, Gregory. 1988. *Hispanic Immigration and Labor Market Segmentation." Industrial Relations* 27(2): 195–214.

———. 1991. *Inequality at Work: Hispanics in the U.S. Labor Force.* New York: Oxford University Press.

Dowdall, George W. 1974. "White Gains from Black Subordination in 1960 and 1970." *Social Problems* 22(2): 162–83.

Duncan, Otis D., and Beverly Duncan. 1955. "A Methodological Analysis of Segregation Indices." *American Sociological Review* 20: 210–17.

Farley, John E. 1987. "Disproportionate Black and Hispanic Unemployment in U.S. Metropolitan Areas: The Roles of Racial Inequality, Segregation, and Discrimination in Male Joblessness." *American Journal of Economics and Sociology* 46(2): 129–50.

———. 1996. *The New American Reality: Who We Are, How We Got Here, Where We Are Going.* New York: Russell Sage Foundation.

————. 1997. "Racial Trends and Differences in the United States Thirty Years After the Civil Rights Decade." *Social Science Research* 26(3): 235–62.

Filer, Randal K. 1992. "The Impact of Immigrant Arrivals on Migratory Patterns of Native Workers." In *Immigration and the Workforce*, edited by George J. Borjas and Richard B. Freeman. Chicago: University of Chicago Press.

Firebaugh, Glenn, and Frank D. Beck. 1994. "Does Economic Growth Benefit the Masses?: Growth, Dependence, and Welfare in the Third World." *American Sociological Review* 59(5): 631–53.

Fix, Michael, and Jeffrey S. Passel. 1991. "The Door Remains Open: Recent Immigration to the United States and a Preliminary Analysis of the Immigration Act of 1990." Discussion Paper PRIP-UI-14. Washington, D.C.: Urban Institute.

Fossett, Mark A., and Cynthia M. Cready. 1998. "Ecological Approaches in the Study of Racial and Ethnic Differentiation and Inequality." In *Continuities in Sociological Human Ecology*, edited by Michael Micklin and Dudley L. Poston Jr. New York: Plenum.

Fossett, Mark A., and K. Jill Kiecolt. 1989. "The Relative Size of Minority Populations and White Racial Attitudes." *Social Science Quarterly* 70(4): 820–35.

Freeman, Richard. 1991. "Employment and Earnings of Disadvantaged Young Men in a Labor Shortage Economy." In *The Urban Underclass*, edited by Christopher Jencks and Paul E. Peterson. Washington, D.C.: The Brookings Institute.

Frisbie, W. Parker, and Lisa Niedert. 1976. "Inequality and the Relative Size of Minority Populations: A Comparative Analysis." *American Journal of Sociology* 82(5): 1007–30.

Hamermesh, Daniel S. 1993. *Labor Demand*. Princeton: Princeton University Press.

Harrison, Roderick J., and Daniel H. Weinberg. 1992. "Racial and Ethnic Residential Segregation in 1990." Paper prepared for the Population Association of America Meetings, Denver, Colo. (May 1992). Washington, D.C.: U.S. Government Printing Office.

Hawley, Amos H. 1945. "Dispersion Versus Segregation: Apropos of a Solution of Race Problems." *Papers of the Michigan Academy of Science, Arts, and Letters*. Ann Arbor: University of Michigan Press.

————. 1950. *Human Ecology*. New York: Ronald Press.

————. 1970. *The Metropolitan Community: Its People and Government*. Beverly Hills, Calif.: Sage Publications.

————. 1986. *Human Ecology: A Theoretical Essay*. Chicago: University of Chicago Press.

Holzer, Harry J., and Wayne Vroman. 1991. "Mismatches and the Urban Labor Market." Urban Opportunity Program. The Urban Institute, Washington, D.C.

Jargowsky, Paul A. 1996. "Take the Money and Run: Economic Segregation in U.S. Metropolitan Areas." *American Sociological Review* 61(6): 984–98.

Juhn, Chinhui, Kevin M. Murphy, and Brooks Pierce. 1991. "Wage Inequality and the Rise in Returns to Skill." *Journal of Political Economy* 101(3): 410–42.

Karoly, Lynn A. 1992. "Changes in the Distribution of Individual Earnings in the United States: 1967–1986." *Review of Economics and Statistics* 74(1): 107–15.

Kasarda, John D. 1985. "Urban Change and Minority Opportunities." In *The New Urban Reality*, edited by Paul E. Peterson. Washington, D.C.: Brookings Institution.

———. 1989. "Urban Industrial Transition and the Underclass." *Annals of the American Academy of Political and Social Science* 501: 26–47.

———. 1995. "Industrial Restructuring and the Changing Location of Jobs." In *State of the Union: America in the 1990s*, edited by Reynolds Farley. New York: Russell Sage Foundation.

King, Allen G., Lindsay B. Lowell, and Frank D. Bean. 1986. "The Effects of Hispanic Immigrants on the Earnings of Native Hispanic Americans." *Social Science Quarterly* 67(4): 673–89.

Kosters, Marvin H., ed. 1991. *Workers and Their Wages: Changing Patterns in the United States*. Washington, D.C.: American Enterprise Institute Press.

Kuznets, Simon. 1977. "Two Centuries of Economic Growth: Reflections on U.S. Experience." *American Economic Review* 67(1): 1–14.

Lalonde, Robert J., and R. H. Topel. 1991. "Immigrants in the American Labor Market: Quality, Assimilation, and Distributional Effects." *American Economic Review* 81(2): 297–302.

Levy, Frank. 1987. *Dollars and Dreams: The Changing American Income Distribution*. New York: Russell Sage Foundation.

———. 1995. "Incomes and Income Inequality." In *State of the Union: America in the 1990s*, edited by Reynolds Farley. New York: Russell Sage Foundation.

———. 1997. *The New Dollars and Dreams: American Incomes and Economic Change*. New York: Russell Sage Foundation.

Lieberson, Stanley. 1980. *A Piece of the Pie: Blacks and White Immigrants Since 1880*. Berkeley: University of California Press.

Massey, Douglas. 1987. "Understanding Mexican Migration to the United States." *American Journal of Sociology* 92(6): 1372–1403.

Massey, Douglas S., and Nancy A. Denton. 1988. "The Dimensions of Residential Segregation." *Social Forces* 67(2): 281–315.

————. 1993. *American Apartheid: Segregation and the Making of the Underclass.* Cambridge: Harvard University Press.

Muller, Thomas, and Thomas J. Espenshade. 1985. *The Fourth Wave: California's Newest Immigrants.* Washington, D.C.: Urban Institute Press.

Nam, Charles B., and Walter E. Terrie. 1986. "Comparing the Nam-Powers and Duncan SEI Occupational Scores." Center for the Study of Population, Working Paper No. 86–27. Tallahassee: Florida State University.

Olzak, Susan. 1992. *The Dynamics of Ethnic Competition and Conflict.* Palo Alto: Stanford University Press.

Park, Robert E., and Ernest W. Burgess. 1921. *Introduction to the Science of Sociology.* Chicago: University of Chicago Press.

Piore, Michael J. 1979. *Birds of Passage: Migrant Labor and Industrial Societies.* New York: Cambridge University Press.

Portes, Alejandro.1995. "Economic Sociology and the Sociology of Immigration: A Conceptual Overview." In *The Economic Sociology of Immigration: Essays on Networks, Ethnicity, and Entrepreneurship*, edited by Alejandro Portes. New York: Russell Sage Foundation.

Quillian, Lincoln. 1996. "*Group* Threat and Regional Change in Attitudes Toward African-Americans." *American Journal of Sociology* 102(3): 816–60.

Reischauer, Robert. 1989. "Immigration and the Underclass." In *The Ghetto Underclass: Social Science Perspectives*, edited by W. J. Wilson. Annals of the American Academy of Political and Social Science 501. Newbury Park, Calif.: Sage Publications.

Ritchey, P. Neal. 1975. "The Effect of Minority Group Status on Fertility: A Re-examination of Concepts." *Population Studies* 29(2): 249–57.

Sassen, Saskia. 1988. *The Mobility of Labor and Capital: A Study in International Investment and Labor Flow.* Cambridge: Cambridge University Press.

————. 1989. "New York City's Informal Economy." In *The Informal Sector: Theoretical and Methodological Issues*, edited by Alejandro Portes, Manuel Castells, and Lauren Benton. Baltimore: Johns Hopkins University Press.

————. 1990. "Economic Restructuring and the American City." *Annual Review of Sociology* 16: 465–90.

Schoeni, Robert F. 1996. "The Effect of Immigrants on the Employment of Wages of Native Workers: Evidence from the 1970s and 1980s." DRU-1408-IF. Santa Monica, Calif.: Rand. Unpublished paper.

Simon, Julian. 1989. *The Economic Consequences of Immigration.* Cambridge, Eng.: Basil Blackwell.

Smith, James P., and Barry Edmonston. 1997. *The New Americans: Economic, Demographic, and Fiscal Effects of Immigration.* Washington, D.C.: National Academy Press.

Stewart, James B., and Thomas Hyclak. 1986. "The Effects of Immigrants, Women, and Teenagers on the Relative Earnings of Black Males." *Review of Black Political Economy* 15(1): 93–101.

Taylor, Lowell Jr., Frank D. Bean, James B. Rebitzer, Susan Gonzalez Baker, and B. Lindsay Lowell. 1988. "Mexican Immigrants and the Wages and Unemployment Experience of Native Workers." Discussion Paper PRIP-UI-1. Washington, D.C.: Urban Institute.

Tienda, Marta, and Ding Tzann Li. 1988. "Minority Concentration and Earnings Inequality: Blacks, Hispanics, and Asians Compared." *American Journal of Sociology* 93(6): 141–65.

Topel, Robert H. 1994. "Regional Land Markets and the Determinants of Wage Inequality." *American Economic Review* 48(2): 17–22.

U.S. Bureau of the Census. 1990. *1990 Census of Population and Housing*. "Public Use Microdata Samples." Machine-readable data files, 5 percent sample. Washington, D.C.: U.S. Government Printing Office.

———. 1993. *1990 Census of Population, Social and Economic Characteristics: United States*. CP-2-1, table 7. Washington, D.C.: U.S. Government Printing Office.

U.S. Department of Labor. 1971. *Monthly Labor Review* 94(3).

———. 1981. *Monthly Labor Review* 104(3).

———. 1991. *Monthly Labor Review* 114(3).

U.S. Immigration and Naturalization Service. 1996. *Statistical Yearbook of the Immigration and Naturalization Service, 1995*. Washington, D.C.: U.S. Government Printing Office.

Waldinger, Roger. 1986. "Changing Ladders and Musical Chairs: Ethnicity and Opportunity in Postindustrial New York." *Politics and Society* 15(4): 369–401.

———. 1989. "Immigration and Urban Change." *Annual Review of Sociology* 15: 211–32.

———. 1996. "The Jobs Immigrants Take." *New York Times*, March 11.

Wilson, William Julius. 1987. *The Truly Disadvantaged: The Inner City, the Underclass, and Public Policy*. Chicago: University of Chicago Press.

———. 1996. *When Work Disappears: The World of the New Urban Poor*. New York: Alfred A. Knopf.

CHAPTER 2

Mexican Immigration, Occupational Niches, and Labor-Market Competition: Evidence from Los Angeles, Chicago, and Atlanta, 1970 to 1990

Michael J. Rosenfeld and Marta Tienda

The burgeoning literature about the labor-market impacts of immigration presents a major paradox. Because there is little evidence that immigrants depress the wages or diminish the employment prospects of native-born workers (see Smith and Edmonston 1997; Borjas 1994, 1995; Greenwood and Hunt 1995; Greenwood and Tienda 1997), most econometric studies conclude that immigrants are not labor-market substitutes for native-born workers. However, case studies of specific industries or occupations generally conclude the opposite (see Martin and Midgley 1994; Greenwood and McDowell 1993; and chapters 6 and 7 in this volume). Several recent case studies argue that immigrants have completely displaced natives in selected occupations. For example, David Grant, Melvin Oliver, and Angela James (1996) and Roger Waldinger (1996) claim that in labor markets with large numbers of recent Mexican migrants, janitorial and domestic service, gardening, and selected factory jobs are now occupied almost exclusively by Mexican nationals. As Mary Waters documents in chapter 6 of this book, black immigrants from the Caribbean have largely (though not quite completely) displaced native blacks from jobs at a food-service company in New York.

The conflicting conclusions between aggregate econometric studies and ethnographic case studies bring into focus several unresolved questions about the extent and nature of competition between immigrants and domestic minority workers. First, how can the apparent lack of aggregate labor-market competition between immigrants and natives be reconciled with evidence that immigrants largely or completely replace native groups in certain occupations? Second, what happens to the "displaced" workers? Do they find work in different industries or occupations in the same labor market, or similar work in different labor markets, or are they virtually crowded out of the labor market? Stated differently, does the ethnic recomposition of an occupation (or industry) necessarily imply displacement, or is occupational succession accompanied by upward and downward mobility? If so, which workers move up and which move down?

It is surprising that so little effort has been made to reconcile these contradictory conclusions, particularly in light of their potentially conflicting policy implications. In part, this state of affairs reflects the limitations of existing data, especially the lack of longitudinal data that allows researchers to witness the process of ethnic succession within and between firms. And, because most case studies of immigrant labor-market competition select jobs that have experienced obvious ethnic succession, they usually ignore the possibility that succession can be accompanied by occupational and geographic mobility of domestic workers. Therefore, our strategy to reconcile the contradictory evidence about labor-market competition between immigrants and U.S.-born minority workers combines aspects of the case study and aggregate approaches. That is, we "map" case studies against changes in the occupational distribution of minority workers and evaluate ethnic occupational succession using multiple indicators.

In this chapter we focus on U.S.-born African Americans and immigrants from Mexico. Our choice of Mexican immigrants rather than all immigrants reflects several considerations. First, Mexico is by far the largest single source of contemporary U.S. immigrants and has been for several years (Rumbaut 1996; Smith and Edmonston 1997; Greenwood and Tienda 1997). Second, Mexican immigrants are highly concentrated geographically—more so than other immigrant groups—and their low rates of internal geographic mobility diminish the possibility that secondary migration will arbitrage their labor-market impacts (Greenwood and Tienda 1997).[1] Third, Mexican immigrants arrive with very low levels of education, which limits the kinds of jobs for which they compete (Greenwood and Tienda 1997; Rosenfeld and Tienda 1997). This narrows the range of occupations we must consider to develop our arguments.

As the largest domestic minority, African Americans also are an important case study of displacement by immigrants. In addition to being the most residentially segregated minority (Massey and Denton 1993), black men lost more ground in the labor market during the 1970s and 1980s than one might expect based on their educational progress (Mare 1995; Wilson 1987, 1996). Immigration has been implicated as one cause of their weakened labor-market position, although empirical evidence of displacement remains weak (however, see Greenwood and Tienda 1997; Hamermesh and Bean 1998). There is tentative evidence, however, that blacks (especially poor blacks) may be negatively impacted by immigration in ways that whites are not. For example, George Borjas (1998) argues that African Americans who own capital benefit from an influx of low-skilled labor, which makes goods cheaper and raises companies' profits. However, because blacks own relatively little capital, they often find themselves competing for jobs with immigrants who have considerably lower levels of formal education and weaker English skills.

Although this argument is directly relevant to questions about job competition and displacement of domestic workers by immigrants, it is also problematic because it defies a basic premise of human capital theory, namely, that skilled workers will fare better in the labor market than workers with less formal training or education. Recent trends in wage inequality favoring more highly educated over less-skilled workers suggest that the labor-market position of Mexican immigrant workers relative to domestic workers should have deteriorated. Yet, despite their favorable educational characteristics in comparison with recent Mexican immigrants, African Americans residing in states that attract the largest numbers of immigrants have consistently lower age-specific labor-force participation rates and higher unemployment rates than Mexicans (Greenwood and Tienda 1997).

Our attempt to reconcile the conclusions from macro- and micro-level analyses is highly descriptive and designed to generate and refine propositions. We argue that case studies of occupations that have experienced occupational succession of natives by immigrants cannot ipso facto be used to draw conclusions about "displacement" more generally. To do so forecloses the possibility that although immigration may displace natives from some jobs, immigration may also create new employment opportunities for natives in other sectors. In what follows, we illustrate how and why this may occur.

To make our case, we examine three labor markets, two of which (Los Angeles and Chicago) have been heavily impacted by immigration since 1970 and one (Atlanta) that has been insulated from immigration. These comparisons show how native blacks fare in specific occupations but under different local immigration regimes. The empirical evidence we provide emphasizes descriptive statistics, but we pay due attention to issues of statistical significance in the appendix, which discusses our methodology in detail.

THE INFLUENCE OF SOCIAL NETWORKS

The ethnographic studies by Mary Waters and Roger Waldinger in the volume (chapters 6 and 7, respectively) offer unique sociological insights into the process of ethnic competition and displacement in the labor market. One key insight from ethnographic evidence is that many low-skill jobs are filled not through a bureaucratic job search that sorts prospective workers among available slots in an open market but rather by the friends and family of the current employees. Network hiring lowers the employer's cost of recruiting potential new employees and also provides the employer some insurance that the new employees will not shirk their duties, because a current worker has vouched for them.

Network recruitment, which is based on the social ties between new and existing employees, makes workplaces more ethnically homogeneous. The tendency toward workplace homogeneity is quite important because in most ethnographic studies the network hiring process appears to work to the disadvantage of native blacks. That is, immigrants seem able to use social networks more frequently and more efficiently than native blacks, and as a result, immigrants have come to predominate in the work sites selected as case studies (such as those described by Waldinger and Waters). It is not entirely clear why the process of network hiring should favor immigrants over native blacks, who, after all, have social networks of their own.

Several explanations are plausible. It is conceivable that immigrants have stronger social networks than native blacks (as suggested by one of Waldinger's respondents). It is also possible that network hiring as implemented in particular firms is intended to favor immigrants over native blacks, presumably because the employers are biased against native blacks (a possibility raised by Waters). Immigrants may also display a stronger willingness to perform menial work for little pay. If so, any recruitment method that minimizes the importance of U.S.-based credentials and education would inevitably favor the immigrants. Yet there must also be cases (as yet undescribed in the ethnographic literature) in which the social context of the workplace favors natives over immigrants. The "old boys' network" of white males in corporate America is one legendary example, but there probably are also black economic niches where immigrants, even if qualified, have a difficult time gaining entry and securing jobs.

OCCUPATIONAL NICHES

Although the concentration of blacks in janitorial and maid work in 1970 was largely a result of the foreclosure of opportunities in other occupations, the emergence of ethnic niches even in menial occupations can confer benefits to an entire group. One important benefit is information about and access to jobs that could provide a temporary safety net in times of unemployment or recession. Citing work by Elijah Anderson, Suzanne Model (1993) argues that the ability of neighborhood adults to find steady (even if menial) employment for young men in the neighborhood was crucial to the maintenance of the adults' authority and hence the social fabric of black neighborhoods. Following Waldinger's (1996) and Model's (1993) arguments, the succession of occupational niches, such as janitorial jobs, from black to immigrant Latino domination means that blacks may have lost the ability to find work as janitors not only during economic downswings but at any time. Taken to its logical conclusion, this reasoning would blame high levels of black unemployment partly or entirely on the presence of immigrant workers.

Some displacement of natives by immigrants in low-skill jobs is to be expected in labor markets like Los Angeles, with large numbers of immigrants, because the immigrant flow is so enormous and because Mexican immigrants have low rates of internal geographic mobility (Greenwood and Tienda 1997). As Mexican immigrants have become a larger share of the workforces of Chicago and Los Angeles, they naturally occupy a higher share of all jobs. The question of competition and displacement hinges on whether the shares of Mexican immigrants in particular jobs exceed their population shares. For example, if blacks and Mexican immigrants were uniformly distributed across occupations, and if changes in both groups' employment paralleled demographic trends, Mexicans' share of all Chicago jobs would have increased from 1 to 3 percent between 1970 and 1990, whereas blacks' presence would have remained roughly constant.

In this chapter we are interested not in occupations that faithfully reflect the local ethnic balance (few such occupations exist anyway) but rather in occupations that reflect domination or at least overrepresentation by one ethnic group. Occupations in which one ethnic group is substantially overrepresented are called niches. Our interest in niches is twofold. First, we want to see how traditional black niches have fared over time with and without the intervention of labor-market competition from immigrants. Second, we want to see how blacks have fared outside of their traditional niches, in sectors of the economy traditionally dominated by whites. We hypothesize that if immigration has created opportunities for some native blacks to climb up the economic ladder, as Grant, Oliver, and James (1996) argue, then we should be able to document increasing black encroachment on traditional white niches in places where immigrants have filled the lowest rungs of the economic ladder.

The simplest operational definition of an ethnic labor-market niche is an occupation or industry in which a particular ethnic group is overrepresented relative to its population share in a designated labor market. This overrepresentation may reflect special skills initially held by members of an immigrant group at the time of its arrival or historically defined differences in the structure of job opportunities when an immigrant group entered the United States (Lieberson 1980, 379).[2] For example, the concentration of Mexican immigrants in U.S. agriculture has long historical antecedents that have left an indelible imprint on the contemporary occupational profile of Mexican Americans (Tienda 1981).

We use the index of representation to define occupational niches, defined as $(n_1/T_2)/(n_3/T_4)$, where the numerator of this formula, (n_1/T_2), represents the number of persons in the labor force of a given ethnic group in a given labor market that works in a particular occupation (n_1) divided by the total number of people in the labor force from the ethnic group (T_2). The denominator of the formula represents the analogous ratio for all other persons in the labor force in that metropolitan area. The statistical appendix provides further discussion of the representation index and the odds ratio, which is a closely related measure. A representation index of 1 indicates that a given ethnoracial group is proportionally represented in a particular occupation.

To illustrate, if blacks make up 10 percent of a metropolitan population and 10 percent of the truck drivers in that metropolitan area, they would have a representation index of 1 for that city and occupation. Alternatively, if the number of black truck drivers exceeded 10 percent, their representation index would be higher than 1. Operationally, we define an occupational niche as a three-digit occupation with a representation index of 2 or higher in a given occupation compared with other groups residing in the same metropolitan area. Thus (to use an example from our case studies), a representation index of 5.58 for blacks in janitorial occupations in Los Angeles in 1970 implies that blacks in Los Angeles in 1970 were 5.58 times as likely as their nonblack contemporaries to be employed as janitors; janitorial work was therefore a black niche in Los Angeles in 1970.

DATA

Our analysis considers three metropolitan areas—Los Angeles, Chicago, and Atlanta—using data from the 1970 and 1990 Public Use Microdata Samples of the U.S. census.[3] The three cities represent

Table 2.1   Ethnoracial Composition of Los Angeles, Chicago, and Atlanta Metropolitan Areas, by Population (in Thousands), 1970 and 1990

| | Los Angeles | | | | Chicago | | | | Atlanta | | | |
| | 1970 | | 1990 | | 1970 | | 1990 | | 1970 | | 1990 | |
	Population	%	Population	%	Population	%	Population	%	Population	%	Population	%
Native, non-Hispanic whites	4,855	69	3,389	41	4,352	73	3,486	60	1,065	76	1,403	65
Native, non-Hispanic blacks	745	11	917	11	1,158	19	1,308	23	307	22	646	30
Mexican Americans	696	10	1,524	18	97	2	295	5	2	0	11	1
Mexican immigrants	138	2	989	12	34	1	183	3	0	0	9	0
Other	590	8	1,451	18	327	5	429	9	23	2	97	4
Total	7,024	100	8,268	100	5,967	100	5,802	100	1,396	100	2,167	100

Sources: 1970 Census 5 percent questionnaire county group files (this is a 1-in-100 sample) and 1990 Census Public Use Microdata Sample 5 percent A file (a weighted 5-in-100 sample).

highly varied contexts of immigration and regional economies. Atlanta was essentially unaffected by immigration during the 1970s and
1980s, whereas Chicago was strongly impacted. In fact, immigration
virtually transformed the ethnoracial composition of Los Angeles
(Waldinger and Bozorgmehr 1996). Our choice of cities was guided
by substantive, theoretical, and practical considerations. On the practical side, we were compelled to select metropolitan statistical areas
(MSAs) with large populations because of our interest in immigrant
and black representation across fine-grained occupational categories.
Only the largest MSAs have sufficient respondents in target occupations in both 1970 and 1990. Second, given our substantive interest
in the labor-market effects of Mexican immigration on blacks, MSAs
with both substantial foreign-born Mexican and domestic black populations narrowed the range of possibilities to Los Angeles and Chicago.

Atlanta provides a fruitful comparison for several reasons. As a labor market containing a large African American population, Atlanta
allows us to address a crucial question, namely, how do blacks fare in
the absence of competition from immigrants? Are the economic prospects of blacks in job categories that have experienced ethnic succession better in the absence of immigration? Of course, we can only
approximate our answer because opportunity structures (the industrial
and occupational mix of jobs) as well as labor-market conditions
(timing and severity of recessions as well as recovery periods) differ.
Unlike Chicago, Atlanta did not experience a collapse of durable-
goods-manufacturing industries that undermined the labor-market
position of blacks. Thus, blacks should have fared better in Atlanta
than in Los Angeles or Chicago because immigration was virtually nil
during the 1970s and 1980s and because manufacturing employment
was not a mainstay of black employment.

Table 2.1 shows summary population statistics for the three metropolitan areas. In 1990, native whites and native blacks combined
made up 95 percent of Atlanta's population, compared with 98 percent two decades earlier. Clearly, Mexican immigrants had not yet
made an appreciable demographic impact in Atlanta by 1990, and
Mexican Americans made up only 1 percent of the metropolitan population. Los Angeles stands in sharp contrast because its Mexican immigrant population grew rapidly during the 1970s and 1980s, from 2
to 12 percent of the metropolitan population. During this period, the
total population also grew rapidly, and Los Angeles surpassed Chicago
as the second largest city in the nation. From 1970 to 1990, Chicago's
Mexican immigrant population grew in relative and absolute terms.
The native black population shares in Los Angeles and Chicago re-

mained stable during the 1970s and 1980s; Atlanta's black population share, however, rose from 22 to 30 percent of the total.

To keep the number of comparisons at a manageable level, most of the detailed tables in this chapter include only native-born non-Hispanic whites, native-born non-Hispanic blacks, and immigrants from Mexico. The exclusion of Mexican Americans (that is, U.S.-born persons of Mexican ancestry) is especially troublesome for Los Angeles, where by 1990 the Mexican American population exceeded 1.5 million persons. The labor-market assimilation of second- and third-generation immigrants requires a separate and detailed analysis of its own; therefore, we can consider Mexican American workers only in places where they seem to have an unusually strong interaction with the supply or demand for Mexican immigrant workers. One final issue that may be important but is impossible to measure with census data is the problem of legal status. In 1990, foreign-born Mexicans included a substantial number of undocumented migrants, but most Mexican migrants enumerated in 1970 were documented. We know that undocumented migrants are especially prone to workplace exploitation because of their precarious legal status (Heer 1990). However, because the census questionnaire does not ask about legal status, we must aggregate the documented and undocumented immigrants together.

Before embarking on a discussion of individual occupations, we present a brief overview of the occupational landscape by broad occupational categories as a way of contextualizing the case studies. Table 2.2 presents the distribution of the male and female labor force by occupational category and by ethnic group. The row percentages are by occupational category. For instance, 88 percent of administrators and managers in Los Angeles in 1970 were white; by 1990 the percentage had dropped to 61 percent. The Mexican immigrant share of administrative work climbed from 0 percent to 3 percent in the same period. The ethnic share of each occupational category do not sum to 100 percent because some ethnic categories are excluded from the table (see table 2.2 note). In the categories of laborers and operators, both native whites and blacks lost ground over the twenty-year period, whereas Mexican immigrants increased their share dramatically in both Los Angeles and Chicago. At first blush, table 2.2 offers some evidence for our basic claim, namely, that in the presence of immigration native blacks experience both upward mobility (into the administrative ranks) and displacement (from factory and laboring jobs). Table 2.2 can offer only superficial evidence, however, because it does not correct for the large demographic changes during the 1970s and 1990s. Neither do these tabulations reveal much about the wages, unemployment rates, skills, and experience that the different ethnic groups have in the same industry. For the more detailed analysis we turn to a series of case studies.

CASE STUDIES

Our selection of occupations for case study is perforce arbitrary, but deliberate. That is, our selection includes occupations that have been the object of previous case studies (janitors in Los Angeles, for example) for which we provide comparative location data. We have provided an extensive discussion of the criteria used to select these occupations elsewhere (Rosenfeld and Tienda 1998). The occupations selected for in-depth scrutiny represent five broad occupational groups, which vary from heavy immigrant influence to the almost total absence of foreign-born workers. These include for men and women, respectively,

1. cleaning services (janitors and maids)
2. factory work (machine operators and assemblers)
3. skilled service occupations (postal clerks and teachers)
4. unskilled service occupations (security guards and nursing aides)
5. office work (managers or administrators and secretaries)

Obviously, this list is not exhaustive, nor can it be in an article-length treatment. However, these ten occupations display a broad range within which the impact of Mexican immigration can be established. These occupations also represent a range with respect to the share of government workers, skill requirements, and relative growth or contraction during the period of investigation.

For each of the ten three-digit occupations examined, we present evidence of changes in group representation, average educational levels of incumbents, occupation-specific unemployment rates, shares of public-sector employment, and annual earnings—indicators germane to our working hypotheses. Although highly descriptive, the evidence presented provides a sound basis for refining propositions and developing appropriate methods to test them. The statistical appendix describes in greater detail the representation index used. The occupation-specific unemployment rate is simply the percentage of workers for that specific occupation who are unemployed. For workers unemployed at the time of the census, "occupation" refers to the last job they worked. Substantive inferences are based on statistically significant comparisons, and criteria used to establish significance are detailed in the appendix.

Table 2.2   Occupational Representation (Two Digit Census Categories) of Native Black, Native White, and Mexican Immigrant Members of the Labor Force, Men and Women, for Los Angeles, Chicago, and Atlanta, 1970 and 1990

| | Los Angeles | | | | | |
| | Native Blacks | | Native Whites | | Mexican Immigrants | |
	1970	1990	1970	1990	1970	1990
Ethnic share of each occupational category (%)						
Admin. and managers	3	8	88	61	0	3
Clerical workers	9	14	76	44	1	6
Craftsmen, building trades	6	7	73	36	2	19
Laborers	13	6	56	22	6	36
Operators, factory workers	12	5	53	14	7	39
Professional and technical	6	8	83	62	0	2
Private household workers	35	5	42	10	6	29
Sales workers	4	7	85	51	1	7
Service workers	17	11	64	29	3	20
Transportation workers	11	13	66	31	2	16
All occupations combined	9	9	73	43	2	13
Occupational distribution for selected ethnic groups (%)						
Administrators and managers	3	12	11	19	1	3
Clerical workers	21	28	22	18	7	8
Craftsmen, building trades	9	9	13	9	13	16
Laborers	6	4	3	3	12	16
Operators, factory workers	17	5	9	3	43	25
Professional and technical	11	16	19	25	1	3
Private household workers	5	1	1	0	3	2
Sales workers	4	9	9	14	3	6
Service workers	20	13	9	7	14	17
Transportation workers	4	4	3	2	3	3
All occupations combined*	100	101	99	100	100	99

Sources: 1970 Census 5 percent questionnaire county group files (this is a 1-in-100 sample) and 1990 Census Public Use Microdata Sample 5 percent A file (a weighted 5-in-100 sample).
*Columns may not sum to 100 percent due to rounding.

Cleaning Services

Because both Waldinger (1996) and Grant, Oliver, and James (1996) discuss janitors in Los Angeles as an instance of black displacement by Latino immigrants, we begin with cleaning-services occupations—janitors, for men, and maids, for women. In 1970, black male Angelinos were more than five times more likely than native whites to work as

Table 2.2   *Continued*

	Chicago						Atlanta					
	Native Blacks		Native Whites		Mexican Immigrants		Native Blacks		Native Whites		Mexican Immigrants	
	1970	1990	1970	1990	1970	1990	1970	1990	1970	1990	1970	1990
	5	10	91	81	0	1	6	16	92	79		0
	15	19	80	68	0	1	15	32	84	65		0
	11	11	82	66	1	6	14	23	85	68		1
	28	18	61	51	1	13	45	39	53	53		2
	25	16	57	38	3	19	31	42	68	50		0
	9	13	85	75	0	0	11	18	9	77		0
	56	20	35	39	0	6	83	65	15	26		0
	6	12	91	78	0	1	3	19	95	76		0
	26	25	65	49	1	7	45	40	53	49		1
	25	23	70	61	0	4	39	41	58	53		0
	16	16	76	67	1	4	20	26	65	68		0
	3	9	9	17	2	3	3	10	13	19		0
	21	23	24	19	9	3	16	22	29	17		0
	9	7	14	10	15	17	9	7	17	8		16
	8	6	4	4	8	16	10	8	4	4		41
	22	7	10	4	49	31	15	5	10	3		1
	8	15	17	20	3	2	9	13	2	21		0
	3	0	0	0	0	0	9	1	1	0		0
	3	9	9	14	4	3	2	11	14	17		0
	18	19	9	9	10	22	21	18	7	8		41
	6	5	4	3	1	3	7	5	3	2		0
	101	100	100	100	101	100	101	100	100	99		99

janitors (see table 2.3). Despite the concentration of blacks in janitorial occupations in 1970, only one-third of all male janitors in Los Angeles were black. Between 1970 and 1990, the janitorial sector in Los Angeles expanded by about 50 percent, from thirty-eight thousand to fifty-two thousand workers, but the number of black male janitors declined from about twelve thousand to about eight thousand. During this period, the number of male Mexican immigrant janitors increased from fewer than one thousand to more than sixteen

Table 2.3   Representation of Native Black, Native White, and Mexican Immigrant Men in Cleaning Services: Janitors in Los Angeles, Chicago, and Atlanta, 1970 and 1990

	1970			1990		
City	Native Blacks	Native Whites	Mexican Immigrants	Native Blacks	Native Whites	Mexican Immigrants
Los Angeles						
Number of workers	12,500	18,100	900	8,304	9,520	16,591
Representation index	**5.58**	*0.32*	1.01	**2.15**	*0.27*	**2.22**
Education (years)	10.20	10.70	3.30	11.70	12.10	7.40
Unemployment rate (%)	5.0	9.0	0.0	16.4	8.0	5.0
Government workers (%)	34	34	0	39	24	6
Income (1989 $)	18,234	18,008	15,707	18,193	19,335	12,158
Chicago						
Number of workers	10,800	24,100	600[a]	11,526	19,974	3,489
Representation index	**2.20**	*0.45*	1.76[a]	**2.24**	*0.45*	1.58
Education (years)	8.6	9.9	7.6[a]	11.2	11.6	7.6
Unemployment rate (%)	4	3	0[a]	21	6	7
Government workers (%)	30	20	0[a]	31	23	8
Income (1989 $)	18,207	22,007	26,145[a]	16,255	19,118	13,873
Atlanta						
Number of workers	3,700	2,000	0	6,471	4,363	162
Representation index	**8.12**	*0.12*	—	**3.95**	*0.24*	1.66
Education (years)	6.7	9.0	—	11.2	12.1	[a]
Unemployment rate (%)	0	5	—	11	5	[a]
Government workers (%)	32	24	—	19	18	[a]
Income (1989 $)	12,329	21,281	—	13,328	16,084	[a]

Sources: 1970 Census 5 percent questionnaire county group files (this is a 1-in-100 sample) and 1990 Census Public Use Microdata Sample 5 percent A file (a weighted 5-in-100 sample).

Notes: Income in 1989 dollars is calculated only for those employed at the time of the census survey; income data from the 1970 census are corrected for inflation, using the CPI. All other statistics include all workers in the labor force (employed and unemployed). Representation indexes greater than 2 are in boldface roman; indexes of less than 0.5 are in boldface italic. Metropolitan area definitions for 1990 have been altered to be identical to the 1970 MSA definitions: Los Angeles includes Los Angeles County; Chicago includes Cook and DuPage Counties; Atlanta includes Dekalb, Fulton, Clayton, Cobb, and Gwinnett Counties.

[a] Sample size is very small, and point estimate may be unreliable.

thousand, surpassing the absolute number of black janitors by a factor of two. This raises the obvious question that inspired case studies of this occupation: Have the Mexican immigrants displaced blacks? The simple answer is yes and no. This is because in 1990 blacks remained overrepresented in janitorial jobs in Los Angeles, even though substantial ground had been lost since 1970. Non-Hispanic native whites in Los Angeles lost about ten thousand janitorial jobs between 1970 and 1990, but most of this loss was a result of the shrinking white population of Los Angeles (see tables 2.1 and 2.2).

In 1990, black janitors in Los Angeles were much more highly represented than Mexican immigrants among government workers, and they earned about 50 percent higher wages. However, black janitors from Los Angeles experienced high unemployment in 1990—16 percent compared with 5 percent among Mexican immigrant janitors[4]— and had higher levels of education than Mexican immigrants—twelve year versus seven years. Thus, in Los Angeles, it appears that Mexican immigrants are succeeding blacks in janitorial occupations, but it is not obvious that this amounts to displacement. Blacks have held on to their janitorial jobs in the government sector, and those who remain are much better compensated than their Mexican counterparts, who work predominantly in the private sector. Although Mexican immigrants have less education and work for less money, they also experience lower unemployment than blacks. Thus, this evidence suggests an alternative interpretation to the conventional displacement story, namely, that blacks now may be overqualified for private-sector janitorial work in Los Angeles. This interpretation is consistent with the stories that Waldinger (1996) tells about immigrants who are more willing than natives (either black or white) to do long hours of menial work at low wage rates. Given their low levels of education, longer hours are one way to make up for their low earning capacity.

In 1990, both blacks and Mexican immigrants were overrepresented in Chicago's janitorial jobs. In absolute terms, there were more than three times as many blacks as Mexican immigrants employed as janitors in Chicago, but this difference reflects the ethnic makeup of Chicago more than different propensities of either group to work as janitors. As in Los Angeles, immigrants in Chicago work almost exclusively in the private sector, receive substantially lower wages, and are much less likely to be unemployed than blacks. Unlike Los Angeles, where the black representation index in janitorial work declined steeply from 1970 to 1990, in Chicago the representation index and the absolute number of black janitors remained fairly constant. Thus, there is little evidence of displacement of blacks by Mexican migrants in Chicago. In both Chicago and Los Angeles in 1990, native whites have far lower unemployment rates than native blacks. These differences suggest the plausible hypothesis that native whites, unlike blacks, have alternative employment avenues open to them such that only men who find adequately compensated (for example, with access to benefits) janitorial work remain so engaged.

Mexican immigrants cannot compete with blacks for Atlanta's janitorial jobs because they constitute a negligible share of the total labor force. It is noteworthy, therefore, that the black index of representation in janitorial jobs decreased there as well—in the absence of any competition with immigrants. Nevertheless, black men residing in Atlanta were four times more likely to work in janitorial services than other Atlanta men. They also experienced a lower unemployment rate (11 percent) than their black counterparts employed as janitors in Los Angeles (16 percent) and Chicago (21 percent). This implies that black janitors residing in areas that do not receive large volumes of new, unskilled migrants may face less intense competition than their counterparts who reside in immigrant-impacted areas. Atlanta's black janitors earn less than their black counterparts in the other cities and also less than white janitors in Atlanta, but 1970 data indicate that this is a long-standing problem and is certainly not attributable to immigration.

In sum, there is some evidence that the janitorial occupation, which was a solid black niche in all three cities in 1970, is under pressure from Mexican migrants. Yet, the comparative evidence indicates that the janitorial occupation has not experienced complete ethnic succession, even in Los Angeles, where black men remain overrepresented in such work. We hypothesize that government employment partly shields black janitors from competition with Mexican immigrants. That whites and blacks earn more than Mexican immigrants employed as janitors also requires further investigation to determine whether wage undercutting is the key mechanism triggering ethnic succession of janitorial jobs; whether the janitorial sector of the economy is becoming split along ethnic lines; and whether lower wages are in fact the result of unequal access to government jobs by black, Mexican, and native white men.

Women in cleaning services are largely concentrated in maid jobs; therefore we consider this occupation for detailed scrutiny of cleaning services. Table 2.4 shows the occupational niche data for maids in the three metropolitan areas under consideration. In Los Angeles, maid jobs have experienced a virtually complete ethnic succession wherein Mexicans have replaced blacks. This is the most dramatic shift for any occupation in the three locations under consideration. In 1970, native black Angelinas were highly overrepresented in the domestic service sector. Although native whites were relatively underrepresented, they still held a sizable portion of all maid jobs. By 1990, Mexican immigrant women had driven most native white and black women out of domestic service jobs. Maid jobs, unlike the janitorial jobs, lack a

Table 2.4 Representation of Native Black, Native White, and Mexican Immigrant Women in Cleaning Services: Maids in Los Angeles, Chicago, and Atlanta, 1970 and 1990

City	1970			1990		
	Native Blacks	Native Whites	Mexican Immigrants	Native Blacks	Native Whites	Mexican Immigrants
Los Angeles						
Number of workers	6,600	5,200	900	1,030	1,115	4,892
Representation index	**7.20**	*0.14*	3.18	0.63	*0.10*	**4.82**
Education (years)	9.20	10.80	8.40	11.70	11.90	7.10
Unemployment rate (%)	4.0	2.0	0.0	8.5	7.1	8.4
Government workers (%)	0	0	0	8	6	4
Income (1989 $)	7,732	9,482	7,134	11,766	10,865	9,197
Chicago						
Number of workers	5,600	2,500	0	3,069	1,917	1,122
Representation index	**7.66**	*0.13*	—	**2.21**	*0.15*	**6.35**
Education (years)	8.4	9.0	—	11.0	11.4	7.2
Unemployment rate (%)	3	0	—	17	4	8
Government workers (%)	0	0	—	8	2	0
Income (1989 $)	7,286	5,773	—	10,409	11,138	9,638
Atlanta						
Number of workers	7,900	700[a]	0	3,718	872	0
Representation index	**30.70**	*0.03*[a]	—	**7.81**	*0.11*	—
Education (years)	8.1	7.4[a]	—	11.3	10.8	—
Unemployment rate (%)	4	0[a]	—	12	4	—
Government workers (%)	0	0[a]	—	6	4	—
Income (1989 $)	5,273	9,313[a]	—	10,745	7,206	—

Sources: 1970 Census 5 percent questionnaire county group files (this is a 1-in-100 sample) and 1990 Census Public Use Microdata Sample 5 percent A file (a weighted 5-in-100 sample).
Notes: Representation indexes greater than 2 are in boldface roman; indexes of less than 0.5 are in boldface italic.
[a]Sample size is very small, and point estimate may be unreliable.

sizable unionized public sector, hence the protective shield we hypothesized for black men in cleaning services is unavailable to protect black women from competition with immigrants.

Mexican immigrant women in Los Angeles, who work for somewhat lower wages than native black women, obtain the lion's share of jobs as maids in Los Angeles, and they appear poised to make considerable inroads in Chicago. Because the volume of Mexican migration to Chicago is appreciably less than that to Los Angeles, Mexican nationals constitute a small share of all maids. Hence, Chicago's native blacks and native whites still maintain substantial footholds in this occupation. In Atlanta, where there was no competition from immigrants, black women held an almost exclusive control of domestic work in 1970 (a representation index of more than 30); this ironclad control has diminished somewhat, but black women remain highly overrepresented among all maid jobs.

For women engaged in cleaning services, the comparison of the three metropolitan areas lends support to the argument that immigrants do replace native blacks in private domestic cleaning services. However, the evidence also leaves open questions about the mechanisms driving the ethnic succession of domestic service jobs. Is it wage competition? The earnings gradient between natives and immigrants is lower for maids than for almost any other occupation because maids who are U.S. natives earn extremely low wages. Women from Mexico do not appear to drive U.S.-born women out of this occupation by working for less, even though the immigrants have much less formal education. The wages of native-born maids were already low in 1970, when there was much less competition from immigrants.

It is conceivable that it is the lack of protection afforded by public-sector employment that permits recent Mexican immigrants to succeed blacks as maids. As Grant, Oliver, and James (1996) point out, being displaced from menial work like domestic service can be advantageous if this opens opportunities higher up in the occupational structure. Whether black and white women who formerly worked as maids no longer do because they found better jobs is an empirical question that has not been addressed. A definitive answer to this question requires longitudinal data.

Factory Work

Historically, factory work has absorbed large numbers of immigrants. For purposes of illustration, and because we are more interested in hypothesis generation than in any particular case study, we consider two typical factory occupations, that of machine operator, for men, and assembler, for women. In both Los Angeles and Chicago, Mexican immigrants have succeeded native whites and blacks in this kind of work, but it is unclear whether succession implies displacement of domestic workers. This is because Mexican immigrants are far less skilled than domestic workers and because the operative jobs that currently exist may require less skill than their predecessors. That Mexican wages in operative jobs have fallen while those of blacks who remained actually rose in absolute terms is consistent with this interpretation.

Table 2.5 Representation of Native Black, Native White, and Mexican Immigrant Men in Factory Work: Machine Operators in Los Angeles, Chicago, and Atlanta, 1970 and 1990

	1970			1990		
City	Native Blacks	Native Whites	Mexican Immigrants	Native Blacks	Native Whites	Mexican Immigrants
Los Angeles						
Number of workers	3,900	11,400	2,000	1,581	3,358	12,143
Representation index	**2.28**	*0.33*	**3.86**	0.78	*0.19*	**4.39**
Education (years)	11.70	11.00	8.70	11.60	12.40	7.30
Unemployment rate (%)	5.0	7.0	5.0	8.0	6.0	5.0
Government workers (%)	12	2	0	15	7	1
Income (1989 $)	24,426	24,723	17,785	28,047	28,594	14,610
Chicago						
Number of workers	5,400	13,200	600[a]	3,045	4,242	4,404
Representation index	1.97	*0.45*	**3.28**[a]	1.33	*0.17*	**6.26**
Education (years)	10.1	10.5	6.8[a]	11.4	11.6	7.6
Unemployment rate (%)	9	2	0[a]	9	8	7
Government workers (%)	2	2	17[a]	4	3	1
Income (1989 $)	21,463	28,159	18,464[a]	25,015	25,841	17,173
Atlanta						
Number of workers	1,100	2,100	0	2,358	1,725	31
Representation index	**2.41**	*0.45*	—	**3.85**	*0.27*	0.85[a]
Education (years)	10.8	9.8	—	11.8	11.8	—
Unemployment rate (%)	15	9	—	5	2	—
Government workers (%)	8	13	—	7	6	—
Income (1989 $)	17,933	22,615	—	20,622	24,789	—

Sources: 1970 Census 5 percent questionnaire county group files (this is a 1-in-100 sample) and 1990 Census Public Use Microdata Sample 5 percent A file (a weighted 5-in-100 sample).
Notes: Representation indexes greater than 2 are in boldface roman; indexes of less than 0.5 are in boldface italic.
[a]Sample size is very small, and point estimate may be unreliable.

In Los Angeles in 1990, native black and white machine operators earn roughly twice as much as Mexican immigrants, but they also average four or more years of schooling (see table 2.5). The earnings differential between natives and immigrants in factory work—unlike that for maids—suggests a split labor market. Edna Bonacich (1972) posits the split labor market in an attempt to explain the sources of ethnic antagonism between native and immigrant workers. In Bonacich's framework, immigrants are willing to work for lower wages than native workers, and the native workers strive either to exclude the immigrants or to insulate themselves from labor-market competition by using legal and social means to segregate and isolate the immi-grants. We have already noted a division of the blue-collar labor mar-ket into a (presumably nonunionized) private sector with a heavy immigrant concentration and a public sector where the natives domi-nate. Bonacich suggests that a split labor market divides immigrant and native workers who do exactly the same work. As we show, how-ever, even within the same factory occupations the natives and immi-grants work in different industries, so that the case for a split labor market is not clear.

Blacks hold the public-sector jobs among operative workers, as in janitorial services. The implicit hypothesis is that the immigrants have displaced the natives from all but the most highly skilled and the union jobs. In Chicago, the 1990 Mexican representation index for machine operators is even higher than in Los Angeles, but the total number of Mexican immigrant machinists is much smaller because Chicago has a much lower population of immigrants than Los An-geles. Whether owing to the smaller scale of immigration to Chicago or to other factors (such as changes in Chicago's manufacturing sec-tor), machinist occupations are less completely bifurcated between highly paid natives and poorly paid immigrants. However, the dra-matic increase in the representation index for immigrants coupled with the declining representation of blacks signals incipient competi-tion that could lead to future displacement of blacks in Chicago. Government employment is unlikely to buffer occupational succes-sion in this instance because only 4 percent of black machine opera-tors are public-sector employees.

Atlanta lacks a manufacturing sector on the scale of Chicago or Los Angeles. More concretely, there were only about one-sixth to one-ninth as many machine operators in Atlanta as in the other cities (about three thousand compared with eighteen thousand in Chicago and twenty-seven thousand in Los Angeles), despite the fact that in 1990 Chicago was only about three times larger and Los Angeles four times larger in population than Atlanta (see table 2.1). Among the relatively small population of male machine operators in the Atlanta area, the number of black workers rose, as did the black representa-tion index—from 2.41 to 3.85 between 1970 and 1990. This is in stark contrast with Chicago and Los Angeles, where Mexican mi-grants have been succeeding blacks in these jobs and by 1990 had achieved a strong occupational foothold.

The loss of factory jobs by native whites in Chicago and Los An-geles is far more severe (in terms of sheer numbers) than the losses sustained by blacks. In Los Angeles the number of white male machine operators declined from 11,400 in 1970 to 3,358 in 1990, and in Chicago the machinist positions held by native whites declined from more than 13,000 to less than 5,000 positions. In all cities, native whites were already underrepresented as machine operators in 1970 (representation indexes of less than 0.5), but their lower representation in this occupation is still dramatic. To the extent that immigrants' job gains in factory work come at the expense of native groups, whites bear the impact as much as or more than blacks.

In Los Angeles, the wages of white and black machine operators increased slightly in real terms between 1970 and 1990. This is a fairly substantial gain at a time that the real wages of high-school-educated workers fell appreciably, although it may be a result of the selection process discouraging whites and blacks from leaving the occupation. In Chicago, the black machine operators who remained in 1990 were better compensated in real terms than their compatriots had been twenty years earlier, whereas white machinists earned less in 1990 than in 1970. However, the largest occupational gap in earnings was that between native and immigrant workers. Mexican machinists have about four years less formal education than native white and black machinists, but this is the same education gap that we find in all the other occupations. Taken at face value, the wage gap provides compelling evidence of a split labor market among factory workers, although more detailed information would be required to determine whether immigrants were paid less for doing the exact same work as natives. Occupational segregation within industries and firms usually precludes a direct test of the split-market hypothesis (Bielby and Baron 1986).

For women factory workers, whose representation we illustrate with the occupation of assemblers (table 2.6), the story is similar to that of male factory workers, in that the lower wages paid to immigrants suggest a split labor market. In Los Angeles and Chicago, Mexican immigrant women made enormous inroads into factory work, but these gains came largely at the expense of whites rather than blacks. Mexican women residing in Los Angeles in 1990 were six times more likely than other women in the metropolitan area to work as assemblers, but they received far lower annual earnings than either blacks or whites. The high rate of unemployment among Mexican assemblers coupled with a more than twofold increase in representation appears to signal growing own-group competition, as social networks continue to channel new immigrants to assembler jobs in a highly volatile segment of the manufacturing sector.

Chicago provides some evidence of intergroup competition. Un-

Table 2.6　Representation of Native Black, Native White, and Mexican Immigrant Women in Factory Work: Assemblers in Los Angeles, Chicago, and Atlanta, 1970 and 1990

City	1970			1990		
	Native Blacks	Native Whites	Mexican Immigrants	Native Blacks	Native Whites	Mexican Immigrants
Los Angeles						
Number of workers	4,400	15,800	1,100	1,576	2,028	9,111
Representation index	1.50	*0.45*	1.85	0.59	*0.12*	**5.99**
Education (years)	11.40	10.80	8.40	12.10	11.20	6.90
Unemployment rate (%)	23.0	14.0	8.0	12.0	16.0	12.0
Government workers (%)	9	3	0	10	2	1
Income (1989 $)	14,958	16,035	10,472	17,176	17,709	10,756
Chicago						
Number of workers	4,500	16,800	700[a]	3,180	4,725	2,688
Representation index	0.88	*0.54*	5.58[a]	**0.99**	*0.22*	8.52
Education (years)	9.7	9.3	7.8[a]	11.3	10.7	7.3
Unemployment rate (%)	10	5	0[a]	21	7	19
Government workers (%)	2	1	0[a]	2	2	2
Income (1989 $)	15,633	15,461	11,387[a]	14,332	16,257	10,455
Atlanta						
Number of workers	700[a]	600[a]	0	1,484	1,239	19
Representation index	**3.1**[a]	*0.26*[a]	—	**2.11**	*0.32*	—
Education (years)	9.4[a]	9.0[a]	—	12.1	10.9	—
Unemployment rate (%)	13[a]	14[a]	—	23	7	—
Government workers (%)	0[a]	0[a]	—	2	7	—
Income (1989 $)	12,667[a]	19,254[a]	—	17,606	16,122	—

Sources: 1970 Census 5 percent questionnaire county group files (this is a 1-in-100 sample) and 1990 Census Public Use Microdata Sample 5 percent A file (a weighted 5-in-100 sample).

Notes: Representation indexes greater than 2 are in boldface roman; indexes of less than 0.5 are in boldface italic.

[a]Sample size is very small, and point estimate may be unreliable.

employment for assemblers increased for every demographic group from 1970 to 1990, as the number of assemblers overall decreased sharply. The Mexican representation index increased over the period under consideration (from 5.60 to 8.52). That factory work, especially assembly work, is almost exclusively private-sector employment gives native groups few protections. By 1990, black unemployment among female assemblers in Chicago was 21 percent, compared with rates of 7 percent among native whites and 14 percent among Mexican immigrants. In Atlanta, with a small manufacturing sector and hardly any immigrants, blacks and whites have maintained their shares of assembler jobs.

In sum, there is mixed evidence about the nature and extent of interethnic competition and displacement among native and immigrant workers holding manufacturing jobs. In Chicago and Los Angeles after 1970, whites lost far more factory jobs than blacks. Small sample sizes preclude firm generalizations from Atlanta's experience, but immigration cannot be a contributing factor to the apparent decline in the wages of white assemblers. To explain the wage gaps between native and immigrant factory workers (both women and men), a more detailed analysis of factory work that combines industry and occupation is necessary. Accordingly, we conducted exploratory analyses of manufacturing jobs by industry.[5]

Mexican immigrants made up 39 percent of factory workers in Los Angeles and 19 percent of factory workers in Chicago in 1990 (see table 2.2). These industrywide representations hold across many individual industries that remain bastions for native workers, such as the blast furnaces and steel mills of Los Angeles and Chicago, where Mexican immigrants hold a representative share of the jobs. Apparel and clothing factories in Los Angeles employ twenty thousand Mexican immigrant women and twelve thousand Mexican immigrant men. Native blacks and whites have negligible shares of the needle-trade jobs, so it is clear that the manufacture of apparel is an industrial niche for Mexican immigrants. This is consistent with historical accounts that describe garment work as an immigrant niche (see also Waldinger 1989). Apparel manufacturing is much less prevalent in Chicago than in Los Angeles (Los Angeles had about six times as many garment workers as Chicago in 1990). Moreover, Asian immigrants are overrepresented in Chicago's garment factories—not Mexicans.

Whereas the Mexican immigrants in Los Angeles are concentrated in the low-wage apparel sector, native white and black males dominate in the highly paid and skill-intensive factories that produce aircraft, aircraft parts, guided missiles, and space vehicles. The Chicago metropolitan area does not have heavy industrial high-technology manufacturing of this kind. According to tables 2.5 and 2.6, the manufacturing wage gap between natives and immigrants is highest for male machine operators in Los Angeles in 1990, where natives earn about twenty-eight thousand dollars a year compared with fifteen thousand dollars for Mexican immigrants. The manufacturing wage gap is steepest in Los Angeles, largely because immigrants dominate in the vast garment industry, although it is native workers who dominate the high-tech manufacturing sector. The industrial segregation of immigrants and natives into low-skill and high-skill manufacturing jobs deflates the hypothesis of the split labor market. Immigrant and native machine operators are in many cases not working on the same kind of machines, nor in the same kind of factories.

Nevertheless, the reality of occupational segregation does not mean that immigrants have not displaced natives from the garment trades in Los Angeles over time (as Waldinger [1989] argues for the case of New York) or that immigrants and natives do not compete for some of the same factory jobs in certain industries. Even detailed occupational codes such as "machine operator" can describe a wide variety of real jobs in which the actual work and the ethnic mix of workers is highly variable and in which little or much intergroup competition can exist.

Skilled Service Occupations

Table 2.7 gives data on postal clerks, a black male occupational niche that has been completely resistant to labor-market pressure from immigrants. Federal civil service jobs generally exclude noncitizens, and although the Postal Service is an independent government agency (and hence has more discretion in hiring policy), the English-language civil service exam and priority hiring for citizen workers combine to limit, if not exclude, immigrants from this occupation. Between 1970 and 1990, black representation among postal clerks in all three cities rose from a representation index of 3.5 in 1970 to an overrepresentation of more than 5.5 in 1990 of all postal workers in Los Angeles and from 6.2 to 9.5 in Chicago. Whites are underrepresented among postal clerks relative to their labor-force shares in all localities, and in Atlanta and Chicago this underrepresentation predates 1970. In Los Angeles, the number of white postal clerks shrunk by almost two-thirds, from forty-seven hundred to seventeen hundred. Although immigrants are excluded from Postal Service employment for a variety of legal and procedural reasons, the dominance of blacks over whites in the post office requires a different kind of explanation. Possible explanations include the power of network hiring and social contacts that allow blacks better information about job openings; a workplace atmosphere that discourages white candidates from applying; and the use of black political resources to maintain control of an occupation that has come to be viewed as rightfully theirs.

Although the position of postal clerk is considered a good job for

Table 2.7   Representation of Native Black, Native White, and Mexican
Immigrant Men in Skilled Services: Postal Clerks in Los
Angeles, Chicago, and Atlanta, 1970 and 1990

	1970			1990		
City	Native Blacks	Native Whites	Mexican Immigrants	Native Blacks	Native Whites	Mexican Immigrants
Los Angeles						
Number of workers	1,800	4,700	0	2,190	1,685	122
Representation index	**3.53**	0.57	—	**5.55**	*0.42*	*0.09*
Education (years)	13.40	12.60	—	13.10	13.50	—
Unemployment rate (%)	10.0	6.0	—	11.0	2.0	—
Government workers (%)	100	100	—	100	100	—
Income (1989 $)	23,720	26,807	—	29,306	29,382	—
Chicago						
Number of workers	3,300	2,700	0	4,200	1,992	24
Representation index	**6.28**	*0.21*	—	**9.50**	*0.21*	*0.06*
Education (years)	12.2	12.5	—	12.6	12.5	—
Unemployment rate (%)	0	7	—	16	0	—
Government workers (%)	100	100	—	100	100	—
Income (1989 $)	27,145	28,773	—	26,310	30,453	—
Atlanta						
Number of workers	1,300	900	0	1,571	557	0
Representation index	**6.65**	*0.16*	—	**9.22**	*0.15*	—
Education (years)	11.8	11.6	—	13.3	13.2	—
Unemployment rate (%)	0	0	—	2	0	—
Government workers (%)	100	100	—	100	100	—
Income (1989 $)	26,736	24,919	—	31,595	28,949	—

Sources: 1970 Census 5 percent questionnaire county group files (this is a 1-in-100 sample) and 1990
Census Public Use Microdata Sample 5 percent A file (a weighted 5-in-100 sample).
Notes: Representation indexes greater than 2 are in boldface roman; indexes of less than 0.5 are in
boldface italic.

high-school graduates, the total number of male postal clerks did not
change much from 1970 to 1990, accounting for fewer than seven
thousand jobs in Chicago, about four thousand in Los Angeles, and
about two thousand in Atlanta at the end of the twenty-year period.
By contrast, the demand for elementary-school teachers—another
largely public-sector occupation—has grown by 42 percent since
1970, to as many as fifty thousand jobs, in both Chicago and Los
Angeles and by 167 percent in Atlanta, to more than twenty-four
thousand positions (see table 2.8). During this twenty-year period, the
population of the Chicago MSA remained stable (balanced by de-
population in the inner city and growth in the surrounding suburbs),

Table 2.8   Representation of Native Black, Native White, and Mexican
Immigrant Women in Skilled Services: Elementary-School
Teachers in Los Angeles, Chicago, and Atlanta, 1970 and
1990

City	1970			1990		
	Native Blacks	Native Whites	Mexican Immigrants	Native Blacks	Native Whites	Mexican Immigrants
Los Angeles						
Number of workers	4,000	31,300	0	8,738	39,940	1,387
Representation index	1.03	1.93	—	1.26	1.81	*0.21*
Education (years)	16.40	16.50	—	15.70	15.80	13.70
Unemployment rate (%)	2.0	3.0	—	1.0	1.0	2.0
Government workers (%)	95	81	—	76	77	81
Income (1989 $)	26,463	24,936	—	27,825	25,327	13,562
Chicago						
Number of workers	4,700	27,000	0	12,081	32,892	225
Representation index	0.78	1.89	—	1.38	1.16	*0.20*
Education (years)	16.1	16.3	—	16.0	16.2	—
Unemployment rate (%)	0	1	—	2	1	—
Government workers (%)	81	72	—	82	65	—
Income (1989 $)	26,061	22,906	—	27,307	23,141	—
Atlanta						
Number of workers	3,200	5,800	0	5,900	18,089	42
Representation index	1.68	0.62	—	0.78	1.43	—
Education (years)	15.9	15.8	—	16.2	16.0	—
Unemployment rate (%)	3	2	—	2	1	—
Government workers (%)	91	93	—	84	83	—
Income (1989 $)	23,146	18,430	—	25,599	21,910	—

Sources: 1970 Census 5 percent questionnaire county group files (this is a 1-in-100 sample) and 1990
Census Public Use Microdata Sample 5 percent A file (a weighted 5-in-100 sample).
Notes: Representation indexes of less than 0.5 are in boldface italic.

whereas that of Los Angeles grew slightly and Atlanta grew about 50
percent (see table 2.1). The growth of teaching positions has far out-
stripped the growth of the population as a whole, signaling increased
demand for teachers.

The figures in table 2.8 indicate that from 1970 until 1990 the
number of black women elementary-school teachers more or less doubled in Los Angeles and Atlanta and almost tripled in Chicago. Although native whites still retain the majority of teaching jobs, the
representation index for black women rose steadily in Chicago and
Los Angeles, although immigrants were virtually excluded from this
occupation. In the Atlanta area, whites have made the greatest relative

gains since 1970, so the representation index for blacks declined even though the number of black female elementary-school teachers almost doubled over this twenty-year period. Unlike that of both Chicago and Los Angeles, whose metropolitan areas lost substantial numbers of whites between 1970 and 1990, Atlanta's white population actually grew by almost 32 percent (see table 2.1).

Teaching in the public schools requires a college degree, a teaching certification, and reasonably strong language skills (even for teacher aides). Thus, there are substantial barriers to the employment of Mexican immigrants, who mostly lack high-school degrees and often lack English skills, as well. What is especially interesting about the case of schoolteachers is that the ranks of schoolchildren in Chicago and, especially, in Los Angeles have been swollen by the children of immigrants. In other words, immigration has been the driving force behind the expansion of school systems in two of the three cities under consideration, and the important job of teaching these children falls almost exclusively to natives (black and white).[6] The literature on the fiscal impacts of immigration has emphasized the fiscal component of public primary education as the main cost that immigration imposes because immigrant families average more children than native families and because public education costs between five thousand and ten thousand dollars per student per year in the larger cities (Clark et al. 1994). Largely ignored by these discussions is the control of teaching jobs by U.S.-born workers. These jobs provide high status, if not high pay, for educated women, who are drawn disproportionately from the ranks of natives. Of course, natives pay the lion's share of local taxes that support public education (because immigrants, especially Mexican immigrants, tend to earn less), but natives also get the vast majority of the best jobs in the school system.

Thus, the case of schoolteachers provides an important lesson about competition and complementarity between native and immigrant workers: The demand for schoolteachers associated with Mexican immigration improves job prospects for college-educated women at the same time that immigrant women are largely excluded from this opportunity, except insofar as second-generation immigrant women become certified for the teaching profession. This case study illustrates strong complementarity between native and immigrant women, who usually find employment in unskilled services. In 1990 black women were more highly represented among teachers in Los Angeles and Chicago (the immigrant-receiving cities) than in Atlanta, a nonimmigrant city (see table 2.8).

Table 2.9   Representation of Native Black, Native White, and Mexican
Immigrant Men in Unskilled Services: Security Guards in Los
Angeles, Chicago, and Atlanta, 1970 and 1990

	1970			1990		
City	Native Blacks	Native Whites	Mexican Immigrants	Native Blacks	Native Whites	Mexican Immigrants
Los Angeles						
Number of workers	1,100	8,200	0	7,123	10,810	1,558
Representation index	1.51	**2.28**	—	**4.02**	0.79	*0.30*
Education (years)	12.6	11.5	—	12.7	13.0	9.4
Unemployment rate (%)	0	4	—	12	7	9
Government workers (%)	36	15	—	15	16	2
Income (1989 $)	17,839	21,980	—	18,388	23,012	11,931
Chicago						
Number of workers	2,500	8,900	0	6,453	8,502	186[a]
Representation index	1.62	0.95	—	**3.95**	0.51	*0.19*[a]
Education (years)	10.80	10.20	—	12.10	12.80	[a]
Unemployment rate (%)	0.0	3.0	—	18.0	4.0	[a]
Government workers (%)	56	13	—	17	9	[a]
Income (1989 $)	21,186	21,018	—	16,883	19,365	[a]
Atlanta						
Number of workers	500	2,200	0	2,962	2,441	17
Representation index	1.05	1.04	—	**3.56**	*0.31*	*0.36*
Education (years)	10.20	8.40	—	12.60	13.10	—
Unemployment rate (%)	0.0	0.0	—	7.0	4.0	—
Government workers (%)	40	23	—	16	21	—
Income (1989 $)	16,147	15,039	—	16,742	22,703	—

Sources: 1970 Census 5 percent questionnaire county group files (this is a 1-in-100 sample) and 1990 Census Public Use Microdata Sample 5 percent A file (a weighted 5-in-100 sample).
Notes: Representation indexes greater than 2 are in boldface roman; indexes of less than 0.5 are in boldface italic.
[a] Sample size is very small, and point estimate may be unreliable.

Unskilled Services

Tables 2.9 and 2.10 present data for two fast-growing service occupations—security guard, for men, and nurse's aide, for women. Few of these jobs attract college graduates, although educational requirements are varied across cities and ethnoracial groups. Most of the employment growth in the security business has gone to blacks, whose representation indexes exceeded 3 in all three metropolitan areas in 1990 but was below 2 in 1970 (see table 2.9). Although most security guard jobs do not require high educational credentials, relatively few Mexican immigrants have been able to encroach on this

Table 2.10 Representation of Native Black, Native White, and Mexican Immigrant Women in Unskilled Services: Nurse's Aides in Los Angeles, Chicago, and Atlanta, 1970 and 1990

City	1970			1990		
	Native Blacks	Native Whites	Mexican Immigrants	Native Blacks	Native Whites	Mexican Immigrants
Los Angeles						
Number of workers	5,200	6,800	100[a]	8,132	7,510	3,800
Representation index	**4.78**	*0.35*	*0.34*[a]	**2.49**	*0.33*	1.18
Education (years)	11.98	11.50	[a]	12.20	12.80	8.70
Unemployment rate (%)	5.0	6.0	[a]	11.0	4.0	7.0
Government workers (%)	29	14	[a]	23	20	15
Income (1989 $)	13,671	11,299	[a]	15,832	16,548	10,006
Chicago						
Number of workers	7,000	6,100	0	12,882	8,120	237
Representation index	**4.16**	*0.25*	—	**4.13**	*0.25*	*0.40*
Education (years)	10.7	11.8	—	12.0	12.8	—
Unemployment rate (%)	2	0	—	12	2	—
Government workers (%)	30	2	—	17	6	—
Income (1989 $)	13,454	9,337	—	13,675	13,075	—
Atlanta						
Number of workers	1,100	600[a]	0	4,849	1,708	0
Representation index	**3.79**	*0.26*[a]	—	**6.16**	*0.17*	—
Education (years)	9.2	9.2[a]	—	12.0	12.6	—
Unemployment rate (%)	8	0[a]	—	13	7	—
Government workers (%)	25	33[a]	—	18	3	—
Income (1989 $)	11,384	9,161[a]	—	13,761	15,184	—

Sources: 1970 Census 5 percent questionnaire county group files (this is a 1-in-100 sample) and 1990 Census Public Use Microdata Sample 5 percent A file (a weighted 5-in-100 sample).

Notes: Representation indexes greater than 2 are in boldface roman; indexes of less than 0.5 are in boldface italic.

[a]Sample size is very small, and point estimate may be unreliable.

traditionally black occupational niche, even in Los Angeles, where the average Mexican immigrant employed as a security guard in 1990 averaged 35 percent lower income and three fewer years of education than the average African American guard.

If lower wages were the primary mechanism enabling Mexicans to compete with blacks, one might predict that this occupation is evolving into a split-market sector. However, it is not possible to determine from census data whether Mexican immigrants have been paid lower wages than native blacks for exactly the same work; it may be that white and black security guards hold more-responsible positions than

Mexicans. That the unemployment rate for white and black security guards rose between 1970 and 1990 in both Chicago and Los Angeles provides evidence for the first stages of immigrant competition. The unemployment rate for security guards also rose in Atlanta, however, where no immigrants were competing for these jobs. Overall, the occupation of security guard has been surprisingly resistant to encroachment from immigrants, even in Los Angeles. The only sign of strain for Los Angeles natives is the declining share of government employment, which suggests a thinner protective buffer from ethnic succession in the future.

For women, the nurse's aide position represents a rapid-growth unskilled service job that remains a black occupational niche in all three cities: Representation indexes were close to 4 as early as 1970 (table 2.10). In Atlanta, where black women face at most limited competition from immigrant women, their representation index rose over time, from 3.8 to 6.2, indicating a higher likelihood of black employment as nurse's aides over time. Their earnings rose slightly in real terms, but so, too, did their average education levels. White nurse's aides made appreciable gains in this occupation, especially in income growth. In Atlanta, this black occupational niche experienced some stress over the period, as indicated by rising black unemployment, but white women remained significantly underrepresented as of 1990.

In Chicago, Mexican immigrant women are virtually excluded from this black occupational niche, in which the average educational level of incumbents is completion of high school. The decline of government-sponsored nurse's aide jobs signals a weakening of black women's niche protection in Chicago. The low educational attainment of Mexican immigrant women limits their access to these jobs, so the black niche does not seem to be under great threat. However, black nurse's aides experienced substantially higher unemployment rates than whites in all three cities in 1990. Black women's control over this occupational niche diminished in Los Angeles as is evident from the lower representation index, higher unemployment rate, and diminished shares of government jobs among nurse's-aide positions in 1990 compared with 1970. Mexican immigrants remained underrepresented in this occupation, but those who secured aide positions had less education and earned lower wages. Although Mexican immigrants in Los Angeles remain underrepresented among nurse's aides, they made significant inroads during the 1970s and 1980s and were above parity in 1990. If our predictions about the pivotal role of public-sector employment in allowing ethnic occupational succession is correct, we would expect encroachment of Mexican immigrants in this occupation in the future.

In sum, the number of nurse's-aide positions has grown over time, but so too has the pool of women seeking these positions. Black unemployment in these positions has risen in all three cities, with the highest increase occurring in Los Angeles, where black women face strongest competition from Mexican immigrants. That the share of government jobs held by black nurse's aides has been declining signals an increasing vulnerability of this traditional black occupational niche to encroachment by white women but also by Mexican immigrant women in the future.

Office Work

Few accounts of labor-market displacement between immigrants and natives consider office work, presuming that this is not an arena where unskilled foreign-born workers compete. Such a presumption is precisely why these occupations are of interest to us here. To determine how the labor-market opportunities of natives respond to immigration, we need to include within our purview occupations that employ natives who can provide services to others (including to immigrants). The growth of immigrant workers in a labor market may permit increasing numbers of native women to enter the workforce, and office work provides numerous opportunities for women, even mothers of young children, to enter the labor force. Managers and administrators (for men) and secretaries (for women) represent the largest three-digit occupations among office workers, and we consider them briefly not only to round out our case studies but also because they have been a major source of employment growth.

The white-collar managers and administrators are the best paid among the occupational groups examined here (see table 2.11), and not surprisingly, this broadly defined occupation has been and continues to be a strongly held white niche. The white index of representation declined somewhat in all three cities between 1970 and 1990, but black and Mexican immigrant workers have not achieved a proportional increase in representation. Only in Los Angeles have blacks achieved a representation index above 0.5 in managerial and administrative occupations. Black earnings in managerial and administrative occupations trail their white occupational counterparts by a significant margin—far more than their educational differentials would predict.

Table 2.11   Representation of Native Black, Native White, and Mexican
Immigrant Women in Office Work: Managers and
Administrators in Los Angeles, Chicago, and Atlanta, 1970
and 1990

	1970			1990		
City	Native Blacks	Native Whites	Mexican Immigrants	Native Blacks	Native Whites	Mexican Immigrants
Los Angeles						
Number of workers	3,900	110,600	300ᵃ	5,701	92,008	4,389
Representation index	*0.38*	**2.96**	*0.1*ᵃ	0.53	**2.62**	*0.17*
Education (years)	12.60	13.40	ᵃ	13.90	14.50	8.60
Unemployment rate (%)	5	5	ᵃ	6	3	6
Government workers (%)	5	1	ᵃ	15	3	1
Income (1989 $)	25,199	56,226	ᵃ	39,181	65,756	24,159
Chicago						
Number of workers	2,800	82,300	0	5,391	81,072	861
Representation index	*0.19*	**3.89**	—	*0.36*	**2.88**	*0.16*
Education (years)	12.2	13.4	—	13.2	14.6	9.7
Unemployment rate (%)	0	0	—	8	2	5
Government workers (%)	4	1	—	16	3	0
Income (1989 $)	28,311	56,837	—	37,553	62,860	31,545
Atlanta						
Number of workers	900	24,500	0	3,687	39,579	0
Representation index	*0.17*	**4.47**	—	*0.30*	**2.73**	—
Education (years)	11.9	13.2	—	13.7	14.5	—
Unemployment rate (%)	0	2	—	2	1	—
Government workers (%)	0	0	—	10	3	—
Income (1989 $)	24,152	50,666	—	36,691	58,383	—

Sources: 1970 Census 5 percent questionnaire county group files (this is a 1-in-100 sample) and 1990
Census Public Use Microdata Sample 5 percent A file (a weighted 5-in-100 sample).
Notes: Representation indexes greater than 2 are in boldface roman; indexes of less than 0.5 are in
boldface italic.
ᵃSample size is very small, and point estimate may be unreliable.

Mexican immigrants are far more excluded from managerial positions than blacks. Their low levels of formal education and limited
fluency in English limit their access even to most low-level managerial
work. Under such circumstances, they cannot possibly compete with
blacks, whose average educational levels are similar to those of whites.
In Los Angeles, where the impact of Mexican immigration has been
the strongest, blacks have climbed the furthest into the managerial
ranks, based on measures of representation and salary. This suggests
the testable hypothesis that the presence of large shares of Mexican

immigrants occupying the most menial jobs actually permits the occupational mobility of black and white native workers (although the representation index for black managers was relatively high in Los Angeles even in 1970, before the current wave of immigration). In Atlanta, where Mexican immigrants are absent, black men's inroads into administrative and managerial positions have been weaker than in Los Angeles or Chicago. A plausible interpretation is that the presence of large numbers of Mexican immigrants increases the demand for all kinds of services and hence increases the need for lower-level managerial and supervisory positions, thereby permitting upward mobility for native workers.

Secretarial work, which in 1970 was firmly a white occupational niche in all three cities, was ethnically transformed during the twenty-year period under consideration (see table 2.12). By 1990 the index of representation for whites fell below 2.0 in all three cities, whereas the black index rose gradually. Nevertheless, blacks remain under-represented in this occupational niche, and Mexican immigrants even more so. These generalizations obtain even in Los Angeles, where blacks, aided by public-sector employment, have achieved better salaries and a higher representation index than blacks in either Chicago or Atlanta.

Because immigrants create their share of paperwork for both government and private corporations, and because immigrants are for the most part excluded from the office jobs where that paperwork is processed, it stands to reason that an influx of immigrants might create new opportunities for native workers in the office occupations. That black workers in Los Angeles have made the strongest inroads in these occupations illustrates one way that immigration can help push native groups further up the occupational ladder. Our evidence is more suggestive than conclusive, however, and warrants further verification. Therefore, we offer this interpretation as a testable hypothesis, among the others previously suggested.

CONCLUSION

The labor-market impact of immigration has been studied intensively in the last few years, but consensus has been elusive. Econometric studies of aggregate effects on a metropolitan labor market generally find little if any labor-market substitution between Mexican immigrants and native blacks. Ethnographic studies such as those by Roger Waldinger have focused on individual occupations or industries in which immigrants are overrepresented. These studies claim that im-

Table 2.12   Representation of Native Black, Native White, and Mexican Immigrant Women in Office Work: Secretaries in Los Angeles, Chicago, and Atlanta, 1970 and 1990

	1970			1990		
City	Native Blacks	Native Whites	Mexican Immigrants	Native Blacks	Native Whites	Mexican Immigrants
Los Angeles						
Number of workers	2,500	87,800	100[a]	12,158	67,250	4,037
Representation index	*0.22*	**2.57**	*0.05*[a]	0.94	1.56	*0.34*
Education (years)	13.20	12.80	[a]	13.20	13.20	12.10
Unemployment rate (%)	4	4	[a]	4	3	3
Government workers (%)	38	11	[a]	21	10	9
Income (1989 $)	19,312	18,265	[a]	21,231	22,043	16,415
Chicago						
Number of workers	5,600	85,300	0	15,228	82,149	699
Representation index	*0.28*	**3.21**	—	0.68	1.71	*0.28*
Education (years)	13.0	12.5	—	13.0	12.9	12.4
Unemployment rate (%)	3	2	—	8	3	5[a]
Government workers (%)	26	7	—	20	8	15[a]
Income (1989 $)	16,505	18,491	—	18,816	18,645	15,122
Atlanta						
Number of workers	1,300	24,000	0	7,237	30,026	0
Representation index	*0.16*	**4.69**	—	0.57	1.79	—
Education (years)	13.8	12.6	—	13.2	13.0	—
Unemployment rate (%)	0	2	—	5	3	—
Government workers (%)	8	14	—	31	12	—
Income (1989 $)	14,498	16,552	—	17,567	18,445	—

Sources: 1970 Census 5 percent questionnaire county group files (this is a 1-in-100 sample) and 1990 Census Public Use Microdata Sample 5 percent A file (a weighted 5-in-100 sample).
Notes: Representation indexes greater than 2 are in boldface roman; indexes of less than 0.5 are in boldface italic.
[a]Sample size is very small, and point estimate may be unreliable.

migrants are good substitutes for native workers and that in some industries or occupations, immigrants completely replace native workers. In this chapter, we offer some idea about how these seemingly divergent conclusions can be reconciled.

As Waldinger's studies have so carefully documented, there exist occupational niches that undergo ethnoracial succession from native control to domination by one or more immigrant groups. Yet even among such occupational niches, only the case of maids in Los Angeles shows complete turnover to immigrant control by 1990. Factory occupations may be destined to complete immigrant control, but as of 1990 blacks maintained a visible foothold in factory jobs. The declining presence of native whites (rather than blacks) has been the most dramatic change in the factories since 1970, but this ethnic recomposition occurred in the absence as well as in the presence of immigration, as our comparison of Atlanta and Chicago shows.

Future work about ethnic occupational succession ought to be balanced, or at least supplemented, by discussion of occupations from which immigrants are largely excluded. This line of inquiry could build on evidence about the occupational upgrading of native whites and blacks and should attempt to decipher whether and how much the better occupational opportunities of both blacks and whites can be attributed to the influx of unskilled immigrants who perform the menial work. Our discussion of skilled service occupations and office work offers clues about the fruitfulness of this line of inquiry.

In both Chicago and Los Angeles (the two immigrant-impacted areas we examined), the positions of postal clerk, security guard, and teacher are occupations that pay living wages, exclude immigrants, and engage disproportionate shares of working-class blacks. To the extent that immigrants in the metropolitan area require education, mail, and security services like other residents, higher immigration probably means more jobs for natives. Mexican immigrants have more children than native families and therefore consume relatively more educational resources (Clark et al. 1994). However, this fiscal burden is at least partly offset by the fact that the new teachers hired to serve them are mostly U.S. natives.

We do not claim that job growth in one industry or occupational sector balances job losses in another sector. The economic calculus of gain and loss is too indeterminate, partly because it is not clear that the displacement of native groups from certain low-skill occupations, like janitor and maid jobs, is necessarily negative for the natives. It may be, as Grant, Oliver, and James (1996) argue, that an influx of low-skilled immigrants can help push some native groups up the occupational hierarchy. Our tabulations also show that blacks have made upward gains in the occupational hierarchy by increasing their numbers and representation in managerial jobs, teaching jobs, and such stable middle-class positions as secretarial work. We have also shown that black workers who remain behind in the low-skill jobs confront fewer job opportunities and sharply increased rates of unemployment. As such, our evidence begins to reconcile the seemingly inconsistent conclusions generated by aggregate econometric analyses and local-area case studies. In other words, there is support for both views of the impact of immigration: that immigrants take low-skill jobs formerly held by natives and that immigrants also help push natives upward in the occupational stratification system. This evidence is consistent with the trivial net impact found in area studies, which appears to be a weighted average of upward and downward moves.

Our case studies provide some evidence that public-sector employment enables blacks to protect their labor-market niches, but not consistently so. Evidence from Atlanta reveals that an influx of immigrants is not a necessary condition to weaken blacks' control of government employment within particular occupational niches. This invites further investigation to determine under what conditions blacks' representation in public-sector employment is vulnerable to encroachment by either Mexican immigrants or native whites. Whether the protections afforded by federal, state, or local government jobs are equally beneficial to blacks and resistant to immigrant succession of occupational niches is another area inviting further research.

Finally, our case studies show large wage disparities between Mexican immigrants and native blacks within a similar (three-digit) occupation. This does not perforce constitute evidence of a split labor market because Mexican immigrants usually have lower skills than their native black counterparts. A simple human-capital explanation of wage disparities would suffice to dismantle claims that Mexican workers undercut wages of blacks or that employers' preferential hiring practices undergird the observed disparities. However, this cannot explain the rising black unemployment in specific occupations where they have been overrepresented in the past, nor can it address why some occupations experience ethnic occupational succession and others remain dominated by native blacks. We believe that further inquiry into the dimensions of market segmentation in the presence of a large volume of immigrants will advance understanding of the nature of competition between Mexican immigrants and native blacks.

APPENDIX

This section describes how the significance of various descriptive statistics from the text can be assessed. (For more examples, see Rosenfeld and Tienda 1998).

The Data

The 1970 census data we use in this chapter are from the county group files of respondents for the 5 percent questionnaire. The public use microdata sample (PUMS) files are a 1-in-100 unweighted national sample. This means that, for instance, when table 2.3 reports that there were 12,500 native black male janitors in Los Angeles in 1970, the PUMS files had exactly 125 such records. The 1990 census data come from the 5 percent PUMS A file, which is a 5-in-100 weighted national sample. Thus, when table 2.3 reports 8,304 native black male janitors in Los Angeles in 1990, the actual number of records in the PUMS was roughly one-twentieth as large (in fact, there were 394 such records).

The Estimates and Their Variance

Unemployment is a binomial variable; that is, every black male janitor in Los Angeles is either employed or unemployed. Of the 394 black male janitors in Los Angeles in 1990 who were captured in the PUMS A file, 70 reported being unemployed. This works out to be an unemployment rate of 17.7 percent, but when the respondents are weighted by the weights that the Census Bureau provides, the weighted mean comes out to be 16.4 percent, which is what is reported on table 2.3. For binomial variables like unemployment, the variance is $p(1 - p)$ for each individual case. In this case N is 394, p is 0.164, and $(1 - p)$ is 0.836, so the variance is 0.1377. The unemployment rate, which is actually an average of 394 individual binomial trials, is normal with a standard deviation equal to the square root of $[(p)^*(1 - p)/N]$ because of the central-limit theorem.

We see from the first case study that the 1990 unemployment rate for black janitors in Los Angeles was 16.4 percent, and for Mexican immigrant janitors, 5.5 percent, but is the difference as significant as it seems to be? The standard error associated with the black unemployment rate is 1.9 percent—that is, the square root of (0.1377/394)—and the standard error for the Mexican immigrant unemployment rate is 0.8 percent—that is, the square root of (0.052/847). The difference between the two normally distributed unemployment rates is itself normally distributed with a mean of 11 percent (16.4 − 5.5 percent) and with a standard deviation of 2 percent—the square root of $[(.019^2) + (.008^2)]$. The difference of 11 percent is 5.41 standard deviations greater than zero, which is to say that we must reject the hypothesis that black janitors and Mexican immigrant janitors had the same chance of being unemployed in Los Angeles in 1990. The high unemployment levels of native black workers, when paired with much lower unemployment levels of immigrants in the same occupation, is fairly good evidence of direct displacement of native by immigrant workers.

Statistical Significance of the Representation Indexes

The representation indexes used in the case studies are calculated using the following formula:

$$\text{Representation index} = \frac{n_1/T_2}{n_3/T_4}.$$

The numerator of this formula (n_1/T_2) represents the percentage of persons (T) in the labor force from the ethnic group in question that works in the particular occupation (n). The denominator of the formula represents the same percentage for all other persons in the labor force in that metropolitan area. For example, from the 1990 census A (weighted) sample there are 5,391 male black managers in the Chicago metropolitan area, from a total of 215,478 black males in the labor force. The numerator of the representation index, n_1/T_2 equals 5391/215478, or 2.5 percent, which means that 2.5 percent of black males in the labor force in Chicago in 1990 were managers. The same data file indicates that there were 90,216 male nonblack managers in Chicago, from a total of 1,289,286 male nonblacks in the labor force, so the denominator, n_3/T_4 equals 90216/1289286, or 6.99 percent. The representation index for this case is 250/699, or 0.36, which we interpret to mean that black males were underrepresented as managers in Chicago.

We use this representation index for its simplicity and its consistency with the measures employed by Roger Waldinger and Mehdi Bozorgmehr (1996). The representation index is not ideal, however, for statistical analysis. For the statistical analysis, we turn to the odds ratio, which is closely related to the representation index.

$$\text{Odds ratio} = \frac{n_1/n_2}{n_3/n_4}.$$

The numerator of the odds ratio represents the odds of working in a particular occupation for a particular group, and the denominator represents the odds of working in the same occupation for all others persons in the labor force. The odds ratio is a ratio of two odds, whereas the representation index is a ratio of two probabilities. The odds are related to the probability in a simple way: Odds = $p/(1 - p)$, where p is the probability. Because we are working here

with three-digit occupations, the probability of being in any one particular category is generally less than 10 percent; as a result, the odds
and the probability do not differ much, because $p/(1 - p)$ is only
slightly greater than p.

To continue with the example of black managers in Chicago, there
were 5,391 black managers in Chicago in 1990. There are 215,478
− 5,391, or 210,087, black males in the labor force besides the managers, so the numerator equals 5,391/210,087, or 2.6 percent. The
denominator of the odds ratio is 90216/1199070, or 7.5 percent. The
odds ratio in this case is 0.34, or just slightly less than the representation index of 0.36.

The natural logarithm of the odds ratio is asymptotically normal
(see Agresti 1996), with a variance of $[(1/n_1) + (1/n_2) + (1/n_3)$
$+ (1/n_4)]$. In this case, n corresponds to the actual number of unweighted observations, rather than the weighted observations, because
the reliability of the estimates depends on the actual number of real
interviews (see Clogg and Eliason 1987 for an explanation of when
and how weights are used in the analysis of categorical data). The
statistical tests of odds ratios serve two purposes: They provide hard
evidence, using a metric of log odds ratios, for the significance of the
differential distribution of groups over selected occupations, and they
provide some substantiation for the statistical significance of selected
comparisons of representation indexes from the text, because the odds
ratio and the representation index tend to be so similar in these cases.

In the text we noted that in 1990 blacks had a greater foothold in
managerial jobs in Los Angeles than in the other cities. The representation index for Chicago was 0.36, and for Los Angeles it was 0.53.
We want to know whether the difference between the two cities on
the log odds-ratio scale is significantly different from zero. The odds
ratio for Chicago is 0.341, and for Los Angeles, 0.476. The log odds
ratio for Chicago is −1.08, with a variance of 0.0054 $[(1/199) +$
$(1/7413) + (1/4000) + (1/51312)]$, and for Los Angeles, −0.74
with a variance of 0.0044 $[(1/242) + (1/6983) + (1/6593) +$
$(1/92584)]$. Because both log odds ratios are normally distributed
(with these large sample sizes, the log odds ratios are almost exactly
normal) and independent from each other, the difference between
them will be a normal variable with a mean of 0.33 (1.08 −
0.74), and a variance of 0.0098 (0.0044 + 0.0054). From this point
it is easy to determine whether the difference is significantly different
from zero: the associated Z-score is 3.354—that is, $0.33/\sqrt{0.0098}$,
which is indeed significantly different from zero at the 0.001 level.
Thus, despite the seemingly narrow difference between the penetra-

tion of blacks into the managerial ranks in Los Angeles and Chicago, the large sample sizes make the difference quite statistically significant; the difference between Los Angeles and Atlanta is stronger and even more statistically powerful. Our claim in the text of this chapter is that the presence of immigrants in the labor force seems to enhance the opportunities for blacks to move up in the occupational hierarchy, and this brief statistical exercise adds substance to that claim.

NOTES

Support for the research for this chapter was provided by the Bi-national study on Mexican-U.S. Migration. We are grateful for institutional support from the Population Research Center of NORC and the University of Chicago and the Office of Population Research, Princeton University.

1. This does not, however, preclude a migration response from domestic workers, which we do not consider.

2. Lieberson (1980, 379) provides numerous examples, noting that among the foreign born in 1950, 3.9 percent of Italians in the civilian labor force were barbers, eight times the level for all white men; and 14.8 percent of Greek immigrant men ran eating and drinking establishments, twenty-nine times the national level.

3. The geographic definitions of the metropolitan areas used here (for 1970 and 1990) follow the 1970 Census Bureau definitions: The Los Angeles metropolitan area includes only Los Angeles County; the Chicago metropolitan area includes Cook and DuPage Counties; the Atlanta area includes DeKalb, Fulton, Clayton, Cobb, and Gwinnett Counties.

4. This difference is statistically significant. See the methodological appendix.

5. Because the Census Bureau records occupation (in hundreds of categories) and industry (in hundreds of categories) for each worker, a cross classification of three-digit occupation by three-digit industry would have far too many cells (and too few workers per cell) to be useful. To streamline the analysis of industries, we aggregated all workers whose occupation was related to factory work and excluded the remaining workers.

6. Not reported in table 2.8 are the U.S.-born women of Mexican origin who in Los Angeles had made substantial inroads into the teaching profession by 1990, with more than six thousand teachers and a representation index of 0.85. That Mexican American teachers average lower educational levels (fourteen years) and lower incomes (about fifteen thousand dollars) than the other native teachers suggests they may fill support-staff

positions or fill slots for bilingual-education instructors. In Chicago, Mexican American teachers remained relatively scarce even in 1990 (fewer than one thousand such teachers and a representation index of 0.58).

REFERENCES

Agresti, Alan. 1996. *An Introduction to Categorical Data Analysis*. New York: John Wiley and Sons.

Bielby, William T., and James N. Baron. 1986. "Men and Women at Work: Sex Segregation and Statistical Discrimination." *American Journal of Sociology* 91(4): 759–99.

Bonacich, Edna. 1972. "A Theory of Ethnic Antagonism: The Split Labor Market." *American Sociology Review* 37(5): 547–59.

Borjas, George J. 1994. "The Economics of Immigration." *Journal of Economic Literature* 32(4): 1667–1717.

———. 1995. "The Economic Benefits from Immigration." *Journal of Economic Perspectives* 9(2): 3–22.

———. 1998. "Do Blacks Gain or Lose from Immigration?" In *Help or Hindrance?: The Economic Implications of Immigration for African Americans*, edited by Daniel S. Hamermesh and Frank D. Bean. New York: Russell Sage Foundation.

Clark, Rebecca L., Jeffrey S. Passell, Wendy N. Zimmermann, and Michael E. Fix, with Taynia L. Mann and Rosalind E. Berkowitz. 1994. *Fiscal Impacts of Undocumented Aliens: Selected Estimates for Seven States*. Washington, D.C.: Urban Institute Press.

Clogg, Clifford C., and Scott R. Eliason. 1987. "Some Common Problems in Log-Linear Analysis." *Sociological Methods and Research* 16(1): 8–45.

Grant, David M., Melvin L. Oliver, and Angela D. James. 1996. "African Americans: Social and Economic Bifurcation." In *Ethnic Los Angeles*, edited by Roger Waldinger and Mehdi Bozorgmehr. New York: Russell Sage Foundation.

Greenwood, Michael J., and Gary L. Hunt. 1995. "Economic Effects of Immigration on Native and Foreign-Born Workers: Complementarity, Substitutability, and Other Channels of Influence." *Southern Economic Journal* 61(4): 1076–97.

Greenwood, Michael J., and John McDowell. 1993. "The Labor Market Consequences of U.S. Immigration." U.S. Department of Labor, Bureau of International Labor Affairs, Division of Immigration and Policy Research. Unpublished report.

Greenwood, Michael J., and Marta Tienda. 1997. "U.S. Impacts of Mexican Immigration." Paper prepared for the Binational Study on Mexico-U.S.

Migration for the U.S. Commission on Immigration Reform. Boulder, Colorado.

Hamermesh, Daniel S., and Frank D. Bean, eds. 1998. *Help or Hindrance?: The Economic Implications of Immigration for African Americans.* New York: Russell Sage Foundation.

Heer, David M. 1990. *Undocumented Mexicans in the United States.* Cambridge: Cambridge University Press.

Lieberson, Stanley. 1980. *A Piece of the Pie: Blacks and White Immigrants Since 1880.* Berkeley: University of California Press.

Mare, Robert D. 1995. "Changes in Educational Attainment and School Enrollment." In *State of the Union: America in the 1990s,* edited by Reynolds Farley, vol. 1. New York: Russell Sage Foundation.

Martin, Philip, and Elizabeth Midgley. 1994. "Immigration to the United States: Journey to an Uncertain Destination." *Population Bulletin* 49(2): 2–45.

Massey, Douglas S., and Nancy A. Denton. 1993. *American Apartheid: Segregation and the Making of the Underclass.* Cambridge: Harvard University Press.

Model, Suzanne. 1993. "The Ethnic Niche and the Structure of Opportunity: Immigrants and Minorities in New York City." In *The Underclass Debate: Views from History,* edited by Michael B. Katz. Princeton: Princeton University Press.

Rosenfeld, Michael J., and Marta Tienda. 1997. "Labor Market Implications of Mexican Migration: Economies of Scale, Innovation, and Entrepreneurship." In *At the Crossroads: Mexican Migration and U.S. Policy,* edited by Frank D. Bean, Rodolfo O. De La Garza, Bryan R. Roberts, and Sidney Weintraub. Lanham, Md.: Rowman and Littlefield.

———. 1998. "Mexican Immigration, Occupational Niches, and Labor Market Competition: Evidence from Los Angeles, Chicago, and Atlanta, 1970–1990." Working Paper Series 98-02, Princeton University, Center for Migration and Development.

Rumbaut, Ruben G. 1996. "Origins and Destinies: Immigration, Race, and Ethnicity in Contemporary America." In *Origins and Destinies: Immigration, Race, and Ethnicity in America,* edited by Sylvia Pedraza and Ruben G. Rumbaut. Belmont, Calif.: Wadsworth.

Smith, James P., and Barry Edmonston. 1997. *The New Americans: Economic, Demographic, and Fiscal Effects of Immigration.* Washington, D.C.: National Academy Press.

Tienda, Marta. 1981. "The Mexican American Population." In *Nonmetropolitan America in Transition,* edited by Amos Hawley and Sara Mazie Mills. Chapel Hill: University of North Carolina Press.

Waldinger, Roger. 1989. *Through the Eye of the Needle: Immigrants and Enterprise in New York's Garment Trades*. New York: New York University Press.

———. 1996. "Who Makes the Beds? Who Washes the Dishes?: Black/Immigrant Competition Reassessed." In *Immigrants and Immigration Policy: Individual Skills, Family Ties, and Group Identities*, edited by Harriet O. Duleep and Phanindra V. Wunnava. Greenwich, Conn.: JAI Press.

Waldinger, Roger, and Mehdi Bozorgmehr, eds. 1996. *Ethnic Los Angeles*. New York: Russell Sage Foundation.

Wilson, William J. 1987. *The Truly Disadvantaged: The Inner City, the Underclass, and Public Policy*. Chicago: University of Chicago Press.

———. 1996. *When Work Disappears: The World of the New Urban Poor*. New York: Alfred A. Knopf.

CHAPTER 3

Ethnic Concentrations and Labor-Market Opportunities

Franklin D. Wilson

This chapter presents results from an analysis of the association of ethnically based concentrations in industry- or occupation-specific employment sectors with labor-market outcomes, such as joblessness, occupational status, and hourly earnings. We ask whether such employment-sector concentrations or ethnic niches provide favorable labor-market outcomes relative to work sites in which workers are not concentrated on the basis of ethnicity. I proceed on the assumption that local labor markets are organized along the lines of gender and ethnic relations and that the relative economic well-being of members of different ethnic populations is substantially affected by the nature of their work sites and by whether or not their work sites constitute employment-sector niches (Waldinger 1996b).

A growing literature examines ethnic niches and their roles in providing employment opportunities for coethnics and in contributing to the dynamism inherent in local labor markets (see Lieberson 1980; Morawska 1990; Model 1993; Logan, Alba, and McNulty 1994; Model and Ladipo 1996; Waldinger 1996b). The term "ethnic niche" is used here to designate employment-sector categories (whether occupation or industry based) in which members of a specific ethnic group are concentrated above the level one would expect based on their share of the total labor force of a local labor market. Sociologically, an employment-based ethnic niche is a social collectivity in which a substantial fraction of its members are known to each other and are a part of a social network formed by common ties of culture, family, religion, race, national origin, and coresidence. Ethnic niches can develop from a variety of sources, including

1. the concentration of coethnic owners and workers in one or more related industries for the purpose of exporting goods or to meet market demand arising internally within the ethnic group

2. businesspeople of one ethnic group acting as middleman minorities in providing goods and services to members of another ethnic group

106

3. concentration and specialization in industrial or occupational activities based on the ability of coethnic members to meet labor demand through social network connections and, in some instances, based on group members possessing some special skills or experience that employers consider relevant to productivity

The first source reflects the development of ethnic economies, including ethnic enclaves if specialization and concentration are involved. There are numerous examples of this in the literature (see Bailey and Waldinger 1991; Aldrich and Waldinger 1990; Logan, Alba, and McNulty 1994; Model 1993; Portes and Bach 1985; Portes and Jensen 1989; Waldinger 1996b), although, as suggested by Richard Alba and Victor Nee (1997), there is still considerable confusion regarding the distinction between ethnic economies and ethnic enclaves. In this case, as with middleman minorities, entrepreneurs are the key actors responsible for promoting the development of ethnic niches, through the establishment of business enterprises that rely on coethnics as a labor supply. Residential concentration and the institutionalization of the provision of resources, goods, and services through social networks facilitate the use of coethnics as a labor supply, particularly if English is not the standard form of discourse.

Much research suggests that labor-market niching is related to the volume and composition of immigration streams to a given destination. Ethnic niches emerge from the interaction between the skills and experiences of members of an ethnic group and the opportunity structure and ethnic diversity of a place as well as from the policies of receiving governments, which can either hinder or facilitate labor-market absorption (see Morawska 1990; Model 1993; Portes and Rumbaut 1996; Waldinger 1996a, 1996b).

Because migration is a network-driven process, immigrants, except perhaps those who arrive with job offers, do not select destinations at random; rather, they move to places where there is an existing network of friends and relatives who can provide them with various forms of assistance, including jobs (see Massey et al. 1994). Moreover, the influence of social networks extends beyond the neighborhood and ethnic enclave, providing employment opportunities in other sectors of the labor market where coethnic owners are not present. Several researchers have taken note of the fact that pioneer migrants may establish a presence in a given labor-market activity—because of prior experience, skills, propensity, or language—and others of similar backgrounds quickly follow suit (see Model 1993; Morawska 1990; Lieberson 1980; Portes and Rumbaut 1996; Waldinger 1996b). Roger

Waldinger (1996b) suggests that through social networking, occupational closure quickly follows the establishment of occupational specialization.

Roger Waldinger (1996b, 24–26) also suggests that labor-market niching enables members of ethnic groups to compensate for background deficits and discrimination through the exploitation of the social capital embedded in their community to promote further employment. Social networks, as a form of social capital, form a critical link between labor supply and demand in a local labor market. It is often through the relations existing between coethnics that information about available employment opportunities is channeled; employers often identify new workers by tapping into the social networks of current employees. Through this process of selective recruitment, niches acquire a group identity and, subsequently, also acquire regulatory mechanisms and procedures to protect the niche against encroachment from members of other groups.

Thus, recently arrived immigrants with coethnics already in residence at the place of destination are often able to secure jobs through current workers who are in a position to sponsor them. This type of employment benefit to members of an ethnic group can continue as long as their niche does not become saturated or, in that event, as long as the excess workers are able to exploit other opportunities. Stanley Lieberson (1980), in a study of the labor-market experiences of African Americans and immigrants from southern and eastern Europe at the beginning of this century, indicates that members of these groups established occupational niches. However, immigration restrictions in the 1920s probably played a significant role in reducing the continued pressure that would have been caused by an otherwise expanding labor supply. The situation for African Americans was quite different, mainly because internal migration is not subject to the same type of policy manipulation and because the limited absorption capacity of their niches forced some African Americans to seek employment in occupations controlled by members of other ethnic groups.

Do employment-based niches provide economic benefits to ethnic group members that they would not have access to if they worked in other areas of a local labor market? Waldinger (1996b, 95) suggests that industrial niches provide a "protected environment" for members of a particular ethnic group because members are more favorably treated with respect to access to employment opportunities and are likely to receive more equitable compensation than members who work in other industries. But, as Waldinger suggests elsewhere, the latter benefit may not apply if the niche is a part of an ethnic economy, because workers may accept low compensation in exchange for the acquisition of a skill or learning how to operate a business (1996b, 24). Workers in ethnic economies who are faced with limited mobility options and who work at low wages may very well seek employment in the general urban market once their initial deficits have been removed or once they are able to access and evaluate information regarding employment prospects outside the ethnic economy (see Nee, Sanders, and Sernau 1994). On the other hand, just as niches may offer a protected environment for members of particular ethnic groups, selective recruiting mechanisms can be perceived by members of out-groups as barriers to employment, because information about jobs and access to jobs through informal channels are closed to them.

Labor-market discrimination faced by members of an ethnic group may lead to the formation of employment niches in sectors of the labor market in which there are few if any discriminatory barriers. For example, among members of the least desired group in the job queue, niches may emerge not just through self-selection but also because group members are more or less forced to accept whatever residual jobs are available once groups higher up in the queue have made their selections. Historically, the concentration of blacks in low-skill and low-wage occupations can be attributed, in part, to limited access to occupational opportunities in labor markets in which they have been concentrated (see Waldinger 1996b). Suzanne Model and David Ladipo (1996), in a comparative analysis of the occupational attainment of selected minority groups in New York and London, suggest that a queueing model offers the most plausible explanation of the differences between the occupational attainment of immigrants from the same origin who immigrated to New York and those who immigrated to London. In New York, the presence of indigenous minorities, namely African Americans and Puerto Ricans, was associated with higher occupational standings for foreign-born Chinese, East Indians, and West Indians than for their counterparts in London, largely because of the absence of such indigenous groups in the latter.

Although recent empirical findings indicate that a substantial number of ethnic group members are employed in ethnic niches, few attempts have been made to determine what share of these groups are actually concentrated in niches, and whether the extent of niche concentration changes as a result of the immigrant share of an ethnic group's total workforce changes over time or, rather, other changes, such as rising educational attainment, might be associated with changes in concentration. These issues direct our attention to the question of whether niching has been pursued as a long-term employment strategy by ethnic groups because of the economic advantages associated with specializing and concentrating in a given activity. Waldinger (1996b) provides a partial answer to this question. He presents results for selected ethnic groups in New York City, indicating the share of the labor supply of each group concentrated in industrial niches since 1940 and the differences in wages between niche and non-niche employment for 1990. At least a third of the workforce of each group, except Italians, were employed in industrial niches in 1990. In the case of Jews, Italians, and blacks, for whom the time trend extends back to 1940, there is a clear pattern of decline in the share of each group's workforce who were concentrated in niches. This pattern did not hold for Jews, whose employment in niches declined to 41 percent by 1980 and then increased to 49 percent in 1990. The decline in niche employment also occurred for West Indians, Chinese, and Dominicans, but the series extends back only to 1970. The volume of immigration for these groups was substantial from 1970 to 1990, and it continues. The recent large-scale migration from non-Anglophonic countries might explain why niche employment for Chinese and Dominicans was still at or greater than 50 percent. The continued concentration of at least a third of the native-born groups in ethnic niches, even considering that each experienced educational upgrading, suggests that these concentrations have economic value as a labor-market strategy (see Waldinger 1996b).

Although employment in niches persisted at a high level for Jews from 1940 to 1990, the industry and occupational composition of the niches changed substantially. Initially, Jewish niches centered on commercial activities (mainly small retail stores), wholesaling, and work in the garment and related industries. During the late 1920s and 1930s, with the entrance of the second generation into the labor market, public-sector employment was added. In the post–World War II period, Jews shifted into the professional service sectors, in higher education, legal and business services, health, publishing, advertising, public relations, and the theater. Along the way, they shed the blue-collar and small-proprietorship niches and moved into highly technical professional niches, as educational attainment increased and labor-market discrimination declined. Thus, the Jewish population did not abandon niching but rather transformed their niches in response to changing labor-market conditions and their position in the labor queue.

In contrast, although niche employment of African Americans and Italians also underwent a transformation from unskilled to skilled blue-collar occupations and employment in the public sector, the share of total employment in niches of each of these groups declined between 1940 and 1990. However, it was still the case that one in three native-born Italians and African Americans were employed in niches in 1990. Overall, these results suggest that native-born groups also concentrate in niches and that the organization of labor-market activities through ethnic niches can continue to provide economic value even to succeeding generations who are regarded as having been assimilated.

Waldinger also presents wage differentials between niche and non-niche employment in 1990 for the ethnic groups he studied to address the question of whether ethnic group members economically benefited from employment in niches. The wages of workers of the three native-born groups (Jews, blacks, and Italians) were higher in industrial niches, whereas the opposite was true for Chinese and Dominicans. Because employment overall in niches declined substantially for Italians and blacks between 1940 and 1990, one could speculate that higher compensation for employment in the remaining niches derived from the specialized and skilled nature of the work involved and the fact that groups may exercise some influence over the recruitment process. As to whether working in a niche lowers the gap between the average wages of members of an ethnic group relative to native-born whites, Waldinger's results indicate that only the gap between black niche workers and whites was reduced more than the gap between black non-niche workers and native-born whites. The favorable wages of black niche workers probably reflects their concentration in public-sector jobs, where barriers to equal opportunities are the least.

THE CURRENT STUDY

Studies by Waldinger, Model, and others (cited in Morawska 1990) raise some important issues regarding economic returns to employment in ethnic niches. The number of ethnic groups, their composition with respect to nativity, their historical mode of insertion into the host economy, available capital resources—financial, human, and social—and their relations with dominant groups have all played a role in structuring the labor-market experiences of their members. If, as previous research suggests, local labor markets are organized around gender and ethnic relations, we would expect a substantial share of individual ethnic populations to be concentrated in labor-market niches, differentiated with respect to industry and occupation.

The current analysis seeks to explore a number of issues relevant to employment in ethnic niches and in employment sectors in general with varying concentrations of immigrants. First, do industry- and occupation-based ethnic niches provide economic benefits with respect to employment, occupational, or earnings attainment? To address this question, I include terms in a model of labor-market outcomes to estimate the effects of ethnic composition of employment sectors and changes therein as well as terms that capture particular features of employment sectors, such as the extent of coethnic control of employment relations and changes therein and whether employment in niches is more beneficial for those with weak English-language skills. I compare labor-market outcomes for ethnic group members working in niches with those of coethnics who work in the general sector of the local economy. If niche employment is more advantageous, one would expect workers in niches to have a lower probability of joblessness and higher occupational and earnings attainment. These effects for niche workers should be enhanced in industries in which there is a high percentage of coethnic owners, managers, and supervisors and reduced for individuals who work in niches but who speak English poorly.

The model estimation used in this chapter assesses the association of labor-market outcomes with changes in the characteristics of employment sectors, including changes in the concentration of coethnics, share of coethnics who are owners, managers, and supervisors, sex composition of the workforce, and the share of the workforce that is foreign born. This makes it possible to determine whether the potential benefits of niche employment rise as the relative number of coethnics increases and as coethnic control of employment relations increases.

Second, are the economic benefits of employment in industry- and occupation-based niches the same for Asians, African Americans, Hispanics and whites? Do some groups benefit more than others from their members being employed in niches? Queuing theory provides some guidance. According to this model, employers follow a preference ordering in selecting their workforces, which in part reflects the skill requirements of jobs, attitudes and work habits of workers, the composition of the existing workforce, and previous experiences of employers with workers from a given group. This suggests that niches occupied by the most favored group would offer greater benefits, and these niches are not likely to be connected to an enclave economy. On the other hand, those groups at the bottom of the labor queue have to make do with the least desirable jobs either in the general or in the enclave economy.

Third, does the foreign-born composition of work sites have an independent effect on labor-market outcomes? Although ethnic groups may provide a large share of the workforce within a given employment sector, there are other employment sectors that may be ethnically heterogeneous but in which the workforce is predominately foreign born. Of course, this may change with time as members of one ethnic group are able to increase their share of employment to a level that enables the group to control the recruitment of new workers. Moreover, the key point I wish to make is that a high concentration of the foreign born, independent of ethnic background, may indicate the operation of a number of forces shaping labor demand, which may, in turn, have an impact on the source of supply of workers.

Factors associated with concentrations of the foreign born in industries connected to ethnic economies are well known (see Logan, Alba, and McNulty 1994; Portes and Rumbaut 1996). Although the workforce in some of these economies may be homogeneous, one can cite numerous examples of employment sectors in these economies that are ethnically mixed (see Waldinger 1996a), with members of different ethnicities forming a division of labor organized around occupations. The owners and managers of these enterprises are driven to keep wages low to remain competitive, and one of the ways in which this can be accomplished is by recruiting an ethnically differentiated workforce based on coethnic identity, skill requirements, and the willingness of workers to accept a given level of compensation. As previously noted, workers may be willing to accept low compensation, either because of low wages linked to conditions at origin or because employment in this sector provides the opportunity for learning and adjusting to the host environment.

Many employers in the general local economy also have strong economic incentives to keep compensation packages low, not only because of competition but also because the goods and services they provide are locally consumed. Their profit margins are low, and they have fewer relocation options available to them and hence cannot move to take advantage of locations where it may be possible to offer lower compensation packages. Employers may be less concerned with the ethnic or immigrant composition of their workforce as long as the offered compensation package is acceptable and workers of different nationalities are able to work together to maintain the desired level of productivity. Whatever the nature of the employment sector, by including in the model a measure of the share of an employment sector's workforce that is foreign born, I am able to estimate whether an increase in the share of the workforce of an employment sector that is foreign born is associated with greater joblessness of native workers and lower levels of occupational and earnings attainment. An analysis of these associations at the level of the employment sector may provide additional insight on the impact of immigrants on the labor-market circumstances of native workers.

DATA AND METHODS

The data for this analysis are derived from the 1980 and 1990 public use microdata sample (PUMS) files, 5 percent sample, for respondents who were at least sixteen years of age, had a job sometime between 1978 and 1980 or between 1988 and 1990, and lived in one of the twenty-three largest (consolidated) metropolitan areas. I use data from both the 1980 and the 1990 files to construct aggregate measures for employment sectors consisting of thirty-two major industry categories and seven major occupational categories, further stratified within metropolitan areas by ethnicity. These aggregate measures are used to identify ethnically based employment niches and to provide summary information for employment sectors in 1980 and 1990 and the changes across the decade. A niche is defined as an employment sector (industry-specific occupational category) with at least five hundred workers in which members of a specific ethnic group are 1.5 times more likely to be concentrated than members of all other ethnic groups. Initially, measures based on the employment sector were constructed for twenty-six ethnic groups, including one African American, six Asian, seven Hispanic, twelve European-ancestry ethnic groups. In this analysis, these groups are aggregated into four major ethnic categories: African American, Asian, Hispanic, and white.

Respondents on the 1990 PUMS who were from nineteen to sixty-four years of age, had worked at least one week since 1989 for wages or salary, and were not in school at the time of the census are used to estimate the association of joblessness, occupational attainment, and hourly wages with selected characteristics of workers, including demographic, labor-market, and employment-sector location in 1980 and changes in these factors from 1980 to 1990. The models used to estimate these associations are of the following form:

$$(3.1) \quad \text{Log } (P/1-P) = \alpha + \Sigma\beta_i V_j + \Sigma\beta_i W_k + \Sigma\beta_i X_l + \Sigma\beta_i Z_m \\ + \Sigma\beta_i V_j W_K + \Sigma\beta_i V_j X_l + \Sigma V_j Z_m$$

and

$$(3.2) \quad \text{Log (SEI) and log (HRWAGE)} = \alpha + \Sigma\beta_i V_j + \Sigma\beta_i W_k \\ + \Sigma\beta_i X_l + \Sigma\beta_i Z_m \\ + \Sigma\beta_i V_j W_k + \Sigma\beta_i V_j X_l \\ + \Sigma\beta_i V_j Z_m + e,$$

where P is the probability that a respondent was jobless (either unemployed or not in the labor force during the census week) rather than employed; SEI is an index of occupational attainment (see Hauser and Warren 1997); HRWAGE is hourly wages for respondents who worked at least one week since 1989; V is a vector of demographic characteristics including age, age-squared, work-limiting disability, marital status, household income other than that of respondent, sex, ethnicity, ability to speak English, duration of residence in the United States if immigrant, immigration before age eleven, immigration after age ten, MSA residence, and whether a college graduate; W is a vector of labor-market-position variables, including major occupation (of which there are seven) and major industry sector (of which there are thirty-two); X is a vector of employment-sector characteristics in 1980, including share of employment sector's labor force that is foreign born, share of ethnic group working in one's own group's niche, share of ethnic group members working in employment sector in which members of another group have established a niche, share of ethnic group (I)'s workforce that are women, index of employment sector concentration for ethnic group (I), and share of coethnics who are owners, managers, and supervisors in an industry; Z is a vector of variables measuring changes in the characteristics of the employment sector, including the ratio of the 1990 to the 1980 index of employment-sector concentration for ethnic group (I), the ratio of the 1990 to the 1980 share of women in the workforce for ethnic group (I), the ratio of the 1990 to the 1980 share of foreign-born workers, and the ratio of the 1990 to the 1980 share of coethnics who are owners, managers, and supervisors; and the product vectors VW, VX, and VZ represent the interaction of ethnicity and sex with a select number of the other variables. Definitions of all variables are reported in appendix A. Household income other than that of the respondent, terms for major occupation, and terms for the interaction of ethnicity and sex with occupation are included only in the logistic equation for joblessness; age-squared is included in the equations for SEI and HRWAGE; and SEI is included in the equation for HRWAGE. In estimating equations (3.1) and (3.2), I use the weights assigned to respondents but divide them by the average sample weight to remove the effect of the 1990 PUMS design.

The specifications included in equations (3.1) and (3.2) provide a means of evaluating a number of hypotheses, including whether working in an ethnic niche and other characteristics of employment sectors influence labor-market outcomes, and whether the foreign-born composition of an employment sector is associated with higher

Table 3.1   Employment in Industry- and Occupation-Specific Niches, 1980 and 1990

| | Employed in a Non-Niche Sector | Employed in a Niche Sector | | | | Ethnic Group's Representation in Survey Group |
| | | Other Group's Niche | Own Group's Niche | | | |
Ethnic Group			Co-Ethnic Only	Multigroup Niche	Total	
African American						
1980	28.8	30.5	25.1	15.6	40.7	12.2
1990	24.5	38.4	20.1	17.1	37.2	12.2
Asian						
1980	27.3	48.7	2.1	22.0	24.1	2.8
1990	20.6	52.8	2.0	24.7	26.7	4.9
Hispanic						
1980	27.0	41.2	8.4	23.4	31.8	8.8
1990	19.1	44.8	6.8	29.3	36.1	12.4
White						
1980	40.7	51.4	3.3	4.7	8.0	76.2
1990	33.3	57.8	2.9	6.1	9.0	70.5
Employment sectors' share in survey group						
1980	37.7	47.9	6.4	8.1	14.5	—
1990	29.8	53.6	5.4	11.2	16.6	—

Sources: 1980 and 1990 Public Use Microdata Samples.
Notes: 1980 sample of 43,720,000 workers; 1990 sample of 51,150,000 workers.

joblessness and low occupational and earnings attainment among workers. Much empirical research suggests the presence of immigrant workers has little or no effect on the labor-market circumstances of native workers (see Wilson and Jaynes 1998). However, most of these studies have focused on the global effects of immigration, ignoring the possibility that the effect of immigrant concentrations within specific industry and occupational sectors may be negative because of labor-supply substitutions. I investigate this possibility here by seeking to determine whether the economic circumstances of native workers are adversely affected by immigrants' shares and changes in shares at the level of employment sectors.

RESULTS

Because employment in industry-specific occupational niches is a central focus of the reported analysis, a general review of the distribution of respondents according to whether or not they work in niches would be useful. Table 3.1 reports the percentage of respondents who work in niches by ethnic identity. The categories were formed by identifying industry and occupational sectors in which members of a particular ethnic group have a 1.5 times greater likelihood of working than members of other groups.

The results reported in table 3.1 indicate that at least one in five workers in each ethnic group worked in the general sector of local labor markets in 1990, but this percentage represents a decline from the 1980 level. The modal category for all ethnic groups is employment sectors in which members of other ethnic groups had established a niche. This does not necessarily mean that these individuals were attached to actual work sites that were dominated by members of other groups, but only that other ethnic groups dominated the employment sector. The percentage of workers in this category was less in the case of African Americans than for the other three groups. At least one in four African American, Asian, and Hispanic workers were employed in niches dominated by coethnics. However, only African Americans had more than 10 percent of their workforce employed in industry and occupational sectors in which only they had established a niche. In 1990, for example, 20.1 percent of the African American labor force, versus 2.0 percent of Asians, 6.8 percent of Hispanics, and 2.9 percent of whites, worked in employment sectors in which only members of their respective groups had established a niche. These percentages are slightly lower than they were in 1980 and may indicate a decline in areas of local labor markets in which only one group dominated. A higher percentage of Asians and Hispanics worked in employment sectors in which at least one other group had also established a niche. From 1980 to 1990, the percentage of workers employed in multigroup-niche sectors increased for all groups but especially for Asians and Hispanics. Further analysis (not reported here) of the industry- or occupation-specific composition of these niches for Asians and Hispanics indicates a high concentration of niches associated with ethnic economies (see Logan, Alba, and McNulty 1994). A substantial amount of employment in enclave economies is driven by ethnic-specific consumer-market demand, a situation known to be associated with recent immigration (see Massey 1985).

One implication of the results reported in table 3.1 is that although ethnicity clearly is an important factor around which employment relations are structured, the majority of workers in each group were not concentrated in employment sectors in which coethnics are also disproportionately concentrated. The estimates of niche employment reported here are lower than expected except, perhaps, for African Americans. This is the case even considering that in constructing the estimates, I used a twenty-five-category breakdown of ethnicity but organized the reporting of results according to the four panethnic categories. However, two caveats are appropriate. First, census data on actual work sites and the organizational context within which employment occurs are not available on the PUMS files; thus, one cannot estimate the extent of undercoverage of labor-force-based niches. Second, because niches were defined as employment sectors with five hundred or more workers, it is highly likely that small and somewhat specialized employment niches have been excluded. These types of niches are not likely to be randomly distributed across ethnic groups; rather, they tend to be concentrated in those groups in which ethnic economies are also likely to be present.

Table 3.2 presents the distribution of ethnic niches by occupation, in the top panel, and the distribution of sample respondents employed in ethnic niches by occupation in the bottom panel for 1980 and 1990; and I combined the data from table 3.1 for employment in one's own group's niche and employment in multigroup niches to focus on employment in niches without regard to whether other groups have established a niche in a given sector. These distributions are summed over industry and metropolitan area of residence. Between 1980 and 1990, all groups except African Americans experienced an increase in the total number of industry- and occupation-based niches. Whites increased from 890 to 994 niches, a 12 percent increase; Hispanics from 586 to 842, a 46 percent increase; and Asians from 202 to 427, a 111 percent increase. The greater percentage for Hispanics and Asians probably relates to the substantial addition to these populations through immigration. The fact that niche formation was higher among Asians may be related to a greater tendency for members of this group to be employed in ethnic economies. African Americans experienced a decline in the number of niches associated with its members from 656 to 614, a 6.4 percent decrease. Whites were overwhelmingly concentrated in niches associated with managerial and professional, technical and sales, and administration and skilled blue-collar (craft and precision manufacturing) occupations. Although Asians were also concentrated in managerial and professional, technical and sales, and administration niches, unlike whites they were also concentrated in services and semiskilled blue-collar (fabricators and operators) occupations. In addition, whites increased their concentration in managerial and professional occupations, whereas the concentration of Asians increased in technical and sales occupations.

The distributions for African Americans and Hispanics who were employed in niches are quite different from those of whites and Asians. African Americans were concentrated primarily in administration, services, semiskilled blue-collar, and unskilled labor occupations. The percentage employed in the latter two categories declined between 1980 and 1990, whereas that in administration increased. It is of particular interest to note that the concentration of African Americans in skilled blue-collar niches in 1990, at 1 percent, was the lowest of all. Hispanics were concentrated in services, blue-collar, and unskilled labor occupations. Their concentration doubled in services and declined in semiskilled occupations by 18 percentage points. Like that of African Americans, Hispanics' concentration in professional and managerial and technical and sales occupations was very low, but unlike that of African Americans, their concentration in administration is also low. In sum, the results in table 3.2 show that the four panethnic groups differ not only in the number of niches formed by their members but also in the distribution of members across niches distinguished by occupation.

Tables 3.3 through 3.5 report selected results from the estimation of equations (3.1) and (3.2). The coefficients for joblessness are odds ratios derived by taking the exponents of the log odds coefficients. Because both equations contain product terms used to test for net shifts in slope coefficients for some variables, such as sex, ethnicity, and occupations, some of the coefficients have been summed to include both the main and interaction effects. The effects of control variables are not discussed and are not reported in tables 3.3 through 3.5, although their effects are reflected in the predicted values, which will be discussed later. The full set of results from equations (3.1) and (3.2) for the log odds of joblessness, occupational attainment, and hourly wages, respectively, are reported elsewhere (see Wilson 1997, appendix tables 3 through 5). However, it is of interest to note that the main and interaction effects of industry and metropolitan residence are substantial and worthy of further review, as they provide insight into the ethnically differentiated character of metropolitan labor markets.

Table 3.3 reports selected results from a logistic regression predicting the odds of joblessness (or not working) at the time of the 1990 census. With respect to variation in joblessness by occupation for men, the results indicate that African American men were substantially more likely to be jobless than white, Asian, or Hispanic men. The odds of joblessness increase slightly as one goes down the list of occupational categories, with laborers having higher odds of joblessness than workers in the other occupations. African American male

Table 3.2 Number and Distribution of Ethnic Populations in Niches by Major Occupation, 1980 and 1990

ETHNIC	TOTAL	MANPROF	TECHSALE	ADMIN	SERVICES	SKILBLUE	SSKLBLUE	UNSKLABR
					Niches			
White								
1980	890	48.2022	16.2921	11.7978	2.9213	12.9213	4.7191	3.1461
1990	994	52.1127	17.9074	9.6579	2.2133	11.0664	4.6278	2.4145
African American								
1980	656	1.5244	3.2012	14.3293	30.6402	3.3537	26.9817	19.9695
1990	614	3.0945	7.8176	17.9153	31.1075	3.4202	21.8241	14.8208
Hispanic								
1980	586	0.5119	1.0239	4.0956	16.3823	13.9932	44.3686	19.6246
1990	842	1.0689	2.2565	5.4632	23.6342	14.1330	35.0356	18.4086
Asian								
1980	202	36.6337	13.8614	14.3564	16.8317	4.9505	11.8812	1.4851
1990	427	33.9578	21.0773	11.7096	16.1593	6.3232	9.8361	0.9368

	Population							
White								
1980	2,649,320	54.5000	16.6428	7.9628	3.6825	11.2104	3.6764	2.3251
1990	3,470,312	62.3713	15.1885	6.2548	3.4210	8.7604	2.6405	1.3635
African American								
1980	2,174,320	2.6068	3.5119	23.3848	35.1650	1.3319	21.5681	12.4315
1990	2,497,904	4.7523	6.3908	27.3365	37.4039	1.2108	15.3653	7.5404
Hispanic								
1980	1,226,620	0.1272	0.4141	2.8534	15.4147	12.8369	52.5591	15.7946
1990	2,462,726	0.3283	2.0062	3.1460	30.6718	13.2803	34.1945	16.3729
Asian								
1980	291,180	33.2784	9.9869	14.6507	22.2062	3.1596	15.7360	0.9822
1990	724,081	31.9863	18.5664	13.2956	20.2890	4.7568	10.6321	0.4737

Sources: 1980 and 1990 Public Use Microdata Sample, 5 percent sample. Include respondents sixteen years of age and over who had worked at least one week since 1978 (for 1980 sample) or 1988 (for 1990 sample).

Notes: For a definition of the attributes please see table 3A.1.

Table 3.3   Factors Associated with the Odds of Being Jobless, 1989

Factors	Total Sample	White	African American	Hispanic	Asian
			Occupation		
Men					
Professionals and managers	—	—	—	—	—
Technical workers and salesmen		1.077	1.943	1.274	1.077
Administrators		1.403	2.001	1.403	1.403
Service workers		1.480	2.346	1.480	1.480
Craft and precision manufacturing workers		1.378	2.250	1.378	1.378
Fabricators and operatives		1.749	2.516	1.749	1.749
Laborers and private household		2.514	4.071	2.114	1.915
Women					
Professionals and managers	—	—	—	—	—
Technical workers and saleswomen		2.508	2.577	3.340	2.084
Administrators		1.806	1.771	2.008	1.501
Service workers		2.673	2.388	2.973	2.221
Craft and precision manufacturing workers		2.490	2.290	2.769	2.069
Fabricators and operatives		3.160	2.559	3.514	2.626
Laborers and private household		3.570	3.256	3.339	2.260
Immigration status					
Nonimmigrant	—				
Immigrated before age 11	1.179***				
Immigrated after age 10	0.972				
Duration of residence	0.993***				
			Employment Sector		
Speak English poorly and work in a niche	0.764***				
Immigrant share, 1980		1.641***	1.641***	1.641***	1.641***
Change in immigrant share from 1980 to 1990		0.000	1.003**	0.995*	0.000
Work in other group's niche, 1980		0.000	0.000	0.000	0.000
Work in own niche, 1980		1.236***	1.019***	1.236***	1.236***
Coethnic owners and managers, 1980		0.000	0.000	0.000	0.000
Change in coethnic owners and managers from 1980 to 1990	0.000				
Share of women, 1980	1.024*				
Change in share of women from 1980 to 1990	0.999*				
Index of concentration, 1980	0.000				
Change in index of concentration from 1980 to 1990	0.999**				

Source: Based on the author's data.
*p < .05; **p < .01; ***p < .001

laborers were four times more likely to be jobless than white men, and this difference was the largest between men and women in any occupation. Among women, the differences between African Americans, whites, and Hispanics were not as great as those observed for men, but note that Asian women clearly stand out as having lower odds of joblessness for most of the major occupations. The differences between men and women were not as great as one would expect, largely because respondents who had not worked since 1988 or earlier were excluded from the sample. This exclusion affected the level of joblessness observed among women more than men, largely because substantially more women of labor-force age were not active in the paid labor force over longer time intervals.

Immigrants who spent their formative years in the United States were more likely to be jobless, whereas other immigrants fared no worse than native workers. The coefficient for duration of residence in the United States, however, suggests that the odds of being jobless is responsive to the length of time an immigrant has spent in the United States, somewhat independent of the age of the person at the time of migration.

The bottom panel of table 3.3 focuses on the association of joblessness with characteristics of the sector of employment. The immigrant share of the labor force of an employment sector in 1980 was associated with substantially increased odds of joblessness, and the association was the same for members of each of the four ethnic groups. More importantly, however, change in immigrant share was not related to the odds of whites or Asians being jobless but slightly increased joblessness for African Americans and decreased it for Hispanics. The slight decline in joblessness among Hispanics in the face of rising immigrant shares implies that members of this group are more likely to have labor-market characteristics similar to that of immigrants. Of course, there is also the distinct possibility that this association is compositional in nature, in that a high percentage of Hispanics are also foreign born.

Is employment in niches associated with the odds of being jobless? Being employed in employment sectors in which other groups had a niche was not associated with the likelihood of being jobless, but being employed in a niche linked to one's own group was associated with high odds of joblessness. The odds of whites, Hispanics, and Asians working in their own group's niches being jobless was 1.24. The odds of joblessness among African Americans was only slightly associated with employment in a niche. One can also note that the proportion of coethnic owners, managers, and supervisors in 1980 in an industry-level employment sector and changes in this proportion from 1980 to 1990 were not associated with the odds of being jobless. Individuals who speak English poorly but work in a niche were substantially less likely to be jobless. It is probable that this coefficient is capturing the benefit to immigrants associated with employment in ethnic niches, particularly those that are part of ethnic economies. These benefits may be crucial for immigrants, who may experience difficulty in securing jobs in employment sectors in which there are few coethnic group members present.

The share of women in the labor force of an employment sector was associated with an increase in the odds of being jobless, but changes in the share of women from 1980 to 1990 was associated with a decrease in the odds. In both instances, however, the coefficients, though statistically significant (at $p < .05$) are rather small. The same can be said for the index of concentration, which was positively associated with the odds of being jobless, but the coefficient is small.

Table 3.4 reports the association of occupational attainment (log of SEI) with selected characteristics of individual respondents and employment sector. As with joblessness, a complete set of estimates derived from estimating equation (3.2) are reported elsewhere (see Wilson 1997). Net of other relevant factors, African American, Hispanic, and Asian men had higher net occupational attainment than white men. The coefficient for Hispanics is almost three times the size of the coefficient for the other two groups of men. The occupational attainment of women was appreciably lower than that of men. White women appear to have had the lowest, and African American women the highest, occupational attainment. Because gross differences in occupational attainment favor whites, its very likely that the lower net coefficient for this group is a function of the heightened responsiveness of occupational attainment to other relevant attributes.

Foreign-born workers had significantly lower occupational attainment, regardless of the age at which they migrated, than native-born workers, but among the foreign born, length of residence in the United States was associated with higher occupational attainment. The latter association appears to offset the effect of being an immigrant in proportion to the number of years someone of foreign birth has been in the United States.

Share of immigrants in the workforce of an employment sector in 1980 was substantially associated with occupational attainment. Ethnic group members working in employment sectors with high immigrant share had lower occupational attainment. This was particularly

Table 3.4   Maximum Likelihood Estimates of Factors Associated with Occupational Attainment, 1990

Factor	Total Sample	White	African American	Hispanic	Asian
Gender and ethnicity					
Men		—	0.033***	0.095**	0.033***
Women		−.042***	−.001***	−.033***	−.023***
Immigration status					
Nonimmigrant	—				
Immigrated before age 11	−.014***				
Immigrated after age 10	−.025***				
Duration of residence	0.011***				
Characteristics of employment sector					
Speak English poorly and work in a niche	−.021*				
Immigrant share, 1980		−.041***	−.102***	−.161***	−.104***
Change in immigrant share from 1980 to 1990		.0005***	−.0001*	−.004***	.0005***
Work in other group's niche, 1980		0.042***	0.145***	−.004***	0.042***
Work in own niche, 1980		−.002	−.184***	−.195***	0.0268***
Coethnic owners and managers, 1980		−.015***	−.037	−.057***	−.020
Change in coethnic owners and managers from 1980 to 1990	−.0005***				
Share of women, 1980	−.085***				
Change in share of women from 1980 to 1990	0.0004***				
Index of concentration, 1980	0.0003***				
Change in index of concentration from 1980 to 1990	0.000				

Source: Table is based on the author's data.
*$p < .05$; **$p < .01$; ***$p < .001$

true of Hispanic workers, followed by African Americans, Asians, and whites. Change in immigrant share between 1980 and 1990 was also associated with lower occupational attainment of African Americans and Hispanics but slightly higher occupational attainment of whites and Asians.

Working in an employment sector in which other ethnic groups had established a niche in 1980 was positively associated with the occupational attainment of African Americans and, to a lesser extent, whites and Asians. The occupational attainment of Hispanics was negatively associated with working in an employment sector in which other groups had established a niche. Working in an employment sector in 1980 in which one's own group had established a niche substantially lowered the occupational attainment of African Americans and Hispanics, raised that of Asians, and had no effect on that of whites. We can also note that workers who speak English poorly and work in a niche had slightly lower occupational attainment.

Hispanics who worked in employment sectors in which coethnic owners, managers, and supervisors were present had lower occupational attainment, which was also true of whites but to a lesser extent. Changes in the proportion of coethnic owners and managers between 1980 and 1990, however, slightly raised the attainment of all workers. The share of women in an employment sector in 1980 was associated with lower occupational attainment, but changes in the share of women in the workplace between 1980 and 1990 slightly increased occupational attainment. Finally, the extent of relative concentration (the index of concentration) of coethnic workers in an employment sector was associated with a slightly higher occupational attainment.

Table 3.5 reports the association of hourly wages (log) in 1989 with selected characteristics of respondents and of employment sectors (see Wilson 1997). As we might expect, the hourly wages of African American, Hispanic, and Asian men were lower than those of white men; surprisingly, however, the net wages of Hispanic men were higher than those of the other two groups. The hourly wages of women were appreciably lower than those of men, regardless of ethnic group affiliation.

The association of immigrant status with hourly wages exhibits the same pattern observed for occupational attainment; namely, immigrants had lower net wages than native workers, but the wages of immigrants increased with length of stay in the United States. Hourly wages were positively associated with occupational attainment, with a 0.5 percent increase in wages associated with a one-unit increase in occupational attainment.

Immigrant share of the workforce of an employment sector was associated with slightly lower wages, and changes in immigrant share was associated with even lower wages. There were no differences among ethnic groups in either of these associations. Being employed in a sector in which other groups had established a niche had no relation to hourly wages, but being employed in one's own group's niche was associated with lower wages for whites, African Americans,

Table 3.5   Maximum Likelihood Estimates of Factors Associated with Hourly Wages, 1989

Factors	Total	White	African American	Hispanic	Asian
Gender and ethnicity					
Men	—	—	−.045***	−.016**	−.045**
Women		−.094***	−.075***	−.082***	−.082***
Immigration status					
Nonimmigrant	—				
Immigrated before age 11	−.043***				
Immigrated after age 10	−.043***				
Duration of residence	0.002***				
Occupational Attainment					
(SEI)	0.005***				
Characteristics of employment sector					
Speak English poorly and work in a niche	−.012*				
Immigrant share, 1980		−.013*	−.013*	−.013*	−.013*
Change in immigrant share from 1980 to 1990		−.001***	−.001***	−.001***	−.001***
Work in other group's niche, 1980		0.000	0.000	0.000	0.000
Work in own niche, 1980		0.012***	−.010***	0.012***	−.013***
Coethnic owners and managers, 1980		−.022***	−.017	−.085***	−.043***
Change in coethnic owners and managers from 1980 to 1990	−.001***				
Share of women, 1980	−.016***				
Change in share of women from 1980 to 1990	−.00001***				
Index of concentration, 1980	0.0001				
Change in index of concentration from 1980 to 1990	−.00001**				

Source: Table is based on the author's data.

*p < .05; **p < .01; ***p < .001

and Asians. Speaking English poorly and working in a niche was associated with reduced wages.

The greater the proportion of coethnic owners, managers, and supervisors in an industry sector, the lower the wages of Hispanics, Asians, and whites (in that order). This variable was not associated with the hourly wages of African Americans. Similarly, increases in

Table 3.6 Mean Predicted Probability of Joblessness by Nativity, Niche Employment, Gender, and Ethnicity, 1990

Gender and Ethnicity	Nonimmigrant[a]			Immigrant[a]		
	Non-Niche Occupation	Niche Occupation Other Group	Niche Occupation Own Group[b]	Non-Niche Occupation	Niche Occupation Other Group	Niche Occupation Own Group[b]
Men						
African American	.146	.142	.138	.120	.127	.122
Asian	.064	.058	.079	.061	.057	.081
Hispanic	.088	.086	.129	.100	.101	.118
White	.070	.061	.119	.065	.063	.121
Women						
African American	.148	.138	.137	.138	.125	.140
Asian	.104	.090	.099	.105	.098	.092
Hispanic	.152	.142	.261	.170	.171	.234
White	.117	.108	.140	.117	.119	.136

Source: Predicted values are based on the coefficient reported in table 3.3.

Notes: Predicted mean probability derived from coefficients estimated from equation (3.3).

[a] Immigrant refers to an individual who migrated to this country after age 10.

[b] The "Own Group" niche category includes occupations in which members of other ethnic groups may have also established a niche.

the proportion of coethnic owners and managers was associated with lower wages. These results, along with those for occupational attainment, raise the possibility that these associations may in large part be reflective of employment conditions in ethnic economies. In this regard, it is interesting to note that with respect to both wages and occupational attainment, the coefficients for African Americans, the group least likely to be employed in an ethnic economy, are not statistically significant. Finally, we can note that a high proportion of women in the workforce of an employment sector in 1980, as well as changes in that proportion, were associated with significantly reduced hourly wages.

Reported results do not provide an unambiguous picture of the role of ethnic niches in promoting economic opportunities and whether the presumed benefits to niche employment differ by ethnic groups. To shed some additional light on this subject, I estimated predicted values for joblessness, occupational attainment, and hourly earnings and organized these estimates by ethnicity, gender, nativity, and niche employment. These results are reported in tables 3.6 through 3.8.

Table 3.6 reports the predicted probability of joblessness by ethnicity, gender, nativity, and whether a respondent worked in a niche in which her or his ethnic group or another ethnic group had established a niche. African American men have the highest probability of joblessness relative to Asian, Hispanic, and white men. In addition, nonimmigrant African American men have higher levels of joblessness than immigrant men, and nonimmigrant Hispanic men working in a niche have a higher probability of joblessness than other nonimmigrant men. There is essentially no difference between nativity groups for Asian and white men. For Asian, Hispanic, and white men the probability of joblessness is higher for those working in coethnic niches. Among women, there do not appear to be any appreciable differences in the probability of joblessness by nativity. However, Hispanic women have the highest level of joblessness, followed closely by African Americans of both sexes. Employment in a coethnic niche does not appear to change the likelihood of joblessness for African American and Asian women. For Hispanic and white women, joblessness among those in a niche occupation is likely to be substantially higher.

Table 3.7 reports predicted occupational attainment values by gender, ethnicity, nativity, and niche employment. In almost every instance, nonimmigrants have higher occupational attainment values than immigrants, and working in a coethnic-based niche is associated

Table 3.7 Mean Predicted Occupational Attainment Scores by Nativity, Niche Employment, Gender, and Ethnicity, 1990

Gender and Ethnicity	Nonimmigrant			Immigrant[a]		
	Non-Niche Occupation	Niche Occupation		Non-Niche Occupation	Niche Occupation	
		Other Group	Own Group[b]		Other Group	Own Group[b]
Men						
African American	31.415	36.408	27.185	30.908	35.743	26.379
Asian	38.799	42.730	34.807	36.837	40.079	29.911
Hispanic	32.183	32.679	21.810	26.863	25.821	19.010
White	36.909	42.045	31.826	35.443	38.547	28.138
Women						
African American	33.971	40.245	28.794	32.028	38.561	26.410
Asian	37.015	40.327	36.327	33.867	35.919	34.441
Hispanic	32.203	33.324	18.684	28.486	25.419	15.831
White	36.203	40.109	35.820	34.076	35.712	33.177

Source: Predicted values are based on coefficient reported in table 3.4.
Notes: Predicted mean derived from coefficients estimated from equation (3.1).
[a] Immigrant refers to an individual who migrated to this country after age 10.
[b] The "Own Group" niche category includes occupations in which members of other ethnic groups may have also established a niche.

with substantially lower occupational attainment. These differences apply to both men and women. The uniformity of this pattern of results suggests that workers may pay a penalty for working in niches. The source of this disadvantage may be restricted opportunities for career mobility. It may also be that a substantial portion of employment in niches results from workers of different groups being channeled into different occupations with few other options available under conditions of labor surplus.

The gaps between men and women are not large and in some instances favor women over men. African American and Hispanic women appear to have higher occupational attainment than men, even among nonimmigrants, particularly in niches. This is an unexpected finding, because conventional wisdom predicts a substantial gap in occupational standing favoring men.

Individuals who work in employment sectors in which another group has established a niche are likely to have the highest occupational status. Why this should be the case, I can only speculate. It may well be that a substantial number of the firms operating in this sector and the non-niche sector follow more bureaucratic procedures for hiring workers, or perhaps workers are better able to secure employment without heavy reliance on coethnic networks.

Table 3.8 reports predicted wages by gender, ethnicity, nativity, and niche employment. In most instances, nonimmigrants are likely to have higher wages than immigrants. This is not the case for African American men employed outside of coethnic niches. The wages of non-niche workers are predicted to be higher than those of niche workers, especially Asian and Hispanic men and Hispanic women. Women uniformly have lower wages than men, although the differences are smaller between African American men and women.

SUMMARY

The results reported in the previous section suggest the following tentative conclusions: Employment in industry- and occupation-based niches composed of coethnics represents a substantial share of the workforce of urban minority workers, including African Americans at 37 percent, Hispanics at 36 percent, Asians at 27 percent, and whites at 9 percent. A majority of African Americans who work in coethnic niches are concentrated in industries and occupations in which no other group has a niche. The larger size of this population and their longer tenure in major metropolitan areas may mean that, until recently, they were the major workforce for many of the low-skill jobs

Table 3.8   Mean Predicted Hourly Wages by Nativity, Niche Employment, Gender, and Ethnicity, 1990

Gender and Ethnicity	Nonimmigrant[a]			Immigrant[a]		
	Non-Niche Occupation	Niche Occupation		Non-Niche Occupation	Niche Occupation	
		Other Group	Own Group[b]		Other Group	Own Group[b]
Men						
African American	10.153	11.909	10.374	10.422	12.312	09.683
Asian	13.029	14.970	10.861	12.255	13.754	09.344
Hispanic	10.344	11.113	08.580	08.799	08.674	07.452
White	13.738	16.983	14.834	14.014	15.983	13.955
Women						
African American	09.172	10.910	08.792	08.903	11.104	07.929
Asian	10.505	11.694	10.294	09.671	10.366	10.521
Hispanic	08.026	08.843	06.572	07.352	06.935	05.736
White	09.436	11.060	10.402	09.615	10.447	09.771

Source: Predicted values are based on coefficients reported in table 3.5.

Notes: Predicted mean weekly wages derived from coefficients estimated from equation (3.5).

[a]Immigrant refers to an individual who migrated to this country after age 10.

[b]The "Own Group" niche category includes occupations in which members of other ethnic groups may also have established a niche.

in the service and manufacturing sectors. Additionally, blacks' concentration in niches is probably a result of historical patterns of exclusion and discrimination, which had the effect of limiting their employment to the least desirable and lowest-paying jobs. Although recent immigrant groups may be moving into some of these jobs, as in, for example, the hospitality industry, these groups are also concentrating in entirely different sectors. Moreover, given the restricted nature of the sample used and the existence of substantial intermetropolitan variation in industry and ethnic composition, additional insight probably can be gained by performing similar analysis for individual metropolitan areas with sufficient sample sizes on the PUMS files.

I find little support for the hypothesis that employment in a niche offers advantages with respect to decreased risk of being jobless and access to high-status jobs that pay wages above what one would expect in the general local labor market. In fact, high joblessness, low occupational status, and low wages are associated with employment in niches (see Model [1997] who reports similar results). In general, immigrants fare worse than nonimmigrants. However, we should take note of the fact that, for those who speak English poorly, working in a niche does lower the odds of being jobless, although the occupation and wages of the individuals remain low. For these individuals, employment in a niche could be a distinct advantage.

With respect to joblessness, African Americans stand out as having the highest level among men, particularly among nonimmigrant men. Indeed, the level of joblessness for nonimmigrants is almost identical to that for African American women. It is clear that high joblessness among African American men and women has little to do with employment in a coethnic niche. This is not the case for Asian and Hispanic men and nonimmigrant women. Given the overall pattern exhibited in table 3.6, coupled with the finding that blacks do not appear to be concentrated in niches in which other groups are present, it seems unlikely that niche formations among the other ethnic groups could have contributed to the high joblessness found among African Americans. However, a clearer picture might emerge if we were to focus on industry- and occupation-specific categories to determine whether the influx of workers from other groups is associated with the outflow of African Americans.

The analysis also addressed the question of whether the immigrant share of the workforce in an employment sector is associated with labor-market outcomes. The results reported here clearly suggest that a high immigrant share in 1980 is associated with the odds of being jobless for African Americans and Hispanics and lower occupational status and wages for all groups. Changes in immigrant shares between 1980 and 1990 are associated with greater joblessness for African Americans and lower joblessness for Hispanics, with lower occupational attainment for blacks and Hispanics, and with lower hourly wages for members of all groups.

These results are consistent with those reported by Franklin Wilson and Gerald Jaynes (1998), who use similar measures, but inconsistent with results reported by others. It is not clear whether these differences are substantive in character or simply the consequence of the use of different measures. Most previous research that assesses the association of immigration flows with labor-market outcome of native workers uses educational attainment of workers as an important stratifying variable. In this chapter, I assess the association of accumulated immigrant stock (immigrant share) with labor-market outcome of local workers in specific industry and occupational groupings. Measures of the flow of immigration, even when observed at the local level, are global in the sense that no effort is made to identify and take account of the specific sectors in which immigrants are seeking employment. A global measure cannot evaluate whether displacement of one group by another is occurring, because such measures are not sector specific. It is possible, however, to make such an evaluation with the approach used in this chapter. Industries and occupations define the activity of the individual in the labor market; thus, it is possible to assess more precisely whether and to what extent immigrants are seeking employment in sectors in which members of other groups are concentrated.

Although reported results establish an association between immigrant shares within an industry- and occupation-specific employment sector and labor-market outcomes, these relations should not be interpreted as causal in nature. The industry and occupational categories are somewhat broad, and thus the composition of an employment sector may have confounded the true relations (see Scott 1996). Similarly, the use of broad panethnic categories may also be a source of confusion, because the individual ethnic groups subsumed under each category are not identical with respect to their relative position in the labor market. We know little about the links between immigrant flows and the development and expansion of ethnic niches except for a few case studies (see Waldinger 1994, and 1996b). A comparative analysis which focuses on a large number of ethnic groups, resident in the same cities, but differing on key attributes such as nativity composition, English fluency, and educational attainment, is what is needed to address many of the issues related to the various strategies used by groups to establish themselves in local labor markets.

APPENDIX

Table 3A.1   Definition of Variables

Characteristics of Respondents

AGE is reported in years, 19 to 64.

AGE^2 is age squared.

DISABLE is 1 if respondent has a work-related disability and 0 otherwise.

OTINCOME is 1 total household income in 1989 minus that of respondent.

MARRIED is 1 if respondent is married and 0 otherwise.

EMARRIED is 1 if respondent has been previously married and 0 otherwise.

SPEAK is a scale measuring English-speaking ability. A value of 1 indicates respondent speaks no English, and a value of 5 indicates respondent speaks only English at home.

SEX is 1 if respondent is a woman and 0 if respondent is a man.

COMGRADE is a scale for years of schooling completed. It has a value of 1 for respondents who completed less than 9 years of schooling and a value of 7 for respondents who completed graduate or professional school.

GRASPK is English-speaking ability of college graduates.

ETHNIC5 is ethnic identification:
African-American (2)
Hispanic (3)
Asian (4)
White (6)

CMSA is metropolitan area of residence (see appendix B).

IMIGR1 is length of residence in the U.S. for immigrants.

IMIGANT1 is 1 if respondent immigrated to the U.S. before age 11.

IMIGANT2 is 1 if respondent immigrated to the U.S. after age 10.

OCCUP is major occupation of employment:
Professional and managerial (MANPROF) (8)
Technical and sales (TECHSALE) (2)
Administration (ADMIN) (3)
Services (except private household) (4)
Craft and precision manufacturing (SKILBLUE) (5)
Fabricators and operatives (SSKLBLUE) (6)
Laborers and private-household workers (SSKLBLUE) (7)

INDUSTY is major industry of employment:
Construction (4)
Food and kindred products (5)
Other durable goods (6)
Textile mill products; apparel and other finished textiles (8)

(Table continues on p. 136.)

Table 3A.1   *Continued*

Characteristics of Respondents

Paper and allied products; printing, publishing, and allied products (10)
Chemical and allied products; petroleum and coal (11)
Lumber, wood, and furniture (13)
Other durable goods (14)
Primary metals; fabricated metals (15)
Machinery, except electrical (17)
Electrical machinery and equipment (18)
Motor vehicles and equipment (19)
Other transportation equipment (20)
Miscellaneous manufacturing; not-specified manufacturing (22)
Railroads; trucks, warehouse, storage; other transportation (25)
Communications (26)
Utilities, sanitary services (27)
Wholesale (28)
Grocery, dairy, retail bakeries (30)
Motor vehicle dealers, and gas stations (31)
Eating and drinking (32)
General merchandise; other retail (33)
Finance, insurance, real estate; banks and credit unions (35)
Business services; legal, engineering, and other professional services (36)
Repair services (37)
Private household (38)
Other personal services (39)
Entertainment and recreation (40)
Hospitals (41)
Health services, excluding hospitals (42)
Elementary and secondary schools; college and university; other education services (45)
Social services, religious, membership (46)
Public administration (48)

Characteristics of Employment Sectors

NATIVE8 is the proportion of the workforce in an industry or occupation (employment) sector that is foreign born in 1980.

CNATIVE is the ratio of the proportion of the workforce in an employment sector that is foreign born in 1990 to the same proportion in 1980.

SEX80 is the share of the workforce of an employment sector that is women in 1990.

CSEX is the ratio of the share of the workforce of an employment sector that is women in 1990 to the same share in 1980.

ODDS80 measures workforce concentration for a given ethnic group. It is the share of a group's workforce employed in a given industry or occupation divided by the share of all other groups' workforce employed in the same employment sector.

CODDS is change in the index of employment sector concentration for a given ethnic group from 1980 to 1990.

SUPER80X is the proportion of a group's workforce employed in an industry who are owners, managers, and supervisors.

Table 3A.1 *Continued*

Characteristics of Employment Sectors

CSUPER is the change from 1980 to 1990 in the proportion of a group's workforce employed in an industry who are owners, managers, and supervisors.

NICH85 is 1 if respondent is employed in an industry or occupation sector in which groups other than his or her own have established a niche and 0 otherwise.

NICH86 is 1 if respondent is employed in an industry or occupation sector in which his or her own group has established a niche and 0 otherwise.

NICHSPK8 is 1 if respondent speaks English poorly and works in a coethnic niche and 0 otherwise.

Note: Most of the variables defined here are not reported in tables 3.3 through 3.5 (see Wilson 1997).

Table 3A.2 CMS and Metropolitan Statistical Areas Included in This Analysis

CMSA/MSA	PMSA	Name
720		Baltimore, Md. MSA
7		Boston, Mass. CMSA
	1120	Boston, Mass. PMSA
	1200	Brockton, Mass. PMSA
	4160	Lawrence-Haverhill, Mass.-N.H. PMSA
	4560	Lowell, Mass.-N.H. PMSA
	7090	Salem-Gloucester, Mass. PMSA
14		Chicago, Ill. CMSA
	620	Aurora-Elgin, Ill. PMSA
	1600	Chicago, Ill. PMSA
	2960	Gary-Hammond, Ind. PMSA
	3690	Joliet, Ill. PMSA
	3800	Kenosha, Wis. PMSA
	3965	Lake County, Ill. PMSA
21		Cincinnati-Hamilton, Ohio-Ind. CMSA
	1640	Cincinnati, Ohio-Ind. PMSA
	3200	Hamilton-Middletown, Ohio PMSA
28		Cleveland, Ohio CMSA
	80	Akron, Ohio PMSA
	1680	Cleveland, Ohio PMSA
	4440	Lorain-Elyria, Ohio PMSA
31		Dallas–Fort Worth, Tex. CMSA
	1920	Dallas, Tex. PMSA
	2800	Fort Worth, Tex. PMSA
34		Denver-Boulder, Colo. CMSA
	1125	Boulder-Longmont, Colo. PMSA
	2080	Denver, Colo. PMSA

Table 3A.2   *Continued*

CMSA/MSA	PMSA	Name
35		Detroit, Mich. CMSA
	440	Ann Arbor, Mich. PMSA
	2160	Detroit, Mich. PMSA
2840		Fresno, Calif. MSA and Salinas-Seaside-Monterey, Calif. MSA (7120)
42		Houston-Galveston-Brazoria, Tex. CMSA
	1145	Brazoria, Tex. PMSA
	2920	Galveston-Texas City, Tex. PMSA
	3360	Houston, Tex. PMSA
49		Los Angeles–Anaheim-Riverside, Calif. CMSA
	360	Anaheim–Santa Ana, Calif. PMSA
	4480	Los Angeles–Long Beach, Calif. PMSA
	6000	Oxnard-Ventura, Calif. PMSA
	6780	Riverside–San Bernardino, Calif. PMSA
56		Miami–Fort Lauderdale, Fla. CMSA
	2680	Fort Lauderdale–Hollywood–Pompano Beach, Fla. PMSA
	5000	Miami-Hialeah, Fla. PMSA
5120		Minneapolis–St. Paul, Minn.-Wis. MSA
70		New York–New Jersey–Long Island, N.Y.-N.J. CMSA
	875	Bergen-Passaic, N.J. PMSA
	3640	Jersey City, N.J. PMSA
	5015	Middlesex-Somerset-Hunterdon, N.J. PMSA
	5190	Monmouth-Ocean, N.J. PMSA
	5380	Nassau-Suffolk County, N.Y. PMSA
	5600	New York, N.Y. PMSA
	5640	Newark, N.J. PMSA
	5950	Orange County, N.J. PMSA
5720		Norfolk–Virginia Beach–Newport News, Va. MSA
77		Philadelphia-Wilmington-Trenton, Pa.-N.J.-Del.-Md. CMSA
	6160	Philadelphia, Pa. PMSA
	8480	Trenton, N.J. PMSA
	8760	Vineland-Millville-Bridgeton, N.J. PMSA
	9160	Wilmington, Del. PMSA
6200		Phoenix, Ariz. MSA
79		Portland-Vancouver, Ore.-Wash. CMSA
	6440	Portland, Ore. PMSA
	8725	Vancouver, Wash. PMSA
6920		Sacramento, Calif. MSA and Stockton, Calif. MSA (8120)

Table 3A.2 *Continued*

CMSA/MSA	PMSA	Name
7320		San Diego, Calif. MSA
84		San Francisco–Oakland–San Jose, Calif. CMSA
	5775	Oakland, Calif. PMSA
	7360	San Francisco, Calif. PMSA
	7400	San Jose, Calif. PMSA
	7485	Santa Cruz, Calif. PMSA
	7500	Santa Rosa–Petaluma, Calif. PMSA
	8720	Vallejo-Fairfield-Napa, Calif. PMSA
91		Seattle-Tacoma, Wash. CMSA
	7600	Seattle, Wash. PMSA
	8200	Tacoma, Wash. PMSA
8280		Tampa–St. Petersburg–Clearwater, Fla. MSA
8840		Washington, D.C. MSA

REFERENCES

Alba, Richard D., and Victor Nee. 1997. "Rethinking Assimilation Theory for a New Era of Immigration." *International Migration Review* 31(4): 826–76.

Aldrich, Howard, and Roger Waldinger. 1990. "Ethnicity and Entrepreneurship." *Annual Review of Sociology* 16:111–35.

Bailey, Thomas, and Roger Waldinger. 1991. "Primary, Secondary, and Enclave Labor Markets: A Training Systems Approach." *American Sociological Review* 56(4): 432–45.

Hauser, Robert M., and John Robert Warren. 1997. "Socioeconomic Indexes for Occupations: A Review, Update, and Critique." In *Sociological Methodology*, edited by Adrian Raftery. San Francisco: Jossey-Bass.

Lieberson, Stanley. 1980. *A Piece of the Pie: Blacks and White Immigrants Since 1880.* Berkeley: University of California Press.

Logan, John R., Richard D. Alba, and Thomas L. McNulty. 1994. "Ethnic Economies in Metropolitan Regions: Miami and Beyond." *Social Forces* 72(3): 691–724.

Massey, Douglas S. 1985. "Ethnic Residential Segregation: A Theoretical Synthesis and Empirical Review." *Sociology and Social Research* 69(3): 315–50.

Massey, Douglas S., Joaquín Arango, Graeme Hugo, Ali Kouaouci, Adela Pellegrino, and J. Edward Taylor. 1994. "An Evaluation of International Migration Theory: The North American Case." *Population and Development Review* 20(4): 699–752.

Model, Suzanne. 1993. "The Ethnic Niche and the Structure of Opportunity: Immigrants and Minorities in New York City." In *The Historical Origins of the Underclass,* edited by Michael Katz. New York: Princeton University Press.

———. 1997. "Ethnic Economy and Industry in Mid-Twentieth Century Gotham." *Social Problems* 44(3): 445–63.

Model, Suzanne, and David Ladipo. 1996. "Context and Opportunity: Minorities in London and New York." *Social Forces* 75(6).

Morawska, Ewa. 1990. "The Sociology and Historiography of Immigration." In *Immigration Reconsidered: History, Sociology, and Politics,* edited by V. Yans-McLaughlin. New York: Oxford University Press.

Nee, Victor, Jimy M. Sanders, and Scott Sernau. 1994. "Job Transitions in an Immigrant Metropolis." *American Sociological Review* 59(2): 485–510.

Portes, Alejandro, and Robert Bach. 1985. *Latin Journey: Cuban and Mexican Immigrants in the United States.* Berkeley: University of California Press.

Portes, Alejandro, and Leif Jensen. 1989. "The Enclave and the Entrants: Patterns of Ethnic Enterprise in Miami Before and After Mariel." *American Sociological Review* 54(6): 929–49.

Portes, Alejandro, and R. G. Rumbaut. 1996. *Immigrant America: A Portrait.* 2d ed. Berkeley: University of California Press.

Scott, Allen J. 1996. "The Manufacturing Economy: Ethnic and Gender Division of Labor." In *Ethnic Los Angeles,* edited by Roger Waldinger and Mehdi Bozorgmehr. New York: Russell Sage Foundation.

U.S. Bureau of the Census. 1989. "Population Estimates by Race and Hispanic Origin for States, Metropolitan Areas, and Selected Counties: 1980–1985." In *Current Population Report.* Series P-25, no. 1040-RD-1. Washington, D.C.: U.S. Government Printing Office.

Waldinger, Roger. 1994. "The Making of an Immigrant Niche." *International Migration Review* 28(1): 3–30.

———. 1996a. "Ethnicity and Opportunity in the Plural City." In *Ethnic Los Angeles,* edited by Roger Waldinger and Mehdi Bozorgmehr. New York: Russell Sage Foundation.

———. 1996b. *Still the Promised City?: African Americans and New Immigrants in Postindustrial New York.* Cambridge: Harvard University Press.

Wilson, Franklin D. 1997. "Ethnic Concentration and Labor Market Opportunities." CDE Working Paper 97-17. Madison: Center for Demography and Ecology, University of Wisconsin.

Wilson, Franklin D., and Gerald Jaynes. 1998. "Immigration and Labor Market Outcomes for Native Workers." CDE Working Paper 95-32 (updated February 1998). Madison: Center for Demography and Ecology, University of Wisconsin.

PART II

ENTREPRENEURSHIP, SOCIAL NETWORKS, AND LABOR MARKETS

CHAPTER 4

Entrepreneurship and Economic Progress in the 1990s: A Comparative Analysis of Immigrants and African Americans

Alejandro Portes and Min Zhou

This chapter continues the exploration of the determinants and consequences of entrepreneurship for immigrant groups and domestic minorities. We update earlier results based on the 1980 census with 1990 data to establish gross and net results of entrepreneurship (defined operationally as self-employment) on the earnings of these various groups. This is followed by an analysis focused on three issues: the determinants of ethnic entrepreneurship; the extent to which ethnic concentration affects the probabilities of ethnic entrepreneurship; and the effect of the rise of immigrant enclaves on the resident African American population.

The creation of entrepreneurial communities by certain immigrant groups and the question of whether these communities represent alternatives to destitution or true vehicles for economic mobility have received considerable attention in the past (Bailey and Waldinger 1991; Light 1972, 1980, 1984; Light and Bonacich 1988; Portes and Jensen 1989; Zhou 1992). Based on data from the 1980 census and our own surveys, we conclude that entrepreneurship represents a major path for individual and collective economic mobility among ethnic minorities. This conclusion is based on four factors:

1. the consistently higher average earnings of the self-employed over employees of the same ethnic background, on both an hourly and a yearly basis

2. the resilience of a positive net self-employment effect on earnings, even after controlling for relevant human capital variables

3. the findings that insignificant or negative self-employment effects on earnings in regression models employing a logarithmic transformation of earnings is seemingly the result of the suppression of positive outliers (high earners), the majority of whom are self-employed (Portes and Zhou 1996)

143

4. historical evidence indicating that the most entrepreneurial immigrant groups in the past have had above-average rates of educational and occupational intergenerational mobility and that their descendants enjoy individual and family incomes higher than the national averages (Portes and Bach 1985; Portes and Jensen 1989; Portes and Zhou 1992, 1996).

Past analyses of national-level data have been supplemented by detailed studies of entrepreneurial immigrant groups that clarify the mechanisms through which business success and economic mobility occur. Within ethnic enclaves, business growth relies on close interdependence between firms such that they supply each other with goods and services and also sell these goods and services in the outside market. Employing a sophisticated analysis of input and output matrices, Kenneth Wilson and Allen Martin (1982) have documented the dense network of business relationships in the Cuban enclave of Miami. They contrast this pattern with the much more atomized situation of black-owned firms in the same metropolitan area.

The capacity of ethnic business concentrations to create informal training systems has been documented by other studies. Alejandro Portes and Robert Bach (1985) theorize that a relationship of reciprocity is established between firm owners and their coethnic employees in which the latter willingly accept low pay, long hours, and often harsh working conditions in exchange for the chance to "learn the ropes" with a view toward establishing their own enterprises at a later date. The study does not document these reciprocity bonds directly but finds that one of the main predictors of self-employment among Cuban exiles arriving in Miami in the 1970s was prior employment in a Cuban enclave firm. Expanding on this theme, Thomas Bailey and Roger Waldinger (1991) directly examine the operation of these informal business apprenticeships in the garment industry. They conclude that bonds of solidarity, in combination with the dynamics of small ethnic firms, provide a key mechanism for the self-sustaining capability of ethnic enclaves. In their words, "Once in place, the immigrant sector has grown as a self-feeding process. Newcomers take up work in immigrant firms, and workers who have gained skills and experience working for co-ethnic owners set up a new business of their own" (Bailey and Waldinger 1991, 443).

In her study of the Chinese enclave in New York, Min Zhou (1992) illustrates how informal reciprocity bonds are established between workers and entrepreneurs and how they function to promote simultaneously the survival of firms, by providing a cheaper and more committed labor force, and the interest of workers, through more flexible work conditions and apprenticeship opportunities. Although when seen from the outside, labor practices in Chinatown may seem exploitative, the study documents that, in reality, many of these arrangements are entered into voluntarily for mutual benefit. Zhou also highlights another aspect of ethnic entrepreneurship neglected in prior studies, namely, its concentration in certain key economic sectors.

Using census data, John Logan, Richard Alba, and Thomas McNulty (1994) systematically examine this aspect in immigrant enclaves nationwide. With the exception of the Cuban case in Miami, where ethnic firms are represented in a wide spectrum of activities, most instances feature a concentration in a few sectors of manufacturing or services. The tendency of ethnic enterprises to cluster in certain key sectors has subsequently given rise to the concept of ethnic niche and to a parallel literature in which overrepresentation of certain minorities, as employers or employees, in particular activities is interpreted as evidence of the existence of an ethnic economy and is used to delineate its composition (Zhou and Logan 1989; Model 1990; Waldinger 1985, 1996).

In general, there is an emerging sociological consensus that ethnic entrepreneurship represents both an important phenomenon and a viable path for economic mobility. Along the way, new knowledge has accumulated on the emergence and self-sustaining character of ethnic enclaves and ethnic niches and on the economic sectors where they are most commonly represented. Comparisons have also been made between the high entrepreneurial dynamism of certain immigrant groups and the relative dearth of such activities among downtrodden domestic minorities. Part of this literature has explored the notable decline of self-employment among the latter groups and examined ways of restoring it as a means for renewing economic mobility (Butler 1991; Green and Pryde 1990; Portes and Zhou 1992; Guarnizo 1994).

Three issues have received relatively less attention: first, the determinants of individual self-employment within specific ethnic groups; second, the extent to which this causal pattern is similar across entrepreneurial immigrant groups and in relation to domestic minorities, particularly African Americans; and third, the effect that the rise of immigrant enclaves in certain cities has on African American earnings and on this group's own propensity toward entrepreneurship. In this chapter, we provide a preliminary analysis of these questions after examining how the most recent national data compare with prior results on the economic consequences of self-employment.

Table 4.1 Socioeconomic Profile of Male Workers by Selected Ethnic Origin, 1990

Characteristic	Chinese	Korean	Vietnamese	Cuban	Dominican	Mexican	Jamaican	African American	White
Speaks English very well (%)	75.3	70.0	77.1	70.5	59.0	53.7	—	—	—
Immigrated after 1984 (%)	21.1	24.1	12.8	5.2	20.2	16.7	18.9	—	—
Married (%)	80.2	86.0	64.3	73.3	67.4	74.9	63.9	58.2	75.0
Mean age (years)	40.6	41.2	37.3	44.1	38.7	36.6	39.2	39.9	40.9
College graduate (%)	50.1	48.7	25.3	19.7	10.0	4.0	17.1	13.4	27.9
Professional occupation (%)	40.5	33.4	20.5	23.0	10.8	5.5	17.8	14.7	28.5
Unemployed (%)	2.9	2.0	4.1	4.3	8.9	7.2	6.6	7.3	3.7
Mean hours worked in 1989	2,078	2,228	1,989	2,090	1,931	1,905	1,890	1,951	2,192
Self-employed (%)	15.3	34.2	9.5	18.2	9.6	6.8	7.3	4.9	14.4
N	14,152	5,896	5,135	10,540	3,257	61,231	3,001	34,200	67,613

Source: U.S. Census of Population, 1990, 5-percent Public Use Microdata Sample.
Notes: Sample restricted to males age 25 to 64 who were in the civilian labor force, worked at least 160 hours, and earned a minimum of $500 in 1989. For individual nationalities, figures are for the total number of foreign-born from each country present in the data. For African Americans, figures are for a three-fifths random sample of persons identified as native-born African Americans. For whites, figures are for a one-tenth random sample of native-born whites.

ENTREPRENEURSHIP AND EARNINGS IN 1990

Table 4.1 presents a socioeconomic profile of seven major contemporary immigrant groups in the United States. Matching samples of native-born whites and African Americans are included for comparison. Although the seven selected groups jointly constitute 42.4 percent of all immigrants who arrived legally between 1971 and 1990, they were chosen not because of their size but as representatives of contrasting situations in terms of socioeconomic background and entrepreneurial orientation. We limit this analysis to males because levels of self-employment among female workers are lower in relation to those of their male counterparts for all groups. This ascriptive difference is theoretically important when examining determinants of entrepreneurship, a point to which we will return later. Three of these immigrant groups have been identified in the research literature as entrepreneurial minorities. Indeed, Chinese, Koreans, and Cubans each had double-digit rates of self-employment in 1990, well exceeding the national average of 9.7 percent. Native-born whites are also quite entrepreneurial, as shown by a self-employment rate among males of 14 percent.

Three other groups—Vietnamese, Dominicans, and Jamaicans—represent intermediate situations, with male self-employment rates around 9 percent. The Vietnamese are the largest group among Southeast Asian refugees and the only one that has developed a sizable business enclave, located just south of Los Angeles in the Santa Ana–Westminster area of Orange County. Dominicans are a fast-growing immigrant group, replacing Cubans as the single largest Caribbean inflow during the last decade. They have also created an identifiable business presence in the Washington Heights section of New York City (Guarnizo 1992, 1994). Jamaicans are another fast-growing Caribbean group, composed mostly of black, English-speaking immigrants. Unlike Dominicans or Vietnamese, they do not have a spatially identifiable ethnic economy, but their average education is higher than that of most other Caribbean and Central American inflows.

Lastly, Mexicans continue to be by far the largest immigrant minority, characterized by low levels of both education and self-employment. At 6.8 percent, the Mexican self-employment rate is higher than that only of native-born African Americans. Table 4.1 also indicates a rough correspondence between rates of self-employment and average levels of education and occupation. Koreans and Chinese, the

Table 4.2 Hourly Wages and Annual Earnings by Type of Employment and Ethnicity, 1990

Characteristic	Chinese	Korean	Vietnamese	Cuban	Dominican	Mexican	Jamaican	African American	White
Mean hourly wages in 1989 ($)	15.7	17.3	12.5	13.9	10.9	9.1	13.1	12.0	16.1
Workers	15.0	15.8	12.5	13.0	10.6	8.9	12.7	11.8	15.4
Self-employed	19.9	20.3	13.2	17.6	13.8	13.0	18.7	15.0	19.7
Mean earnings in 1989 ($)	31,772	34,865	24,505	28,335	19,503	16,506	23,439	22,506	34,197
Workers	29,721	29,902	24,116	26,510	19,212	16,084	23,105	22,268	32,897
Self-employed	43,151	44,419	28,209	36,558	22,239	22,295	27,704	27,128	41,949
Net effect of self-employment[a]									
On hourly wages ($)	3,524***	3.103***	.177	3.168***	2.400***	2.677***	3.858***	1.793***	2.420***
On annual earnings ($)	8,959***	8,771***	3,331***	7,492***	2,054*	3,916***	2,985**	3,948***	5,455***
N	14,152	5,896	5,135	10,540	3,257	61,231	3,001	34,200	67,613

Source: U.S. Census of Population, 1990, 5-percent Public Use Microdata Sample.

Notes: For sample definition, see footnote in table 4.1.

[a]OLS unstandardized regression coefficients of earnings equations that include the following variables: self-employment, education (high-school graduate; some college; college graduate); age; age squared; occupation (professional or executive occupation; technical occupation; service occupation); marital status; knowledge of English; recency of immigration; full-time year-round employment; public sector employment; presence of children; number of adults in family; and residence in the South. Full regression results are available from the authors upon request.

***Coefficient is significant at the .001 level.

most entrepreneurial groups, have the highest proportions of college graduates and of professional workers, exceeding on both counts the native white averages. They are followed, in turn, by Cubans and Vietnamese. Dominican and Mexican immigrants and African Americans come at the bottom in both variables.

The same rank order is present in table 4.2, in which we turn to the question of average earnings. The purpose of this analysis is not to compare earnings between different ethnic groups but rather to examine the effect of self-employment within each group. In other words, we seek to establish whether entrepreneurship has a consistent effect on earnings across such different ethnic categories and, if this effect exists, whether it corresponds to past expectations. To answer these questions, the table presents results of two analyses. First, we compare average hourly wages and annual earnings of employees and the self-employed within each ethnic group to establish whether a gross effect exists. Second, we regress hourly and annual earnings on a standard human capital function plus a dummy variable for self-employment to establish the net effects of the latter.

Results are impressive in their consistency both across ethnic categories and over time. They can be readily compared with published findings based on the 1980 census that show essentially the same pattern (Portes and Zhou 1992, 1996). Without exception, self-employed workers have average earnings superior to those of their salaried coethnics. With samples this large, all such differences are statistically significant; hence, it is preferable to concentrate on their absolute size. For annual earnings, the gap ranges from approximately three thousand dollars for Dominicans to more than ten thousand dollars for Chinese, Koreans, and Cubans. The latter figure represents close to one-third of the average annual earnings for each of these groups.

These absolute differences provide enough empirical groundings to consider the issue of entrepreneurship as theoretically important. Unquestionably, male workers who have acquired their own firms surpass their salaried counterparts economically and, though this advantage varies, it hold across all ethnic groups. A valid caveat, however, is that these gross differences do not accurately reflect reality because they do not take into account the different human capital profiles of self-employed and salaried workers. The alternative argument, commonly advanced by economists at this point, is that because of their human capital advantage, the self-employed would be as well off if they were salaried workers. Some authors have gone as far as to assert that, once these factors are controlled, self-employment exercises a negative effect on earnings (Borjas 1986, 1990; Bates and Dunham 1991; Bates 1994).

The bottom panel of table 4.2 examines the tenability of this argument. In line with published results for 1980, we find that human capital variables account for a substantial proportion of the variance in average earnings and significantly reduce, but do not eliminate, the effect of self-employment. The magnitude of this reduction is approximately one-half of the gross difference for most groups. Nonetheless, the net effect of self-employment on hourly wages and annual earnings remains positive and, in all but one case, significant. For annual earnings, it ranges from about two thousand dollars for Dominicans to almost nine thousand dollars for Chinese and Koreans. These figures can be tentatively interpreted as the economic advantage of being self-employed above and beyond those derived from different human capital endowments.

The debate on the economic effects of ethnic entrepreneurship then gets tangled into a number of questions concerning the proper functional form of the earnings equation, the endogenous versus exogenous character of hours worked, and other technical issues. As in other areas of social science inquiry, the overelaboration of the analysis ends up by obscuring its fundamental findings. Past research, supported by present results, can be summarized in three conclusions, once these various controversies are taken into account:

1. Entrepreneurs derive an absolute advantage from their economic activities over coethnic salaried workers. Entrepreneurs are disproportionately represented among high earners, a fact commonly obscured by the log linear functional form of the earnings equation (Portes and Zhou 1996).

2. Entrepreneurs consistently work more hours; this is part of the reason for their higher annual earnings. However, the advantage of self-employment is not derived exclusively from higher work effort, as shown by net differences in hourly wages.

3. Although superior absolute returns to self-employment are present among all ethnic categories, the advantage tends to be larger among the most entrepreneurial immigrant groups; that is, the higher the self-employment rate, the larger the absolute and net earnings gap in favor of entrepreneurs. This last difference raises the question of whether determinants of self-employment also vary across different ethnic communities.

DETERMINANTS OF ENTREPRENEURSHIP

A number of studies have analyzed differential propensities for self-employment between ethnic minorities (Aldrich, Zimmer, and

McEvoy 1989; Fratoe and Meeks 1985; Light 1984). The complementary question of employment differences *within* specific groups has received less attention. The question is significant because only a minority of working males, even within the most entrepreneurial communities, become self-employed. The process of causation at the individual level may hence be quite different from that determining variations between groups. Economists who have dealt with this issue have modeled individual probabilities for self-employment as a human capital outcome, employing the same set of predictors as in earnings equations. Their rationale is that such variables as education and work experience should increase the skills necessary to open a new business. Among the foreign born, years since immigration and knowledge of English are expected to operate in the same direction (Borjas 1986, 1990; Stevens and Chen 1984).

Less attention has been paid to demographic variables such as gender, marital status, and household compositions. George Borjas (1986) notes, however, that marriage resolves the "shirking" problem created when strangers are hired as employees in small firms and successfully incorporates this variable into his model of self-employment.[1] From a different perspective, Alejandro Portes and Leif Jensen (1989) stress the importance of gender differences in self-employment and the fact that the core of ethnic entrepreneurs is composed of middle-aged married men. They argue that small entrepreneurship is primarily a family affair in which men claim the firms as "theirs" but which represents, in reality, a collective family endeavor. Although women seldom declare business ownership, their participation is crucial to the success of these firms.

In their analysis of determinants of self-employment among Cubans in Miami, these authors find that gender, when it is introduced into the equation, overpowers the effects of all other predictors, rendering them insignificant (Portes and Jensen 1989). Portes and Jensen's analysis, restricted to males, reveals strong positive effects of marriage and the number of children present in addition to human capital variables. The effect of other adults in the household, however, turns out to be negative, indicating that entrepreneurship is not promoted by a simple addition of hands and that it is primarily a nuclear-family affair.

It is possible to reproduce this analysis for different ethnic groups nationwide on the basis of 1990 census data. This exercise seeks to answer three questions: What is the role of human capital and family variables as potential determinants of self-employment? How does this causal pattern vary among ethnic groups, in particular between entrepreneurial immigrants and native-born minorities? What is the

role of ethnic clustering in promoting or discouraging entrepreneurship?

Table 4.3 present logistic regressions of self-employment on the
relevant variables present in the census files. Education is represented
by three dummy variables, with "less than high school" as the omitted
category. Because the data do not provide educational attainment in
years, we substitute actual age for work experience. Age is also given
in two cohorts, with "less than thirty-five" as the reference category.
Recency of immigration is indicated by two dummy variables for the
foreign born, with immigration before 1980 as the omitted category.
Other predictors include knowledge of English, marital status, presence of children, number of adults in household, and area of residence. Results are presented for the three most entrepreneurial immigrant groups—Chinese, Cubans, and Koreans—as well as for native-
born whites and African Americans.

The table illustrates a series of notable findings: First, entrepreneurship is mainly the business of older men, as indicated by the
consistently positive coefficients for older age across every group. It is
also the occupational preserve of the more educated, although effects
of education are not linear for all ethnic categories. A college degree
or postgraduate education significantly increases the chances of self-
employment among native whites, African Americans, and Cubans
but not among the two Asian groups. For the latter, a high-school
diploma or some years of college education suffice. Among the Chinese a postgraduate degree actually decreases the probability of self-
employment. Overall, the less educated (those with less than a high-
school diploma) are least likely to become entrepreneurs for all
groups, but the causal relation is not consistent.

A common effect for all immigrants is that of recency of immigration, which greatly reduces chances for self-employment. This is reasonable and reinforces the impression, conveyed by the age effects,
that ethnic firms are run primarily by settled and more experienced
men. In particular, immigrants during the past five years appear to be
at a major disadvantage in terms of gaining access to their own enterprises. The last human capital variable—knowledge of English—does
not increase the probability of self-employment for any group and
actually decreases it among Korean and Cuban men. This result indicates that more-acculturated immigrants in these groups are less likely
to choose independent business as an occupational alternative. Combined with the negative effect of postgraduate education for the Chinese, these results lend support to the argument advanced by some
authors that self-employment is resorted to in the absence of suffi-

cient human capital to succeed in the mainstream labor market (Bates and Dunham 1991).

By far the most important finding in these data, however, is the effects of the family variables. The characterization of ethnic enterprise as a family affair holds for all three immigrant groups, among whom being married has one of the strongest effects on the probability of self-employment. The same is true for native whites but not for African Americans, the single group among whom married men stand no better change than single men of becoming entrepreneurs. To the extent that the creation and survival of small firms is supported in all other cases by the contribution of spouses, the chances for African American entrepreneurship appear to be weakened accordingly.

Although a quantitative analysis cannot directly demonstrate the means through which marriage contributes to business creation among different ethnic groups, a wealth of ethnographic evidence supports this relation. Qualitative studies of Cubans in Miami (Fernández-Kelly and García 1989; Perez 1986), Koreans in Los Angeles (Light 1980; Light and Bonacich 1988), and Chinese in various cities (Wong 1998; Zhou 1992), as well as earlier studies of Jewish and Japanese small firms (Bonacich and Modell 1980; Howe 1976; Petersen 1971; Rischin 1962), consistently indicate the decisive role of wives in the capitalization and operation of the businesses that husbands come to claim as their own.

Consistent with results reported by Portes and Jensen (1989), the presence of children has a positive net effect for all immigrant groups under study but not for native whites and blacks. This result highlights again the role of the nuclear family in promoting immigrant entrepreneurship. Less consistent, however, is the effect of other adults living in the household. For Koreans, by far the most entrepreneurial group, the presence of other adults in the household also increases self-employment, but this effect does not materialize among either Chinese or Cuban men.

To summarize results so far, entrepreneurship consistently involves older males and, among immigrants, those more settled in the country. It is consistently a family affair, with the notable exception of African Americans. The effects of human capital are not entirely consistent. Education increases the probability of self-employment for most groups, though this effect is not linear in all cases. Controlling for education, immigrants who are less fluent in English are more likely to pursue this career line. A final question is the extent to which clustering of an immigrant group in a given area increases the

Table 4.3   Determinants of Self-Employment Among Selected Ethnic Groups, 1990

Predictor[a]	Chinese			Cuban		
	B[b]	EXP (B)[c]	Δ[d]	B[b]	EXP (B)[c]	Δ[d]
Age						
35+	.669**	1.95	.11	.547***	1.73	.10
	(.069)			(.070)		
55+	.711***	2.04	.12	.385***	1.47	.06
	(.092)			(.087)		
Education						
High-school graduate	.234***	1.26	.03	−.108	—	—
	(.082)			(.077)		
Some college	.199*	1.22	.03	−.073	—	—
	(.083)			(.075)		
College graduate or more	−.240**	.79	−.03	.164*	1.18	.03
	(.076)			(.077)		
Recency of immigration						
After 1984	−1.010***	.36	−.10	−.909***	.40	−.10
	(.082)			(.149)		
1980 to 1984	−.275***	.76	−.03	−.308***	.73	−.04
	(.059)			(.072)		
Proficiency in English	.004	—	—	−.279***	.76	−.04
	(.068)			(.068)		
Family						
Married	.465***	1.59	.07	.302***	1.35	.05
	(.083)			(.071)		
Presence of children	.117*	1.12	.02	.209**	1.23	.03
	(.056)			(.059)		
Number of adults in household	.025	—	—	.003	—	—
	(.020)			(.022)		
Area of Residence						
Los Angeles PMSA	.328***	1.39	.05	—	—	—
	(.062)					
New York PMSA	−.206***	.81	−.02	—	—	—
	(.074)					
Miami-Hialeah PMSA	—	—	—	.371***	1.45	.06
				(.054)		
Constant	−2.516***			−2.145***		
N	14,152			10,540		

Source: U.S. Census of Population, 1990, 5-percent Public Use Microdata Sample.
[a]For sample definition, see footnote in table 4.1.
[b]Standard errors of regression in parentheses.
[c]Net effects on the odds of self-employment. Positive effects > 1.00.
[d]Net probabilities evaluated at the mean of the distribution for each ethnic group (equals net increase or decrease in the probability of self-employment).
*p < .05; **p < .01; ***p < .001.

	Korean			White			African American	
B^b	EXP (B)^c	Δ^d	B^b	EXP (B)^c	Δ^d	B^b	EXP (B)^c	Δ^d
.715***	2.04	.17	.527***	1.69	.08	.668***	1.95	.04
(.074)			(.028)			(.064)		
.684***	1.98	.17	.882***	2.42	.14	.923***	2.52	.07
(.113)			(.038)			(.088)		
.232	—	—	−.075	—	—	−.252***	.78	−.01
(.120)			(.037)			(.067)		
.377**	1.46	.09	.002	—	—	−.230***	.80	−.01
(.121)			(.037)			(.071)		
.209	—	—	.091**	1.10	.01	.227**	1.25	.01
(.115)			(.037)			(.076)		
−.850***	.43	−.16	—	—	—	—	—	
(.085)								
−.187**	.83	−.04	—	—	—	—	—	—
(.070)								
−.179*	.84	−.04	—	—	—	—	—	—
(.073)								
.742***	2.10	.18	.328***	1.39	05	.107	—	—
(.111)			(.033)			(.061)		
.238***	1.27	.06	.002	—	—	−.040	—	—
(.070)			(.026)			(.059)		
.143***	1.15	.03	−.077***	.93	−.01	−.028	—	—
(.026)			(.015)			(.021)		
.324***	1.38	.08	—	—	—	—	—	—
(.068)								
.014	—	—	—	—	—	—	—	—
(.095)								
—	—	—	—	—	—	—	—	—
−2.327***			−2.316***			−3.361***		
5,135			67,613			34,200		

chances for self-employment. The theory of ethnic enclaves would suggest that it does, by creating larger, culturally defined markets and pools of coethnic labor. In addition, the functioning of enclaves as informal training systems should have its strongest influence in the areas of greater ethnic concentration. On the other hand, a more individualistic perspective would suggest that chances for self-employment are determined primarily by the person's own human capital and the support received from immediate family members.

The bottom panel of table 4.3 addresses this question for the three immigrant groups in the analysis. As is well known, Cubans concentrate in the Miami-Hialeah metropolitan area. As of 1990, 56.6 percent of Cubans in the United States lived in this area. The two Asian groups are more dispersed. The Koreans' principal concentration is in the Los Angeles metropolitan area, where 23.6 percent live. Los Angeles also contains the major identifiable Korean business enclave in the country, known as Koreatown and located close to downtown. The Chinese are found in two major clusters—Los Angeles (16.3 percent) and New York (14.9 percent). San Francisco, a city with a historically famous Chinatown, currently harbors less than 10 percent of the foreign-born Chinese in the United States.

Coefficients corresponding to the major areas of ethnic concentration tend to support the predictions of enclave theory. Chinese and Koreans living in the Los Angeles–Long Beach area, and Cubans living in the Miami-Hialeah area, all have a distinct advantage toward becoming entrepreneurs, relative to their more dispersed fellows. Comparing the data to that reported in table 4.1, we see that the net probability of self-employment among Chinese in Los Angeles, their principal ethnic and business concentration, rises 5 percentage points above the national average, to 20 percent. The self-employment rate for Cubans nationwide is 18.2 percent, but the probability increases to 24 percent in Miami, controlling for other variables. The story repeats itself with the Koreans in Los Angeles, whose net probability of self-employment increases by 8 percent over the national average, reaching a remarkable 42 percent.[2]

An anomaly in these results, however, is the negative coefficient for residence in New York among the Chinese. Because the reference category is Chinese immigrants living in less dense concentrations elsewhere, enclave theory would predict that the New York coefficient should be positive and second in strength only to that corresponding to Los Angeles. On the contrary, however, the effect is negative and significant. After additional analysis, we believe that the main reason for this lies in the contrasting educational profiles of the Chinese

Table 4.4   Education, Occupation, and Self-Employment Among Chinese Immigrants, 1990

Characteristics	New York PMSA	Los Angeles–Long Beach PMSA	Other United States
Education			
Less than high school	37.3	19.1	16.6
High-school graduate	19.4	13.0	11.7
Some college	15.3	20.2	16.2
College graduate or more	28.0	47.7	55.5
Occupation			
Executive or professional	22.6	38.9	44.8
Technical	13.5	16.8	15.8
Sales or clerical	49.0	35.9	33.0
Laborer	14.9	8.4	5.4
Effect on self-employment: college graduate and place of residence interaction[a]			
B[b]	.670***	.605***	—
	(.155)	(.122)	—
EXP (B)	2.01	1.83	—
Δ[c]	.11	.10	—

Source: U.S. Census of Population, 1990, 5-percent Public Use Microdata Sample.
Notes: For sample definition, see footnote in table 4.1.
[a]Interaction term: "college graduate or more" times "residence in each metropolitan area," controlling for all predictors listed in table 4.3.
[b]Standard errors in parentheses.
[c]Net increase or decrease in the average probability of self-employment.

foreign-born population in New York, Los Angeles, and the rest of the country. Recall that, though those with advanced degrees tend to follow other career pursuits, entrepreneurship among the Chinese still requires a good education, being significantly and positively associated with high-school graduation and some years of college. Table 4.4 presents the educational distribution of the Chinese population in Los Angeles, New York, and the rest of the country. It clearly shows the lower average educational levels of the Chinese settling in the New York area. This lower level of human capital can neutralize the positive effects of ethnic concentration, leading to lower entrepreneurial rates in the aggregate.

Put differently, to the extent that business creation requires some education, the relative absence of advanced education among the New York Chinese lowers the collective capacity for business development and, hence, the ability to make use of the advantages of a large coethnic population. This line of reasoning has an obvious and testable implication. Although self-employment levels are relatively low for the average Chinese in New York, this should not be the case for the better educated. Indeed if predictions from enclave theory hold, we should find a positive interaction effect between level of education and ethnic concentration. As seen previously, the best-educated Chinese tend to leave self-employment, but this tendency should be weaker in areas of dense ethnic concentration, because these areas offer the best opportunities for business success.

The bottom panel of table 4.4 presents the relevant results. They show a strong interaction effect between college or postgraduate education and living either in New York or Los Angeles. Controlling for all other predictors, the probability of self-employment increases by 10 percent for Chinese living in Los Angeles and by 11 percent for Chinese living in New York, provided that they are college educated. The pattern actually extends to San Francisco, the third largest Chinese concentration, where the interaction with high levels of education also yields a strong positive effect on self-employment (1.09; $p < .001$).

These results have two implications. First, they support the enclave hypothesis indirectly by showing that immigrants with high levels of human capital are attracted to entrepreneurship in areas of ethnic concentration, where opportunities and resources for business creation exist. Second, they further clarify the negative effect of residence in New York on Chinese self-employment. Those with college degrees are as inclined to become entrepreneurs in New York as in Los Angeles or San Francisco—there are just fewer of them. The original New York coefficient reflects their scarcity and the relative dominance of immigrants with relatively low skills.

In sum, there are significant similarities in the profile of the self-employed among three entrepreneurial immigrant groups and native whites. Compared to the cohort under thirty-five, older and married men with relatively high levels of education dominate these positions. Based on reliable logistic coefficients evaluated at the mean of the distribution, older men have a probability of becoming entrepreneurs that ranges between 15 and 35 percent above that of their coethnics in each group examined. Among immigrants, longer periods of residence in the United States reinforce this dominance. In every case, the least educated are also the least likely to become self-employed. Ethnic concentration strongly supports entrepreneurial development among immigrants, with the important exception of the Chinese in their second area of concentration. We interpret this result as a consequence of the distinct human capital profile of Chinese immigrants in New York City, which places them at a collective disadvantage relative to their counterparts in Los Angeles or in the rest of the country. For the college educated, however, New York is as attractive a business site as other areas of Chinese concentration.

Comparative analysis for native whites reproduces the significant effects of age, education, and marital status in all their essentials. For African American men, however, marriage and other family variables bring no measurable returns to entrepreneurship, placing this group at a relative disadvantage. It is possible that the absence of a family effect on African American entrepreneurship has to do with the relatively low marriage rate among men from this group. At 58 percent, the marriage rate for African American adult males is 15 percentage points below that for Cubans and 28 points below that for Koreans. Among the self-employed, the gap is even larger: The marriage rate for African American men in this group is 64 percent, compared with 80 percent for Cubans, 81 percent for whites, 91 percent for Chinese, and 94 percent for Koreans. The gap again reflects the overwhelming predominance of married men among the most entrepreneurial groups.

IMMIGRANT AND AFRICAN AMERICAN SELF-EMPLOYMENT

What effect does the rise of immigrant business enclaves have on the condition of the largest domestic minority, African Americans? A number of studies in the past have investigated whether the absolute number of immigrants in specific areas affects the employment chances and earnings of this minority (Bean, Lowell, and Taylor 1987; Borjas 1987; Muller and Espenshade 1985; Taylor et al. 1988). In the present analysis, we focus on a different question, namely, whether the emergence of a sizable concentration of immigrant firms in a metropolitan area affects chances for self-employment among African Americans and the earnings returns of African American entrepreneurs and workers.

A school of thought drawing inspiration from Edna Bonacich's concept of "middleman minorities" would argue that the rise of sizable concentrations of immigrant business conspires against a similar development among African Americans by usurping business opportunities and competing directly with existing minority firms (Bonacich 1973; Waldinger 1994). "Middlemen" can endow their enterprises with levels of financial capital and business expertise that native groups seldom have, thus displacing them from business sectors catering to the majority market and even taking over business opportunities in minority neighborhoods themselves. Accordingly, in those cities where immigrant enterprise concentrates, we would expect deleterious effects both on the creation of African American businesses and on the returns to African American self-employment.

An alternative argument builds on the economic notion of agglomeration effects and the sociological concept of role modeling to predict higher levels of domestic minority business in cities with large immigrant enclaves. The idea is that ethnic enterprise is not a zero-sum game but rather "a rising tide" that lifts all boats. Immigrant enterprise can spin off new kinds of economic opportunities, with direct consequences for the entire working population of the area (Portes and Zhou 1992). The presence of successful small immigrant firms can also provide an incentive for others to try their hand at the same lines of businesses and multiple examples of how to do this (Aldrich and Waldinger 1990). Accordingly, cities where immigrant economies are prominent should also have higher rates of African American entrepreneurship and higher economic returns for those choosing this career path.

We examine the relative merit of these ideas on the basis of two sets of data. The first focuses on African American self-employment in three metropolitan areas known to hold the largest immigrant enclaves at present. The second set systematically pursues the same question by examining African American self-employment and earnings in the nation's sixty-two largest metropolitan areas. New York, Los Angeles, and Miami are the target cities for the first part of the analysis. As is generally known, these cities are not only the three principal recipients of contemporary immigrants but are also the areas where immigrant business concentrations have become most developed and most visible.

Los Angeles is home to a Koreatown, a Chinatown, and large suburban Chinese and Vietnamese enclaves such as Monterey Park and Westminster (Fong 1994; Light, Kwon, and Zhong 1990; Min 1987). It also includes other expanding immigrant economies, such as the Iranian and Israeli (Gold 1997). New York has several identifiable enclaves. The most notable are Chinatown, Washington Heights (for Dominicans), and Brighton Beach (for Russians). In addition, there are smaller and commonly mixed business concentrations of Colombians, Peruvians, Dominicans, and East Indians in Jackson Heights; Chinese, Koreans, and East Indians in Flushing; and West Indians in Brooklyn (Guarnizo 1994; Mollenkopf and Castells 1991; Zhou

1992). Miami is dominated by the Cuban enclave, but around it there has been a rapid growth of firms owned by Colombians, Brazilians, Argentines, and other Latin Americans. There is even a small Haitian business district (García 1996; Portes and Stepick 1993; Stepick 1989). Clearly, any bearing that the growth of immigrant enterprise has on African American economic outcomes should be evident in these cities.

Table 4.5 presents the relevant findings. African American self-employment in New York is close to the national level, but it is significantly higher in the Los Angeles–Long Beach and Miami-Hialeah areas. The net effect of residence in these two cities on African American self-employment is positive in both cases but significant only in Los Angeles. In line with the analogy of a rising tide for all, the net probability of African American self-employment in Los Angeles is a full 2 percentage points above the national average. Average annual earnings for African Americans are also higher in Los Angeles, especially for entrepreneurs, whose earnings exceed the national average for all native whites (see table 4.2).

In agreement with previous findings, self-employed African Americans surpass the average earnings of their salaried counterparts in every city. Furthermore, net effects of self-employment, controlling for other predictors of earnings, are positive and significant in all three cities. Note that the net economic advantage conferred by self-employment on black entrepreneurs exceeds the national average by a factor of two in Miami, three in Los Angeles, and close to four in New York. Because these figures are the result of regressions within each city, they are not attributable to intercity differences in average earnings.

Overall, these results suggest that the effects of the concentration of immigrant businesses in major U.S. metropolitan areas are not deleterious to the economic returns of African Americans. Although the evidence at this point is neither consistent nor compelling, the pattern of findings indicates that areas containing large immigrant enclaves have a mostly benign effect on black entrepreneurship and on its economic returns. The positive association shown in these findings does not demonstrate that immigrant business concentration causes higher rates of African American entrepreneurship or higher returns for the self-employed. Examining possible causal relationships between the two types of ethnic enterprise is beyond the scope of the available data. Results do indicate, however, that the rise of immigrant enclaves does not prevent African American business creation or its positive economic effects.

Table 4.5   Self-Employment and Earnings Among Native-Born African Americans in Cities of Immigrant Business Concentration, 1990

Metropolitan Region	African American Self-Employment (%)	Net Effect of Residence on African American Self-Employment[a] B	Net Effect of Residence on African American Self-Employment[a] EXP (B)	African American Earnings ($1,000s) Total	African American Earnings ($1,000s) Workers	African American Earnings ($1,000s) Self-Employed	Net Effect of Self-Employment on African American Earnings[b] ($1,000s)
Los Angeles–Long Beach PMSA	6.8	.381** (.122)	1.46	29.9	29.0	42.5	9.9***
New York PMSA	4.5	−.102 (.139)	—	27.3	26.6	42.7	15.6***
Miami–Hialeah PMSA	5.8	.237 (.246)	—	21.7	21.6	23.3	6.1*
United States	4.9	—	—	22.5	22.3	27.1	3.9***

Source: U.S. Census of Population, 1990, 5-percent Public Use Microdata Sample.

Note: For sample definition, see footnote in table 4.1.

[a]Logistic regression for native-born African Americans, controlling for the set of predictors included in table 4.3.

[b]Regression for native-born African Americans in each metropolitan area, controlling for the set of predictors included in table 4.2

*$p < .05$; **$p < .01$; ***$p < .001$.

Table 4.6   Correlations Between Average Immigrant and African
American Self-Employment in the Sixty-Two Largest
Metropolitan Areas, 1990

Variable	Immigrant Rate of Self-Employment	Immigrant Average Annual Earnings from Self-Employment
African American rate of self-employment	.058	−.076
African American average annual earnings from self-employment	.196	−.112
African American total annual earnings	−.077	.228*

Source: U.S. Census of Population, 1990, 5-percent Public Use Microdata Sample.
Notes: For sample definition, see footnote in table 4.1. See appendix for the names of PMSAs included in this analysis.
*$p < .05$.

To explore this issue further, we present intercorrelations between average immigrant and African American self-employment and earnings in the sixty-two largest metropolitan areas in 1990 (these cities are listed in the appendix to this chapter). The question that these series seek to answer is whether there is any general relationship between these variables beyond those observed in the three main areas of immigrant business concentration. Table 4.6 presents the results. With cities as units of analysis, the rate of immigrant self-employment is positively correlated with rates of African American self-employment and annual earnings of African American entrepreneurs but negatively correlated with total African American earnings. These correlations are all weak and statistically insignificant. The only significant correlation is between immigrant business earnings and total earnings of African Americans, and it is positive, thereby supporting the hypothesis of a benign relationship.

This analysis can be extended by controlling for additional predictors at the city level. Our initial explorations in this direction confirm the same trend of mostly feeble net associations between immigrant and African American enterprise. These findings lead to the conclusion that the rise of immigrant business concentrations does not have a strong effect on the economic outcomes for African Americans living in the same cities. In particular, there is no evidence of a "middleman" pattern of interethnic exploitation. On the contrary, whatever weak correlations exist point to a positive association between immigrant self-employment and African American entrepreneurship and earnings.

CONCLUSION

Advantages accruing to an ethnic community by virtue of widespread business development extend beyond the economic success of individual business owners. A cadre of successful entrepreneurs provides accessible role models to others in the same community and generally contributes to the development of ethnic institutions. Bounded solidarity tends to be high among groups that define themselves and are defined by others in terms of their distinct physical or cultural characteristics (Light 1984; Rischin 1962; Portes and Sensenbrenner 1993). For this reason, the economically and professionally successful within these groups tend to support their own, a pattern that creates significant multiplier effects. This is especially the case when economic success has been built on coethnic networks facilitating access to capital, labor, or markets.

The analysis of individual-level census data cannot demonstrate these collective processes, and, for this reason, it conveys an impoverished image of the character and consequences of ethnic entrepreneurship. Among other things, it promotes relatively sterile debates about whether the self-employed gain or lose when their work effort is factored in or when the earnings equation employs a logarithmic transformation. Such debates are beside the point when the goal is to examine the collective consequences of a particular social process. More relevant at this level are historical and contemporary case studies that document the community-level advantages noted previously. The multiplier effects of independent business creation are present not only among immigrants but among other solidary groups, as well, whether these are defined in terms of class, culture, or race. The rise of industrial districts in the Red Belt of central Italy, the continent-spanning commercial activities of the overseas Chinese, the tight control of underground industrial production in the former Soviet Republic of Georgia by orthodox Jews, and the successful Otavalan indigenous economy in the Ecuadoran Andes are so many disparate examples illustrating this common pattern (Altman 1983; Capecchi 1989; Granovetter 1995; Kyle 1995).

The finding in our data that the rise of immigrant enclaves does not detract from African American entrepreneurship, and may actually support it, provides a point of departure for a final reflection. All too often, scholarly analyses and policy prescriptions to ameliorate the plight of African Americans discard entrepreneurship as a viable option. They concentrate instead on issues of spatial segregation or advocate solutions as modest as a minimum-wage public-works scheme. We do not believe that African American enterprise, at least as a partial answer to the condition of this minority, should be so easily disregarded. Although it is clear that the social and economic bases that sustain immigrant enclaves are commonly absent in areas of African American concentration, there is no a priori reason they can not be promoted or functional equivalents identified.

A key finding of the previous analysis is the absence of a positive marriage effect on African American self-employment, which thus comes to depend on the age and education of would-be entrepreneurs. Here is an area where identification of functional substitutes to resources made available by the nuclear family may yield fruit. Alternatively, successful policies that promote family stability may indirectly support entrepreneurial ventures. The work of several scholars, primarily John Butler (1991), documents the existence of vibrant black economies in a number of southern cities at the turn of the century. Although it would be naive to attempt their resurrection under present conditions, they offer a suitable point of reference as programs in support of new African American entrepreneurship take hold.

A history of systematic discrimination and enforced disadvantage has left many African American communities unable to undertake these transformations by themselves. The requisite resources are simply not there. Hence, advocating entrepreneurship as one potentially viable path for African American economic mobility should not be confused with conservative calls for bootstrapping and self-reliance. At least at the start, such efforts would require considerable external support. Affirmative action programs that protect and encourage minority entrepreneurs, currently under attack, represent a key step in the right direction. These market reserves should be supplemented by targeted training programs and business credit facilities.

A common misconception of past programs in support of minority business development is that such firms must be sizable in order to make a difference. This is not the case, as the experience of many immigrant enclaves makes clear. It is rather the proliferation of small firms, often not employing more than immediate family members, that creates the necessary environment for the self-sustaining capacity of an entrepreneurial community. The lesson that comes from these experiences is to start small and involve as many people as possible. Several other valuable lessons for the promotion of African American enterprises can also be derived from the study of immigrant enclaves and individual businesses. Research on the topic can thus make a significant contribution by going beyond simple comparisons across groups to examine the transferability of those features that support the remarkable success of certain immigrant communities.

APPENDIX: THE SIXTY-TWO LARGEST METROPOLITAN AREAS, 1990

Albany-Schenectady-Troy, N.Y.
Anaheim-Santa Ana, Calif.
Atlanta, Ga.
Austin, Tex.
Baltimore, Md.
Bergen-Passaic, N.J.
Birmingham, Ala.
Boston, Mass.
Boulder, Colo.
Buffalo, N.Y.
Charlotte, N.C.
Chicago, Ill.
Cincinnati, Ohio
Cleveland, Ohio
Columbus, Ohio
Dallas, Tex.
Dayton-Springfield, Ohio
Denver, Colo.
Detroit, Mich.
El Paso, Tex.
Fort Worth, Tex.
Greensboro, Nebr.
Honolulu, Hawaii
Houston, Texas
Indianapolis, Ind.
Jersey City, N.J.
Kansas City, Mo.
Los Angeles–Long Beach, Calif.
Louisville, Ky.
Memphis, Tenn.
Miami-Hialeah, Fla.
Middlesex, N.J.
Milwaukee, Wis.
Minneapolis, Minn.
Monmouth, N.J.

Nashville, Tenn.
Nassau-Suffolk, N.Y.
Newark, N.J.
New Orleans, La.
New York, N.Y.
Norfolk, Va.
Oakland, Calif.
Oklahoma City, Okla.
Orange County, N.J.
Philadelphia, Pa.
Phoenix, Ariz.
Pittsburgh, Pa.
Portland, Ore.
Richmond, Va.
Riverside, Calif.
Rochester, N.Y.
Sacramento, Calif.
Salt Lake City, Utah
San Antonio, Tex.
San Diego, Calif.
San Francisco, Calif.
San Jose, Calif.
Seattle, Wash.
St. Louis, Mo.
Tampa, Fla.
West Palm Beach, Fla.
Washington, D.C.

NOTES

1. Borjas defines as "shirking" the self-interested behavior of hired employees that runs contrary to the interest of the firm. Hiring family members including spouses resolves this problem because of their common interest in the firm.

2. These new probabilities are computed on the basis of the net probability columns in table 4.3 for each ethnic group in its main areas of residence.

REFERENCES

Aldrich, Howard, and Roger Waldinger. 1990. "Ethnicity and Entrepreneurship." *Annual Review of Sociology* 16: 111–35.
Aldrich, Howard, C. Zimmer, and D. McEvoy. 1989. "Continuities in the

Study of Ecological Succession: Asian Business in Three English Cities."
Social Forces 67(4): 920–44.

Altman, Jonathan. 1983. "A Reconstruction Using Anthropological Methods of the Second Economy of Soviet Georgia." Ph.D. diss., Middlesex Polytechnic Institute, England.

Bailey, Thomas, and Roger Waldinger. 1991. "The Changing Ethnic/Racial Division of Labor." In *Dual City: Restructuring New York*, edited by John Mollenkopf and Manuel Castells. New York: Russell Sage Foundation.

Bates, Timothy. 1994. "Social Resources Generated by Group Support Networks May Not Be Beneficial to Asian Immigrant–Owned Small Businesses." *Social Forces* 72(3): 671–89.

Bates, Timothy, and Constance Dunham. 1991. "The Changing Nature of Business Ownership as a Route to Upward Mobility of Minorities." Paper presented to the Urban Institute Conference on Urban Labor Markets and Labor Mobility. Arlie House, Va. (March 7–8).

Bean, Frank D., B. Lindsay Lowell, and Lowell J. Taylor. 1987. "Undocumented Migration to the United States: Perceptions and Evidence." *Population and Development Review* 13(December): 671–90.

Bonacich, Edna. 1973. "A Theory of Middleman Minorities." *American Sociological Review* 38(5): 583–944.

Bonacich, Edna, and John Modell. 1980. *The Economic Basis of Ethnic Solidarity: Small Business in the Japanese American Community.* Berkeley: University of California Press.

Borjas, George J. 1986. "The Self-Employment Experience of Immigrants." *Journal of Human Resources* 21: 485–506.

———. 1987. "Self-Selection and the Earnings of Immigrants." *American Economic Review* 77: 531–53.

———. 1990. *Friends or Strangers: The Impact of Immigrants on the U.S. Economy.* New York: Basic Books.

Butler, John S. 1991. *Entrepreneurship and Self-Help Among Black Americans: A Reconsideration of Race and Economics.* Albany: State University of New York Press.

Capecchi, Vittorio. 1989. "The Informal Economy and the Development of Flexible Specialization." In *The Informal Economy: Studies in Advanced and Less Developed Countries*, edited by Alejandro Portes, Manuel Castells, and Lauren Benton. Baltimore: Johns Hopkins University Press.

Fernández-Kelly, M. Patricia, and Anna M. García. 1989. "Informalization at the Core: Hispanic Women, Homework, and the Advanced Capitalist State." In *The Informal Economy: Studies in Advanced and Less Developed Countries*, edited by Alejandro Portes, Manuel Castells, and Lauren Benton. Baltimore: Johns Hopkins University Press.

Fong, Timothy P. 1994. *The First Suburban Chinatown: The Remaking of Monterey Park, California.* Philadelphia: Temple University Press.

Fratoe, Frank A., and Ronald L. Meeks. 1985. "Business Participation Rates of the Fifty Largest U.S. Ancestry Groups: Preliminary Report." Minority Business Development Agency, U.S. Department of Commerce, Washington, D.C. Mimeographed.

García, María Cristina. 1996. *Havana, U.S.A.: Cuban Exiles and Cuban Americans in South Florida.* Berkeley: University of California Press.

Gold, Steven J. 1997. "Transnationalism and Vocabularies of Motive in International Migration: The Case of Israelis in the United States." *Sociological Perspectives* 40(3): 409–27.

Granovetter, Mark. 1995. "The Economic Sociology of Firms and Entrepreneurs." In *Essays on Networks, Ethnicity, and Entrepreneurship*, edited by Alejandro Portes. New York: Russell Sage Foundation.

Green, Shelly, and Paul Pryde. 1990. *Black Entrepreneurship in America.* New Brunswick, N.J.: Transaction Books.

Guarnizo, Luis E. 1992. *One Country in Two: Dominican-Owned Firms in New York and the Dominican Republic.* Ph.D. diss., Johns Hopkins University.

———. 1994. "Los 'Dominican Yorkers': The Making of a Binational Society." *Annals of the American Academy of Political and Social Science* 533(May): 70–86.

Howe, Irving. 1976. *World of Our Fathers.* New York: Harcourt Brace and Jovanovich.

Kyle, David. 1995. *The Transnational Peasant: The Social Structures of Economic Migration from the Ecuadoran Andes.* Ph.D. diss., Johns Hopkins University.

Light, Ivan. 1972. *Ethnic Enterprise in America: Business and Welfare Among Chinese, Japanese, and Blacks.* Berkeley: University of California Press.

———. 1980. "Asian Enterprise in America: Chinese, Japanese, and Koreans in Small Business." In *Self-Help in Urban America*, edited by Scott Cummings. New York: Kennikat Press.

———. 1984. "Immigrant and Ethnic Enterprise in North America." *Ethnic and Racial Studies* 7(2): 195–216.

Light, Ivan, and Edna Bonacich. 1988. *Immigrant Entrepreneurs: Koreans in Los Angeles, 1965–1982.* Berkeley: University of California Press.

Light, Ivan, Im Jung Kwon, and Deng Zhong. 1990. "Korean Rotating Credit Associations in Los Angeles." *Amerasia* 16(2): 35–54.

Logan, John R., Richard D. Alba, and Thomas L. McNulty. 1994. "Ethnic Economies in Metropolitan Regions: Miami and Beyond." *Social Forces* 72(3): 691–724.

Min, Pyong Gap. 1987. "Factors Contributing to Ethnic Business: A Comprehensive Synthesis." *International Journal of Comparative Sociology* 28(3–4): 173–93.

Model, Suzanne. 1990. "The Ethnic Economy: Cubans and Chinese Reconsidered." University of Massachusetts, Amherst. Unpublished paper.

Mollenkopf, John H., and Manuel Castells, eds. 1991. *Dual City: Restructuring New York*. New York: Russell Sage Foundation.

Muller, Thomas, and Thomas J. Espenshade. 1985. *The Fourth Wave: California's Newest Immigrants*. Washington, D.C.: Urban Institute Press.

Perez, Lisandro. 1986. "Immigrant Economic Adjustment and Family Organization: The Cuban Success Story Reexamined." *International Migration Review* 20(1): 4–20.

Petersen, William. 1971. *Japanese Americans: Oppression and Success*. New York: Random House.

Portes, Alejandro, and Robert L. Bach. 1985. *Latin Journey: Cuban and Mexican Immigrants in the United States*. Berkeley: University of California Press.

Portes, Alejandro, and Leif Jensen. 1989. "The Enclave and the Entrants: Patterns of Ethnic Enterprise in Miami Before and After Mariel." *American Sociological Review* 54(6): 929–49.

Portes, Alejandro, and Julia Sensenbrenner. 1993. "Embeddedness and Immigration: Notes on the Social Determinants of Economic Action." *American Journal of Sociology* 98(6): 1320–50.

Portes, Alejandro, and Alex Stepick. 1993. *City on the Edge: The Transformation of Miami*. Berkeley: University of California Press.

Portes, Alejandro, and Min Zhou. 1992. "Gaining the Upper Hand: Economic Mobility Among Immigrant and Domestic Minorities." *Ethnic and Racial Studies* 15(4): 491–522.

———. 1996. "Self-Employment and the Earnings of Immigrants." *American Sociological Review* 61(2): 219–30.

Rischin, Moses, 1962. *The Promised City: New York Jews, 1870–1914*. Cambridge: Harvard University Press.

Stepick, Alex. 1989. "Miami's Two Informal Sectors." In *The Informal Economy: Studies in Advanced and Less Developed Countries*, edited by Alejandro Portes, Manuel Castells, and Lauren Benton. Baltimore: Johns Hopkins University Press.

Stevens, Richard, and Gary Chen. 1984. "Minority-Owned Business Problems and Opportunities: A 1983 Update." Report to the Research Division. Minority Business Development Administration, U.S. Department of Commerce, Washington, D.C.

Taylor, Lowell J., Frank D. Bean, James R. Rebitzer, Susan Gonzalez Baker, and B. Lindsay Lowell. 1988. "Mexican Immigrants and the Wages and Unemployment Experience of Native Workers." Discussion paper PRIP-UI-1. Washington, D.C.: Urban Institute.

Waldinger, Roger, 1985. "Immigration and Industrial Change in the New York City Apparel Industry." In *Hispanics in the U.S. Economy*, edited by George J. Borjas and Marta Tienda. New York: Academic Press.

————. 1994. "The Making of an Immigrant Niche." *International Migration Review* 28(1): 3–30.

————. 1996. "Ethnicity and Opportunity in the Plural City." In *Ethnic Los Angeles*, edited by Roger Waldinger and Mehdi Bozorgmehr. New York: Russell Sage Foundation.

Wilson, Kenneth, and W. Allen Martin. 1982. "Ethnic Enclaves: A Comparison of the Cuban and Black Economies in Miami." *American Journal of Sociology* 88(July): 135–60.

Wong, Bernard. 1998. *Ethnicity and Entrepreneurship: The New Chinese Immigrants in the San Francisco Bay Area*. Boston: Allyn and Bacon.

Zhou, Min. 1992. *Chinatown: The Socioeconomic Potential of an Urban Enclave*. Philadelphia: Temple University Press.

Zhou, Min, and John R. Logan. 1989. "Returns on Human Capital in Ethnic Enclaves: New York City's Chinatown." *American Sociological Review* 54(5): 809–20.

CHAPTER 5

Minority Niches and Immigrant Enclaves in New York and Los Angeles: Trends and Impacts

John R. Logan and Richard D. Alba

In the 1960s, the simple concept of a dual economy was a useful device for referring to the concentration of minority workers in certain low-wage industries (Edwards, Reich, and Gordon 1975). The revival of large-scale immigration has highlighted another feature of the twentieth-century metropolis: the immigrant proclivity toward small-scale business enterprise as an alternative source of livelihood. The enclave strategy appears to many observers to be a viable means of moving more quickly up the economic ladder, though one seldom taken. Select immigrant minorities have succeeded in establishing local ethnic economies in certain places, including the Cuban enclave in Miami (Wilson and Portes 1980), Koreans in Los Angeles (Bonacich and Light 1988), and Chinese in New York (Zhou 1992). Other immigrant groups—such as Mexicans—are as unlikely as African Americans or Puerto Ricans to form enclaves based on concentrated ownership in any metropolitan area (Logan, Alba, and McNulty 1994). What opportunities are lost for this reason? What have been the gains to those groups or group members who take the entrepreneurial route?

To begin to answer this question, we investigate ethnic segmentation of the labor force in New York and Los Angeles in 1980 and 1990. We study African Americans in both metropolitan areas, as well as the largest Latino group in each region: Puerto Ricans, in New York, and Mexicans, in Los Angeles. As a contrast, we study the most entrepreneurial immigrant groups, the Koreans and Chinese, in both regions. For members of these groups we analyze what difference it makes whether they are business owners or work for others and whether they are located in sectors where their group has created a specific ethnic niche. Does it enable them to work longer hours? Does it result in a higher hourly income? In other words, does the enclave strategy pay off? Most relevant to public policy, is there reason to believe that some minorities would enjoy substantial advancement in the long term from a strategy of enclave development based on small business?

THE BENEFITS OF ETHNIC ECONOMIES

We presume that to some degree we will find that members of immigrant and minority groups are concentrated in specific industrial sectors in each region but that there will be differences in the character of these concentrations. Some will be the employment niches of the familiar dual economy: sectors where black and Hispanic minorities have traditionally found public-sector jobs or work in firms that are owned and managed by whites. Others will be ethnic enclaves, such as Cuban Miami, where group members are concentrated as both owners and workers in certain activities. A third situation will be sectors where the group predominates as owners and among the self-employed but without relying particularly on coethnic workers. We refer to these as entrepreneurial niches. (Robert Jiobu [1988] has referred to this as a situation of "ethnic hegemony." The "middleman minority" business owner—serving another minority group's consumer market or relying on workers of another group [see Bonacich 1973; Zenner 1991]—is one possible basis for such entrepreneurial niches.)

Members of racial and ethnic groups have often congregated in similar jobs because group members govern access to them by some combination of ownership, control of labor unions, control of information about openings, or other privileged participation in labor recruitment (Lieberson 1980; Model 1993; Waldinger 1996b). Public jobs, for example, have been a particularly important sort of niche throughout this century because of their overall growth and their relative security of employment. Niches in sectors controlled by powerful craft unions are another example. On the other hand, disproportionate representation of a group in the labor force of a particular industry can also reflect the group's lack of resources, a "ghettoization" into undesirable jobs. Hence, Roger Waldinger's (1996b, 100) analysis of the earnings payoff for working in a group's employment niche in New York in 1990 shows wide variations among groups. Italians, whose niche by now is mainly in professional and technical sectors, and African Americans, because of their concentration in public jobs, did better in their niche than outside of it. New immigrant groups, including Chinese, Dominicans, and West Indians, earned considerably less in their niche jobs, even after controlling for background characteristics. In a similar analysis for Los Angeles, where background characteristics were not controlled, Waldinger (1996a) found a comparable degree of variation: Chinese and Mexicans born in the United States earned more in their niches than outside of them, whereas immigrant Chinese and Mexicans (and also immigrant Koreans) in the group studied earned more outside their niches.

More attention has been given recently to enclave economies than to employment niches. An enclave economy is a complex of economic sectors (perhaps interrelated among themselves) in which a group predominates both as owners and in the workforce. It is widely believed that ethnic enclaves provide benefits to both sides. Thomas Bailey and Waldinger (1991) suggest that from the employer's perspective a coethnic labor force provides assurance that investments in training will be repaid by loyalty and (in one form or another) reduced labor costs. Kenneth Wilson and Alejandro Portes (1980) emphasize the advantages to workers: Within a sheltered ethnic economy, workers may find employment despite their deficits (such as poor English, lack of formal education, or unfamiliarity with the labor market), and those with better qualifications are more likely to find jobs commensurate with their skills.

Although enclave participation may improve opportunities for getting a job, taking into account the sometimes limited qualifications of new immigrants, the payoff from an enclave job is uncertain. Min Zhou's generally positive portrait of New York's Chinatown acknowledges that "relative to the mainstream economy, the enclave economy, as a whole, represents the basic characteristics of the broader competitive sector," including limited earnings (Zhou 1992, 118). John Logan, Richard Alba, and Thomas McNulty (1994) have found that most enclaves of nonwhites in 1980 consisted of a thin cluster of economic sectors with low levels of investment and low average wages. Suzanne Model (1997) studied enclave economies between 1940 and 1970 of several groups in New York. She found that group members had no income advantage, compared with nongroup members, within their enclave sectors. Some sectors in which enclaves could be identified provided higher than average earnings to employees of any ethnicity. This was the case with respect to government in 1940 and 1950, when it was an Irish sector, and apparel manufacturing in 1940 and 1950, when it was predominantly Russian. These sectors offered no income advantage by 1970, however, by which time they had passed over to other groups (blacks and Italians, respectively). Some other sectors—for example, retail trade—were never advantageous to any particular racial or ethnic group.

A question that is closely related to the desirability of the enclave economy is whether the entrepreneurial activity on which it is based is well rewarded. Certainly most immigrant or minority small businesses operate with relatively low capitalization, relying in part for their profitability on the long hours that self-employed people are willing to commit to work (Light and Rosenstein 1995). Yet some evaluations of enclave economies emphasize their capacity to promote entrepreneurship as a form of social mobility (Portes and Bach 1985). In addition, although the evidence on this point is mixed (see Borjas 1990), some recent research indicates that self-employment may improve annual earnings (net of other background characteristics) for Cubans and Koreans, though not for Chinese or blacks (Portes and Zhou 1996; also Waldinger 1996a, 451).

These previous studies leave doubt as to whether the ethnic economy is really consequential for a group's success. Niches and enclaves may have different effects, a niche in public employment may have a better return that a private-sector niche, effects for some groups may be different from effects for others, and special attention needs to be given to the impact of self-employment.

RESEARCH DESIGN

Sectoral concentration is measured here as an overrepresentation of group members as owners or workers in particular economic sectors. Overrepresentations are calculated as odds ratios, applying the methodology introduced by Logan, Alba, and McNulty (1994). For this purpose, all private-sector workers in each metropolitan statistical area (MSA) have been classified by type of worker (owner or self-employed versus employed by someone else, including unpaid family workers) and by industry sector. The odds ratio for owners is the ratio of the odds of a group member's being an owner or self-employed in a particular sector (versus being an owner or worker in any other sector) to the odds of a nongroup member's being an owner in this sector (versus being an owner or worker in any other sector). The odds ratio for workers is the equivalent ratio. These measures have the advantage of being independent of the sizes of groups and of industry sectors, as well as being unaffected by the overall distribution of owners across sectors. An odds ratio of 1.00 indicates that a group is neither overrepresented nor underrepresented in a sector. Following current practice, we identify instances in which the value is 1.50 or above (and where the sample number of group workers or owners is three or greater) as concentrations.

Because of its importance for some groups, we introduce civilian public employment into the analysis even though it fits neither an owner nor a worker categorization. The odds ratio for public employment is the ratio of the odds that a group member is a public employee (versus an owner or worker in any other sector) to the odds that a nongroup member is a public employee (versus an owner or worker in any other sector). We consider odds ratios above 1.50 as evidence of an employment niche in the public sector.

We use these indicators of sectoral specialization to answer the following specific questions:

1. How can we characterize the mode of incorporation for each group? Do its members tend to be found in public jobs, employed by others in the private sector, or owners?

2. To the extent that a group has achieved concentrated ownership or self-employment in certain sectors, what are these sectors? How have they changed since 1980? Which of them include complementary concentrations of group members as workers (thus constituting the classic form of enclave economy)?

3. How large a share of the group's workforce is found in these "owner" sectors? For comparison, what share is found in public employment or in private-sector employment niches? How have these shares changed since 1980?

Each of these questions addresses a slightly different aspect of ethnic segmentation, but taken together they offer a firm basis for comparing groups. (For a similar analysis of a larger sample of metropolitan areas, see Logan, Alba, and Stults 1999.)

In the second phase of the analysis, we analyze the effects of sectoral location—in enclaves, employment niches, entrepreneurial niches, or the mainstream economy—on hours worked and income. We have estimated several versions of these models, sensitive to debates over the most appropriate forms. We present results for men (though in most respects the same results are also found for women). Our income equations use logged annual income as the dependent variable, including hours worked as a predictor. An alternative specification, where the dependent variable is income per hour, yields almost identical results for other predictors but conceals the important effect of hours worked. Another alternative uses the nonlogged value of income or income per hour, as recommended by Portes and Zhou (1996). We prefer the logged form because it is a better-fitting model. The main difference in results, as also reported by Portes and Zhou, is that self-employment generally has a positive or neutral effect on non-

Table 5.1   Odds Ratios (and Counts) of Group Members as Public Workers, Self-Employed, and Private-Sector Workers in New York and Los Angeles, 1990

Ethnic Group	Public Workers		Self-Employed		Private-Sector Workers	
			New York			
African American	2.29	(245,558)	0.32	(30,305)	0.71	(565,079)
Puerto Rican	1.42	(67,383)	0.35	(10,181)	1.01	(212,086)
Chinese	0.43	(11,152)	0.96	(10,991)	1.76	(103,826)
Korean	0.16	(1,381)	3.18	(9,615)	1.00	(29,643)
			Los Angeles			
African American	3.06	(105,460)	0.47	(20,807)	0.57	(251,277)
Mexican	0.66	(94,050)	0.45	(56,761)	1.92	(838,829)
Chinese	0.83	(11,967)	1.37	(15,109)	0.92	(82,924)
Korean	0.45	(4,247)	3.81	(20,454)	0.52	(43,303)

Source: Data from Census of Population 1990.
Note: Totals given in parentheses.

logged earnings, because of the very high earnings of some business owners, but a negative effect on logged earnings. We conclude that self-employment has a positive impact on earnings through its effect on working hours, and we find that this effect is not limited to the highest earners.

ETHNIC SEGMENTATION AND SECTORAL CONCENTRATION

Table 5.1 reports on the composition of the labor force of each group by class of worker. These data reveal that some groups are unusually entrepreneurial. The odds ratio for Koreans are greater than 3.0 for self-employment in both regions. At the other extreme, African Americans, Puerto Ricans, and Mexicans have odds ratios for self-employment in every case below 0.50. Two groups—most of whose members have the advantage of citizenship at birth—have a strong tendency toward public employment: blacks (well above 2.0) and Puerto Ricans (just below the 1.5 threshold). Mexicans are strongly overrepresented as workers in the private sector.

This contrast helps us to identify two poles of economic incorporation. One is strictly "entrepreneurial"—many overrepresentations as owners but few as public or private employees. The other is "public- or private-sector dependence." The Chinese seem to fall in between.

Table 5.2   Sectors of Ownership Overrepresentation for Non-Hispanic African Americans, Puerto Ricans, and Mexicans, 1980 and 1990

	Odds Ratios			
	New York		Los Angeles	
Ethnic Group and Sector	1980	1990	1980	1990
African Americans				
Transportation		1.56		
Private household services	*3.67*			
Hospitals		*1.67*		*1.65*
Social services		*1.95*		
Transportation equipment				1.74
Trucking				*1.68*
Utilities				2.62
General merchandising				2.33
Schools				2.30
Puerto Ricans				
Food stores	1.54			
Mexicans				
Agriculture			*1.54*	*2.31*
Apparel		2.66		
Eating places		1.54		

Sources: Data from Census of Population 1980 and 1990.
Note: Italics indicate sectors in which the group is overrepresented both as owners and as workers.

Tables 5.2, 5.3, and 5.4 list all sectors in which a group was concentrated as owners in either 1980 or 1990 (with their odds ratio for each year). The tables further distinguish "enclave" sectors (those in which group members are also overrepresented as workers) from "entrepreneurial" sectors by italicizing the odds ratio in the former instance. As implied by the low rates of ownership, African Americans, Mexicans, and Puerto Ricans have few sectors of concentrated entrepreneurial activity. Table 5.2 reveals a few such sectors for blacks. There were three in 1990 in New York: transportation, hospitals, and social service organizations. In Los Angeles there were six—all new in 1990, suggesting the emergence of a black enclave economy in this region. Among Mexicans in New York there has also emerged an enclave based on apparel manufacturing and restaurants, a replication of the earlier Chinatown economy, but the only Mexican sector in Los Angeles remains agriculture. Puerto Ricans had no owner sectors in either region in 1990.

By contrast, both the Koreans and Chinese had several established

Table 5.3   Sectors of Ownership Overrepresentation for Chinese, 1980 and 1990

| | Odds Ratios | | | |
| | New York | | Los Angeles | |
Sector	1980	1990	1980	1990
Textiles				4.89
Apparel manufacturing	*4.09*	*3.93*	*10.61*	*4.75*
Manufacturing, not specified				2.62
Machinery				1.55
Electrical equipment				1.89
Transportation equipment				1.78
Transportation	2.27			1.92
Wholesale			2.15	3.51
General merchandising				2.85
Retail stores			1.84	1.86
Food stores		1.92	*5.84*	1.61
Eating places	*7.62*	*7.46*	*8.19*	*4.63*
Food products	8.25	3.39		5.12
Insurance and real estate			2.28	
Printing				1.77
Banking and credit services				*1.64*
Health services				1.90
Personal services	3.40	1.66	2.20	1.89

Sources: Data from Census of Population 1980 and 1990.
Note: Italics indicate sectors in which the group is overrepresented both as owners and as workers.

sectors of business ownership in 1980, and by 1990 both had experienced a marked expansion of ethnic enclaves. This phenomenon implies a growing gap in the mode of economic incorporation between various minorities, with one set remaining dependent on others for employment and another developing stronger entrepreneurial or enclave economies.

The Chinese (see table 5.3) had clearly established enclave economies by 1980 in New York and Los Angeles. In each case the core of the enclave was in restaurants and the garment industry (with corresponding worker concentrations), supplemented in varying degrees by food stores, personal services, and others for a total of nine ownership sectors. By 1990, despite population increases of 70 percent or more in New York, there was essentially no change in this constellation. The existing enclave was maintained. In Los Angeles, however, where the Chinese population also increased substantially (from about 95,000 to nearly 250,000), the Chinese economy experienced a tre-

Table 5.4   Sectors of Ownership Overrepresentation for Koreans, 1980 and 1990

| | Odds Ratios | | | |
| | New York | | Los Angeles | |
Sector	1980	1990	1980	1990
Textiles		3.78		
Apparel manufacturing		*2.19*	*13.41*	*10.17*
Manufacturing, not specified			12.96	2.46
Miscellaneous manufacturing		2.66		
Transportation equipment				2.99
Transportation	4.11			1.56
Wholesale	3.84	2.30	3.89	4.22
General merchandising		7.82		
Retail stores	11.69	*5.42*	5.22	*8.99*
Food stores	*30.70*	21.85	11.71	*21.35*
Eating places		3.19	6.15	8.92
Food products				6.19
Agriculture			1.58	
Construction				1.54
Automobile and gasoline dealers			5.79	5.45
Communications				1.70
Insurance and real estate	2.37			
Printing			2.62	
Banking and credit services				2.43
Business services				1.54
Health services			2.55	1.91
Personal services	3.30	*7.42*	*2.73*	4.46
Repair services		1.55	2.36	
Hospitals		3.02	5.69	
Schools				8.59

Sources: Data from census of Population 1980 and 1990.
Note: Italics indicate sectors in which the group is overrepresented both as owners and as workers.

mendous boom. (See Horton [1995] for a discussion of the growth of the Chinese economy in Los Angeles and its linkages with investment capital from the Far East.) From seven ownership sectors, the economy grew to seventeen. Complementary worker concentrations in apparel manufacturing and eating places were retained, and one in food stores was replaced by another in banking and credit. Several of the new sectors were in manufacturing sectors where Chinese appeared only as owners, a broad expansion of entrepreneurial niches.

The Koreans, too, expanded an already strong ethnic economy in

Los Angeles (with nearly 150,000 Koreans by 1990, more than double the 1980 number) and New York (where there were 76,000). In both regions we could consider the Korean economy to be an ethnic enclave (see table 5.4). In New York the enclave sectors (combining owner and worker concentrations) in 1990 include one manufacturing sector (apparel, as in Los Angeles), as well as food stores, other retail, and personal services. As it is well known that Korean groceries serve a largely non-Korean clientele, this could also be considered an "export sector" in the sense that Zhou (1992) uses the term.

The Korean enclave economy in Los Angeles in 1980 was even more impressive. It encompassed enclaves in apparel manufacturing and personal services and entrepreneurial niches in fully eleven other sectors. By 1990 owner odds ratios and complementary worker overrepresentation were very high in three sectors: apparel, food stores, and other retail. Although the ownership odds ratio declined below 1.50 in five sectors, this was more than counterbalanced by the addition of seven new ones. More important, the gains included such key sectors as banking and credit, communications, schools, and business services, sectors that are more typically controlled by whites. Thus, the Los Angeles enclave was strengthened over the decade.

THE SIZE OF ETHNIC ECONOMIES

The analyses of ethnic economies in the preceding sections are based entirely on odds ratios. These show the relative degree of concentration or representation of groups as owners or workers in particular sectors. They do not, however, reveal the size of these sectors. Now we shift to this dimension: How many group members—that is, what percentage of group members of those in the labor force—did the ethnic economies in the study involve?

To gauge the size of ethnic economies we take several steps. First, for each case we calculate what percentage of group members in the private sector (including owners) worked in those sectors in which the group had owner concentrations (combining enclave sectors and entrepreneurial niches). To test whether this figure is really distinctive, we compare it with the percentage of nongroup members in the region who work in the same sectors. Second, to reflect the ethnic economy for those groups who have few owner concentrations, we present similar figures for group members in sectors where the group is overrepresented as workers but not as owners—private-sector employment niches. Third, to place private-sector concentrations into a larger context, we list the proportion of total civilian workers who

Table 5.5   Distribution of Employees Across the Public Sector,
Owner Sectors, and Worker Sectors, 1980 and 1990
(Percentage)

Ethnic Group and Year	Group Members			Nongroup Members		
	Public Sector	Owner Sectors	Worker Sectors	Public Sector	Owner Sectors	Worker Sectors
	New York					
African American						
1980	30.1	3.5	35.2	15.4	0.5	20.0
1990	29.2	19.5	17.7	15.3	11.0	9.4
Puerto Rican						
1980	19.9	3.7	25.1	17.7	2.5	12.7
1990	23.3	0.0	9.0	17.6	0.0	4.9
Chinese						
1980	6.5	52.4	0.0	18.1	15.0	0.0
1990	8.9	41.4	3.0	18.3	12.5	1.7
Korean						
1980	10.3	57.2	18.8	17.9	28.9	10.1
1990	3.4	66.0	0.2	18.2	33.4	0.1
	Los Angeles					
African American						
1980	29.1	0.0	30.3	12.3	0.0	17.4
1990	27.9	21.5	22.8	11.2	12.2	14.1
Mexican						
1980	10.1	1.6	33.1	14.6	0.8	11.5
1990	9.5	2.8	46.4	13.7	0.9	22.4
Chinese						
1980	12.3	47.4	12.7	13.9	28.5	7.2
1990	10.9	63.7	2.2	12.8	48.0	1.2
Korean						
1980	4.0	62.1	1.4	14.0	38.0	0.4
1990	6.2	73.3	0.0	12.8	56.1	0.0

Sources: Data from Census of Population 1980 and 1990.

were employed by government (presenting information from table 5.1
in a different form from before). Table 5.5 provides these data for
both 1980 (based on enclaves and niches identified in 1980) and
1990 (based on sectors overrepresented at that time).

For each group this table allows us once again to characterize the
ethnic economy in each region, but now from a different perspective:
In terms of percentages of the workforce involved, are group members
found in the enclave or entrepreneurial economy, in private-sector

employment niches, or in public employment? How did the pattern change between 1980 and 1990, if at all? We do not expect the answers to these questions to diverge greatly from what we already learned from analyses of odds ratios, but perhaps some new aspects of the situation will emerge: The number of owner sectors, after all, does not necessarily determine their size.

Let us discuss each group in the same order as in the previous section. Table 5.1 shows the heavy (though slightly declining) over-representation of blacks in public employment. Second, only a small share of blacks are working in sectors of black ownership, but this share is growing over time. As shown in table 5.2, private household services was the only black owner sector in New York in 1980; by 1990, these had been replaced by transportation, hospitals, and social services. About 19 percent of blacks worked in these latter three sectors in 1990 (twice the proportion of nonblacks in the same sectors). What changed over time for blacks is not the importance of these as sources of employment, because even in 1980 the three sectors employed 18 percent of blacks, but rather that they became loci of black business ownership. Nevertheless, the black enclave covers only a moderate share of total black employment, about the same proportion as in the remaining private-sector employment niches and less than in public employment.

Puerto Ricans, like blacks, have larger shares of public employment than most other groups, and this advantage is growing over time. (Especially in New York, they are not far below the black percentage in public jobs, and we consider public employment now to be a Puerto Rican niche even though the odds ratio is slightly below our 1.50 threshold value.) Very few Puerto Ricans are employed in Puerto Rican owner sectors, but many more are found in employment niches. In this case, however, there has been a decline in the latter category in New York, reflecting a dispersion of Puerto Ricans out of their older niches and into new areas as workers.

Mexicans present yet another variation on the theme of small enclaves. Mexicans are actually underrepresented, compared with other groups, in the public sector. In Los Angeles, where Mexicans are found in large numbers, few are found in owner sectors and many—a growing number now reaching nearly half the Mexican population—are found in employment niches. In New York, however, where the Mexican community is small but recently growing, the share in Mexican owner sectors has jumped to nearly a third, with a corresponding drop in employment niches. In this respect, New York's Mexicans resemble blacks more than Puerto Ricans.

By 1990 the share of both Chinese and Koreans in employment

niches was insignificant, whereas the share in owner sectors ran from 41 percent for Chinese in New York to a range of 60 to 75 percent in other cases. By another criterion—the difference between them and nongroup members in the same sectors—the Koreans in New York stand out even more: the Korean percentage in the group's owner sectors in 1990 are 33 percentage points above those for non-Koreans. This reflects the fact that Korean owners employ disproportionate shares of Korean workers.

This review of the size of ethnic sectors reinforces and refines some conclusions based on the odds ratios alone: the extent of black (and to a lesser degree, Puerto Rican) dependence on public employment, the emergence of moderate enclave economies for a few non-entrepreneurial groups (including Mexicans in New York and blacks in both regions), and the extreme concentration of the Korean and Chinese labor force in enclave economies.

EFFECTS OF NICHE AND ENCLAVE EMPLOYMENT

With a clear picture of the character of ethnic segmentation in these two regions, we can now pose more clearly our questions about its impacts. In their large enclave sectors and entrepreneurial niches, do the Koreans and Chinese find opportunities to work longer hours and earn higher incomes than in other sectors of the economy? Do blacks in New York and Los Angeles, where they have established small enclaves, benefit from placement in these sectors, and how does the return in these new enclaves compare with what blacks receive in their more traditional niche in the public sector? Do Puerto Ricans in New York and Mexicans in Los Angeles, concentrated in employment niches (and, in the Puerto Rican case, in public employment) do less well in these niches? More broadly, does self-employment itself enhance income, directly or indirectly?

To answer these questions, we estimate separate multivariate models for each group in each metropolitan area. Results of these models are reported in tables 5.6 (for hours worked) and 5.7 (for logged income). Our choice of samples and variables and our methodology largely replicate the analyses presented by Portes and Zhou (1996), except that we estimate separate equations for hours and income. Our samples include all men in the civilian labor force in the New York or the Los Angeles–Long Beach MSA, aged twenty-five to sixty-four, who had positive earnings and worked at least 160 hours in 1989.

Variables are defined as follows: Income is the sum of wages or salary and self-employment income in 1989. Hours worked is an annual total; as an independent variable it is scaled in terms of hundreds of hours per year. Self-employment includes the self-employed and business owners. Marriage is a dummy variable distinguishing those currently married from single, divorced, and widowed persons. Work experience is computed as the difference between age and years of schooling. Education is represented as a set of dummy variables for some high school, some college, and some postgraduate education based on number of years of schooling, with fewer than eight years as the reference category. English-language ability is a dummy variable contrasting those who speak English only or well with those who speak English poorly or not at all. Immigration is included as a contrast between the most recent immigrants (those arriving in the previous five years) and all others. Living with children is a dummy variable identifying those who live together with their own children under the age of eighteen.

Labor-force variables are based on the analyses of ethnic segmentation reported earlier. Position in the labor force is represented by three mutually exclusive dummy variables—working in the group's enclave sectors, entrepreneurial niches, and employment niches—with placement in all other sectors as the reference category. In the equations for blacks and Puerto Ricans, where we identified important public-sector employment niches, these are separately represented as an additional dummy variable, so that possible differences between private- and public-sector employment niches could be tested.

The tables present unstandardized regression coefficients. To compensate for the great difference in the size of groups, which would influence tests of statistical significance, we began by selecting random samples of 10,000 working men and women of each group in each region. The analyses include only men, with sample sizes in a fairly narrow range of 4,452 to 6,264. Similar results are found in analyses of the samples of women, which are not reported here. The tables also present predicted values of hours worked and income for a particular "standard" worker, varying labor-force sector. These values are based on a married man living with children, not a recent immigrant, who speaks English well, has some college, works two thousand hours per year as an employee (approximately full time), and has twenty years of work experience.

The models predicting hours worked have low levels of explained variance, ranging from as little as .016 (for blacks and Puerto Ricans in New York) to .120 (for Koreans in Los Angeles). Another interesting descriptive finding in table 5.6 is that differences among these

Table 5.6 Predictors of Annual Hours (100s) Worked, for Men in Selected Groups in New York and Los Angeles

Predictor	New York				Los Angeles			
	Korean	Chinese	Black	Puerto Rican	Korean	Chinese	Black	Mexican
Selected coefficients								
Self-employed	3.145**	4.150**	0.117	1.179**	3.554**	2.558**	0.209	0.635*
Enclave	2.846**	2.248**	-0.106	—	3.088**	0.542	-0.495	-1.283**
Entrepreneurial niche	2.689**	2.440**	0.528	—	0.412	0.053	0.758*	—
Employment niche	—	3.957**	-0.351	-0.074	—	-2.708**	-0.224	-0.298
Public employee	—	—	0.507*	0.021	—	—	0.184	—
Constant	21.497**	19.271**	17.168**	18.158**	15.047**	18.807**	18.270**	18.086**
R-squared	.076	.056	.016	.016	.120	.078	.033	.035
N	6,102	5,424	4,452	5,573	5,797	5,494	4,830	6,264
Predicted values								
Mainstream worker	20.44	20.28	19.86	20.16	21.01	21.09	21.15	21.61
Employment niche worker	—	24.24	19.51	20.09	—	18.38	20.92	21.32
Entrepreneurial niche worker	23.13	22.72	20.38	—	21.42	21.14	21.90	—
Enclave worker	23.29	22.53	19.75	—	24.09	21.63	20.65	20.33
Public worker	—	—	20.36	20.18	—	—	21.33	—
Unadjusted mean annual hours	22.84	21.03	19.42	19.72	21.78	20.57	20.01	19.79

Source: Data from Census of Population 1990.
*p < .05; **p < .01.

groups are also small: The unadjusted average values fall between 1,942 (for black men in New York) and 2,284 (for Koreans in New York). These differences are smaller after controlling for other background characteristics.

Self-employment has a positive effect on hours worked for Koreans and Chinese in both regions. The effect is large, enough to increase total hours by 15 to 20 percent per year. Whatever else it represents, working for oneself now represents a means for Koreans and Chinese to work more. It has much smaller effects, however, for Puerto Ricans and Mexicans and nonsignificant effects for blacks.

The other main finding from these analyses is that a person's sector of employment has no uniform effect on hours worked. The most positive case for a beneficial impact of enclave employment is that of Koreans, with coefficients of 2.846 and 3.088 (because hours are measured in hundreds, this is an advantage of about three hundred extra hours for those in the enclave sectors). There is a comparable effect for Chinese in New York but not in Los Angeles. The effects for other groups are either nonsignificant or negative. Working in an entrepreneurial niche also has mixed effects: positive for Koreans and Chinese in New York, for example, but nonsignificant for these groups in Los Angeles. Neither does working in the group's employment niche necessarily increase working hours: for Chinese, the effect is strongly positive in New York but negative in Los Angeles. For other groups the effects are not significant. Even public employment, reputed for offering job security, provides only small positive effects for blacks in New York and none in Los Angeles.

Rather than uniform effects, then, these sectoral variables have differential effects by group and by region. Those Koreans and Chinese who work in group enclaves and niches in New York work considerably more hours. In Los Angeles it is only the Korean enclave that produces more hours. Blacks, Puerto Ricans, and Mexicans reap little benefit in working hours in either region by being in their ethnic sectors.

The unadjusted mean incomes, reported at the bottom of table 5.7, reveal somewhat greater differences among groups in income than those we found in working hours. There are, however, some surprises in the relative ranking of groups. In New York, the highest mean income is for blacks (nearly twenty-seven thousand dollars). In Los Angeles the ranking is very different: Koreans and Chinese have average incomes above thirty-three thousand dollars, blacks are somewhat lower, and Mexicans much further behind (below twenty-two thousand dollars). Of course, these figures provide only a partial pic-

Table 5.7 Predictors of Logged Annual Income, for Men in Selected Groups in New York and Los Angeles

	New York				Los Angeles			
	Korean	Chinese	Black	Puerto Rican	Korean	Chinese	Black	Mexican
Selected coefficients								
Yearly hours (100s)	0.030**	0.044**	0.055**	0.054**	0.033**	0.050**	0.063**	0.056**
Self-employed	0.034	−0.145**	−0.257**	−0.063	0.101**	0.029	−0.032	−0.090**
Enclave	−0.249**	−0.472**	−0.045	—	−0.218**	−0.327*	0.000	−0.240**
Entrepreneurial niche	−0.193**	−0.301**	0.052	—	0.046	−0.052*	0.225**	—
Employment niche	—	−0.265**	0.126**	−0.096**	—	−0.238**	−0.070**	−0.015
Public employee	—	—	0.212**	0.144**	—	—	0.081**	—
Constant	8.588**	8.448**	8.041**	8.181**	8.525**	8.343**	8.014**	7.982**
R-squared	0.238	0.417	0.286	0.299	0.273	0.429	0.358	0.415
N	6,102	5,424	4,452	5,573	5,797	5,494	4,830	6,264
Predicted values								
Mainstream worker	24,175	26,308	24,823	26,265	28,374	30,104	26,096	26,324
Employment niche worker	—	20,188	28,161	23,851	—	23,717	24,320	25,930
Entrepreneurial niche worker	19,924	19,464	26,161	—	29,705	28,565	32,694	—
Enclave worker	18,844	16,413	23,727	—	22,827	21,700	26,092	20,704
Public worker	—	—	30,672	30,327	—	—	28,290	—
Unadjusted mean income	24,802	23,593	26,970	24,424	33,874	33,798	30,160	21,596

Source: Data from Census of Population 1990.
*p < .05; **p < .01.

ture of groups' relative standing. They differ also in labor-force participation and in the composition of households (especially the number of wage earners per household). Black incomes reflect advantages of nativity, the income of many men among the other groups being depressed by recent immigration or poor English skills. Nevertheless, among those men who work at least part of the year, it is revealing that the "successful" and certainly entrepreneurial Koreans and Chinese do not outperform blacks in earnings in New York.

Our main concern is the impact of self-employment and sectoral location on income. (Because hours worked is now included as a control variable, we are effectively studying hourly income.) Effects of self-employment are again mixed but mostly negative: It is a positive factor for Koreans in Los Angeles (a 10 percent boost), which reinforces the higher number of working hours of self-employed Koreans found in the previous table (adding perhaps another 10 percent to their earnings in this way). In other cases, however, it is small at best, and it is clearly negative in some instances. The most severe disadvantage from self-employment is experienced by blacks in New York: These men earn 25 percent less than comparable black men working for others and do not compensate at all by longer working hours. It is also negative for Chinese in New York and Mexicans in Los Angeles, though at least here the effect is counterbalanced by longer hours.

Effects of sectoral location are also mixed. The only consistently positive effect (compared with working in the mainstream economy) is that of public employment for blacks and Puerto Ricans (an 8 to 21 percent boost); clearly, this is a beneficial employment niche for these groups. By contrast, working in the Korean or Chinese enclave or niche sectors generally depresses wages for these groups. We might have expected low average earnings in these sectors simply for compositional reasons: They are the sectors more likely to include recent immigrants, with lower education and less English-language ability. Indeed, there are very strong effects of immigration, education, and language (not shown here). Having controlled for the effects of these human capital variables, enclave and entrepreneurial sectors still provide substantially lower income—as much as 47 percent less in the case of Chinese in their New York enclave.

Which groups, then, offer particular benefits to their members who work in the group's enclave or niches? Inspection of the predicted values in this table, which are intended to standardize for background characteristics, provides at least one kind of answer. In New York, the highest predicted incomes are for blacks and Puerto Ricans in their public-sector niche. The highest predicted incomes for Koreans and Chinese are found in mainstream sectors; owner sectors are less well paid. In Los Angeles, the pattern is somewhat different. The public sector has a fairly high return for blacks, but so does employment in the small black entrepreneurial niche. Los Angeles Koreans in their entrepreneurial niche earn as much as those in the mainstream economy, though Koreans in the enclave are very disadvantaged. Chinese and Mexicans in their enclave jobs are also poorly rewarded.

DISCUSSION AND CONCLUSION

In the two regions we studied, there has been considerable flux in the location of ethnic economic boundaries. Whites maintained predominant ownership in many sectors; but, although many of their ownership concentrations weakened, those of other groups tended to grow selectively. At one extreme are very large and long-established minority groups—Mexicans in Los Angeles and Puerto Ricans in New York—who have extremely low levels of self-employment. They concentrate increasingly in certain employment niches (in the public sector for Puerto Ricans, in the private sector for Mexicans), though many group members are dispersed throughout the economy, working for others. Some groups with low levels of ownership nonetheless have established new sectoral concentrations. The prime example is blacks, who are shifting toward self-employment in sectors where they were already concentrated as workers. At another extreme are those new immigrant groups—especially the Koreans and Chinese—who have been able to establish and expand large and diverse enclave economies, providing employment to a large share, often more than half, of group members.

The deep divide between these two extremes could be portrayed in terms of relative success and relative failure. Waldinger (1996a, 449–50), referring specifically to Los Angeles, concludes that "the region's pattern of ethnic specialization also constitutes a system of inequality. . . . Niching is pervasive, but not every niche proves rewarding. Some do, notably those concentrations that provide opportunities for self-employment. . . . For African Americans, government is an advantageous niche. . . . By contrast, Mexicans and Central Americans seem to have been herded into niches that constitute mobility traps." Our analyses of the tangible rewards of sectoral concentrations, however, lead to somewhat different conclusions.

First, the enclave strategy of economic incorporation has had variable payoffs. If it is successful for any group, that group is Koreans, who have established a large enclave and entrepreneurial niche in both regions. On the positive side, self-employed Koreans work about 15 percent longer hours than those who work for others, and those in the Korean enclave or entrepreneurial niche gain as much as 15 percent more in income. The result of working more hours, though, is counterbalanced by low hourly income. Korean self-employed earn between 3 and 10 percent more, controlling for hours. Those in the Korean enclave, however, earn as much as 25 percent less than those in the mainstream economy. The result is similar, though slightly less favorable, for the Chinese in New York but decidedly worse for the Chinese in Los Angeles. In this latter case, those in the owner sectors do not work more than Chinese in the mainstream economy. Furthermore, controlling for hours, they earn less. We emphasize, then, that the payoff from the enclave is variable for these more entrepreneurial groups.

Second, other kinds of ethnic concentrations can have positive effects for minority groups. As Waldinger has also stressed, the now-familiar black and Puerto Rican concentrations in the public sector provide security in working hours and a better than average income. In New York, the nongovernmental employment niche of blacks—where blacks are concentrated as workers for other groups—provides better hourly earnings than does work in the mainstream economy, an enclave sector, or entrepreneurial niche. Similarly, the employment niche of Mexicans in Los Angeles provides only slightly lower working hours or hourly earnings than does the mainstream economy (and neither difference is statistically significant).

Third, neither blacks nor Mexicans have reaped special rewards from a more entrepreneurial strategy. Mexicans in Los Angeles gain slightly higher working hours from self-employment, but at the cost of lower hourly earnings. Their only sector of concentrated ownership is in agriculture, and here they suffer both fewer hours and lower earnings. Blacks in both regions have modest sectors of ownership, providing employment for about as many blacks as does their non-government employment niche. Black self-employment has no positive effects in either region. Otherwise, the situation in Los Angeles is mixed: Black enclave sectors offer no special returns, but the entrepreneurial niche (in transportation equipment and utilities) does have a better payoff in hours and earnings. In New York, however, neither the enclave nor the entrepreneurial niche offers better hours or wages than the mainstream economy.

The ethnic fragmentation of the metropolitan economy is quite clear, and it is evident that the boundaries between groups have not diminished in the past decade. Our research leads us to be more cautious, though, about the consequences of the segregated labor market. The particular route through which Koreans and Chinese have made a place in the metropolis gives them a very visible social role. Apart from their high levels of education and other personal characteristics, however, it has not given them much advantage. In light of the mixed returns to self-employment and sectoral specialization, it would seem unlikely to offer a solution for those groups, like Mexicans, who now find themselves at the bottom of the economic hierarchy. Of the alternatives we have described, public employment may be the best option, and it certainly has proved to be beneficial to blacks and Puerto Ricans in these two regions.

This said, we do not consider wages and working hours to be the whole story. There are other ways in which the enclave strategy may prove to be more advantageous: as a means of absorbing a high volume of non-English-speaking immigrants, as a family strategy of self-exploitation, or as a complement to other dimensions of group solidarity in an immigrant or minority community. Possibly it will turn out that there are other longer range implications: that small business owners will have higher rates of wealth accumulation, or that their children will find a wider range of opportunities for career mobility. It would be premature to discount this mode of incorporation; what we propose, rather, is caution in presuming its virtues.

NOTES

The research for this chapter was supported by the National Science Foundation (grant number SBR95-07920). The Center for Social and Demographic Analysis, State University of New York at Albany, provided technical and administrative support through grants from NICHD (P30 HD32041) and NSF (SBR-9512290).

REFERENCES

Bailey, Thomas, and Roger Waldinger. 1991. "Primary, Secondary, and Enclave Labor Markets: A Training Systems Approach." *American Sociological Review* 56(4): 432–45.

Bonacich, Edna. 1973. "A Theory of Middleman Minorities." *American Sociological Review* 38(5): 583–94.

Bonacich, Edna, and Ivan H. Light. 1988. *Immigrant Entrepreneurs: Koreans in Los Angeles, 1965–1982.* Berkeley: University of California Press.

Borjas, George. 1990. *Friends or Strangers: The Impact of Immigrants on the U.S. Economy.* New York: Basic Books.

Edwards, Richard, Michael Reich, and David Gordon. 1975. *Labor Market Segmentation*. Boston: D. C. Heath.

Horton, John. 1995. *The Politics of Diversity: Immigration, Resistance, and Change in Monterey Park, California*. Philadelphia: Temple University Press.

Jiobu, Robert M. 1988. "Ethnic Hegemony and the Japanese of California." *American Sociological Review* 53(3): 353–67.

Lieberson, Stanley. 1980. *A Piece of the Pie: Blacks and White Immigrants Since 1880*. Berkeley: University of California Press.

Light, Ivan, and Carolyn Rosenstein. 1995. *Race, Ethnicity, and Entrepreneurship in Urban America*. New York: Aldine de Gruyter.

Logan, John R., Richard D. Alba, and Thomas L. McNulty. 1994. "Ethnic Economies in Metropolitan Regions: Miami and Beyond." *Social Forces* 72(3): 691–724.

Logan, John R., Richard D. Alba, Michael Dill, and Min Zhou. 1999. "Ethnic Segmentation in the American Metropolis: Increasing Divergence in Economic Incorporation, 1980–1990." *International Migration Review*, forthcoming.

Model, Suzanne. 1993. "The Ethnic Niche and the Structure of Opportunity: Immigrants and Minorities in New York City." In *The "Underclass" Debate: Views from History*, edited by Michael Katz. Princeton: Princeton University Press.

———. 1997. "Ethnic Economy and Industry in Mid-Twentieth-Century Gotham." *Social Problems* 44(4): 445–63.

Portes, Alejandro, and Robert L. Bach. 1985. *Latin Journey: Cuban and Mexican Immigrants in the United States*. Berkeley: University of California Press.

Portes, Alejandro, and Min Zhou. 1996. "Self-Employment and the Earnings of Immigrants." *American Sociological Review* 61(2): 219–30.

Waldinger, Roger. 1996a. "Ethnicity and Opportunity in the Plural City." In *Ethnic Los Angeles*, edited by Roger Waldinger and Mehdi Bozorgmehr. New York: Russell Sage Foundation.

———. 1996b. *Still the Promised City?: African Americans and New Immigrants in Postindustrial New York*. Cambridge: Harvard University Press.

Wilson, Kenneth L., and Alejandro Portes. 1980. "Immigrant Enclaves: An Analysis of the Labor Market Experiences of Cubans in Miami." *American Journal of Sociology* 86(21): 295–319.

Zenner, Walter. 1991. *Minorities in the Middle: A Cross-Cultural Analysis*. Albany: State University of New York Press.

Zhou, Min. 1992. *Chinatown: The Socioeconomic Potential of an Urban Enclave*. Philadelphia: Temple University Press.

CHAPTER 6

West Indians and African Americans at Work: Structural Differences and Cultural Stereotypes

Mary C. Waters

When Colin Powell was toying with the idea of running for president in 1994, media stories used his West Indian background to explain his success. In his autobiography, Powell himself uses his Jamaican parents' values and his West Indian roots to explain the development of the good parts of his character (Powell and Persico 1995). As the son of Jamaican immigrants, Powell is not alone as a successful West Indian American. In fact, many black luminaries in the United States are actually immigrants or the children of immigrants from the Caribbean, including Marcus Garvey, James Weldon Johnson, Claude McKay, Stokely Carmichael, Shirley Chisholm, Malcolm X, Kenneth Clark, James Farmer, Roy Innis, W. Arthur Lewis, Harry Belafonte, Sidney Poitier, and Godfrey Cambridge.

But the actions and behaviors of other black Americans who are also of West Indian origin are rarely tied to their West Indian backgrounds. Louis Farrakhan is also the child of a West Indian immigrant; his family is from Barbados. Yet the American image of the successful West Indian is helpful in explaining Colin Powell and not so helpful in explaining Farrakhan—who is as disliked and rejected by white Americans as Powell is liked and accepted. This cultural stereotype of black immigrants as more successful than native-born black Americans is deeply ingrained in American society. The question of the relative success of West Indians versus black Americans is also a hotly debated academic and political question. Academics find West Indians to be an interesting case because they share a visible minority racial status with black Americans, yet they also have an ethnic and immigrant background that makes them a separate group. Politically, the differential success of West Indians has been used as proof that racism is not responsible for the problems of black Americans. If West Indians are successful despite their black skin, some commentators argue, policies such as affirmative action designed to help black Americans are not necessary.

This chapter begins with a brief review of the current scholarly evidence on West Indian socioeconomic status. I then describe a case study of exactly the population that is so intriguing in the statistical portrait of West Indians in America: low-skilled, poorly educated workers who nevertheless have high labor-force participation rates—much higher, in fact, than native African Americans. The case study is based on participant observation in a Wall Street corporate cafeteria and in-depth interviews with its African American and West Indian workers, as well as with white managers and supervisors. The cafeteria's workforce used to be predominantly African American. In the fifteen years preceding the study however, the workforce had gradually become primarily West Indian. This case study provides a micro-level window into two important questions: How do demographic shifts in the composition of the labor force come about? How do participants—both managers and workers—understand these demographic shifts?

I argue that unskilled, uneducated West Indians do better in the labor market than comparable African Americans largely for structural reasons, including network hiring, employer discrimination in favor of immigrants, and differential appreciation of low-level jobs by immigrants and natives. Yet the white managers of the cafeteria and the immigrants who work there interpret the demographic shift as reflecting negative characteristics of African Americans. The social implications of these labor-market dynamics are found in both the genesis and the reinforcement of stereotypes, in the minds of whites, native blacks, and West Indians, of the latter as "successful," especially compared with African Americans. This case study cannot settle the debate between those who argue that niche employment improves conditions for African Americans and those who argue that it reduces their employment (see chapters 2 and 3 in this volume). It does, however, show that the subjective psychological interpretations expressed by the participants in this demographic turnover can have long-term negative impacts for African Americans. Regardless of whether the displaced African Americans from this cafeteria go up or down in the social stratum, the cultural explanations used by both white managers and the immigrants to understand the demographic changes are negative in their implications for African Americans.

HOW THE WEST INDIANS ARE DOING IN THE AMERICAN ECONOMY

Authors from Ira Reid in the 1930s to Nathan Glazer and Daniel Patrick Moynihan in the 1960s to Thomas Sowell most recently have described West Indians as more successful than American blacks and have devised a number of theories to explain why (Glazer and Moynihan 1963; Reid 1939; Sowell 1978).[1] Some of those who tout West Indian success argue that this shows that racism and discrimination is not an explanation for the relative lack of success of African Americans in the United States (Sowell 1978). Other authors have questioned the "myth" of West Indian success or questioned the theories put forward to explain that success (Steinberg 1989). Lately the debate has become more technical, with academics arguing about whether black immigrants do in fact do better than African Americans (Farley and Allen 1987; Kalmijn 1996; Model 1991, 1995, 1997). This is a politically charged debate, and the estimates of, and explanations for, West Indian success tend to reflect political differences. Conservative writers such as Thomas Sowell tend to see large differences and to stress cultural explanations. Liberal writers such as Stephen Steinberg tend to see little or no difference and to stress structural explanations for the differences they do find.

Perhaps the best known of the analyses of West Indian success is Thomas Sowell's argument that first- and second-generation black immigrants have higher levels of income, occupational status, and business ownership than native-born African Americans. He also cites the lower crime rates and fertility rates of West Indians. He concludes that this shows that "color alone, or racism alone, is clearly not a sufficient explanation of income disparities . . . between the black and white populations" (Sowell 1978, 43).

In addition to his claims about first-generation West Indians, Sowell uses 1970 census data on birthplace of parents to analyze the relative success of second-generation West Indians. He finds that second-generation West Indians in New York City, who are unlikely to have an accent that would enable a white employer to distinguish them from native blacks, "exceeded the socioeconomic status of other West Indians, as well as that of native blacks—and of the United States population as a whole—in family income . . . education . . . and proportion in the professions" (ibid., 44). He concludes that the relative success of West Indians "undermines the explanatory power of current white discrimination as a cause of current black poverty" (ibid., 49).[2]

The argument that foreign-born blacks are more successful than American-born blacks can be traced to the work of Ira Reid, a sociologist who conducted a study of foreign-born blacks in the 1930s, entitled *The Negro Immigrant: His Background Characteristics and Social Adjustment, 1899–1937*.[3] Reid's work was the source for Glazer and Moynihan's oft-quoted argument that West Indians were success-ful because "the ethos of the West Indians, in contrast to that of the Southern Negro, emphasized saving, hard work, investment, and edu-cation" (Glazer and Moynihan 1963, 35).

More recent academic debates have centered on whether the immi-grants who have arrived in the United States since 1965 and their children can also be called a black success story. Researchers have examined data from the 1970, 1980, and 1990 U.S. censuses to an-swer the following question: Do black immigrants outperform African Americans? Data from the 1970 census gave a resounding yes as the answer. Based on a multivariate study that controlled for background characteristics, economist Barry Chiswick concludes that foreign-born blacks who have been in the United States at least ten years have higher annual earnings than native-born blacks (Chiswick 1979). Subsequent analyses of 1980 census data by economist Kristin Butcher and another by sociologist Suzanne Model, using the same techniques, find no earnings advantage when foreign-born and na-tive-born blacks with the same background characteristics are com-pared, but these analyses do find an employment and an occupational advantage for the foreign born (Butcher 1994; Model 1991).

The debate in the literature has centered on whether West Indians have an earnings advantage over American blacks. Some analyses find a slight advantage; others, using different statistical controls, none. In an analysis of 1990 census data, limited to urban blacks, both native and foreign born, age twenty-six to sixty-four with positive annual earnings in 1989, sociologist Mathias Kalmijn finds a distinct advan-tage in earnings and occupational outcomes for British-origin Carib-beans. He finds that black immigrants and their descendants from English-speaking Caribbean countries are more educated and more likely to be married and have higher prestige occupations and higher earnings than native-born African Americans with no Caribbean an-cestry (Kalmijn 1996). Suzanne Model also finds that West Indians are less likely to be on public assistance than comparable African Americans (Model 1995).

The literature on the socioeconomic performance of West Indians agrees that the foreign born have higher labor-force participation rates than native-born blacks. This is true of both West Indian men and women but most striking among the West Indian women. Foreign-born West Indian women who are heads of household and thus (if they are legal) eligible for welfare, and foreign-born West Indian men who are disabled, are far more likely to be in the labor force than comparable African American men and women (Model 1995, 543).

The high labor-force participation of foreign-born black women is remarkable—they are more likely to be in the labor force than any other major demographic group in New York. In 1990 foreign-born West Indian men exceeded native-born African Americans in labor-force participation rates by 12.3 percentage points (89.1 percent versus 76.8 percent). Among women, the foreign born exceeded the native born by 12.1 percentage points (81.3 percent versus 69.2 percent) (ibid., 542). Philip Kasinitz (1992) reports that households headed by single women are less common among West Indians than among African Americans. Even among the more deprived single-female-headed households in 1980, the West Indian female households are less likely to be on welfare and more likely to be employed. This high labor-force participation rate is all the more remarkable as recent West Indian immigrants were overrepresented in the very lowest education categories.[4]

Scholars who stress cultural differences between African Americans and West Indians as explanations for the latter's success point to a difference in the historical conditions of slavery and freedom in the Caribbean and the United States. For instance, Ira Reid argues that the higher ratio of Africans to slaves born in captivity in the Caribbean led to a higher degree of resistance and a stronger sense of family among the Caribbean slaves and their descendants: "Coming from the slave clearing house for the United States, the Caribbean Negro has developed into a spirited, aggressive culture type, whose program and principle of accommodation has been singularly different from that of the American Negro" (Reid 1939, 49). He also stresses that because there were few poor whites in the islands, slaves and free blacks were trained in skilled work there, whereas in the American South the black codes and other restrictions led to fewer skilled workers among the American slaves and their descendants (ibid., 84).[5]

Dennis Forsythe argues that West Indians do so well in the United States because they have been indoctrinated in the Protestant ethic, which he defines as including "a strong belief in self-discipline, drive, and determination." This ethic developed, he argues, "because of the West Indians' schooling in the British educational system, their majority status in the Caribbean, and the wider 'role frontier' available there" (Forsythe 1976, 65). Others argue that majority status provides role models and leads West Indians to grow up believing that anything is possible and that their dreams can be fulfilled only through hard work (Parris 1981, 10).

Of course, cultural explanations for differences in outcomes between groups are hard to pin down. They often rely on stereotypes that affect the way in which the analyst interprets behavior and beliefs.[6] The debate about West Indian success has often relied on stereotypes about native-born blacks, including assertions that they do not value education, are less ambitious for their children, and are less likely to believe in the American dream. Careful analysis of an exhaustive amount of survey data on this topic by political scientist Jennifer Hochschild has disproved many of these stereotypes (Hochschild 1995, 160). Suzanne Model argues that class differences in the Caribbean have created different cultures within local societies and that historical differences across islands have also led to different cultural adaptations. Which of these many Caribbean cultures, she asks, is the culture that was supposedly brought with the immigrants and is responsible for their successes (Model 1995)?

Those who stress structural explanations for West Indian success tend to focus on the selectivity of immigration, the psychological and structural consequences of immigration, and the preference some employers reportedly have for foreign-born over native-born blacks. Immigration is a selective process in a number of ways. Legal restrictions on who can immigrate selected for literacy in earlier years and, since 1965, for certain occupations, especially nurses coming from the West Indies (although most immigrants in the post-1965 era come in under family reunification and not under occupation-immigrant categories).

Immigration is also selective in ways that are less easily measured. Even when immigrants and those who stay behind do not differ on measurable characteristics such as education or skill level, immigrants are generally those with the ambition and drive to move to a place where they think opportunities will be better. The personality characteristics this selects for might not be measurable in large data sets, but they could easily lead to aggregate differences across groups.[7]

The psychological and structural consequences of immigration have strong effects on the social organization of immigrant communities in the United States. These structural conditions have consequences that can also explain some of the differences between American blacks and West Indians. Immigrants are more likely to accept low-wage, low-status jobs than are natives in a country, because the immigrant's sense of self is not as bound up with the job as is the native's (Piore 1979). Immigrants judge jobs based on comparisons with the opportunities available to them in their native country, and despite low pay, the conditions in secondary labor-market jobs often look good to them. They also do not perceive the same stigma attached to low-status jobs, because their sense of self is tied to a societal status system in the home country.

Immigrants are embedded in networks that can provide information and referrals to job opportunities in a way that natives often are not. Because immigration proceeds along chains of networks, most immigrants in an established stream have a chain of contacts that can bring them valuable information and referrals (Massey, Goldring, and Durand 1994; Portes 1995; Tilly 1990). Both of these factors—the ready-made networks and the lack of aversion to low-status jobs—could explain the much higher labor-force participation rates among unskilled and poorly educated West Indians relative to unskilled and poorly educated native-born blacks.

Finally, discrimination in favor of the foreign born on the part of white employers can certainly be a factor. Analysts of the situation of West Indians in the United States have documented the belief of West Indians that they receive better treatment from whites when it is known that they are foreign born (Foner 1987; Lowenthal 1972; Reid 1939; Stafford 1987). As Roy Bryce-Laporte writes, "The white landlord, the white shopkeeper, and the white boss will also tell them of their moral superiority over the American black and distinctiveness of their accent, and if British, the grammatical correctness of their English or American—leaving them to believe that they are the recipients of exceptional favors" (Bryce-Laporte 1972, 46). In the discussion that follows of the dynamics of employment among low-skilled West Indians in one workplace in Manhattan, I argue that there are clear structural reasons that explain the legendary capacity for and commitment to work among West Indians—the very attributes that are most often used to argue for a cultural explanation for their success.

THE CASE STUDY: AMERICAN FOOD COMPANY

Most West Indians in New York City work in the service economy. They are concentrated in the health services (22 percent of Caribbean New Yorkers work in hospitals, nursing homes, and home health care) but are represented in a number of other service sectors of the economy (Waldinger 1996, 121).

American Food Services is an international food-service company that runs restaurants and cafeterias throughout the country. It employs 170 employees in its United States Financial cafeteria, in Manhattan. About fifteen managers and office staff manage the operation. We conducted in-depth interviews with sixty-five employees, including nine whites (three male and six female), all of whom were managers, fifteen American blacks (six male and nine female), including two supervisors, and thirty-four West Indian immigrants (eleven males and twenty-three females) including six supervisors and two managers. In addition we interviewed three Puerto Rican males, two Puerto Rican females, one Peruvian female, and one Bangladeshi male, all of whom were workers.[8] The interviews lasted between one and two hours, and all covered the same core sets of issues—family background, ethnic and racial identity, job history, attitudes and interactions with other ethnic groups, neighborhood characteristics, and political attitudes. In addition, we asked the managers about hiring decisions and their assessments of the strengths and weaknesses of the workforce. The respondents were told that the study was about the impact of immigration from the Caribbean on life in New York City.

The in-depth interview was my primary way of gathering information, but my research assistant and I were present during every workday for about two and a half months; thus, we were able to observe the dynamics of the workplace apart from the formal interview situation. When we were not interviewing we spent time in the main office, where employees came in to punch the time clock, or we sat in a corner of the kitchen area, observing the workers, or in the cafeteria, where we were able to talk informally with employees on their breaks. We were thus able to observe some of the dynamics in the workplace—which workers took breaks together, how people got along with each other and with their supervisors. In all, we interviewed almost all the white and American black employees in the establishment and about one-third of the English-speaking Caribbean immigrants.

Network Hiring

Management was unwilling to give us access to personnel records, but we were able to get a consistent account of the changes the workplace had experienced over the previous twenty years. Since 1970, the cafeteria's workforce has changed from one made up of black American men and women, and older white women who were returning to work after raising families, to a workplace that in 1991 was about 90 percent foreign born. The physical plant had also changed. Before the construction of the current modern skyscraper, United States Financial was located in an older New York office building, also in the Wall Street area. The cafeteria and dining room were run in-house by the financial-services company. American Food took over the running of the food services for the company in 1981, two years before the move to the current building in 1983. The older building was more accessible to people looking for a job from the street; in fact, some of the older employees who have the longest service with the company originally got their jobs by "pounding the pavement." In my sample, these workers include a white male manager, several American black females, and an immigrant female.

Both managers and workers report that hiring used to be done through newspaper advertisements and employment agencies specializing in food-service workers. In the early 1980s this began to change, and at the time of the interviews the company had not placed an advertisement in a newspaper in more than nine years. Occasionally an agency was hired to find a skilled worker—a chef's assistant, for example; however, almost all hiring for the previous nine years had been through current employees' social networks—despite the official company rule against hiring relatives to work together. The rule is broken constantly, because network hiring is easier for the managers. They generally believe that they get a higher-quality worker, and they have more control over the workforce, because the worker who gave the recommendation has an interest in the new hire's performance. One manager explained the benefits of network hiring thus:

> If a position opens up, and then Ingrid says, "My brother needs a job," we won't look at the applications, we tell her to bring her brother. We do it undercover, because you're really not supposed to have brothers and sisters and husbands and wives in there. But it makes it a little bit more manageable [because] when they do bring somebody in, they tend to be a little bit better workers because of—well, somebody like Ingrid [has] been here for ten years. You know? Her brother needs a job. Her brother comes here, he says, "I'm not gonna let my sister look bad. She's been here for ten years and now I'm gonna jerk around and make her look bad? I mean, that's part of her career." (White male manage, age forty)

The remarkable change at American Food in both hiring practices and the demographics of the workforce does not seem to have been a conscious choice by management. Rather, the switch from employing American blacks and a few white women to employing West Indians and other immigrants occurred in the following fashion: Each worker is allowed to recommend someone for a position. If the new person does not work out, then that person cannot recommend any more friends or relatives. If the new hire performs well, then not only can

Table 6.1 Characteristics of Food-Service Workers

Characteristic	American Black		West Indian	
	Females	Males	Females	Males
N^a	9	5	17	9
Average age	46	31	36	35
Number with food-service training	4	2	0	1
Number not hired through network[b]	5	0	1	1
Years in United States	—	—	12.1	8.1
Years at present job	7.1	4.6	5.7	4.8

Source: Data from a study of the American Food Company conducted by Mary Waters.

[a]*N* does not equal total number interviewed because managers were not interviewed about their method of hire and because interviews with some workers did not include this information.

[b]Number of workers of each nativity group who were initially hired through formal means, not through recommendation of friends and relatives.

the original person recommend another prospect, but the new hire can as well. Because of the different value placed on these low-skill, low-pay jobs by immigrants and by Americans, this rule tends to cut off the networks of the American workers and increase the number of hires from the immigrant networks. Although no statistics were supplied to us, the managers claim that the turnover is much lower among the immigrants than among American blacks or among the white American women. The preponderance of West Indians also does not seem to have been a conscious choice. Because of their knowledge of English, they are preferred over other immigrants for jobs that involve contact with customers. The kitchen jobs are often filled by Hispanics and others, such as Thai and Bangladeshi immigrants. In addition, the company's personnel policy encourages minority hiring, and the West Indians count as black employees for these purposes.

The overall characteristics of the workers we spoke with are reported in table 6.1. There are several striking differences among the groups. The American black females were the oldest and had been on the job the longest, at a mean of 7.1 years. The American black males were more recent hires and also were younger. The foreign-born males and females were also more recent, but both groups had been there slightly longer than the American black males. Perhaps the most striking differences were in the method of hire of the workers and the percentage of workers with previous training in food services. Five of the nine American females we interviewed got their current jobs through some formal avenue, whereas all of the black American males and the vast majority of the foreign-born males and females got their jobs through networks. The American black females who got their jobs through formal means either applied by walking in off the street at the old building, answered a newspaper ad, were referred by an agency, or, in the case of two women, were placed in this job after completing food-service training programs in an attempt to get off welfare.

The American black males, on the other hand, all got their jobs through recommendations from friends. In two cases, the friends who recommended them were foreign-born black males they knew through intermarriages in their families. This gender difference in method of hire also reflects the different periods in which these people were hired: The American black females were survivors from the early days when it was possible to be hired through a formal mechanism; the American black males were more recent hires.

The difference in formal training is also striking. The American blacks were more likely to have received training in food services either in school or in previous corporate settings. Because both managers and workers agreed in their interviews with us that no skills were necessary for these jobs, that everything could be taught to workers in a few days' time, it could be that these differences reflect the statistical discrimination of this firm's hiring practices. In general, the managers prefer immigrants, for reasons that will be discussed later. Given this preference, and the fact that many unskilled workers are turned away from these jobs, the American blacks who are hired must in some way impress the person hiring them during the interview. As the managers made clear, all things being equal, they would rather hire an immigrant. It may be that the American blacks who are on the job had some previous training that functioned to get them in the door to interview for the job. This reflects patterns in hiring that have been found in a number of other studies, all of which conclude that for blacks, formal hiring mechanisms work better than network hiring practices, because they provide more objective criteria for employers to make hiring decisions and less opportunity for employers to practice "statistical discrimination" (Holzer 1987; Kirschenman and Neckerman 1991; Neckerman and Kirschenman 1991).[9]

The microprocesses described here freeze out African Americans from entry-level jobs. Roger Waldinger's book, *Still the Promised City?* (1996), shows on a large scale how network hiring can adversely affect low-skilled African Americans, in effect driving them out of the

labor force, at the same time as the labor force absorbs large numbers
of poorly educated immigrants. Waldinger argues that patterns of network hiring lead to the formation of racial and ethnic niches in employment—the concentration of racial and ethnic groups in industries or sectors of the economy beyond what one would expect, given
their proportions in the population.

Waldinger traces the patterns of niche formation and succession in
New York City over the past fifty years for a number of immigrant
groups, including West Indians and African Americans.[10] He argues
that West Indians have been able to expand their presence in New
York's economy in recent decades while the African Americans presence has declined because the West Indians were poised to do well in
New York's growing postindustrial service economy. Although both
groups started in 1940 with a concentration in personal services—
notably, domestic services and laundering—by the 1970s and 1980s,
West Indians had established strong concentrations in the expanding
health-care industry. By 1990 employment in the niches of hospitals,
nursing homes, and health services provided employment to 22 percent of Caribbean New Yorkers.[11] By contrast, African Americans
moved into public-sector employment.[12] This shift in opportunities
put a larger premium on education: Most public-sector jobs required
formal education, which was also increasing dramatically among African Americans during this period.

This has had differential effects on educated and uneducated African Americans. Employed, skilled African Americans are doing well
in the niche of public-sector employment, with many of them holding jobs in managerial or professional occupations. Unskilled African
Americans, however, have been locked out of the networks that provide
entrée to unskilled entry-level jobs because their group no longer controls those niches. Those jobs have been taken over by immigrants—
both black immigrants and other immigrants. Although Waldinger's
aggregate statistics show that unskilled and poorly educated West Indians are concentrated in health care and personal services, the role of
ethnic networks in hiring among food-service workers interviewed is
similar to other niche employment. Networks get uneducated immigrants jobs and freeze out uneducated African Americans.

Entry-level jobs at American Food Service paid, in 1991, about
$5.25 an hour, or $210 a week. This would yield a gross income of
$840 a month for a strenuous forty-hour week. A full-time worker's
yearly income would be $10,080. The fact that the job is with a
major corporation with an internal labor market, that it includes
health insurance for full-time workers, and it pays slightly better than

the minimum wage makes it a better-than-average unskilled entry-level job. However, the low pay and general lack of opportunities to advance in salary or job position make it a dead-end job, and the wages earned consign the employee to the ranks of the working poor for the rest of his or her life. For the vast majority of workers, who will not be promoted, the job provides a forty-hour workweek of hard work, with little control over working conditions and a precarious employment situation dependent on economic conditions. However, there is a steady supply of immigrants eager to land these entry-level jobs, enough so that one female manager called the immigrant network her "upstairs agency":

> We have a guy in here who calls us almost every other week— "You need anybody, you need anybody? I've got somebody for you, you know." I mean, why go outside? Just go to my agency upstairs and say, "Got anybody for me this week?" (White female manager, age thirty-three)

Skills are generally not a requirement in hiring. Entry-level jobs include washing dishes, serving food on the cafeteria line, fixing drinks, and making sandwiches as well as general cleanup activities in the kitchen. These jobs can be learned in a matter of minutes or hours. Some slightly more skilled jobs, such as chopping vegetables for salads or cooking soups, can be learned in a day or less. The managers are explicit, however, that they are looking for certain characteristics, if not skills, in employees, especially reliability, loyalty to the job, and the ability to take orders and be "flexible." These characteristics are important enough that they even outweigh relevant experience.[13]

When native-born applicants manage to get a referral to a manager for a screening interview for one of these entry-level jobs, the quest for these characteristics puts them at a distinct disadvantage. Native-born applicants are less likely than immigrants to accept the manager's request for a commitment to an unspecified set of tasks. Rather than seeing the employment as a favor for which he or she would promise loyalty to the company, and to the manager, the American worker sees the job situation as a contract. For instance, this white female manager stated that in the initial interview with an applicant she asks, "'Are you willing to do anything?' And, if they say yes, I hire them."

Q: Are there people that say no?

A: Yes. I had people come in for a dishwashing job and give me a resume. "Does this mean that you wouldn't scrub the floor if I ask you to?" And he said, "Well, if it's not in my job description, no." You know I didn't hire him. (White female manager, age fifty-three)

In fact, this issue of "flexibility" is a source of contention among the workers who are on the job. Many of the Americans told us that the immigrants create a situation where everyone is exploited because they do not insist on job descriptions. For instance, this black American worker believed that because the immigrants do not stand up for their rights, all the workers at American Food suffer:

Q: Are there any negative aspects of your job?

A: Well, yes. Because I think, all of the main focus is focused on dealing with foreigners. Because see, they don't know the American system, you know, and they feel they must be cautious because they don't want to do anything wrong. Basically, they don't know their rights, you know? And then, at the job, see, they get the feeling that everybody don't know their rights. So, it causes problems . . . like sometimes, the company's policies are not written, it just seems like they make them up as they go along. You see, they [the immigrants] do a lot of things that they don't have to do, to try to, I guess, ease their way, you know? Sort of like, to make less problems for themselves. I guess they would figure the less problems for them, the better. But then you have to look at what you consider a problem, you understand? Because, if someone's gonna mistreat you, you know, by taking away your rights, I mean, that's a problem right there as far as I am concerned. (American black male worker, age twenty-eight)

How West Indians and American Blacks Perceive the Job

Although managers and supervisors at American Food do not set the wages for the new hires, the way the proprietor of a small shop would, they seem to prefer to deal with the West Indian immigrants, who do not complain about the low wages and who are not constantly seeking higher wages.

Americans wouldn't do what immigrants do. They wouldn't do the work without questions, you know. Immigrants will do anything because they're here, they have no money, and they're willing to work for their money. They're willing. Americans, I think, have it to easy, you know. And I just feel like, you hire an immigrant, right, you pay him three dollars an hour. You hire an American, he won't work for three dollars an hour. He won't. He'll want seven dollars an hour. That's why a lot of immigrants get hired, because they'll work cheaper. (White female manager, age fifty)

The immigrants are willing to work for less and to commit themselves to entry-level jobs because they use a different metric to measure the value of these jobs. This twenty-nine-year-old Guyanese immigrant, explaining why she enjoys her job, noted,

That show—*In Living Color*[14]—and it's true, most people that came from the West Indies, they always do more than one job, and it's true. Because you come here with one intention—that you want a better living and you want to have things that you never had before. So you don't mind working for it because back home we work real hard. So when you come up here it's like— the job up here compared to Guyana is like nothing. So you don't mind working hard, you know. To the Americans, it's too much work. And for us it won't be like too much work. . . . You buy yourself things that you never had. You get to do a lot of things. I never had a car in Guyana. Now I have two cars. I never had a lot [of] things but now I have it. Life is much better. Much easier. (Guyanese female worker, age twenty-nine, in the United States nine years)

Similarly, the low status of these jobs does not bother the immigrants as it would a person born in this country. Because the immigrants are between two societies—their homeland and the United States—their sense of self is not tied to the work they do as it would be at home or if they had grown up in the United States (Piore 1979; Waldinger 1987). As one thirty-nine-year-old Guyanese immigrant observed,

In America, no job is degrading. No job is degrading. . . . In America, when you are a tradesman, you are a big man. More than those who sits in an office. But in my country, everybody wants to have an office job. In America, the main thing is earning, and earning it honestly. (Guyanese male worker, age thirty-nine, in the United States six years)

Although working in a cafeteria all day may not be a great job, many compare it with cutting cane in the tropical sun or working long hours for much lower wages in an economy where the prices of imported goods have skyrocketed. The immigrants came to the United States expecting the streets to be paved with gold. This sense that the future will be better and that America is a land of opportunity contrasts with the outlook of the native workers doing the same jobs. Not only did the black Americans see their jobs as a necessary evil that did not hold much promise for the future, many of them also thought the presence of the immigrants significantly affected their working conditions, making it harder to rise in the company and harder to improve their wages. In the assessment of a black American worker, his future at American Food looks bleak:

> I hear people are in there for five to ten years and they doing the same thing. They might make a little bit more money but, I mean, fifteen years and all you get is a plaque, or a dollar bonus or something like that. That's not money, so I don't think you'll move too far in this American Food, so that's why I won't stay long. (American black male worker, age thirty-three)

Some black Americans were very much aware of the ways in which the immigrants and the Americans view the same job differently. This worker argued that the immigrants are in the United States on a "work program," which allows them to accept low wages they should scorn:

Q: So do you think wages would be higher at a place like American Food if there weren't immigrants around to work there?

A: Yes, I think so. I think so. I think the base salary would be. I think the base salary would be considerably higher. And then like the foreigners always say, well, you Americans lazy, you Americans this, you Americans that. Due to the fact that we won't work for low wages. I feel that is unfair, I mean, we being Americans, I mean, we shouldn't have to work for this less amount of money when we know that we could or should be earning more. And then, see, what the foreigners fail to realize, they come to this country to make a living, too, and then they always talking about going back to their country. So they're mostly here like on a work program. So, I mean, when you come into a country under those circumstances, I guess you would have to take whatever you can get. But, being an American in this country, then, you know, we don't feel that way. (American black male worker, age twenty-eight)

All of the black American workers agreed that the way to be hired at American Food was to know someone. Because of the low wages and the low status of the job, it would be easy for many people to walk away from the job should some other alternative arise. Although the Americans were entitled to recommend friends and relatives for jobs, most described the ways in which their networks had been cut off because the people they had recommended had not worked out.

> They won't let me bring nobody else in because of my brother. Like when I was at the old shop, I got him on, we was working together. That was during the wintertime, during the summer he got in school. He had like a day class. So he had to make a choice between his job and the school. So I told him, "Go to school, man." So you know, after a while, I couldn't bring nobody in. Because you know, he took school over the job. So I was telling them, "He wants to go to school." [They said,] "No, you don't bring no responsible people in." I said, all right. I'm still working, so what am I gonna worry about somebody else for, you know. Let them stand. You know, you can't do that to me 'cause he decided to go to school. (American black male worker, age thirty-seven)

This worker agreed that his brother should choose school over this low-level job, but effectively it cut off his ability to recommend any other friends or family members for jobs at American Food. Yet even though the rule covering recommendations for hiring provides a rational explanation for why American Food increasingly hires only immigrants, many of the African American respondents had heard that there was a systematic bias in favor of hiring the foreign born. The African American workers told us they believed that whites and West Indians, if given the chance, would hire West Indians over American blacks.

White Employers' Preference for Immigrant Workers

The managers were not at all reticent about describing their preference for immigrants over Americans. White native-born Americans are not employed as workers at all in the site and do not apply for jobs there, so when the managers contrasted Americans and immigrants, they were generally contrasting American blacks with foreign-born blacks and Hispanics. Although only one white manager actually described herself and her racial opinions in overtly racist language, all of the managers had a clear preference for the immigrant blacks over the natives.

A: If I had one position and if it was a West Indian versus an American black, I'd go with the West Indian.

Q: And that's because of your experience working with people?

A: Yes. Their reliability, their willingness to do the job or what has to be done.

Q: Are there concrete statistics on this?

A: I don't have them. I just—it's just experience that they have a different drive than American blacks (White male manager, age forty-two)

It is clear that the substitution of immigrants for native workers in this workplace has come about for structural reasons. The company wants flexible workers who give loyalty to the company, appreciate low pay, and obey managers and supervisors when they give orders. However, from the American blacks' perspective, these jobs should command no loyalty. They believe that the pay is very bad; that workers should not have to do whatever they are asked to do; that they have a right to a job description; and that their immigrant coworkers, because of their willingness to work without benefits and guarantees, undermine the position of native-born workers. For the immigrants, the bargain offered by American Food does not seem on the face of it to be a bad one. It seems to offer a shot at the American dream—if not for them, then for their children. (Perhaps I should say it offers them a chance at the Guyanese dream, because it is in reference to home conditions and pay that the job looks attractive.)

This difference of perception about the relative worth of these jobs, and about the treatment workers have a right to expect on the job, is understandable, given the different structural situations of the immigrant workers and the African American workers. The devaluation of these jobs and the desire of the Americans to limit the power of management is not, however, understood by the white managers or the West Indians as a rational response to a bad job with limited opportunities for mobility. Rather, the whites and the West Indians interpret these reactions as moral failings of American blacks as individual workers.

THE USE OF CULTURAL STEREOTYPES

The workers and managers at American Food all noticed the substitution of immigrants for African Americans, but their interpretations of why this happened differed. The whites and the immigrants had similar reactions to these developments. They blamed African Americans workers for losing their jobs and praised the immigrants for their ability to work hard. The African Americans tended to see the change as rooted in the bad quality of the jobs themselves. Familiar cultural stereotypes in American society of lazy black Americans and hardworking immigrants provided a ready language for whites and West Indians to explain this workplace dynamic. African American workers were also aware of these stereotypes, and they struggled to provide a different interpretation. This led to a great deal of tension and competition between the immigrants and the African American workers.

The Whites' Perception

We asked the white managers specifically why there were so few American blacks working in the corporation now, compared with twenty years ago. They claimed that black Americans preferred welfare to entry-level jobs like the ones in the cafeteria, that black Americans lacked a work ethic and the discipline to hold on to the jobs, and that black Americans wanted more money than these jobs paid. When we asked about white ethnic groups and why they did not come in for these jobs, we got very different answers. For instance, the supervisor of waiters in the restaurant thought that American blacks do not come in because they are lazy and lack discipline but that Italians do not come in for these jobs because they have other options: "You know, a lot of them go into construction or into their fathers' businesses, or they go into Italian restaurants where mostly they deal with Italian customers and Italian bosses."

It was striking that although the managers were aware of how much they relied on network hiring, they still attributed American blacks' lack of success in the cafeteria jobs to lack of discipline and work ethic.

> Very few American blacks have applied for work that I've seen. . . .
> And the ones we get, they were not successful in retaining their
> employment. And the conjecture I make in my own mind is, they
> don't have the self-discipline to hold the job. Have I encountered
> that among non-American blacks? Yes. But not nearly as signifi-
> cant[ly]. (White male manager, age forty-two)

These whites generally hold a very low opinion of ghetto blacks, distinguishing them from "good blacks"—meaning middle-class or hardworking African Americans. Yet they described most of the blacks they came in contact with at work as ghetto blacks.[15] Many spoke with disdain of women who left their cafeteria jobs because they could live better on welfare. The black American workers who are hardworking and reliable, whom these whites see every day, do not disconfirm the stereotypes the managers hold.[16] Instead, these hardworking blacks are seen as exceptions to the general rule that inner-city blacks are criminal, welfare dependent, and have too many children.

All the whites interviewed stated that before working in this work site they had been unaware of differences between foreign-born and American-born blacks and that they were surprised when they first encountered the differences. For instance, one white male manager described a Jamaican employee whose parents were upset when she dated a black American because they felt all black males were worthless. He recalled being surprised by this, because, to him, all blacks were the same. Another manager described what he learned from his employees over the years about differences between the two groups:

I know that the West Indian blacks don't like the American blacks 'cause they get put into the same position as American black people. And they tend more to shy away from doing all of the illegal things because they have such strict rules down in their countries and jails. And they're nothing like here. So they're really paranoid to do something wrong. They seem to be very, very self-conscious of it. No matter what they have to do, if they have to try and work three jobs, they do. They do all kinds of things. They make crafts and try and sell them to each other and whatever. They won't go into drugs or anything like that. Whereas the American black people, right away. I mean, you talk about the ghetto black, you talk about the guy's running around with a gun and drugs. These people don't want to be affiliated with that. But, if you see somebody black, everybody's black, everybody's a junkie or everybody's got a gun. They don't like that. They really don't like it. They want to be distinguished as Trinidadians, and I even here them talk about American black people. They really don't like them. They really don't like them. . . . They try to keep their children away from American blacks. I think that the parents know enough to keep them away from American blacks because they see the American black as being a bad person, and they don't want their children to fall into this. (White male manager, age forty)

Although the whites reported that they only recently became aware of differences between foreign-born and American-born blacks, they described what they perceived as different values and behaviors between the groups. The whites saw the West Indians as more ambitious, more hardworking, and less troublesome than the African Americans. They also thought the West Indians were less materialistic than the Americans.

> I work closely with this one girl who's from Trinidad. And she told me when she first came here to live with her sister and her cousin, she had two children. And she said, "I'm here four years and we're reached our goals." And what was your goal? For her two children to each have their own bedroom. Now she has a three-bedroom apartment and she said that's one of the goals she was shooting for. Four years it took her to get there. Now if that was an American, they would say, "I reached my goal, I bought a Cadillac." Like, that's what they would say. Or, "I bought a diamond ring or a watch." This one got her son and daughter each their own bedroom. Now that is a difference. (White female manager, age fifty-three)

The managers use the immigrants' immigration experience and ethnic experiences as explanations for both good and bad behaviors at work. For instance, whereas American blacks are blamed for their lack of work ethic and for not showing up for work on Mondays, the immigrants are often allowed cultural or ethnic explanations for why they behave in a particular way. One manager explained that new immigrants sometimes reverted to "island time," and if they were late or did not show up for work when it rained, he generally forgave them, on grounds that they just did not understand the American way of work.

The whites also made analogies to their own immigrant and ethnic past to understand the experience of the black ethnics. All the managers were themselves second- or third-generation descendants of immigrants, and they viewed the West Indian workers through the lens of their own parents' and grandparents' immigrant experiences, including the difficulties of assimilation and the inevitable sacrifices made for the success of their children.

> I remember, like, seeing movies and listening to my grandfather and all. When he came here, they would call him guinea and this and that. He couldn't get work and all of that stuff. You know? It's the same as that. And now these people are coming— I think that it is just like myself and my son. I didn't let him go

amuck. It's the same thing as I think with the Trinidadians. As long as they have both their parents, and their parents are good, I think they'll keep raising them just like that. I think [with] that the Trinidadians—the same thing. They're gonna take care of their children and they're gonna try to tend to them, keep them away from trouble. (White male manager, age forty)

Even managers who expressed negative opinions about American blacks made many spontaneous comments about how similar their immigrant ancestors and the current West Indian immigrants are. In effect, these whites saw themselves in the immigrants, even as they saw the American blacks as "the other."

The Immigrants' Perceptions

The immigrants we spoke with were generally well aware of their employer's preference for immigrants as workers, and they tended to share the whites' perceptions of the superiority of West Indians to black Americans. In fact, the West Indians were apt to chronicle even minute differences between themselves and black Americans. Drawing on their experiences in their neighborhoods, their children's schools, on public transportation, and in the media, as well as on the job, the West Indians found black Americans lacking in basic values and achievements.

At American Food, the line manager in charge of day-to-day functioning of the cafeteria is a thirty-eight-year-old Trinidadian woman who has worked for the company for seventeen years. She thought that many of the top managers were prejudiced against black people. However, she found that once people found out she was from Trinidad, they were more likely to appreciate her work. She thought that on the job her immigrant identity took precedence over her race:

A: My ex-boss, he was white, and he would rather have a staff like this with a lot of West Indians because of the problems [he had] when he would hire Americans. He would say, "It's a waste." On a Monday morning when he looking for his job to be done, they're not here. And he always say he liked West Indian people. And I think I did benefit from that. I think this is why I'm in this position right now through him, you know? And probably because I'm black, maybe he wouldn't appreciate me that much. If you're working for a place and there's openings for a job, them big firms, they like to take West Indians faster than a black American.

Q: Why do you think that is?

A: Because as I was saying, most people know most Americans is lazy.
Black Americans. (Trinidadian female manager, age thirty-eight, in
the United States twenty-two years)

Because of the positive reactions to her national background she
has received at work and at school in the United States, she has consciously decided to keep her accent:

> I used to go to beauty school and I can remember going there,
> it was about three years after I came here, and I would not open
> my mouth to say a thing. Because it was a lot of Americans and
> I was afraid to speak. And I remember when it was time for
> graduation, everybody have to get up and introduce their self
> and stuff like that. And when I started to speak the class went,
> oh! You know? And the teacher said, "You have such a nice
> accent and you hardly ever speak." And then the kids, they
> started saying the same thing and after that, you know, be my
> friend and all this and speak to me. And I was all embarrassed
> about my accent and here somebody appreciate it and then I
> decided that I wouldn't try to lose it.

This suspicion that people will be against them because they are
foreigners is a typical experience among the immigrant workers. They
are usually pleasantly surprised to get a more positive reaction, but
this reaction is usually limited to whites. When it comes to relations
with black Americans, the immigrants report a very different reception, as this same manager related:

> American people, especially black Americans, they think that
> West Indian people come here to take their jobs. But the way I
> feel, this is their place, and they have all the opportunities, and
> they supposed to, you know, use it up, but we come from the
> outside, and we see the opportunities and we grab at it and they
> get upset about us. The average black American will not come
> here and work for five dollars an hour. They would rather stay
> home or hang out. But to me, I would take the five dollars and
> make it do. You know what I mean? And they hate us for that,
> and that's wrong, I think, because we are not here to take any-
> body's job. Most of the jobs that the West Indian people have
> here, the Americans wouldn't do it. . . . I was talking to one of
> the employees, and she always say, "You need to get Americans
> inside here." But, you hire the Americans and they goof off, and
> they like time off, too. The Americans work for one month

straight, and then after that they start—within a week—they call out sick, late. Most of the employees here is West Indian. (Trinidad female manager, age thirty-eight, in the United States twenty-two years)

These beliefs were not held only by the managers. The immigrant workers themselves were also highly critical of their American black co-workers. The welfare system figures prominently in the immigrants' explanations of Americans' seeming unwillingness to work.

The majority of the black Americans—what I say is, either they're lazy or they don't like to work. I might be wrong, but judging from places where you work along with them, if they need something, they work for it. When they get it, that's it. They don't—the majority of them, like, they don't have a plan about what they need with their life. I think this welfare system encourages it. 'Cause in my country, there is no such thing. You gotta work for a living. There is no social security and welfare, nothing like that. (Guyanese male worker, age thirty-nine, in the United States six years)

Part of the reason the welfare system seems to figure so prominently in the explanations of the workers is their accurate observation that a single mother is financially better off on welfare than working at American Food. One foreign-born woman who was working in the cafeteria told me she made five dollars an hour, or $200 a week. After carfare and deductions to her paycheck for insurance, she was better off financially on public assistance. On welfare, she had received $219 every two weeks, along with food stamps and subsidized housing. She chose work over welfare, but for her own sense of pride, not for financial reasons.

The immigrants believe in the American dream of upward social mobility and find themselves in what they perceive to be the strange position of teaching Americans about how to achieve that American dream. This Trinidadian supervisor described an argument she had with an American worker about the fact that the supervisors are mostly immigrants. This woman contrasts her individual success with what she perceives to be his lack of understanding of what it takes to get ahead:

I said to him, "I didn't come here as a supervisor. I came here, and I was poor, I wasn't rich. I started from scratch. . . . I was always interested in learning new things, and now I'm a supervisor." So I said to him, "If I had to come in here and stand washing the pots, I would have started washing the pots. Because I would have told myself that I'm not gonna be washing these pots all the time, right?" He said, "I don't want to go through all of that to be a supervisor. I think I should be a supervisor." I said, "Supervise what? How can you supervise if you don't know the job yourself? You have to know the job yourself first before you can become a supervisor. . . . . You haven't done anything." So he was, like, "Yeah, you come here from Trinidad." I said, "Well, you're wrong. Because if I was you, I would be the supervisor because I'm the American, and I wouldn't be the person who was washing the pots." So I said, "The immigrant should be the one washing the pots. And you should be the supervisor because you were born here. You let somebody come and take away your stuff from you, so you're wrong." (Trinidadian female supervisor, age thirty-six, in the United States nineteen years)

The immigrants see themselves as disciplined hard workers, and they attribute that quality to their strict island upbringing. However, when contrasting West Indians in America with those back home, and in contrasting their own lives back home and in the United States, most people readily described a more laid-back life in the islands, where people do not work very hard. In Trinidad, this respondent explained, life was much more easygoing and more fun. If it rained, she argued, you did not have to go to work:

Yes, here it is, "You work!" Down there, you go to work, you miss work, and, "Hey, you wasn't feeling good yesterday?" and you say, "Nah, I wasn't feeling good," and you stay home. If the rain falls too hard and you feel like staying home, you stay home. But not here. You come out. 'Cause it's—I guess here they make you feel more independent and more responsible than home. You just sit down, you relax, and here, they make you feel more responsible. (Trinidadian female worker, age thirty, in the United States ten years)

The West Indian immigrants simultaneously believe that people back home have it easy or do not work as hard as people in the United States and that some inbred trait among them allows them to be superior workers; they do not acknowledge that it is because they are immigrants that they work so hard. Like the whites who conveniently forget about the hardworking American blacks who disconfirm their stereotypes, the West Indians selectively construct and remember cultural traits about themselves that serve to confirm their own stereotypes and self-images. Thus, West Indian immigrants are able to maintain a view of themselves as hardworking because they are West Indian even as they describe their frustrations with the laziness of West Indians when they return home for a visit.

The American Blacks' Perceptions

The immigrants and the whites interviewed believed that there were few blacks at American Food because black Americans do not work hard. This American black worker agreed with the widespread opinion that the Americans would not work as hard as the West Indians, but he questioned why the West Indians would work so hard at jobs that offer so little in return:

Q: Why do you think that there are so few black Americans working at American Food?

A: 'Cause they don't like to work as hard as the West Indians or people that come from another country. . . . There are a lot of West Indians here because they like to bust their butt. You know, they work hard because they need this job. The Americans feel that they don't have to work hard because this is their home, you know, this is where they was raised. A lot of them work too hard. That's sometimes what I see, too hard. You know, 'cause they, like, young, and they shouldn't be working that hard. That's how I feel. Got a lot of time to go before you gotta go kill yourself like that. (American black male worker, age twenty-three)

In addition to their resentments that the immigrants are surpassing them economically, the American blacks hear the immigrants complaining about Americans. This leads to strong tensions between the two groups:

Q: Have you noticed any tensions at all between West Indians and American blacks in New York?

A: Oh, yes. Oh my God. Are you kidding? Ah. This is ridiculous. I mean, it's really ridiculous because a lot of it is pure ignorance. . . . They don't like us. And myself, included. They think that we're lazy. We don't try to get out and do things for ourselves. We just sit back and complain about the white man. What the white did. . . . I think you have the confrontation between the black Americans and the black islanders because the black Americans are not trying to understand the islanders and the islanders are not trying to understand the black Americans. So I listen to them, and I try to explain things to them, and they explain things to me. . . . You know, one thing about me, if they want to say all those things, I don't get uptight about that. I say, "No, don't feel bad. If that's the way you feel right now, it's all right to say it. You can call me a Yankee, I don't get offended. Because I know my people have called you people a lot of things." (American black female worker, age fifty)

Black Americans' awareness of the stereotypes the immigrants hold of them makes it difficult to have normal relations with co-workers. They know the immigrants think they are lazy and that they do not like them very much. Even the Americans who said they did not personally have a problem with the "island people" described a fairly high level of tension on the job. For instance, this woman describes the interactions she has had on the job:

They can be nasty when they want to be as far as like their attitudes, you know. Some time they just—a lot of times they don't like American people. They say we have a chip on our shoulder about them. It's like they're not too friendly. Like when I first started working here, you know, everybody wanted to know where I was from, you know, they were asking, you know, the first couple of days I was working, where you from, where you from. I said, "I'm from here," you know. And then I could see the change like the following day. It's like, you know, I go and I say good morning and it's like, "Hm, morning"—like if they didn't really want to say it. (American black female worker, age twenty-two)

A common complaint of the West Indians is that the Americans tell them to go back to their country and do not welcome them to the United States. One of the workers who acknowledges saying those things to the immigrants explained why he feels that way:

I hate it when they put this country down. I'll be ready to send them back. You can live, man, but don't put this country down, 'cause it's helping you. It gets me a little upset. . . . I tell them, "What you doing here, then?" Yeah, and they always telling me how the sun is shining and all that. Yeah, but they ain't got an economy, man. (American black male worker, age thirty-seven)

Competition for jobs was cited by both immigrant and American blacks as the source of many of the tensions that existed.

> They always cursing the West Indians. I don't think they like West Indians. . . . They feel that we come here to take away what they have, you know. I mean, they here all the time, you know, and there is so many things that they could be doing, and we come here and we see the opportunity and we go for it. So, there is always some American who would be cursing us, "You better go back to where you come from. You only come to take"—you always hear that. (Guyanese female worker, age twenty-nine, in the United States nine years)

American workers often reminded the immigrants that the islands they were from are poor and underdeveloped. This was a way for the Americans to feel superior to the obviously more successful immigrants on the job. The immigrants reacted by taunting the Americans with their dominance in the workplace, which they knew annoyed and embarrassed the Americans.

> The black American that we have working here will always put down immigrants. And he say the thing which is the stereotype, saying, "They come here and take our jobs." But as I see it, if he had adapted himself, or adapted different things to get what he wanted, he would have gotten it. Other people say to him, "We are immigrants and we are waiting on tables and working in a kitchen. How does that make you feel as an American doing the same? Don't you feel less of yourself?" (Trinidadian male worker, age twenty-six, in the United States four years)

CONCLUSION

The West Indian immigrants who work at American Food have done very well compared with their American black co-workers. Numerically, they are now the majority on the job. They are told by management that they are valued because they are hardworking, in explicit contrast with American blacks, who do not last long on the job. The American blacks the immigrants encounter on the job tell them to go back where they came from and accuse them of coming to take American jobs. The immigrants also face these hostilities in encounters with American blacks on the streets, on subways, and in stores. The immigrants perceive this situation as a violation of the natural order of things: By rights, they think, the American blacks should be doing better. The immigrants are seizing opportunities that the majority of American blacks, who are poor, seem to be passing by.

Most of the immigrants used their limited experience with inner-city black Americans and the readymade cultural stereotypes prevalent in the mass media to explain the behaviors and attitudes of their American black co-workers. Thus, the immigrants compared their own hardworking, planning, friendly, upward-striving selves with the lazy, welfare-dependent, unfriendly, bitter, black Americans. Although their beliefs did not stop the immigrants from developing friendships, romantic relationships, or uneasy alliances with African Americans, the social patterns among the workers were divisive, and very rarely did American blacks and "island people" sit together at lunch breaks or see each other outside work. The network hiring that created and recreates the workforce also means that the immigrants often have family and friends at work who look out for one another and with whom to socialize.

It may be that at the macroeconomic level, immigrants do not "take jobs" from native workers (Smith and Edmonston 1997). It may even be that many of the African Americans who used to work at this cafeteria are now in better jobs, perhaps in the African American niche of government employment. Yet, the dynamics in this workplace suggest that although structural causes are used to explain the turnover, cultural explanations are used by those involved to understand the changes. These perceptions and intergroup tensions find their way into policy debates about immigration and affirmative action. The whites in these workplaces use the experiences of successful West Indian blacks to conclude that policies such as affirmative action are not needed for American blacks. Most of all, these perceptions become a self-fulfilling prophecy as successful later-generation black Americans, like Colin Powell, are noted for their ethnicity, and controversial figures of the same origin, like Louis Farrakhan, blend into the category of American blacks.

This research was supported by a grant from the Russell Sage Foundation and by a John Simon Guggenheim Fellowship. I am grateful for research support from Kayode Owens, Jimmy Phillipe, and Tomas Jimenez, and for comments on an earlier draft from Frank Bean, Stephanie Bell-Rose, and two anonymous reviewers.

NOTES

1. Also see Coombs 1970; Forsythe 1976; Raphael 1964; Smith 1985.

2. The second generation in 1970 were the offspring of immigrants who came to the United States in the earlier part of the century. They were a select group in terms of their characteristics and behaviors.

3. Reid's work, the only book-length comprehensive study of the black immigrant to date, is a valuable and highly engaging study. However, Reid was also faced with the limited data available on the West Indians. He based a great deal of his book on entries by West Indians to a life-history essay contest in which contestants entered essays about their experiences as immigrants and described their reactions to specific situations, like employment and discrimination.

4. Roger Waldinger's figures on education among foreign-born and native-born black New Yorkers also show a pattern of declining educational attainment over time for the foreign born and increasing educational attainment for the native born. For instance, in 1970, West Indian immigrants were 1.51 times more likely to have graduated from college than all other New Yorkers, while native-born blacks were 70 percent less likely. By 1990, West Indians were about half as likely as all other New Yorkers to be college graduates (odds = 0.56), whereas native blacks were also almost half as likely (odds = 0.48). In 1970 native-born and foreign-born blacks were about equal in their odds of having less than a high-school education (1.23 for native born and 1.22 for foreign born). While African Americans increased their education levels so that by 1990 they were almost on a par with all other New Yorkers in the odds, they were in the lowest education category (odds = 1.09); West Indians were more concentrated in the least educated group with odds = 2.03 that they were among the least educated (Waldinger 1996, 76).

5. Owens Smith (1985, 24) points out that the economic vacuum created after slavery was abolished in the Caribbean created opportunities for skilled black craftsmen and artisans. This did not happen in the American South because large numbers of poor whites were available to take those jobs. White owners in the South created political and legal barriers to black advancement into those jobs in the form of the black codes and the like.

6. One study by Oscar Glantz shows some distinct attitudes of West Indians that fit with cultural stereotypes, but it was based on a very small

and nonrandom sample. Glantz, comparing the beliefs of West Indian students at Brooklyn College with those of white Catholics and Jews, finds that "the West Indian group expressed more trust in the responsiveness of the economic reward system, more faith in the value of hard work at school and in the value of hard work generally, and less negativism in their orientation toward the electoral system in the United States" (Glantz 1978, 200).

7. Evidence to support the importance selectivity plays in explaining differences between West Indians and African Americans comes from Kristin Butcher's analysis. Butcher finds that when West Indian immigrants are compared with African Americans who moved across a state line from where they were born, the West Indian advantage evaporates. She concludes that is it the selectivity of movers, whether internal migrants or international immigrants, that explains their higher performance (Butcher 1994). Stanley Lieberson also argues that internal migration among American blacks produces a migrant selectivity advantage (Lieberson 1978, 1980).

8. We asked to interview whites, blacks, and West Indians, but these other workers were referred to us early in the process for interviews, and it would have seemed unfair to refuse to interview them. They provided valuable information from an alternative perspective on ethnic and race relations in the workplace and on working conditions overall.

9. Joleen Kirschenman and Kathryn Neckerman (1991, 204) define statistical discrimination as "employers' use [of] group membership as a proxy for aspects of productivity that are relatively expensive or impossible to measure." They go on to note that "those who use the concept disagree about whether employers' perceptions of group differences in productivity must reflect reality."

10. Waldinger defines West Indians as immigrants from the Anglophone Caribbean, excluding immigrants from Haiti, other Francophone countries, and the Dutch West Indies. He defines the native-born African American niche as those industries and occupations in which the concentration of native African Americans was at least 50 percent higher than their share of the economy (Waldinger 1996, 106–22).

11. These areas of concentration, however, employ mostly West Indian women—in 1990, 73 percent of the employees in West Indian niche employment were women. Men were more dispersed throughout the economy, with only 20 percent of West Indian men working in the Caribbean niche (Waldinger 1996, 120–21).

12. "Twenty-eight percent of all employed African Americans worked in public sector black niches; another nine percent worked in other areas of

the public sector where the black concentration was not so high" (Waldinger 1996, 111).

13. Kirschenman and Neckerman (1991) find in a study of Chicago-area employers that they too place a high premium on "character" and personal characteristics in hiring workers for entry-level jobs.

14. More than a few West Indian immigrant workers mentioned with pride the situation comedy, *In Living Color*. The show had a Jamaican character who was satirically depicted as having twenty-eight jobs, working constantly. The satire was lost on the immigrants, who talked with pride about the character.

15. This is similar to statements made by many of the employers interviewed by Kirschenman and Neckerman (1991).

16. There is a large literature in psychology on the genesis and maintenance of stereotypes. One consistent finding is how resistant to change stereotypes are once they are established. When a person holds a stereotype about another person or thing, an instance of a person that does not meet the stereotypical expectation is seen not as evidence to disconfirm the stereotype; rather, the person who does not fit is seen as an "exception that proves the rule." In similar fashion, these managers keep a stereotype of African Americans as lazy even as they encounter many hardworking African Americans (Eberhardt 1993; Eberhardt and Fiske 1998).

REFERENCES

Bryce-Laporte, Roy. 1972. "Black Immigrants: The Experience of Invisibility and Inequality." *Journal of Black Studies* 3(1): 29–56.

Butcher, Kristin. 1994. "Black Immigrants in the United States: A Comparison with Native Blacks and Other Immigrants." *Industrial and Labor Relations Review* 47(2, January): 265–84.

Chiswick, Barry R. 1979. "The Economic Progress of Immigrants: Some Apparently Universal Patterns." In *Contemporary Economic Problems, 1979*, edited by William Fellner. Washington, D.C.: American Enterprise Institute Press.

Coombs, Orde. 1970. "West Indians in New York: Moving Beyond the Limbo Pole." *New York Magazine* 13, July: 28–32.

Eberhardt, Jennifer. 1993. "Where the Invisible Meets the Obvious: The Effects of Stereotyping Biases on the Fundamental Attribution Error." Ph.D. diss., Harvard University.

Eberhardt, Jennifer, and Susan Fiske, eds. 1998. *Racism: The Problem and the Response*. Thousand Oaks, Calif.: Sage Publications.

Farley, Reynolds, and Walter R. Allen. 1987. *The Color Line and the Quality of Life in America.* New York: Russell Sage Foundation.

Foner, Nancy. 1987. "The Jamaicans: Race and Ethnicity Among Migrants in New York City." In *New Immigrants in New York*, edited by Nancy Foner. New York: Columbia University Press.

Forsythe, Dennis. 1976. "Black Immigrants and the American Ethos: Theories and Observations." In *Caribbean Immigration to the United States*, edited by R. S. Bryce-Laporte and D. M. Mortimer. Washington, D.C.: Smithsonian Institution.

Glantz, Oscar. 1978. "Native Sons and Immigrants: Some Beliefs and Values of American-Born and West Indian Blacks at Brooklyn College." *Ethnicity* 5(2): 189–202.

Glazer, Nathan, and Daniel Patrick Moynihan. 1963. *Beyond the Melting Pot.* Cambridge: MIT Press.

Hochschild, Jennifer L. 1995. *Facing Up to the American Dream: Race, Class, and the Soul of the Nation.* Princeton: University Press.

Holzer, Harry J. 1987. "Informal Job Search and Black Youth Unemployment." *American Economic Review* 77(3): 446–52.

Kalmijn, Matthijs. 1996. "The Socioeconomic Assimilation of Caribbean American Blacks." *Social Forces* 74(March): 911–30.

Kasinitz, Philip. 1992. *Caribbean New York: Black Immigrants and the Politics of Race.* Ithaca: Cornell University Press.

Kirschenman, Joleen, and Kathryn M. Neckerman. 1991. "'We'd Love to Hire Them But . . .': The Meaning of Race for Employers." In *The Urban Underclass*, edited by Christopher Jencks and Paul Peterson. Washington, D.C.: Brookings Institution.

Lieberson, Stanley. 1978. "Selective Black Migration from the South: A Historical View." In *Demography of Racial and Ethnic Groups*, edited by F. D. Bean and W. P. Frisbie. New York: Academic Press.

———. 1980. *A Piece of the Pie: Blacks and White Immigrants Since 1880.* Berkeley: University of California Press.

Lowenthal, David. 1972. *West Indian Societies.* London: Oxford University Press.

Massey, Douglas, Luis Goldring, and Jorge Durand. 1994. "Continuities in Transnational Migration: An Analysis of Nineteen Mexican Communities." *American Journal of Sociology* 99(6): 1492–1533.

Model, Suzanne. 1991. "Caribbean Immigrants: A Black Success Story?" *International Migration Review* 25(Summer): 248–76.

———. 1995. "West Indian Prosperity: Fact or Fiction?" *Social Problems* 42(November): 535–53.

———. 1997. "An Occupational Tale of Two Cities: Minorities in London and New York." *Demography* 34(November): 539–50.

Neckerman, Kathryn, and Joleen Kirschenman. 1991. "Hiring Strategies, Racial Bias, and Inner City Workers." *Social Problems* 38(4): 433–47.

Parris, D. Elliott. 1981. "The Contributions of the Caribbean Immigrant to the United States Society." *Journal of Caribbean Studies* 2(1): 1–13.

Piore, Michael. 1979. *Birds of Passage: Migrant Labor and Industrial Societies.* New York: Cambridge University Press.

Portes, Alejandro. 1995. *The Economic Sociology of Immigration: Essays on Networks, Ethnicity, and Entrepreneurship.* New York: Russell Sage Foundation.

Powell, Colin L., and Joseph E. Persico. 1995. *My American Journey.* New York: Random House.

Raphael, Lennox. 1964. "West Indians and Afro Americans." *Freedomways* 4(3): 433–45.

Reid, Ira de A. 1939. *The Negro Immigrant: His Background Characteristics and Social Adjustment, 1899–1937.* New York: Columbia University Press.

Smith, James P., and Barry Edmonston. 1997. *The New Americans: Economic, Demographic, and Fiscal Effects of Immigration.* Washington, D.C.: National Academy Press.

Smith, Owens. 1985. "The Politics of Income and Education Differences Between Blacks and West Indians." *Journal of Ethnic Studies* 13(3): 17–30.

Sowell, Thomas. 1978. "Three Black Histories." In *Essays and Data on American Ethnic Groups*, edited by Thomas Sowell. Washington, D.C.: Urban Institute Press.

Stafford, Susan Buchanan. 1987. "The Haitians: The Cultural Meaning of Race and Ethnicity." In *New Immigrants in New York*, edited by Nancy Foner. New York: Columbia University Press.

Steinberg, Stephen. 1989. *The Ethnic Myth: Race, Ethnicity, and Class in America.* Boston: Beacon Press.

Tilly, Charles. 1990. "Transplanted Networks." In *Immigration Reconsidered: History, Sociology, and Politics*, edited by Virginia Yans-McLaughlin. New York: Oxford University Press.

Waldinger, Roger. 1987. "Changing Ladders and Musical Chairs: Ethnicity and Opportunity in Postindustrial New York." *Politics and Society* 15(4): 369–401.

———. 1996. *Still the Promised City?: African Americans and New Immigrants in Postindustrial New York.* Cambridge: Harvard University Press.

CHAPTER 7

Network, Bureaucracy, and Exclusion: Recruitment and Selection in an Immigrant Metropolis

Roger Waldinger

Network theory represents at once the most distinctively sociological and the most successful sociological contribution to our understanding of international migration. Admittedly, network theory does not explain the activation of migration streams; but as it identifies a feature common to most, if not all, migrations and tells us why those migrations, once begun, persist, its explanatory power is great, indeed. The argument is simple: Networks provide the mechanisms for connecting an initial, highly selective group of seedbed immigrants with a gradually growing base of followers back home. Those connections rely on social relationships, developed before the decision to migrate is made, in which trust is taken for granted. Consequently, the networks provide durable, efficient conduits for the flow of information and support.

Resource flows through the networks change in a twofold process. On one hand, the early immigrants, the "veterans," consolidate their place in the host society, reducing the costs undergone in providing information and support and thus widening the pool of candidates they can help. On the other hand, a growing proportion of the home communities find themselves linked to settlers in a position to give assistance, lowering the costs and risks of movement and thus increasing migration's net expected returns. Very quickly, network consolidation and expansion make migration a self-feeding phenomenon, as ties to settlers diffuse so broadly that almost everyone in the home society enjoys access to a contact abroad.[1]

For all its power, however, network theory never quite explains why the structures function as they do. It offers a supply-side theory of immigration, emphasizing a "universal logic [that] takes hold as the network is extended and elaborated, binding [home country] institutions more tightly to specific destinations in the United States" (Massey et al. 1987; 169). It may be the case, as Douglas Massey and his collaborators argue, "that *all that is necessary* for a migrant network to develop is for one person to be in the right place at the right time and obtain a position that allows him to distribute jobs and favors to others from his community" (ibid.). But this formulation suffers from its inevitabilism: that "eventually someone achieves a position of authority . . . and begins to recruit fellow townspeople for work" (Massey, Goldring, and Durand 1994, 1528, 1501). More importantly, it begs a logically anterior question: how does it happen that such authority positions open up to socially stigmatized outsiders, such that they can hand out valued resources to needy friends and kin? Note that the specification of the argument implies an inherently expansionary thrust, requiring us to explain not simply why veterans find positions for janitors or dishwashers but also why their leverage extends to ever higher reaches of the economic ladder.

Part of the problem involves the explanation itself: As an explanation, network theory provides an account of social reproduction. First, however, we need to understand how outsiders get inserted into a structure from which they have previously been excluded, and to answer that question, we need an explanation of social discontinuity. As I have tried, elsewhere, to address that question (see Waldinger 1994), considerations of economy and simplicity allow me to bracket the question of which factors, and under what conditions, open up "the right place." We can safely assume that all workers at the very bottom of the labor market engage in a good deal of churning; on the other hand, we can expect that immigrants will apply for these entry-level jobs at higher rates than anyone else. Consequently, the number of people with contacts and with the ability to help get a job and keep it quickly increases. Over time, the ranks of low-level kitchen workers increasingly come to be filled through immigrant networks; given bosses' natural preference to recruit from inside, the immigrant presence automatically grows.

This type of explanation tells us why there are lots of immigrant sweepers and kitchen helpers; network theories, however, stake grander claims, contending that migration involves a self-feeding process (for example, Massey et al. 1987, 171). In that case, the networks must constantly expand their ambit; one wonders how.

Arguments from the "economic sociology of immigration" (Portes 1995) provide one answer to the puzzle. The same connections that span immigrant communities constitute a source of social capital, providing social structures that facilitate action—in this case, the search for jobs and the acquisition of skills and other resources needed to move up the economic ladder. Networks tying veterans to newcomers allow for rapid transmission of information about openings in workplaces or opportunities for new business start-ups. Networks also provide better information within workplaces, reducing the risks associated with initial hiring and similarly connecting coethnic entrepreneurs, who take membership in the community as an index of trust (Bailey and Waldinger 1991). Once in place, the networks are self-reproducing, because each incumbent recruits friends or relatives from his or her own group, and entrepreneurs gravitate to the cluster of business opportunities that their associates in the community have already identified. Relationships among coethnics are likely to be many-sided, rather than specialized, leading community effects to go beyond their informational value and engendering both codes of conduct and the mechanisms for sanctioning those who violate norms (Portes and Sensenbrenner 1993). Put simply, network prevails over market, providing the more efficient mechanism for reducing the costs and risks associated with hiring.

Note, however, that the argument links the embeddedness of employment in immigrant communities to two distinct aspects of immigrant connections: Networks provide a conduit for high-quality two-way information flows; and, thanks to their potential for social closure, they also furnish a structure for enforcing behavioral expectation. Clearly, the potential for social closure of immigrant networks is a property valued by employers: In some instances, informal hiring practices perform more efficiently than more open, formal processes (Tilly and Tilly 1994, 301). By definition, social closure involves the exercise of power; for that reason, the social-closure potential of immigrant networks can also serve to increase opportunities for one group of ethnically distinctive workers at the expense of another. This effort to expand rewards by restricting access to resources and opportunities to a limited circle of eligibles generates an expansionary thrust, extending the penetration of immigrant networks beyond the range defined by considerations of an efficiency sort.

Exclusionary closure, to borrow the terminology coined by the British sociologist, Frank Parkin (1979), occurs when ethnically distinct insiders attempt to monopolize job opportunities for members of their core network and restrict outsiders. Although social relations embed economic behavior in an ethnic community and thereby enhance the ease and efficiency of economic exchanges among community members, those same connections implicitly restrict outsiders. Indeed, the more embedded are ethnic economic actors in dense, many-sided relations, the stronger the mechanisms for excluding outsiders, and the greater the motivations for doing so. Network recruitment offers the opportunity to detach the hiring process from the open market, allowing insiders to ration openings to their referrals;

consequently, one ethnic group's ability to mobilize resources through social structure serves as a strategy for limiting another group's chances for advancement. The effort to work with others of one's own kind provides further impetus for the spread of network recruitment.

Thus, the social connections among workers, and between workers and employers, facilitate economic action; network recruitment is so extensive because it improves the quality and quantity of information that both workers and employers need and also shapes the employment relationship by imparting a set of understandings common to workers and employers. Once imported into a workplace, however, immigrant networks can be turned to other ends; it is precisely because they are so powerful that they are hard to uproot and difficult to control.

Thus, factors related to efficiency and power explain why the implantation of ethnic networks among formally "open" organizations enlarges opportunities for low-skilled ethnic insiders while reducing access to outsiders. However if network hiring is extensive, it is not pervasive. After all, networks connect immigrants to organizations; it is the distinctive features of the organizations employing immigrants that set the upper bounds on network penetration.

Emphasizing network over organization is a common sociological theme. The network phenomenon offers proof that the earlier antinomies posited by modern sociology—gemeinschaft versus gesselschaft, modernity versus traditionalism, formal versus informal—do not hold. After all, what could be more gemeinschaftlich, more traditional, than the reappearance of entire family groups within a workplace that maintains all the other appurtenances of bureaucratic management? The pattern at the top of the organization does not necessarily look all that different—even if "old boy" connections and club memberships are not quite as important as they were a mere two decades ago.

We can agree on the reality of a backstage life to organizations, in which social connections among employees—and between employees and the communities to which they are linked—remain alive and well. However, it is one thing to argue that networks ward off the pressures toward formalization that the earlier literature describes so well and quite another to ignore those pressures altogether. Recall that modern personnel management arose, in part, out of an effort to reduce the role of personalistic ties in hiring and promotion. That effort cannot be judged a full success and may well be doomed to partial failure, as the modern organizational literature would suggest. Nonetheless, it remains the case that organizational practices circumscribe the scope for network recruitment, for reasons having to do with formalization, on one hand, and the maintenance of legitimacy, on the other.

In either case, organizational features affect the conditions under which workers are selected—an issue to which network theory does not attend. Network theory provides two variants on the ways in which workers are matched to jobs, both focusing exclusively on recruitment. The variant favored by the migration literature tells a story about the strength of strong ties; most network studies, by contrast, accent a different element, namely, the strength of weak ties (Granovetter 1973). Whatever its virtues, the weak-ties story does not seem to provide an explanation for the behavior of the information giver: after all, why provide valuable information to someone to whom one has a slight, perhaps even just a passing, connection? More to the point, weak ties are unlikely to serve as two-way channels of communication, telling job seekers about opportunities (with uneven degrees of accuracy) but not reassuring bosses about the appropriateness of applicants' traits. In any case, the strength of weak ties is not a plausible theory of sponsorship, an act for which weakly tied associates have neither the means nor the motivation.

Thus, the strength of weak ties is essentially an argument about the ways in which social networks alter the information available to job seekers while doing nothing to alter the information needed by employers when making a decision about hiring. Strong ties may not do much to diversify information flows. They seem likely to function better as conduits for two-way flows of information, because members of dense networks know their associates well and maintain the ongoing relations needed to ensure that network associates perform as predicted. Consequently, the strength of strong ties is a viable theory of sponsorship, as it explains how social connections can also alter the employer's calculus.

For strong ties to actually deliver a job, the employer's informational needs must be fully met by the intelligence provided through the referral network—and those conditions cannot always be fulfilled. The interests of workers and employers are hardly symmetric: under conditions of job scarcity, workers may seek to maximize employment opportunities for their kin and associates, a goal that could well distort the quality of information provided to employers. Let us even suppose that sponsors have pure motivations or identify their interests with those of their employers; still, they will be at best imperfect judges of an applicant's qualifications, having limited knowledge of both the job and the applicant's suitability. The nature of the job will also come into play: It is one thing to trust a sponsor's word when the tasks are relatively simple and the work is closely supervised, quite another matter for a function involving greater complexity and more autonomy. For all these reasons, organizations are likely to screen the persons who apply for the job; the degree to which organizations screen applicants, and implement their own selection criteria, limits the scope of informal, network-based recruitment. The more formal and the more extensive the screening process, the lower the dependence on referral networks—which, for the subject matter of this chapter, implies that bureaucracy will mitigate the exclusionary effects of network recruitment.

Classical organizational theory tells us that bureaucracy selects with an eye toward prediction; the need to ensure consistent performance, according to a set of standardized criteria, drives the substitution of formal, impersonal means of selection for those based on ongoing, particular relationships among persons. However, organizations also need to maintain their legitimacy among the clients they serve, as well as the workers who staff the ranks. From this perspective, network recruitment is a possible threat, yielding excessive, unwanted homogeneity, which, in turn, may suggest that the organization treats some groups of workers and customers differently from others. Hence, the need to maintain legitimacy provides additional impetus for bureaucratic hiring procedures, which, by their very nature, reduce the scope for network recruitment.

Let me be clear: In highlighting the contrast between network and bureaucracy, I am not seeking to add yet another dualistic scheme to the binary oppositions of primary versus secondary or formal versus informal practices. Bureaucracies are permeated by networks; and as relatively few immigrants work in the black market, bureaucratic factors exercise at least some influence on immigrant employment outcomes. Rather, I am invoking network and bureaucracy as sensitizing concepts, trying to introduce greater depth to our understanding of the labor-market reality in the immigrant metropolis by drawing our attention to variations in the mechanisms by which workers are matched to jobs and to the difference that those differences make.

EMPLOYMENT OUTCOMES AND ETHNIC SOCIAL STRUCTURE

If organizations differ in the mechanisms used for recruiting and selecting workers, the labor force is also made up of categorically distinctive groups that also vary, not just in skills but in the informal social structures that might increase access to information and support. In general, strong ties of the sort described above are embedded in the migration experience itself: Those without close connections to settlers are far less likely to engage in migration than those with strong, preexisting ties; and the tendency of immigrants to move under the auspices of settlers and their subsequent interdependence fosters a reciprocal flow of exchanges, leading premigration connections to endure.

Thus, strong ties are likely to be more powerful and more pervasive among immigrants than among natives. That generalization seems to provide a particularly apt description of the principal immigrant and native-born groups with which this chapter is concerned, namely, Mexican and Central American immigrants, on one hand, and African Americans, on the other. Networks play a particularly important role in the immigrant streams in question, because the newcomers are especially low skilled, possessing few resources other than the help provided by kin and compatriots. Moreover, the social structures established in the United States point to the potential for activating informal help. For example, high rates of marriage, large households, and the presence of subfamily units within households suggest that the family is likely to provide an important resource. Similarly, convergence on burgeoning barrios characterized by high employment rates, notwithstanding the low skills of the residents, implies access to local sources of help.

By contrast, the social structures of less skilled African Americans appear to be more diffuse, more fragmented, and less effective. Certainly, the family is much less likely to be an effective resource, given the much lower marriage rates, the much higher incidence of single headship, and the much smaller family size. Although we still know too little about how the distinctive social structure of the African American population might exercise an independent effect on economic outcomes, other studies have documented the ways in which internal fragmentation and competition have reduced the potential for mobilizing the informal resources needed for business formation. As I have found in my own previous work comparing African American, Caribbean, Korean, and Euro-American construction contractors, African Americans have had the greatest difficulty in mobilizing and securing the loyalty of their coethnics (Waldinger 1996, chap. 8). Similarly, as we shall see later, the employers in the low-skilled sector also perceive African Americans to differ from immigrants in their ability to access informal help in much the same terms.

However, arguing that the social structure of less skilled African

Americans is less dense and cohesive than the pattern found among Mexican and Central American immigrants does not imply anomie. The tendency of African American workers to converge on a narrow set of niches, discussed in other chapters of this book as well as in my own previous research (Waldinger 1996; Waldinger and Bozorgmehr 1996), provides implicit testimony to the strength of African American social networks: At the very least, African Americans observe the disparity of their coethnics in specialized sectors of the economy and use that information as a signal for action. Indeed, we know that more is involved: As I have shown in my case study of the ethnic politics of municipal jobs (Waldinger 1996, chap. 7), black civil servants assiduously activate social connections to place their kin and associates in government work.

Yet it does appear that those social networks function most effectively in organizations with other incentives to increase the employment of African American workers. Government, the prime black niche, is both an employment structure of great transparency and one that is responsive to electoral pressure, which increases the pressure for monitoring. In the private sector, African Americans are likely to concentrate in those sectors dominated by large organizations—in which bureaucratic practices reduce the importance of close ties in the hiring process and size increases visibility and, therefore, the incentives to monitor. Thus, the more heavily an organization depends on informal recruitment practices and the less institutionalized its personnel function, the more likely immigrants will find room to exercise exclusionary closure against African Americans.

METHODOLOGY

Although this paper builds on my earlier case studies of immigrant employment (Waldinger 1996), the approach taken here is inspired by Joleen Kirschenman and Kathryn Neckerman's (1991) research on employer hiring practices in Chicago: Interested in discrimination, Kirschenman and Neckerman opted for in-depth interviews with a relatively small sample of employers, focusing directly on hiring practices. Their findings have drawn considerable attention, because they discovered that employers often take race and ethnicity quite explicitly into account in hiring decisions. However, the methodology has also proved attractive, because in-depth interviews with employers offer considerable advantages over the more conventional statistical analyses of large-scale microdata sets. As Philip Moss and Chris Tilly have noted, "Face to face, open-ended interviewing . . . generates rich, detailed data, and has the flexibility to accommodate and follow up on responses that are unexpected or do not fit predetermined categories. The informal, conversational tone of the interview helps to get respondents involved and interested, and creates a situation in which employers are more likely to speak freely about sensitive subjects such as race" (Moss and Tilly 1991, 3).

This chapter is based on in-depth interviews, conducted in 1993 and 1994, with managers and owners in 230 establishments in Los Angeles County: 44 restaurants, 46 printers, 41 hotels, 39 furniture manufacturers, 24 department stores, and 36 hospitals.[2] The industries selected allow for comparison along a number of dimensions, including size, bureaucratization, and degree of immigrant and African American representation. With the exception of the restaurant sample, which was drawn from the Yellow Pages and designed to include both chains (varying in size from 3 to 55 units) and single-owned operations, the sample was drawn randomly from business directories.[3] The organizations were located in a variety of areas within Los Angeles County, both within the central city and in more suburbanized areas. The interviews were arranged with the highest-ranking person involved in the hiring process, and they were structured by an instrument involving a mix of fixed and open-ended questions. In the beginning of the interview, we identified the largest category of low-skilled jobs and then focused the remainder of our discussion on those jobs and the workers who filled them. The interviews lasted from an hour and a half to three hours. In some cases, interviews were recorded and subsequently transcribed; in other instances, detailed notes were made of interviewees' responses.

NETWORKS AND EXCLUSIONARY CLOSURE

Network Versus Market

Managers and owners viewed referrals favorably for a variety of reasons, a number of which had to do with deficiencies of the alternative methods. Those shortcomings had little to do with the volume of applicants. "They walk in regularly," the human resources manager at a hotel explained; a retailer in the San Fernando Valley observed that "you get them all the time." One of the hospital informants reported that "It's just because people, I mean, we have so many people just coming in off the street a day. I guess it's just the access, you know, coming in. You get members who come for doctor's appointments, end up here lost, and then they see our job board. Those kinds of things."

Although yielding considerable traffic, walk-ins were less likely to produce the right applicant mix. "We know that the people are out there, but higher caliber people aren't walking in." As one interviewee noted, job seekers with the time to canvass employer after employer are more likely to be jobless for good reason. "The disadvantage of walk-ins is that the people are unemployed. It sounds funny, but the most employable person has a job. If you want to attract employable people, you would want to attract people with a job."

Employers unable to do more than select from the flow of applicants drawn in off the street were unlikely to be pleased with the results, forced to "tak[e] what is there" and left reliant on either the local labor supply or else less-skilled help than was desired. Some entry-level positions were so simple and dead-end that recourse to the least desirable help mattered little; other entry-level jobs, although unattractive as such, stood at the bottom of the job ladder, making employers eager to hire people who might move up. An entry from my field notes reports of one company that "under normal times, they'll take one or two joggers per year. 'They don't line up at the door.' Some college students consider that work beneath them. At times, they can't get entry-level people who also have the potential to grow. So referrals are important."

More problematic were matters related to information. Thanks to their size and visibility, the larger, more public facilities—like the department stores or hospitals—attracted a sizable applicant flow with little or no effort; but sorting through all the job hunters was an unenviable task, forcing employers "to fish through about one hundred applicants," as one retailer noted discontentedly. The effort often proved unproductive: "I don't see the specific skills for different departments with walk-ins." Moreover, random job seekers rarely arrived with an appropriate orientation toward the job. "Many of the applicants do not understand what the job entails, the hours involved, nor the fact that it is a service industry," grumbled a discounter. Some walk-ins, not sufficiently knowledgeable, also sent the wrong signals. "If a person doesn't know much about our store, and we ask them, 'What brought you here,' they will usually mention the pay, the benefits, the employee discount. We're not interested in those people. We want people who are prepared to do hard work. Someone who's referred knows what goes into working here."

More important were information inadequacies on the employer side. Perceiving walk-ins as "coming out of the woodwork," employers found assessments of the job match hard to make. "I will ask one of the waiters for a referral before hiring a walk-in," said the owner of an upscale restaurant on the West Side of Los Angeles. "I don't know someone who comes in through the door." Because most jobs entail some degree of interdependency, compatibility between incumbents and employees of unknown quality was also a worry. "With the walk-ins, you don't really know their personalities, and maybe if there is a conflict or a difference of opinion this person might freak out."

Advertisements in newspapers generate a bigger draw, "bring[ing] in the most numbers,"as one discounter noted. "I just think that they reach a larger population." They also spanned the entire market, attracting a crowd of applicants that was likely to be more diverse than those who just walked in off the street. Those features were not equally valued by all, however. Those employers who gave newspaper advertising bad reviews complained about costs entailed in paying for an ad—not a trivial consideration when advertising in the *Los Angeles Times,* which, in any case, was better suited for "attracting skilled workers who at least read the *L.A. Times* and have to buy it." More displeasing were the administrative pains entailed in absorbing the large flow of applicants that an advertisement inevitably generated. Stirring up the labor force only complicated life for those employers who drew their labor force from the bottom of the labor market. "If I put an ad in a newspaper, I get one hundred applicants for every one position," groused a hotel manager, whose counterpart in an upscale hotel explained, "I can do without getting the numbers of people in here. For a position like steward or housekeeping, we get over two hundred applicants in (a) four-hour period." For all these reasons, employers of the least skilled help were likely to view advertising as a last resort.

For many, however, it was preferable to the "huge time factor" involved in the volume of interviewing walk-in applicants. Advertising was a more serviceable tool for attracting the right type of applicants than passive reliance on the flow of workers off the street: "If we run an ad and are very specific about what we are looking for, we often get a better-quality candidate than if we rely on walk-in traffic." The larger audience reached through advertising had a similar appeal, as noted by a retailer who contrasted a suburban store—which got by through reliance on random job seekers—and a downtown location, where "we have to do a lot more because the walk-in candidates are not necessarily qualified." Nonetheless, advertisements often failed to send the right signals, or perhaps did not send the signals in ways that were effectively received, producing inquiries from applicants who lacked the desired characteristics. One printer noted that advertisements were very successful in generating lots of applicants, mainly because "they don't understand the ad." "We get a lot of people who'll call in and want to know about a job, and they have no experience," exclaimed a restaurant owner. "I wonder why they called, since the ad specifies 'experienced waitress.'" Nor did advertising do much to ensure selectivity, "bring[ing] in the numbers, but not the qualifications." Having to "fish through one hundred applications to find three or four [with] what we're looking for," as noted by a discounter, left many managers unhappy.

Not only did employers have to grapple with the costs entailed in sifting through the large number of recruits generated by advertisements, they then had to deal with the issue of how to screen those applicants who seemed eligible. Because newspapers directed "quite a bit of flakes" toward employers' doors, problems related to the quality of information loomed large. "We don't know much of the person," explained a personnel manager of a furniture factory with two different locations in the Los Angeles area. "It is difficult to know whether that person will turn out to be good or not."

To resolve informational uncertainties, the employer had to verify the details of an applicant's record, which involved no small effort. In many cases, there was little or no information to be had, as noted by one hospital manager, who contrasted professional positions—"where there are resumes and references and other things that we use, as well"—with the situation of a janitor, "especially a walk-in, [where] we typically don't have a lot of information except what we have in the application and through the interview process." Employers intent on digging into an applicant's background also had to be prepared to bear the costs: "If you're trying to get five people, you have to make sure the information is complete, review the applications, screen. It's more time-consuming than when someone makes a referral." Many employers were still disposed to make that effort, but not for all classes of labor, as noted by a factory owner who distinguished between truck drivers, for whom background checks "were much more critical," and warehouse workers, for whom references were "not important." In addition to skill and responsibility, organizational factors came into play; the larger, more bureaucratized organizations were the most likely to insist on a formal screening. Nevertheless, large numbers in all six industries were abandoning the attempt to secure references; for example, a retailer claimed that "trying to get information about past employment was a waste of time"; a manufacturer said that "we generally don't call references on those kinds of jobs because you usually don't get an honest reply"; and a hospital manager still did reference checks "when available. In this day and age, 'Oh, the company went out of business.' You know, that gets really tough."

For most organizations, the informational problem boils down to social structure—or, rather, its absence among employers in the metropolis, which makes opportunism rife. It is one thing to "get information informally from people we have a relationship with," explained a restaurateur, quite another thing to expect to get "quality references with a cold phone call." Informal connections helped: One owner, for example, contrasted the human resources department of a large firm, which "might just confirm that the former employee did work there," with "smaller companies [that] tend to be more cooperative." In some cases, employers were part of a "grapevine" through which they could directly or indirectly access the relevant information. "Printers are a close-knit group," explained a vice president for manufacturing. "We talk among ourselves. If you know the company, you can call them and ask what kind of an employee the person was."

Better yet were referrals from current employees, who have an interest in opening up, as opposed to "a lot of companies [that] are not willing to release any information." A printing plant in East Los Angeles carefully checked references for skilled workers brought in from the outside but saw no reason to follow the same practice when hiring workers at the entry level, who were typically brought in through referrals: "Our people wouldn't put someone in here who just wants to get a paycheck because they're concerned about their own well-being." Similarly, the manager of a steak house, which relied on references from a tight-knit group of Mexican workers to fill kitchen jobs but engaged in more formal procedures when hiring waiters, called references for the front-of-the-house jobs but rarely bothered to do the same for workers in the back. For many employers—especially the smaller outfits and the manufacturers—personal contacts obviated the need to collect information through official channels. "I don't call previous employers," noted the president of a manufacturing concern, "because to a certain extent my employees are doing the screening for me." Asked if the foreman of his company calls previous employers to check out a reference, one respondent replied, "If the position is important, yes; if not, no. For the machine operator, no. We're more interested in his attitude, his basic moral charge. Another employee recommended him, that to us is good enough. And most of the time, if there is something negative, they will usually tell us. We don't have a problem with having someone who's just spent six months in jail because he had a parking ticket or something that he didn't take care of."

Network Hiring as Social Reproduction

Thus far, the material tells a familiar story: The social connections among workers, and between workers and employers, facilitate economic action. "Hiring is a risk," as a department store manager pointed out, and the search for risk reduction leads to network recruitment, which improves both the quality and the quantity of information that workers and employers need. Efficiency is all to be valued, and especially by sociologists when they find that a social, as opposed to market, process provides the more useful container. As is often the case, however, efficiency involves an equity trade-off; in this case, workers without contacts to incumbents lose out when it comes to access to job information.

Exclusion is the natural by-product of reliance on referrals, if only because network recruitment inherently involves a process of social reproduction. Thus, the employers we interviewed were quick to point to a basic network principle—homophily, or the tendency of socially similar people to band together. "Friends of friends, friends of employees, word of mouth, it's as if they've all worked together, they all, it's a community type of thing, it's a networking type of thing." Similarity among persons within the same recruitment network means that referrals are likely to originate from an appropriate applicant pool. "All these people know someone who has been working in the related industry, and when they become aware that jobs are available, they will bring a brother, cousin, or neighbor in." Given a tight community where "you get the same people who are working together kind of hanging around in the same area, when the job opening occurs they do communicate with one another, saying that there's a job opening." In this situation, word of mouth ensures that information leaks out to the appropriate occupational community. "Almost everyone who applies here has worked in some other furniture company," explained a plant manager, and as for those without comparable experience, "we don't look at them." "Lots of waitresses, that's all they've been doing," noted the owner of a coffee shop. "I just ask them and they call their friends or co-workers." Both kitchen workers and waiters seem to have privileged access to a supply of qualified workers: "They [my workers] know everybody in the business. It's a very tight community. All you have to do is ask one of your workers or your cooks if they know someone in the market, and they'll always satisfy the needs. I don't know someone who comes in through the door. They [the workers] know if a guy's a thief or rude to customers because of socializing outside." A furniture manufacturer similarly noted that referrals pull in candidates from other factories, too. "We rely a lot on employee referrals. Because they know people who work in other factories that are unhappy."

The tendency to hire persons socially similar with respect to occupational backgrounds carries over to ethnic backgrounds as well—no surprise, considering that the common predilection for convergence on an ethnic niche steers groups toward some economic specializations and not others. "Once one has one Hispanic you have two or three more, and this brings about a chain reaction. The same thing happened with our accounting department: Once we hired an Asian, they seemed to be all Asian." Hotels display a distinct ethnic division of labor, with Mexicans and Central Americans dominating housekeeping and the kitchen; blacks in security, parking, and the front office; Filipinos working as accountants, night managers, and clerical workers; and whites employed as waiters in restaurants and bars. Manufacturing plants tend to have a heavily Hispanic tilt on the shop floor; office operations frequently look different, however, as in one furniture manufacturer where the "entire accounting department is from the Philippines." The ethnic consequences of network hiring are even more vividly seen in the restaurants; relying on two hiring strategies—walk-ins, to fill front-of-the-house jobs, and referrals, to get kitchen workers—yields a pattern in which "the front is a little bit of everything, whites, blacks, Asians" whereas the kitchen is an exclusively Latino world. In general for the managers we interviewed, the past served as prologue, favoring ongoing recruitment from the established source, regardless of the group involved. Thus, even black workers in the hospital industry—an industry with relatively high levels of African American employment—found that network recruitment could work in their favor, as in the case of a public hospital in South Central Los Angeles in which a human resources manager told us that "at the hospital, in this area, it's predominantly black. Most people out here are from the area. It's hard to get into unless you know someone's sister, uncle, aunt." Similarly, a private hospital that employed a large black workforce experienced a high black applicant rate but could secure Latino workers only through active recruitment efforts and an affirmative action program.

Although all groups displayed a tendency toward convergence on particular occupational or industrial niches, employers emphasized the immigrant factor. "Many are immigrants, and they seem to look out for each other. These immigrants network much more than any other group." Given the demographic diversity of Los Angeles, "immigrant" can refer to any number of groups. Our interest, however, was focused on entry-level jobs; when we asked employers why they recruited through referrals, they were most likely to respond with reference to the Mexican and Central American workforce—"the Mexican Mafia," to quote a regional fast-food executive—that dominated bottom ranks and which "nine times out of ten provides someone the next day."

In explaining the pattern, employers highlighted two types of factors, one of which falls under the rubric of embeddedness. A preference for ongoing relations, for accepting the referrals produced by incumbents with track records, simply led to more of the same. "When we do the networking with our current Hispanic workforce," noted one furniture manufacturer, "they are bringing in other Hispanics"; another explained that "90 percent of our workforce out there is Hispanic, and all of these people know someone who has been working in the related industry, and when they become aware that jobs are available, they will bring a brother, cousin, or neighbor in."

In the employers' eyes, the ability to furnish referrals was also related to the structure of the networks and communities to which Mexican and Central American workers were attached. A furniture manufacturer told us that "over the years, reliance on referrals has led us to a largely Hispanic workforce. They are very social. I don't want to sound racist, but I never met a lonely Mexican. They all have extended families." A printer struck the same note, explaining that "a Hispanic household has extended family—friends, neighbors. They always know someone who needs a job." A restaurant manager told me, "The back is filled almost strictly from referrals. The kitchen workers have a lot of friends and cousins. And we don't have much turnover. They have ten people waiting in the wings. We opened a new restaurant this summer. I hired all the waiters from walk-ins; all the back-of-the-house workers came from referrals."

Put somewhat differently, these employers valued the strength of strong ties for their predictive value; for that reason, if no other, groups with stronger ties were more likely to benefit from a preference to hire from within. Whatever the precise motivation to mobilize connections to the Latino workforce, one result was a work world in which "everyone knows each other," to quote a Euro-American factory owner. A furniture manufacturer described his factory as a "grandfather, father, son situation." "We have a very large Hispanic population," recounted the production manager in an East Los Angeles printing plant, "and they all have cousins and uncles. Everyone in the open web department is related. The sisters are in the bindery, and some of them are related to people in the open web department." A production manager estimated that "almost 60 percent of the workers are family related. Many of them are compadres and comadres because they have known each other for so long." One Christmas, a hotel discovered that it "gave everyone turkeys [before] realizing that we gave the same family twenty turkeys. At least half of the maids are from one family, and the other half probably is from another. The executive housekeeper's assistant is her sister."

Network Hiring as a Self-Activating Process

Employers' accounts often suggested that they consciously mobilized connections between incumbents and outsiders to secure the desired workforce. The information flows are also activated by employees, whose contacts invariably extend to people looking for jobs. Just as social connections secure jobs for persons who are not actively looking—a conceptual problem of nontrivial importance for the job-search literature—social networks produce applicants for employers who do not yet have vacancies to fill. "Fifty percent of our people come from referrals," explained the human resources manager for a VA hospital: "They know someone, tell someone, have a friend fill out the application. We have a lot of people who have friends with applications already filled out; we have encouraged them to do that. If you can't come everyday, have someone keep a lookout for you. They will give in an application the day the notice is posted. Then the supervisor could get the person that day and hire that day."

As this example suggests, incumbents keep themselves busy—or are kept busy—finding places for their associates. "If he [a brother of an employee] is not working, they'll approach us. 'Do you need a new polisher?'" "We usually have a waiting list of friends from the existing employees," explained a factory owner. "Most of the time we have people waiting to come to work." A production manager told us that "there are always people looking for a job who know people here and would like to get a foot in the door."

Ongoing relationships between job seekers outside the organization and incumbents, with inside information about hiring needs, means that control over hiring patterns often slips out of management's hands. In larger, more bureaucratic establishments, contacts between incumbents and job seekers are crucial for finding a place on the line before the rest of the world finds out; in smaller establishments, workers have access to more information than bosses, which means that incumbents take care of any recruitment before an employer realizes that vacancies might arise. "Referrals occur before the vacancy appears," a printer told us. "Everybody out there knows about it before we do. People put an application in on the first day, and then the brother reminds us of it." Connections among co-workers yield another source of inside information. "Around here," noted one of the respondents in our hotel sample, "someone says, 'I'm going to resign in two weeks,' and the next day I have applications for a job that may or may not be vacant." Often, the workers know better than their bosses, who report that "the least amount of knowledge the [workers] can share [with the bosses], the happier they are." A furniture factory manager reported, "I have people coming to apply for jobs and I say there is no openings out there and they say but Jose is going to quit; they have already heard about it before I even have the job posted."

Moreover, the self-activating nature of network recruitment often makes it resistant to management's efforts at short-circuiting the process, regardless of the formality of the hiring process and the particular organizational context. One of the hospitals we visited, which surveyed its employees twice a year, found that 95 percent of the new hires came from employee referrals; the personnel manager explained that "we do place a lot of ads but it usually ends up that somebody is a friend of somebody who works here, and that's how they've gotten in." Similarly, a small community hospital posts job openings with the private industrial council and the employment service but to no avail, because applications from in-house postings arrive first. "The employees really keep a good eye 'cause they want to bring their families and friends in." For reasons of equity—"It's not fair to just go out there and tell the good worker about a vacancy"—a furniture factory puts a "Help Wanted" sign in front of the plant when new workers are needed; but, as the plant manager noted, "It's the same as telling the employees." One factory owner switched from network recruitment to newspaper advertising as a means of upgrading the labor force, but this required running a blind ad with no mention of the factory's name, address, or phone number. "When the name of the company was in the ad," the owner pointed out, "the existing referrals would bring the people in." Ties between incumbents and applicants are so powerful that a reliance on recruitment methods of the formal kind fails to shut down the mechanics of informal hiring networks. One public-sector human resources official relates that

we have a lot of family members that work, you know, everybody's cousin works here, and sister, and, you know, brother-in-law and stuff like that. So I think there is a lot of. . . . Because what we do is if we have a job posted over at the employee's cafeteria, saying, you know, ITCs, you know, "Open testing soon, please apply," something like that. So people call up all their friends and go, "Hey, they're hiring." So probably there were a lot more referrals than we know of.

BUREAUCRACY AND THE LIMITS TO
NETWORK PENETRATIONS

Thus far, I have told a story about networks and the ways in which the penetration of ethnic networks into formally "open" organizations enlarges opportunities for ethnic insiders while reducing access to outsiders. As I argued in the introduction, however, hiring involves selection as well as recruitment. In some cases, organizations make little or no effort at selection, or they rely on the networks to select the desired labor force; but any attempt to implement formalized selection procedures will inevitably reduce the range of network penetrations.

Formalization

Many of the organizations studied dispensed with bureaucratic means of selection, if only because networks can often provide more and better quality information than that obtained through bureaucratic means. "The supervisor does an interview—a 'marginal' one. The employee referring the applicant has already been asked if the applicant will fit in" (quoted from my field notes). The nature of the job and the characteristics of the organization itself come into play, as well. Restaurants, for example, seemed to do little to sort out applicants, whether referred by their existing kitchen workforce or not. "I talk to the person over the counter for forty-five seconds, literally," said one fast-food operator. "I can decide rather quickly whether this person has the needed qualities." Time pressures, and the need to add bodies quickly, also led employers to skimp on screening, as the manager for a regional chain pointed out. "Are they available? Can they work the schedule? Can you work Saturdays from three to closing. If you say yes, that takes care of a lot of things from the manager's point of view."

The situation in manufacturing was not all that different. Referral networks certainly gave applicants with connections a foot in the door; the manufacturers were particularly likely to value the information provided by incumbent workers, leading them to dispense with more formal checks and, in some cases, with any other effort at screening. Although most manufacturers did more, almost always choosing to interview, those efforts generally took a rudimentary form. Screening procedures were apt to be informal, relying on a manager's or owner's intuition and varying from one situation to the next. Smaller manufacturers rarely maintained a specialized personnel function, instead delegating hiring decisions to a supervisor who was likely to have come up from the ranks, as well. Beyond the interviews, some firms also engaged in an informal, skills-related assessment, but performance-related assessments of a more formal sort were relatively infrequent. Even the smallest firms were unlikely to be equally lax when hiring for more-skilled jobs—small size, traditional organizational forms, and industry subcultures notwithstanding. As long as "you can tell in a day if they are going to be any good"—a statement that seemed to hold true for the many entry-level production jobs "where if you don't cut it in a week, you're gone"—the nature of work at the lowest level rarely demanded a more intensive effort at selection.

Screening procedures were likely to be more elaborate in the hotels, with efforts to assess an applicant's potential more extensive the larger and more high-priced the hotel. As sizable units of large, often international chains, hotels typically maintained a human resource office, and the presence of a personnel function yielded considerable standardization in screening efforts. To be sure, referral networks played an important role in recruitment, but then personnel took over. Although the jobs were unskilled, they offered ample opportunity for theft and, as in the case of housekeepers, involved work of considerable autonomy; consequently, hotel managers consistently checked references, even though that procedure yielded little information, as personnel officials unhappily acknowledged. "We try to get as much information as we can," complained one human resource director, "but people increasingly just give out data, position held, length of employment. This is often hard to get over the phone." Consequently, the interview also served as a crucial selection tool, though one that hotel managers wielded with more care than their counterparts in restaurants or manufacturing. A common practice is to "use a behavioral interviewing process, giving specific examples of when they did this or that. 'Describe the time you got upset at a co-worker, what did you do?'" Procedures have also been designed to assess more directly how an applicant is likely to interact with others. One hotel, for example, conducted group interviews; another did a team inter-

view, in which an applicant was interviewed by a manager, a supervisor, and an hourly worker at the same time. "The hourly employee
can relate experiences, can ask questions that the department head or
supervisor won't ask as quickly." In most cases, personnel screened the
applicants, making an initial recommendation to a functional manager, who also interviewed and then selected a candidate.

Hotels thus followed a standardized and formalized procedure for
screening applicants, though as the chief tool involved a face-to-face
interview, the method inevitably contained a certain informal element. By contrast, the department stores and larger hospitals, in particular those in the public sector, used screening procedures of an
even more formalized sort, with extensive reliance on testing as well
as the usual background checks and interviews. Of course, any interpersonal situation, such as the interview, always involved considerable
informality, in which decisions were usually made by rule of thumb.
If the interview and the selection criteria followed a nonstandardized
format, the department stores interviewed consistently, systematically,
and at great length—in contrast with restaurants and manufacturers.
Moreover, screening typically involved multiple steps, which, in turn,
reduced the advantages enjoyed by members of a referral network.
Typically, successful hires first underwent a review by a lower-level
personnel officer, next an interview with the human resources manager, then an interview with the relevant department manager, and, in
some cases, final interviews with the big bosses themselves. Along the
way, most applicants were forced to submit to a variety of tests designed not so much to assess skills as to forecast behavior in jobs, such
as selling, that involved considerable autonomy and unpredictable interactions with customers.

Thus, for reasons having to do with organizational features and the
characteristics of the jobs, screening among department stores took a
highly elaborated form, making bureaucracy rather than network the
critical factor whereby workers were matched with jobs. Hospitals
presented a similar, though distinctive, pattern. Procedures were likely
to be standardized, with a preference for application forms, background checks, and interviews with personnel as well as line officials.
Notwithstanding the size and complexity of the institutions, however,
informality often ruled when it came to the criteria used to select
bottommost help. "If it's an entry-level person," explained a manager
for one of the region's major nonprofit HMOs (health management
organizations), "more often than not, the manager or the supervisor
that's interviewing those people, he's going to, you know, get a fairly
good gut feeling for that individual" and do no more. Tests were also

not a commonplace for such entry-level jobs as janitor or dietary aide, though more prevalent when used to pick clerical help.

As the only one of our six industries with a sizable public-sector component, hospitals offer a particularly good example of formalized selection procedures, and their effects on hiring outcomes. Because the civil service framework gives individual institutions limited flexibility in their hiring, it severely curtails the influence of ethnic networks. In some cases, managers lose autonomy altogether, as in the case of a veterans' hospital, where the office of personnel management "took away direct hiring, because people started looking to work for the Feds. We weren't using OPM's people. None of us were." Even when hiring does not follow the exam route, other restrictions, such as an imperative to hire veterans wherever possible, sometimes constrain managers' decision making.

More importantly, perhaps, the civil service framework keeps job requirements high, in part because the high volume of the applicant flow yields no pressure to lower demands.

A: (resp. 1) Here, we did an exam for clerk, it was a temporary clerk, but it had no experience required.

Q: And no typing?

A: (resp. 1) And no typing. And we got 800 applications in two days.

A: (resp. 2) But that doesn't mean. . . . We only have probably thirty, forty vacancies, if that.

A: (resp. 1) It was just amazing that we got that many applications.

A: (resp. 2) Because typically we would like a little bit more of a skill, because that gives us the flexibility of utilizing someone. And almost everyone needs them to have some kind of keyboard knowledge.

A: (resp. 1) But even on the exam process, even though we got 800, only 140 passed the exam.

Q: Is that the normal ratio?

A: (resp. 1) Well, it wasn't in the past, but today it is. Yeah, that's reading and comprehension and spelling, and it becomes a major issue in terms of having these skills needed just to pass an exam. Shows a change in skill level. Coming out of the schools.

A: (resp. 2) Coming out of the schools. And it is unfortunate. And it's something we're concerned about.

Whereas these managers in a local public hospital system were satisfied that, because the exam had been officially validated, it tested fairly for the competencies required by the job, other respondents were not quite so sure. A respondent at a hospital in the same system told us that "the clerk [exam] is a high rate of fail, probably the highest" and also noted that "people would get so bogged down with the math, they couldn't get to the end of the test." Likewise, a human resources manager in a military-related hospital contended that "some people with reasonable clerical skills don't take the test well," and noted that "when we were able to examine directly, the quality was better."

Of course, all these characteristics mean that civil service requirements and procedures make government an effective institutional barrier to competition from most immigrants. Rules are rules, and they generally work well in excluding newcomers, who lack the credentials, experience, or even English-language facility that public-sector hospitals require.

> The only requirement is they pass both the tests, and then they're put on the eligibility list. So we have some people who have made out the application, passed the test, passed the typing test, we send them to interview, and they're absolutely, we don't know, we can't figure how they passed the test. They can't even talk. I mean they, it's kind of like, especially Asians, we don't know how they passed the test. Because it's kind of like they can't speak English. You ask them a question and they don't know what the hell you're talking about. Yet they pass the exam, they can read. Because the exam is held under very strict [procedures], we have proctors there to make sure that nobody takes the test for somebody else. And we have to have their driver's license there. I mean it's a very extensive closed exam. And we sit in on interviews and we get people and they say, "How did that person pass the test?" Because they can't put two sentences together. So they don't ever get hired, ultimately hired.

Note that the same procedures that keep immigrants out of entry-level public-sector jobs affect less skilled African Americans in just the same way.

Legitimacy

Despite its many virtues, network hiring is a practice that not every employer has rushed to embrace. As noted, network hiring reproduces the characteristics of the existing labor force, yielding the "'like-me' syndrome," as the manager of a fast-food chain pointed out. Not all employers sought to pursue this goal. "With referrals you get very homogeneous groups," noted the owner of a South Bay furniture factory. "There is a problem with only one group." One problem was of particular concern to some employers: the fact that referral networks "tend to have biases and traits, and you are forced in that direction." As one factory owner explained,

A: If you are not careful you end up with all Hispanics. And I am a little bit nervous that I have too many Hispanics and not enough blacks.

Q: Nervous in what sense?

A: Are you familiar with affirmative action terminology? We will end up with a concentration of Hispanics and an underutilization of blacks. And I think in areas I have that. I don't have any government contracts, I am not an affirmative action employer, but it is something that I am sensitive about.

The anxiety quotient was not high enough to drastically change practices in this one factory, though the employer was at pains to ensure that the Hispanic clerical workers did not control the flow of new hires. Other employers did much more. Conceding that referrals were more likely to be "good workers, they're usually just, I mean, real reliable, dependable," hospital managers knew that dependence on referrals would inevitably, and undesirably, give their workforce a distinctive cast.

A: Sometimes it gets too tight like the old Boeing network . . . and we have to remember to remain diverse. So that's one problem because a lot of times you're just referring certain ethnic groups or something like that.

Q: But so you take steps to deter that from happening?

A: Right, right.

Q: What kind of—so that would just be not taking any more referrals?

A: Or, no, not necessarily, but if some, if you just start getting a lot of referrals, then your affirmative action goal is something else. You just have to do outside recruiting. You can't take those referrals.

Hospital managers were also conscious that reliance on referrals could change the balance of power, often in ways that did not suit management's interests. "I, really, I try to keep a pretty broad spectrum of ethnic groups in the kitchen so we don't get too many cliques. It would be real easy to have an all Filipino kitchen."

Both the department stores and the hospitals were at particular pains to avoid the pattern of single-group dominance found at the back of the house in kitchens or hotels and on furniture factory floors. Both industries sought to serve a diverse clientele, and that imperative pushed them toward outreach while also breeding an aversion to reliance on hiring through workers' contacts. "Diversity is in both our customers and our workforce, and we want to bring it [further] into our workforce," explained a department store manager. A unit of one of the region's most important HMOs saw diversity "as a reality based on, from the personnel standpoint, on our applicant pool; from a business standpoint, from our membership. You want to have a workforce that's representative and can respond to the needs of our members." A department store manager told us that clientele and employees "parallel each other steadily. You need to truly understand that you have a melting pot in your workforce, and you have to look at your workforce and clientele objectively as a marketing group." For these reasons, the pool of employees should "reflect the cultural diversity of your clientele. If I could hire 10 percent black, 10 percent Filipino, 8 percent white, 7 percent Hispanic, and really get it in line with what's really going on, as far as how people live in this area . . . what more could you ask for?" Although the ethnic composition of the clientele can vary—yielding, in one case, a workforce that is "white, because it matches the demographics of the area"—that same consideration of seeking "to match our store to the people who come to the store" motivates managers to "try hard to have Spanish-speaking people, and the Middle Eastern language group (Iranians, Afghans, Armenian)."

One should not take from this that hospitals or department stores had been bitten by the multicultural bug; rather, they were simply listening to the marketplace, which told them that sensitivity to ethnic matters counted, and then responding in appropriate ways. Customers "don't just notice the merchandise," explained a manager at an old-line department store, "they look at the people who are working there." That consideration made diversity desirable: "When you are out hiring folks . . . make sure to, consciously make sure, that we have a wide variety of people working at the store, so many blacks, so many Hispanics, and that seems to help business a lot." Not only do customers pay attention to the composition of the people trying to service their needs; they are also willing to express their unhappiness about the faces they do (or do not) see. A top-of-the-line department store in the South Bay received "letters from African American customers asking, 'Where are the African American employees?'"; the firm is "now training to focus on an African American base." Noting that "the biggest challenge I have is getting the right candidate into the store," one manager underlined the impact of customers' ethnic preferences: "I have customers in Huntington Beach who do not want someone who is Korean and Vietnamese waiting on them. . . . Conversely I have a customer in West Covina who is East Asian or Hispanic, and sometimes they are extremely uncomfortable in being waited on by someone who is Caucasian." Considerations such as these led stores not only to recruit among a diverse pool but also to engage in monitoring practices that would ensure adequate representation of the different components of the customer base. "I like to have a balanced workforce," explained a department store manager. "It's always on our mind. We get monthly printouts on hiring and diversity, so we know if we're short."

Thus, the search for a workforce that mirrors the customer base necessarily leads employers away from a reliance on network hiring. Dependence on referrals yields a homogeneity that is doubly unwanted, as it reduces organizations' ability to deal effectively with their diverse clientele and makes the clientele suspect that the organization treats some groups of workers and customers differently from others. But the need to achieve balance can still have exclusionary consequences in a context where one group's numbers are at best holding steady while another's are swelling. Such is the case in hospitals, where the need to service a growing non-English-speaking population—"we have a lot of Spanish-speaking members that come in, and we call for translation a lot"—swells demand for a skill likely to be unevenly shared among the region's demographic groups. "We desperately need bilingual people," reported a manager in a facility with a very large black workforce, and indeed, many hospitals viewed bilingualism as a plus, sufficiently so that it moved bilingual applicants higher up in the hiring queue: "Many of the positions that we have is [sic] bilingual. So I will look at, do they speak Spanish? Yep, well then, they go into another stack. Not that I discriminate based on bilingual, but it's something that is a skill that is used here, required of many jobs."

Although demands to service customers who do not speak English will only grow, so too will the availability of bilingual speakers. Moreover, the children of immigrants with the baseline skills needed to work as dietary aides or housekeepers are entering the labor market in growing numbers, and to the extent that they have some facility in two languages, they will increasingly have an advantage over native-born blacks: "We have a large ethnic patient population, and to an extent our patients' access to medical care has improved with having people that they can communicate with. So one of our objectives is having a diverse workforce, which mirrors our diverse patient population."

The need for bilingual speakers is particularly acute in precisely that sector where blacks are most overrepresented—namely, the public hospitals—because these are the facilities most heavily used by Latino immigrants. Although dominated by poorly educated Mexicans and Central Americans, the region's foreign-born population is very diverse; higher-skilled newcomers from Asia or the Middle East are more likely to have adequate competency in English and also possess other skills that hospitals want. Moreover, the demand for English is more a soft than a hard constraint in its impact on the influx of the foreign-born. The hospitals already abound in the use of languages other than English, and that trend will only increase as the demography of the region increasingly reflects the presence of the foreign-born—yet another factor weakening African Americans' hold on this traditional niche.

CONCLUSION

The social connections among immigrants get good play in the sociological literature, in part, no doubt, because of the analytic power that the concept of the immigrant social network packs. The networks can be accurately characterized as structures "with history and continuity that give [them] an independent effect on the function of economic systems," as James Coleman has maintained (Coleman 1988, S97). There is probably also an affinity between the sociologists' professional biases and the virtues they detect in the networks they seek to describe. After all, the dominant picture is one in which embeddedness in ethnic networks and communities leads to cooperative, if not conformist, behavior among ethnic economic actors. Although *homo societas* may be preferable to *homo economicus*, an undue emphasis on cooperation, conformity, and solidarity is a source of analytical weakness, as sociology as learned in the past.

Moreover, the now conventional wisdom about immigrants' social capital fails to unravel the most puzzling aspect of the immigrant employment scene: It is one thing to observe, with Walter Powell and Laurel Smith-Doerr (1994), that "even the disadvantaged can turn to networks to provide access to opportunities not available on the open market" (374) and quite another to explain why those networks should so consistently expand their reach. After all, the network structures are "wrong," in that weak, not strong, ties are the key to gaining access to new sources of employment; and the network associates are of the "wrong" type, as well, because their socioeconomic characteristics make them unlikely to form those weak ties to others in positions of influence, which the network literature tells us is a must. Immigrants, however, are rich in strong ties—and it is a good thing, too, because jobs and job information are too scarce to be distributed to one who is weakly connected. Furthermore, employers turn to immigrant networks not simply for reasons of mimesis or filtering (DiMaggio and Powell 1983) but because the social-closure potential of immigrants' networks generates additional predictive value. Thus, the repeated action of network hiring leads to the cumulation of informal immigrant resources; over time, immigrant workers gain the potential for the exercise of power, as network associates can mobilize their connections in ways inimical to the interests of outsiders.

Clearly, exclusionary closure is not a property of immigrant networks alone; the same processes of social reproduction evident in immigrant-dominated industries recur in those segments of the economy—such as the public sector—where African Americans are overrepresented. However, as immigrant densities in the low-skill sector grow, so too do the obstacles to less-skilled African American workers. The implantation of immigrant networks tends to detach vacancies from the open market, for reasons having to do with efficiency as well as the social-closure potential of immigrant networks. To be sure, some black workers nonetheless find a way in. However, the environment in industries like hotels, restaurants, and furniture manufacturing is not good: Tension between African Americans and Latinos is rife, as I have reported elsewhere (Waldinger 1997a); and that spells trouble for blacks, who find themselves not just a sociological but a quantitative, often very small, minority, needing to get along in a workplace where Spanish, not English, is often the lingua franca (Waldinger 1997b) and depending on others to learn skills and get jobs done.

Bureaucracy has a different effect, opening doors that networks close. From the standpoint of the immigrants, and of those who study them, networks generate social capital for newcomers poor in all other resources and, for that reason, attract applause. However, the repeated action of network hiring favors those with ties to insiders—an outcome that those lacking the same connections are likely to view as unfair. One is hard put to quarrel with that judgment; those organizations serving diverse clienteles are in no position to do so, as the customer base will not tolerate a workforce dominated by a single group.

Of course, selecting a mixed group is easier when the hiring process has undergone some degree of formalization. Concerted efforts at selection are related to organizational size and complexity, with the larger organizations more likely to have established formalized selection procedures. Although size has an effect regardless of industry, in my sample, size and other organizational characteristics correlate strongly with industry; hence, screening efforts are more extensive and more formalized in hotels, hospitals, and department stores than in printing, furniture manufacturing, and restaurants. The nature of the job matters, as well: Regardless of size, organizations take more care in filling jobs entailing autonomy and some level of unpredictability than those in which supervision is direct and tasks invariant. Although this conclusion implies that efficiency concerns motivate organizational behavior, those responses can have an additional, unintended effect—that is, they may yield more equitable outcomes.

That, however, is not always the case. If fairness implies workforce representativeness, then bureaucratic means of selection signal future difficulties for black workers, as African Americans constitute a relatively small portion of the Los Angeles population and are overrepresented in a number of sectors servicing a heavily immigrant clientele. Moreover, few organizations function as Max Weber (1978) suggests that they should. Selection almost always involves a personal element; those personal interventions allow considerable scope for discretion and thereby for the intrusion of bias—which, in the current climate, is unlikely to favor African Americans.

One suspects that even the more impersonal means of selection will not do much to assist those low-skilled African Americans displaced by the workings of immigrant networks. Any effort to check for a criminal record—a screening activity common to almost all the department stores we surveyed—will have the greatest negative impact on the members of the group with the highest rate of arrests. In Los Angeles, African Americans comprise the group most vulnerable to such checks and far more so than their foreign-born Latino counterparts.[4]

Moreover, bureaucratic means of selection tend to artificially raise hiring criteria, just as Weber notes. Selection is most impersonal in the civil service—a factor making public employment less permeable to immigrants but also to less skilled African Americans. Moreover, the ramifications of both the civil service system and its requirements redound with much greater force among blacks, given the degree to which the public sector has long been the most favorable source of African American employment. Referrals, as noted, work less well in accessing public-sector jobs, making the buildup of African American employment in such government workplaces as hospitals less efficient as a source of useful information and assistance to job seekers. Because the high job requirements exclude the least-skilled members of the African American community in Los Angeles, they also hurt the chances of those persons most exposed to immigrant competition elsewhere in the market. As well, the attractiveness of public-sector jobs yields an additional source of competition—not, in this case, from immigrants but from a broader pool of better-skilled natives who seek the security and compensation available to those who work on the public payroll.

In the end, network and bureaucracy can both be characterized as systems of social exclusion each operating according to its own principle. Those differences notwithstanding, the victims of exclusion are most likely to be black.

NOTES

Thanks to the John Randolph Haynes and Dora Haynes Foundation for the generous funding which supported collection of the data on which this study is based.

1. These two paragraphs do no more than present a stylized summary of a now vast literature; for a lucid discussion of network theory, with ample references, see Massey et al. 1993.

2. All employers are single-counted, even if they were owners or managers of multiunit operations. Three of the hospital interviews involved persons not directly employed by hospitals; these were with the vice president of a company supplying contract housekeeping services to hospitals; an official in a large public-sector-hospital workers' union; and two personnel officials in a local government department responsible for general health care services.

3. Our list of acute-care medical hospitals in Los Angeles County was taken primarily from a local street guide, supplemented by a regional business directory.

4. For example, the Los Angeles Survey of Urban Inequality found that 37 percent of African American men with a high-school education or less

reported some experience in reform school, a detention center, jail, or prison, as opposed to 10 percent of their foreign-born Latino counterparts (Johnson, Oliver, and Bobo 1991).

REFERENCES

Bailey, Thomas, and Roger Waldinger. 1991. "Primary, Secondary, and Enclave Labor Markets: A Training Systems Approach." *American Sociological Review* 56(4): 432–45.

Coleman, James. 1988. "Social Capital in the Creation of Human Capital." *American Journal of Sociology* 94 (supplement): S95–120.

DiMaggio, Paul, and Walter Powell. 1983. "The Iron Case Revisited: Institutional Isomorphism and Collective Rationality in Organizational Fields." *American Sociological Review* 48(12): 147–60.

Granovetter, Mark. 1973. "The Strength of Weak Ties." *American Journal of Sociology* 78(6):1360–80.

Johnson, James, Melvin Oliver, and Laurence Bobo. 1991. "Proposal for a Los Angeles Study of Urban Inequality." University of Michigan and University of California, Los Angeles. Unpublished paper.

Kirschenman, Joleen, and Kathryn M. Neckerman. 1991. "'We'd Love to Hire Them, But . . .': The Meaning of Race for Employers." In *The Urban Underclass*, edited by Christopher Jencks and Paul Peterson. Washington, D.C.: Brookings Institution.

Massey, Douglas, et al. 1987. *Return to Aztlan*. Berkeley: University of California Press.

Massey, Douglas, Joaquin Arango, Graeme Hugo, Ali Kousouci, Ana Pellegrino, and J. Edward Taylor. 1993. "Theories of International Migration: A Review and Appraisal." *Population and Development Review* 19(3): 431–66.

Massey, Douglas, Luis Goldring, and Jorge Durand. 1994. "Continuities in Transnational Migration: An Analysis of Nineteen Mexican Communities." *American Journal of Sociology* 99: 1492–1533.

Moss, Philip, and Chris Tilly. 1991. "Raised Hurdles for Black Men: Evidence from Interviews with Employers." Paper presented to the annual conference of the Association for Public Policy Analysis and Management. Bethesda, Md.

Parkin, Frank. 1979. *Marxism: A Bourgeois Critique*. New York: Columbia University Press.

Portes, Alejandro. 1995. Introduction to *The Economic Sociology of Immigration: Essays on Networks, Ethnicity, and Entrepreneurship*. New York: Russell Sage Foundation.

Portes, Alejandro and Julia Sensenbrenner. 1993. "Embeddedness and Immigration: Notes on the Social Determination of Economic Action." *American Journal of Sociology* 98(16): 1320–50.

Powell, Walter, and Laurel Smith-Doerr. 1994. "Networks and Economic Life." In *The Handbook of Economic Sociology*, edited by Neil Smelser and Richard Swedberg. New York: Russell Sage Foundation.

Tilly, Chris, and Charles Tilly. 1994. "Capitalist Work and Labor Markets." In *The Handbook of Economic Sociology*, edited by Neil Smelser and Richard Swedberg. New York: Russell Sage Foundation.

Waldinger, Roger. 1994. "The Making of an Immigrant Niche." *International Migration Review* 28(1): 3–30.

———. 1996. *Still the Promised City?: African Americans and New Immigrants in Postindustrial New York*. Cambridge: Harvard University Press.

———. 1997a. "Beyond the Sidestream: The Language of Work in an Immigrant Metropolis." Working Paper, Lewis Center for Regional Policy Studies. Los Angeles: UCLA.

———. 1997b. "Black/Immigrant Competition: New Evidence from Los Angeles." *Sociological Perspectives* 40(2):365–86.

Waldinger, Roger, and Mehdi Bozorgmehr, eds. 1996. *Ethnic Los Angeles*. New York: Russell Sage Foundation.

Weber, Max. 1978. *Economy and Society: An Outline of Interpretive Sociology*. Berkeley: University of California Press.

PART III

MIGRATION, LABOR MARKETS, AND POPULATION CHANGE

Newly Emerging Hispanic Communities in the United States: A Spatial Analysis of Settlement Patterns, In-Migration Fields, and Social Receptivity

James H. Johnson Jr., Karen D. Johnson-Webb, and Walter C. Farrell Jr.

A host of recent studies has drawn attention to the increasing diversity of the United States population. Driven in large part by heightened immigration—legal and illegal—principally from Mexico, other parts of Latin America, and Southeast Asia and by high rates of natural increase among these newly arrived immigrants, recent population projections indicate that people of color—Asians, blacks, and Hispanics—will numerically constitute the majority of the U.S. population by the fifth decade of the twenty-first century.

This demographic change is well under way in Los Angeles, New York, Miami, and other port-of-entry communities, where large numbers of these new immigrants have settled over the past quarter century. Research indicates that the new immigration, as it has been characterized, is dramatically changing the complexion and composition of all social, economic, educational, and political institutions (for example, neighborhoods, workplaces, schools, and governments) and in the process has prompted a range of noteworthy responses from indigenous, native-born residents (see Valbrun 1999; Frey et al. 1993a; Johnson, Farrell, and Guinn 1997; National Research Council 1997).

At one level, studies indicate that both well-off and poor non-Hispanic whites and non-Hispanic blacks are fleeing these port-of-entry communities in large numbers. William Frey (1996; and Frey et al. 1995a) argues that this type of response is contributing to a "balkanization" of the U.S. population, because those leaving are settling most often in destination communities that are segregated along the lines of class and race.

On another level, research shows that the new immigration has generated considerable tension and conflict between the native born left behind in these communities and the various newly arrived immigrant groups over jobs, housing, and other scarce social and economic resources (see Oliver and Johnson 1984; Johnson and Oliver 1989; Johnson, Farrell, and Guinn 1997; Johnson-Webb and Johnson 1996). Studies reveal that conflicts between the native-born and the new immigrants (that is, those arriving since 1965) have undergirded nearly all of the civil disturbances that have occurred in U.S. cities in the post-1980 period (Johnson and Oliver 1989; Johnson and Farrell 1993; Johnson, Farrell, and Guinn 1997), paralleling the 1960s, when U.S. cities were rocked by conflagrations triggered by racial antagonisms between whites and blacks.

Nowhere was this more apparent than in the Los Angeles civil unrest of 1992, characterized as the nation's worst urban insurrection of this century. Although the videotaped beating of a black motorist by three white police officers was the spark, the findings of recent research indicate that the civil unrest was rooted in smoldering tensions among three nonwhite ethnic minority groups: native blacks and recently arrived Asian and Hispanic immigrants.

This chapter seeks to broaden the current state of knowledge and understanding of the new immigration by focusing on two related, but heretofore largely neglected, facets of Hispanic population growth and change in the U.S. The first pertains to the changing migration behavior of the Hispanic population, and the second relates to the reception of the Hispanic migrants in destination communities.

With respect to changing migration behavior, evidence is mounting that Hispanics, not unlike native-born blacks and whites, are beginning to move down the urban hierarchy to small- and medium-sized cities and towns in states that traditionally have not been magnets for either Hispanic immigration or internal Hispanic population redistribution (Johnson-Webb and Johnson 1996; Holmes 1998). To illustrate this emergent trend, we focus here on eight states that experienced relatively high Hispanic population growth between 1990 and 1994. We also devote specific attention to the origin, size, and composition of the flows into specific destination communities within these states.

With respect to the receptivity of the communities into which Hispanics migrate, media accounts and anecdotal evidence suggest that the same kinds of tensions and conflicts that have characterized Hispanic immigration into port-of-entry communities are being reproduced in small- and medium-sized cities and towns. Here, we attempt to provide insight into the nature and magnitude of the tensions and conflicts that have accompanied the influx of Hispanics into the selected destination communities in the eight targeted states.

To illustrate the changing migration behavior, we draw upon data from a range of census reports and databases, including the 1990 Public Use Microdata Sample (PUMS, 5 percent sample) and 1994 census estimates of the U.S. population by state and by race or ethnicity derived from administrative records (U.S. Bureau of the Census 1993, 1995). We draw principally from media coverage of the Hispanic influx into these destination communities to assess the social receptivity toward in-migrating Hispanics.

For our purposes here, we employ the U.S. Bureau of the Census definition of Hispanics as those who classified themselves in one of the specific Hispanic-origin categories listed in the 1990 census questionnaire—"Mexican," "Puerto Rican," "Cuban," "Dominican," "Central American," or "South American"—as well as those who indicated that they were of other Spanish or Hispanic origin. The latter category includes those who came from Spain and those identifying themselves in the census questionnaire as Spanish, Spanish American, Hispanic, Hispano, Latino, and so on (U.S. Bureau of the Census 1993).

HISPANIC SETTLEMENT PATTERNS IN THE UNITED STATES: A GENERAL OVERVIEW

Between 1980 and 1995, the Hispanic population of the United States grew at a much faster rate than the population of the nation as a whole. During the 1980s, it increased by nearly 50 percent—from 14.6 million to 21.9 million—while the total population increased by only 9.8 percent (see table 8.1). In the early 1990s, the Hispanic population increased by 28 percent, reaching 28 million in 1994. By comparison, the U.S. population, according to estimates compiled by the Census Bureau, increased by only 6 percent between 1990 and 1994.

Historically, the Hispanic population (mainly Mexicans and Mexican Americans) has settled primarily in the southwestern United States (Bean and Tienda 1987). As of 1994 Hispanics still constituted relatively large proportions of the populations of several of the states that make up this region: California (28 percent), Texas (27 percent), Arizona (20 percent), and New Mexico (39 percent) (see figure 8.1). Beyond the Southwest, only three states had Hispanic concentrations above 10 percent in 1994: New York (13.7 percent), New Jersey (11.0 percent), and Florida (13.4 percent).

The figure highlights the areas in which the Hispanic population has traditionally settled in the United States, but statistics on the rates of Hispanic population change by state between 1990 and 1994 sug-

Table 8.1   Total and Hispanic Population Change in the United States and in Selected States, 1980, 1990, and 1994

Place	Total Population			Hispanic Population		
	From 1980 to 1990					
	1980	1990	% Change	1980	1990	% Change
United States	226,545,805	248,718,291	9.8	14,603,683	21,900,089	49.9
Port-of-entry states	76,587,401	90,505,397	18.2	11,757,000	17,823,338	51.6
California	23,667,902	29,760,021	25.2	4,541,300	7,687,950	69.2
Arizona	2,718,215	3,665,228	34.2	444,102	688,335	56.1
New Mexico	1,302,894	1,515,069	16.1	477,051	579,227	21.4
New York	17,558,072	17,990,455	2.4	1,660,901	2,213,932	33.4
Florida	9,746,324	12,937,926	31.0	858,105	1,574,136	83.5
Texas	14,229,191	16,986,510	18.6	2,982,583	4,339,900	45.3
New Jersey	7,364,803	7,730,188	4.8	494,096	739,858	50.4
New Hispanic magnets	25,917,751	28,419,666	9.7	315,953	534,563	69.2
Arkansas	2,286,435	2,350,725	2.8	16,976	19,876	17.1
Georgia	5,463,105	6,478,216	18.6	60,974	108,923	78.6
Iowa	2,913,808	2,776,755	−4.7	26,274	32,645	24.2
Maryland	4,216,975	4,781,468	13.4	63,196	125,106	98.0
Minnesota	4,075,970	4,375,099	7.3	32,115	53,884	67.8
Nebraska	1,569,825	1,578,385	0.5	28,262	36,969	30.8
Nevada	800,493	1,201,833	50.1	54,130	124,418	129.9
Tennessee	4,591,120	4,877,185	6.2	34,026	32,742	−3.8
	From 1990 to 1994					
	1990	1994	% Change	1990	1994	% Change
United States	248,718,291	263,641,389	6.0	21,900,089	28,032,113	28.0
Port-of-entry states	90,585,397	95,565,193	5.5	17,823,338	20,669,401	16.0
California	29,760,021	31,430,901	5.6	7,687,950	8,939,192	16.3
Arizona	3,665,228	4,075,088	11.2	688,335	823,587	19.7
New Mexico	1,515,069	1,653,537	9.1	579,227	645,801	11.5
New York	17,990,455	18,172,614	1.0	2,213,932	2,498,526	12.9
Florida	12,937,926	13,950,777	7.8	1,574,136	1,872,002	18.9
Texas	16,986,510	18,378,280	8.2	4,339,900	5,022,338	15.7
New Jersey	7,730,188	7,903,996	2.3	739,858	867,955	17.3
New Hispanic magnets	23,542,481	30,165,917	28.1	534,563	711,562	33.1
Arkansas	2,350,725	2,452,671	4.3	19,876	26,621	33.9
Georgia	6,478,216	7,055,336	8.9	108,923	140,322	28.8
Iowa	2,776,755	2,829,252	1.9	32,645	43,215	32.4

Table 8.1   *Continued*

Place	Total Population			Hispanic Population		
	From 1990 to 1994					
	1980	1990	% Change	1980	1990	% Change
Maryland	4,781,468	5,006,265	4.7	125,106	162,604	30.0
Minnesota	4,375,099	4,567,267	4.4	53,884	71,520	32.7
Nebraska	1,578,385	1,622,858	2.8	36,969	48,387	30.9
Nevada	1,201,833	1,457,028	21.2	124,418	175,631	41.2
Tennessee	4,877,185	5,175,240	6.1	322,742	43,262	32.1
	From 1980 to 1994					
	1980	1994	% Change	1980	1994	% Change
United States	226,545,805	263,641,389	16.4	14,609,000	28,032,113	91.9
Port-of-entry states	76,954,000	95,565,193	24.2	11,457,000	20,669,401	80.4
California	23,771,000	31,430,901	32.2	4,544,000	8,939,192	96.7
Arizona	2,731,000	4,075,088	49.2	441,000	823,587	86.8
New Mexico	1,305,000	1,653,537	26.7	477,000	645,801	35.4
New York	17,575,000	18,172,614	3.4	1,659,000	2,498,526	50.6
Florida	9,874,000	13,950,777	41.3	858,000	1,872,002	118.2
Texas	14,321,000	18,378,280	28.3	2,986,000	5,022,338	68.2
New Jersey	7,377,000	7,903,996	7.1	492,000	867,955	76.4
New Hispanic magnets	25,917,731	30,165,917	16.4	315,953	711,562	125.2
Arkansas	2,286,435	2,452,671	7.3	16,976	26,621	56.8
Georgia	5,463,105	7,055,336	29.1	60,974	140,322	130.1
Iowa	2,913,808	2,829,252	−2.9	26,274	43,215	64.5
Maryland	4,216,975	5,006,265	18.7	63,196	162,604	157.3
Minnesota	4,075,970	4,567,267	12.1	32,115	71,520	122.7
Nebraska	1,569,825	1,622,858	3.4	28,262	48,387	71.2
Nevada	800,493	1,457,028	82.0	54,130	175,631	224.5
Tennessee	4,591,120	5,175,240	12.7	34,026	43,262	27.1

Source: U.S. Bureau of the Census, Population Division, Population of States and Counties, Census of Population and Housing, Summary Tape File 1c.
Note: Population figures for 1994 are estimates.

gest that a redistribution trend is under way (figure 8.2). During this period, eight states experienced rates in excess of the national rate of Hispanic population change (28 percent): Nevada experienced the highest rate of Hispanic population growth (41 percent), followed by Arkansas (34 percent), Minnesota (33 percent), Iowa (32 percent),

Figure 8.1   Distribution of Hispanic Population by State, 1994

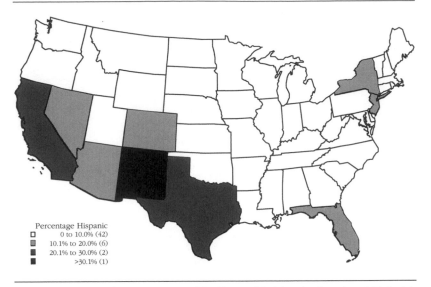

Percentage Hispanic
□   0 to 10.0% (42)
▨   10.1% to 20.0% (6)
▦   20.1% to 30.0% (2)
■   >30.1% (1)

Source: Based on data from U.S. Bureau of the Census, Administrative Records and Methodology Research Branch.
Note: Population estimates as of July 1, 1994.

Figure 8.2   States Experiencing Rapid Hispanic Population Growth, from 1990 to 1994

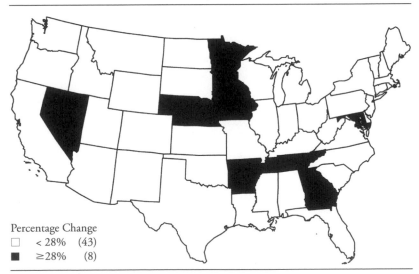

Percentage Change
□   < 28%   (43)
■   ≥28%   (8)

Source: Based on data from U.S. Bureau of the Census, Administrative Records and Methodology Research Branch.
Note: Population estimates as of July 1, 1994.

Tennessee (32 percent), Nebraska (31 percent), Maryland (30 percent), and Georgia (29 percent).

In terms of absolute growth, as table 8.1 shows, the greatest gains in Hispanic population during this period were seen in Nevada (51,213), Maryland (37,498), Georgia (31,399), and Minnesota (17,636). In 1994, their Hispanic populations totaled 175,631, 162,604, 140,322, and 71,520, respectively. Three of the remaining high-growth states experienced absolute increases in their Hispanic populations in excess of 10,000 between 1990 and 1994: Iowa (10,570), Nebraska (11,418), and Tennessee (10,520). During this period, Arkansas (6,745) was the only one of these high-growth states with an absolute increase in its Hispanic population of less than 10,000.

That Nevada was the top-ranking state in terms of both the absolute and the relative growth of its Hispanic population is not surprising, given its interior location relative to the border states (California, Arizona, New Mexico, and Texas) that make up the traditional heartland of Hispanic immigration and settlement in the Southwest region of the country. However, the burgeoning rates—absolute and relative—of Hispanic population growth in the other seven states, especially Georgia, Maryland, and Minnesota, are noteworthy. Geographically removed from the historical core of Hispanic settlement in the Southwest, these states traditionally have not been magnets of Hispanic immigration or internal migration.

Signs that these states were emergent strongholds of Hispanic population growth actually were evident during the 1980s (see table 8.1). However, little systematic research attention has been devoted to this population redistribution trend. According to the 1990 census, four of these states experienced large relative and absolute increases in their Hispanic populations between 1980 and 1990: Nevada (130 percent, or 70,288), Maryland (98 percent, or 61,910), Georgia (79 percent, or 47,949), and Minnesota (68 percent, or 21,769). Nebraska (31 percent, or 8,707), Iowa (24 percent, or 6,371), and Arkansas (17 percent, or 2,900) experienced more modest rates of growth in their Hispanic populations during the 1980s; however, despite lower relative rates of growth than in the former four states, their absolute Hispanic population increases during the late 1980s totaled 36,969 (Nebraska), 32,645 (Iowa), and 19,876 (Arkansas). This finding is salient because a few locations have served as the "magnets" for most of the Hispanic population growth within these states between 1980 and 1995.

In sum, over the fourteen-year period ending in 1994, dramatic changes occurred in the migration behavior of the Hispanic population in the United States. The Hispanic population of the nation as a whole increased by 92 percent between 1980 and 1994, but the rates of growth in the previously identified eight states, which traditionally have not been areas of Hispanic settlement, were much higher. With their Hispanic populations more than doubling during this fourteen-year period, Nevada (225 percent, or 121,500), Maryland (157 percent, or 99,400), Georgia (130 percent, or 79,400), and Minnesota (122 percent, or 39,400) led the way, followed in rank order by Nebraska (71 percent, or 20,100), Iowa (65 percent, or 17,000), Arkansas (57 percent, or 10,000), and Tennessee (27 percent, or 9,000) (table 8.1).

For our purposes here, what is important about these trends is that there is no overlap between the seven port-of-entry states with large concentrations of Hispanics (California, Arizona, New Mexico, New York, Florida, Texas, and New Jersey) and the eight states that experienced the highest rates of Hispanic population growth between 1990 and 1994 (Arkansas, Georgia, Iowa, Maryland, Minnesota, Nebraska, Nevada, and Tennessee). Nor is there any overlap, except for Georgia, between the eight states experiencing high rates of Hispanic population growth during the early 1990s and those states identified by William Frey (1995) as magnets of immigration (California, Illinois, New York, New Jersey, Georgia, and Massachusetts) and magnets of internal migration (Washington, Arizona, Florida, North Carolina, and Virginia) during the late 1980s, as figure 8.3 shows.

Finally, it should be noted that the eight states experiencing high percentage increases in their Hispanic populations also registered sizable increases in their non-Hispanic black and Asian populations from 1980 to 1994 (Johnson and Roseman 1990; Johnson and Grant 1997; Frey et al. 1993a, 1993b; Barringer 1993; Newbold 1997). What is most significant about this finding is that, in the midst of this growth in their nonwhite populations, these states experienced, overall, relatively slow growth in their non-Hispanic white populations. Thus, to the extent that these states experienced net gains in total population between 1980 and 1994, it was attributable, in large measure, to the influx of people of color.

Research suggests that these and other states in the Midwest and the Sun Belt have emerged as migration magnets for Hispanics and other people of color, owing to their recent economic restructuring experiences (Kanter 1995; Labich 1994). Following the devastating

Figure 8.3   Comparison of Frey's Classifications (1990) and Census
Estimates of Hispanic Population Change (1994)

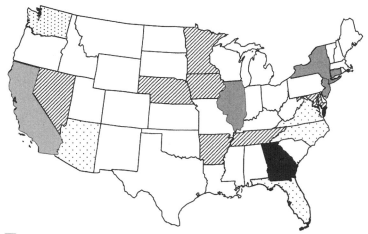

▪ States with High Immigration Rates (Frey 1995)

⬚ States with High Internal-Migration Rates (Frey 1995)

▨ States with High Change in Hispanic Population (estimated 1994)

■ States with High Change in Hispanic Population (estimated 1994) and
   High Internal-Migration Rates (Frey 1995)

Sources: William H. Frey, "Immigration and Internal Migration 'Flight' from US Metropolitan
Areas: Toward a New Demographic Balkanization," *Urban Studies* 32(4–5): 733–57. U.S. Bu-
reau of the Census, Administrative Records and Methodology Research Branch.
Note: Population estimates as of July 1, 1994.

deindustrialization of the 1970s and 1980s, the economies of many of
the midwestern states to which Hispanics (and other people of color)
have flocked in significant numbers in recent years have experienced a
dramatic economic turnaround (Labich 1994; Melcher and Kelly
1994). Over the past decade or so, local and state governments in the
Midwest have made extraordinary efforts to attract new businesses
and to become more competitive in the global marketplace, and the
efforts of their labor have paid off (Havenmann 1998).

   Beginning in the late 1980s and continuing through the early
1990s, according to Melcher and Kelly (1994), the economies of the
Midwest grew at a faster rate than the national economy. Among
other factors, the region's economic revival was the result of:

1. the growth of high technology and "knowledge-driven" industries in metropolitan areas like Minneapolis–St. Paul;

2. the increasing concentration of the meat-packing industry (especially beef and hog processing) in small metropolitan areas and rural communities in Iowa, Minnesota, and Nebraska; and

3. sharp increases in export activities across a variety of economic sectors in metropolitan communities throughout the region (Minnesota Planning 1996, 1997; Stull, Broadway, and Griffith 1995; Kaplan and Schwartz 1996; Havenmann 1998)

The economic revival of the Midwest has occurred in the wake of the ongoing economic boom in the Sun Belt, which actually began in the 1970s and accelerated during the 1980s and early 1990s (Foust and Mallory 1993). During this period, the Atlanta, Georgia, Metropolitan Statistical Area (MSA) emerged as the regional economic hub of the South (as defined by the Census Bureau), leading it to be rated as the fourth-best metropolitan area in the world in which to do business in 1994 (Saporito 1994). More recently, Las Vegas, another Sun Belt city, has been rated the number-one city for employment growth for several years running (Oliver 1996; Daniels 1997). Communities in Arkansas, Georgia, and Maryland have emerged as centers of poultry production, and local communities throughout the region have reengineered their business recruitment strategies in an effort to successfully compete for both domestic and foreign direct investment in their local economies (Kanter 1995; Kaplan and Schwartz 1996). Among other locational advantages, local chambers of commerce and other officials in Sun Belt states have leveraged the region's lower cost of living and warmer climate to attract business, including traditional manufacturing (for example, automobile-manufacturing plants), high technology, and advanced-services-sector firms, to their communities (Cole and Deskins 1998; Mair, Florida, and Kennedy 1988; Howlett 1995; Pins 1997; Molpus 1997; Daniels 1997).

Over the past fifteen years, in short, most of the employment growth in the United States has not occurred in the traditional centers of economic activity—major metropolitan centers in the so-called industrial heartland of the Northeast and Midwest. Rather, it has occurred in small- and medium-sized metropolitan areas and rural communities in the Midwest and the Sun Belt. Attracted by, and in some instances recruited as a consequence of, severe labor shortages, Hispanics—American citizens and noncitizens alike—and other people of color are flocking to these new areas of economic opportunity in significant numbers. In the process, they are dramatically changing the social geography of the local landscape. Contrary to the assertions of some researchers (for example, Peterson and Rom 1990), Hispanics and other people of color are moving to these areas not to take advantage of liberal welfare benefits but to find good jobs (Johnson, Grant, and Farrell 1994; Frey et al. 1995a; Johnson and Grant 1997).

HISPANIC POPULATION CONCENTRATIONS WITHIN HIGH-GROWTH STATES

Where within these high-growth states have Hispanics settled? Are they highly concentrated in specific communities, or are they dispersed throughout these states? To answer these questions, we compiled a set of maps that depict the percentage distribution of Hispanics by county within each of the eight high-growth states in 1994. These maps illustrate the degree or extent to which the Hispanic population is clustered within each of these states and specifies the metropolitan or nonmetropolitan status of the communities in which they have elected to settle. What is immediately apparent in these maps is that Hispanics have settled primarily in metropolitan areas within these high growth states.

Minnesota's Hispanics are concentrated in the Minneapolis–St. Paul MSA (figure 8.4). In Iowa, Hispanics are concentrated in the Davenport, Iowa–Moline–Rock Island, Illinois (Scott County) and Des Moines MSAs (Polk County) (figure 8.5). Nevada's primary concentration of Hispanics (more than 70%) is in the Las Vegas MSA (Clark County), and its second major concentration can be found in the Reno MSA (Washoe County) (figure 8.6). Nebraska's Hispanic population is concentrated mainly in the Omaha MSA (Douglas County) in the eastern part of the state and in the Lincoln MSA (Lancaster County), which is just southwest of Omaha. There is also an additional Hispanic concentration in Scotts Bluff County, a rural county in the extreme western panhandle of the state (figure 8.7).

Maryland's Hispanic population is concentrated mainly in Montgomery and Prince Georges counties, suburban communities adjacent to Washington, D.C.; as figure 8.8 shows, there is a second major concentration in the Baltimore MSA (Baltimore and Anne Arundel counties). In Tennessee, Hispanics are concentrated in several MSAs: Memphis, Clarksville, Nashville, Chattanooga, and Knoxville (figure 8.9).

The Little Rock MSA (Pulaski County) contains the highest concentration of Hispanics in the state of Arkansas; in 1994, there were

(*Text continues on p. 277.*)

Figure 8.4   Distribution of Hispanics in Minnesota, by County, 1994

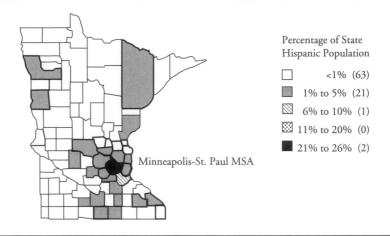

Percentage of State
Hispanic Population

☐   <1% (63)

▨   1% to 5% (21)

▨   6% to 10% (1)

▧   11% to 20% (0)

■   21% to 26% (2)

Minneapolis-St. Paul MSA

Sources: U.S. Bureau of the Census, Administrative Records and Methodology Research Branch, April 1990; Office of Management and Budget, 1997.
Notes: Population estimates as of July 1, 1994. Bold boundary indicates metropolitan county as of 1997.

Figure 8.5   Distribution of Hispanics in Iowa, by County, 1994

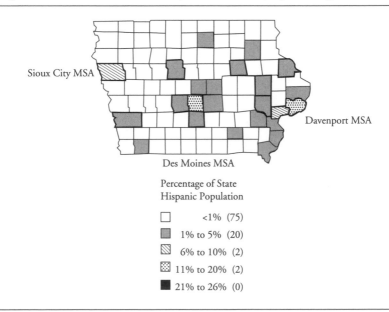

Sioux City MSA

Davenport MSA

Des Moines MSA

Percentage of State
Hispanic Population

☐   <1% (75)

▨   1% to 5% (20)

▨   6% to 10% (2)

▧   11% to 20% (2)

■   21% to 26% (0)

Sources: U.S. Bureau of the Census, Administrative Records and Methodology Research Branch, April 1990; Office of Management and Budget, 1997.
Notes: Population estimates as of July 1, 1994. Bold boundary indicates metropolitan county as of 1997.

Figure 8.6   Distribution of Hispanics in Nevada, by County, 1994

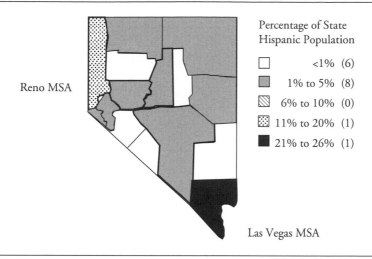

Reno MSA

Percentage of State
Hispanic Population

☐   <1% (6)

▨   1% to 5% (8)

▧   6% to 10% (0)

▨   11% to 20% (1)

■   21% to 26% (1)

Las Vegas MSA

Sources: U.S. Bureau of the Census, Administrative Records and Methodology Research Branch, April 1990; Office of Management and Budget, 1997.
Notes: Population estimates as of July 1, 1994. Bold boundary indicates metropolitan county as of 1997.

Figure 8.7   Distribution of Hispanics in Nebraska, by County, 1994

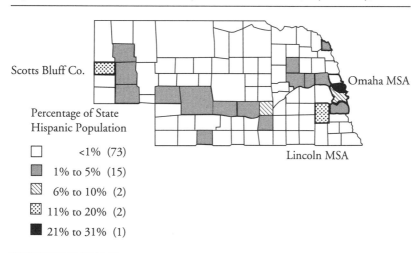

Scotts Bluff Co.

Omaha MSA

Percentage of State
Hispanic Population

☐   <1% (73)

▨   1% to 5% (15)

▧   6% to 10% (2)

▨   11% to 20% (2)

■   21% to 31% (1)

Lincoln MSA

Sources: U.S. Bureau of the Census, Administrative Records and Methodology Research Branch, April 1990; Office of Management and Budget, 1997.
Notes: Population estimates as of July 1, 1994. Bold boundary indicates metropolitan county as of 1997.

Figure 8.8   Distribution of Hispanics in Maryland, by County, 1994

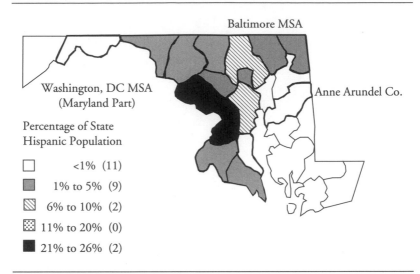

Baltimore MSA

Washington, DC MSA
(Maryland Part)

Anne Arundel Co.

Percentage of State
Hispanic Population

☐   <1% (11)

▨   1% to 5% (9)

▨   6% to 10% (2)

▧ 11% to 20% (0)

■ 21% to 26% (2)

Sources: U.S. Bureau of the Census, Administrative Records and Methodology Research Branch, April 1990; Office of Management and Budget, 1997.
Notes: Population estimates as of July 1, 1994. Bold boundary indicates metropolitan county as of 1997.

Figure 8.9   Distribution of Hispanics in Tennessee, by County, 1994

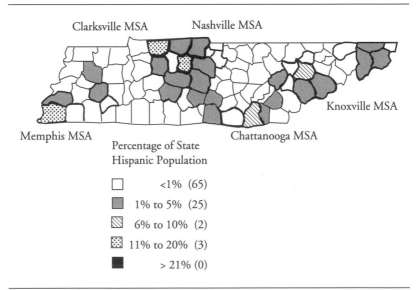

Clarksville MSA   Nashville MSA

Knoxville MSA

Memphis MSA   Chattanooga MSA

Percentage of State
Hispanic Population

☐   <1% (65)

▨   1% to 5% (25)

▨   6% to 10% (2)

▧ 11% to 20% (3)

■   > 21% (0)

Sources: U.S. Bureau of the Census, Administrative Records and Methodology Research Branch, April 1990; Office of Management and Budget, 1997.
Notes: Population estimates as of July 1, 1994. Bold boundary indicates metropolitan county as of 1997.

Figure 8.10 Distribution of Hispanics in Arkansas, by County, 1994

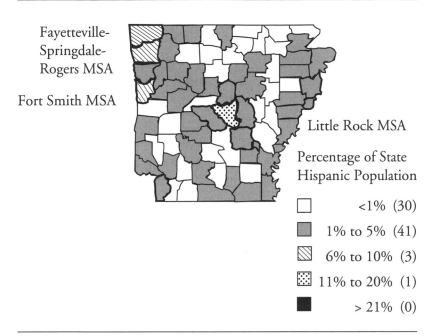

Fayetteville-
Springdale-
Rogers MSA

Fort Smith MSA

Little Rock MSA

Percentage of State
Hispanic Population

☐ <1% (30)

▨ 1% to 5% (41)

◩ 6% to 10% (3)

▦ 11% to 20% (1)

■ > 21% (0)

Sources: U.S. Bureau of the Census, Administrative Records and Methodology Research Branch, April 1990; Office of Management and Budget, 1997.

Notes: Population estimates as of July 1, 1994. Bold boundary indicates metropolitan county as of 1997.

secondary concentrations in the Fayetteville-Springdale-Rogers and Fort Smith MSAs (Figure 8.10). Within the state of Georgia, Hispanics are concentrated in the Atlanta MSA, principally in the city of Atlanta (Fulton County), and also in the two adjacent suburban counties of Cobb and Dekalb (figure 8.11).

ORIGINS OF HISPANIC NEWCOMERS TO HIGH-GROWTH STATES

Where did the Hispanics who settled in these eight states come from? Did they come principally from other U.S. communities, or did they come from abroad and settle in these communities? To answer these questions, we employ the concept of an immigration field (Roseman 1977), which is defined here as any Public Use Microdata Area

Figure 8.11   Distribution of Hispanics in Georgia, by County, 1994

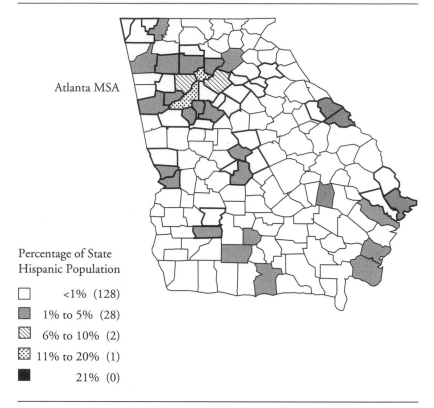

Atlanta MSA

Percentage of State
Hispanic Population

☐   <1% (128)

▨   1% to 5% (28)

◩   6% to 10% (2)

▦   11% to 20% (1)

■   21% (0)

Sources: U.S. Bureau of the Census, Administrative Records and Methodology Research Branch, April 1990; Office of Management and Budget, 1997.
Notes: Population estimates as of July 1, 1994. Bold boundary indicates metropolitan county as of 1997.

(PUMA) sending one hundred or more Hispanics to one or more specific communities in any of the eight case-study states between 1985 and 1990.

As figure 8.12 shows, the Minneapolis–St. Paul MSA emerged as the only place in Minnesota that received significant flows of Hispanics between 1985 and 1990. Chicago (230) and New York (143), both traditional port-of-entry communities for Hispanic immigrants, contributed the largest flows. There was also significant Hispanic in-migration from Vancouver, Washington (115), Boulder, Colorado

Figure 8.12   Distribution of Hispanic Migrants from PUMA In-
Migration Fields to Minnesota Metropolitan Areas,
from 1985 to 1990

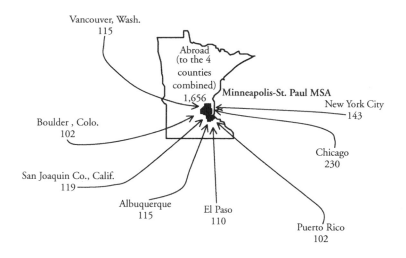

Source: U.S. Bureau of the Census, 1990 Public Use Microdata Samples (5 percent), issued July 1993; Washington, D.C.

(102), and San Joaquin County, California (119), as well as Albuquerque, New Mexico (115) and El Paso, Texas (110). The PUMS data indicate that 1,656 Hispanics from abroad and 102 from Puerto Rico also settled in the Minneapolis–St. Paul MSA between 1985 and 1990.

In Iowa, Hispanics have settled primarily in two metropolitan communities: Davenport and Des Moines (see figure 8.13). Most of the Hispanics settling in Des Moines came from abroad (703). Among U.S. jurisdictions, Chicago (247), Puerto Rico (147), and the North Texas Panhandle (105) sent Hispanics into Des Moines. In the case of the Davenport MSA, the largest flow of Hispanics came from nearby Rock Island County (207), a community in the Illinois portion of the Davenport MSA, and several rural counties in Texas (138).

The Hispanic newcomers to Nebraska settled in three of the state's metropolitan areas: Lincoln, Omaha, and Sioux City (figure 8.14). Between 1985 and 1990, the majority of the Hispanics settling in

Figure 8.13   Distribution of Hispanic Migrants from PUMA In-Migration Fields to Iowa Metropolitan Areas, from 1985 to 1990

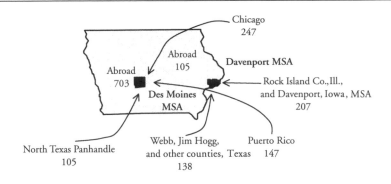

Source: U.S. Bureau of the Census, 1990 Public Use Microdata Samples (5 percent), issued July 1993; Washington, D.C.

Figure 8.14   Distribution of Hispanic Migrants from PUMA In-Migration Fields to Nebraska Metropolitan Areas, from 1985 to 1990

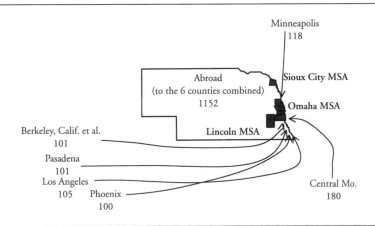

Source: U.S. Bureau of the Census, 1990 Public Use Microdata Samples (5 percent), issued July 1993; Washington, D.C.

Figure 8.15   Distribution of Hispanic Migrants from PUMA In-
Migration Fields to Arkansas Metropolitan Areas, from
1985 to 1990

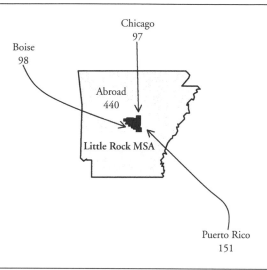

Source: U.S. Bureau of the Census, 1990 Public Use Microdata Samples (5 percent), issued July 1993; Washington, D.C.

these three metropolitan areas came from abroad (1,152). Among these three MSAs, Omaha was the only one to experience a significant influx of Hispanics from another U.S. jurisdiction. As the figure reveals, there were Hispanic migrant streams into Omaha from Berkeley (101), Pasadena (101), and Los Angeles (105), California; Phoenix, Arizona (100); Minneapolis, Minnesota (118); and a set of rural counties in central Missouri (Audrain, Callaway, Cole, Cooper, Howard, Montineau, and Osage) (180).

The Little Rock MSA is the only community in the state of Arkansas to receive salient flows of Hispanic newcomers, as defined in this study, during the late 1980s. As figure 8.15 illustrates, 440 Hispanics from abroad settled in Little Rock between 1985 and 1990. Among U.S. jurisdictions, there were Hispanic migrant flows from Puerto Rico (151), Boise, Idaho (98) and Chicago, Illinois (97).

In the state of Nevada, the Hispanic newcomers settled primarily in two MSAs: Las Vegas and Reno. In both of these metropolitan areas, a large number of the Hispanic settlers came directly from abroad: 7,680 (Las Vegas) and 4,429 (Reno) (see figure 8.16). There

Figure 8.16   Distribution of Hispanic Migrants from PUMA In-Migration Fields to Nevada Metropolitan Areas, from 1985 to 1990

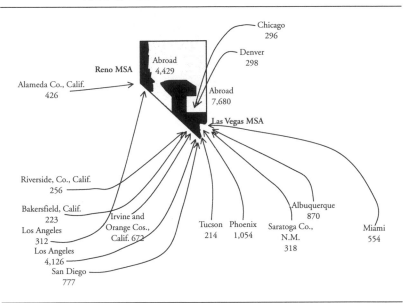

Source: U.S. Bureau of the Census, 1990 Public Use Microdata Samples (5 percent), issued July 1993; Washington, D.C.

was a strong regional character to the flows from other U.S. jurisdictions, with most originating in the nearby states of California, Arizona, and New Mexico. Between 1985 and 1990, there were significant Hispanic flows into Reno from Alameda County (426) and Los Angeles (312), California. A much broader group of communities in California and other states sent Hispanics to Las Vegas: Los Angeles (4,126), San Diego (777), Irvine and Orange County (672), Riverside County (256), and Bakersfield (223), California; Phoenix (1,054) and Tuscon (214), Arizona; Albuquerque (870) and Saratoga County (318), New Mexico; and Denver, Colorado (298). Outside of these nearby states, Las Vegas attracted sizable numbers of Hispanic newcomers from Dade County, Florida (554) and Chicago, Illinois (296).

Four metropolitan areas in the state of Tennessee received significant flows of Hispanics between 1985 and 1990: Memphis MSA, Clarksville MSA, Nashville-Davidson MSA and Chattanooga MSA (see figure 8.17). In the case of Memphis, all of the Hispanic mi-

Figure 8.17   Distribution of Hispanic Migrants from PUMA In-Migration Fields to Tennessee Metropolitan Areas, from 1985 to 1990

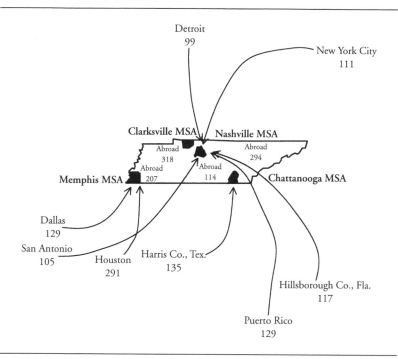

Source: U.S. Bureau of the Census, 1990 Public Use Microdata Samples (5 percent), issued July 1993; Washington, D.C.

grants from other U.S. jurisdictions originated in two Texas communities: Dallas (129) and Houston (291). An estimated 207 Hispanic newcomers from abroad also settled in Memphis between 1985 and 1990. Nashville drew Hispanics from a much wider set of communities than did Memphis. In addition to the 294 who settled there from abroad between 1985 and 1990, Nashville also received Hispanic migrants from San Antonio, Texas (105), Detroit, Michigan (99), New York City (111), Hillsborough County, Florida (117, part of the Tampa–St. Petersburg–Clearwater MSA), and Puerto Rico (129). With respect to the Chattanooga MSA, there were two streams between 1985 and 1990: one was from abroad (114), and the other was from Harris County, Texas (135), which is part of the Houston MSA. However, the Clarksville MSA only received Hispanics from abroad (318); there were no domestic immigrants.

In the state of Georgia, Hispanic newcomers settled in significant numbers in six different metropolitan communities: Atlanta, Albany, Athens, Augusta, Columbus, and Savannah. Among the eight case-study states, Georgia had perhaps the most diverse set of Hispanic immigration fields—that is, specific communities from which there were salient flows of Hispanics into one or more of the state's metropolitan communities—between 1985 and 1990. Because of the large number of sending communities and for ease of presentation, flows of Hispanic migrants into the Atlanta MSA are depicted separately from those into the other five Georgia metropolitan areas.

As figure 8.18 illustrates, a significant number of the Hispanic newcomers to Atlanta came from abroad (8,398). In terms of U.S. jurisdictions, communities in the states of Texas (Houston [2,000], Dallas [886], San Antonio [572], Austin [292], San Angelo [260], Waco [148], and the border communities of Brownsville [149] and Hidalgo Co. [225]); California (Los Angeles [582], Orange County [272], San Francisco and Oakland [238], Lynwood and Southgate [227], and San Jose [197]); New York (New York City [1,414]); Florida (Miami [813], Ft. Lauderdale [305], and Hialeah [226]); and Puerto Rico (1,158) all contributed significant streams of Hispanic migrants to the Atlanta MSA. Between 1985 and 1990, significant numbers of Hispanics also settled in Atlanta from New Orleans, Louisiana (394), Reno, Nevada (109), Clarksville, Tennessee (249), Chicago, Illinois (370), Washington, D.C. (129), and Amherst, Massachusetts (184).

The other five Georgia MSAs—Albany, Augusta, Athens, Columbus, and Savannah—received Hispanic newcomers from a variety of origin communities (figure 8.19). Among the five, Savannah received the greatest number—from Colorado Springs, Colorado (269), Charleston, South Carolina (143), Miami, Florida (144), Honolulu, Hawaii (112), and Puerto Rico (171). Savannah also received a significant number of Hispanic newcomers from abroad (714). The Columbus MSA received a large flow of Hispanics from abroad (1,649) and significant flows from the following U.S. jurisdictions: Clarksville, Tennessee (145), Austin, Texas (145), Hardin and Meade Counties (188) (these rural communities border the Louisville MSA, in Kentucky), and Camden, Laclede, Miller, Morgan, and Pulaski Counties, Missouri (172) (a set of rural communities in central Missouri). Another Hispanic migrant flow into Columbus originated in a North Carolina military community, Fayetteville and Fort Bragg (114).

The Augusta MSA had three salient flows of Hispanics between

Figure 8.18   Distribution of Hispanic Migrants from PUMA In-
Migration Fields to Atlanta, Georgia, Metropolitan
Area, from 1985 to 1990

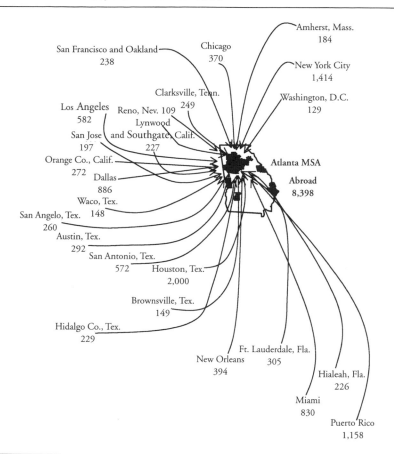

Source: U.S. Bureau of the Census, 1990 Public Use Microdata Samples (5 percent), issued July 1993; Washington, D.C.

1985 and 1990: from San Diego (109) and Puerto Rico (250) and from abroad (393). The Albany MSA had salient flows from the Marion–Muncie, Indiana, MSA (106) and from the Tidewater region of North Carolina (103). As the figure shows, the Athens MSA had only one major flow—from abroad (291).

Hispanic newcomers have settled in three metropolitan areas in Maryland: the Washington, D.C., MSA (Maryland part), the Bal-

Figure 8.19   Distribution of Hispanic Migrants from PUMA In-
Migration Fields to Five Georgia Metropolitan Areas,
from 1985 to 1990

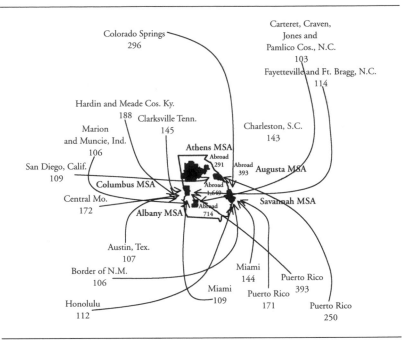

Source: U.S. Bureau of the Census, 1990 Public Use Microdata Samples (5 percent), issued July 1993; Washington, D.C.

timore MSA, and the Cumberland MSA. However, the largest number of Hispanic newcomers to the Washington, D.C., MSA (Maryland part) came from abroad (16,290) (figure 8.20). Among U.S.
jurisdictions, the largest flows originated in the city of Washington,
D.C. (3,460), the Virginia part of the Washington, D.C., MSA
(1,473), and Puerto Rico (1,335). There were also large flows from
New York City (1,022), Chicago (432), and Jersey City, New Jersey
(334), between 1985 and 1990. In addition, communities in California (Los Angeles [476], Coronado and San Diego [102], and Santa
Cruz [115]), Texas (Houston [507], El Paso [309], Dallas [148], and
San Antonio [120]), and Florida (Miami [621]) were responsible for
Hispanic migrant streams into the Maryland part of the Washington,
D.C., MSA during this period.

Figure 8.20   Distribution of Hispanic Migrants from PUMA In-
Migration Fields to Maryland Metropolitan Areas, from
1985 to 1990

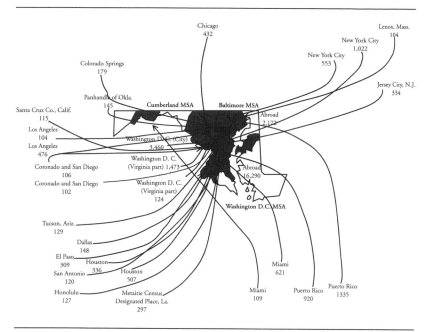

Source: U.S. Bureau of the Census, 1990 Public Use Microdata Samples (5 percent), issued July
1993; Washington, D.C.

Compared with the Washington, D.C., MSA (Maryland part), the
Baltimore MSA received a much smaller flow of Hispanic newcomers
from abroad (2,172). Most of the Hispanic newcomers to the Baltimore MSA were from Puerto Rico (920), New York City (533),
Houston, Texas (336), Metairie CDP (census designated place), Louisiana (297), Colorado Springs, Colorado (179), the Oklahoma Panhandle (145), Tucson, Arizona (129), Honolulu, Hawaii (127),
Miami, Florida (109), Coronado and San Diego (106) and Los Angeles, California (104), and Lenox, Massachusetts (104).

PROFILE OF HISPANIC NEWCOMERS
TO HIGH-GROWTH STATES

Who are the Hispanic newcomers to these destination communities?
To answer this question, we focus on three demographic identifiers—

ethnicity, citizenship status, and occupational status—using data from the 1990 PUMS.

Ethnic Composition

Figures 8.21 to 8.28 depict the distribution of Hispanics by ethnicity in each of the case-study states. In every state except Maryland, Hispanics of Mexican ancestry predominate. Eighty-four percent of the Hispanic newcomers to Nebraska (figure 8.23), 60 percent of those settling in Minnesota, Iowa, Arkansas, and Nevada (figures 8.21, 8.22, 8.24, and 8.25, respectively) and close to half of those arriving in Tennessee (figure 8.26) and Georgia (figure 8.27) (46 percent each) were of Mexican decent. Between 1985 and 1990, either Puerto Ricans or "other" Hispanics constituted the second-largest ethnic group settling in each of these seven states.

In contrast with the foregoing seven states, the ethnic composition of Maryland's Hispanic population is far more diverse. Central Americans constituted the largest group of the state's Hispanic newcomers (27 percent), followed closely by South Americans (21 percent). Mexicans and Puerto Ricans each accounted for about 14 percent of the Hispanic newcomers to Maryland (figure 8.28). Relative to the other case-study states, it is noteworthy that Maryland had the largest percentage of Dominicans (2 percent) and Georgia (figure 8.27) the largest percentage of Puerto Ricans (16 percent). Tennessee (figure 8.26) had the largest percentage of Cubans (9 percent) and other Hispanics (21 percent).

Citizenship Status

Figures 8.29 to 8.36 illustrate the citizenship status of the Hispanic newcomers. The five categories of citizenship were as follows: U.S. born, not a U.S. citizen, naturalized, born abroad to American parents, and born in a U.S. territory. The 1990 PUMS data reveal that in each state, the majority of Hispanic newcomers were born in the United States, Puerto Rico, or another U.S. territory. This is especially true for Hispanics who settled in the case-study midwestern states between 1985 and 1990. It is also true for those who moved into Tennessee (figure 8.34) and Arkansas (figure 8.32).

More than 70 percent of Hispanics settling in Minnesota, Iowa, Nebraska (figures 8.29, 8.30, and 8.31, respectively), Arkansas, and Tennessee during this period were born in the United States or one of its territories. Significantly smaller percentages of the Hispanic popu-

(*Text continues on p. 296.*)

Figure 8.21   Ethnicity of Hispanics in Minnesota, 1990

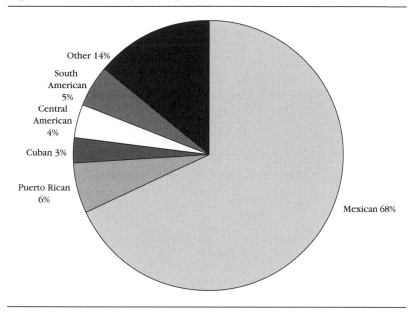

Source: U.S. Bureau of Census, 1990 Public Use Microdata Samples (5 percent) issued July 1993; Washington, D.C.

Figure 8.22   Ethnicity of Hispanics in Iowa, 1990

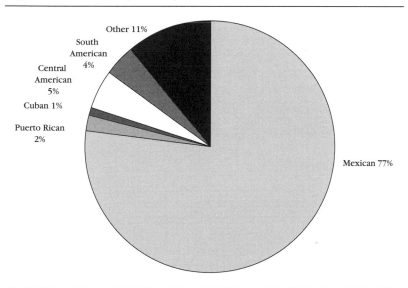

Source: U.S. Bureau of Census, 1990 Public Use Microdata Samples (5 percent) issued July 1993; Washington, D.C.

Figure 8.23   Ethnicity of Hispanics in Nebraska, 1990

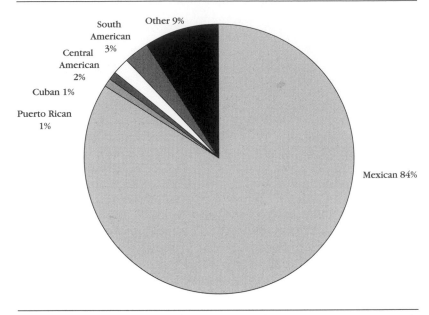

Source: U.S. Bureau of Census, 1990 Public Use Microdata Samples (5 percent) issued July 1993; Washington, D.C.

Figure 8.24   Ethnicity of Hispanics in Arkansas, 1990

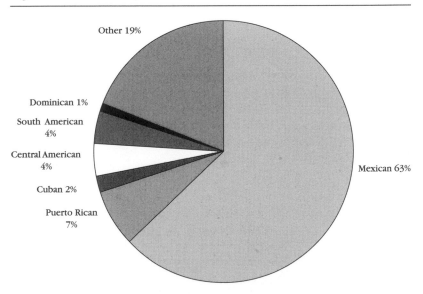

Source: U.S. Bureau of Census, 1990 Public Use Microdata Samples (5 percent) issued July 1993; Washington, D.C.

Figure 8.25   Ethnicity of Hispanics in Nevada, 1990

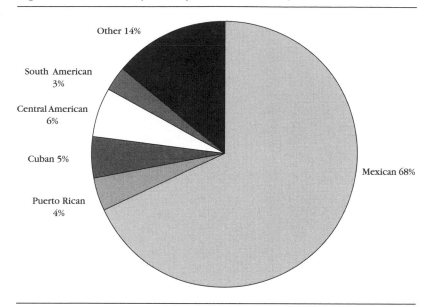

Source: U.S. Bureau of Census, 1990 Public Use Microdata Samples (5 percent) issued July 1993; Washington, D.C.

Figure 8.26   Ethnicity of Hispanics in Tennessee, 1990

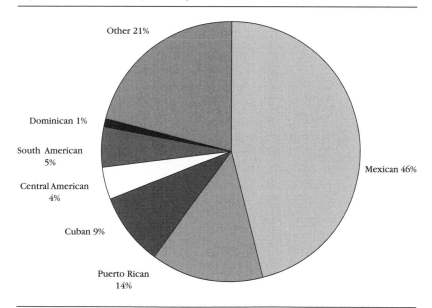

Source: U.S. Bureau of Census, 1990 Public Use Microdata Samples (5 percent) issued July 1993; Washington, D.C.

Figure 8.27   Ethnicity of Hispanics in Georgia, 1990

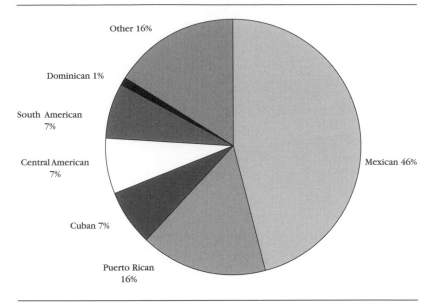

Source: U.S. Bureau of Census, 1990 Public Use Microdata Samples (5 percent) issued July 1993; Washington, D.C.

Figure 8.28   Ethnicity of Hispanics in Maryland, 1990

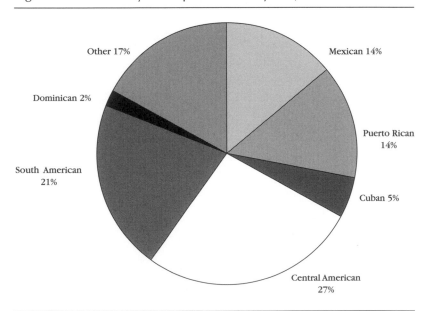

Source: U.S. Bureau of Census, 1990 Public Use Microdata Samples (5 percent) issued July 1993; Washington, D.C.

Figure 8.29   Citizenship of Hispanics in Minnesota, 1990

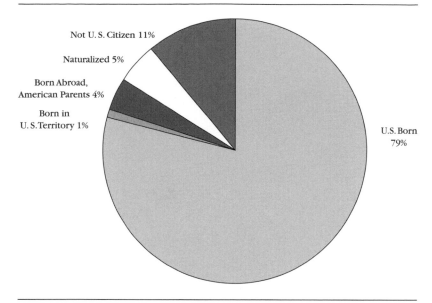

Not U. S. Citizen 11%

Naturalized 5%

Born Abroad,
American Parents 4%

Born in
U. S. Territory 1%

U.S. Born
79%

Source: U.S. Bureau of Census, 1990 Public Use Microdata Samples (5 percent) issued July 1993; Washington, D.C.

Figure 8.30   Citizenship of Hispanics in Iowa, 1990

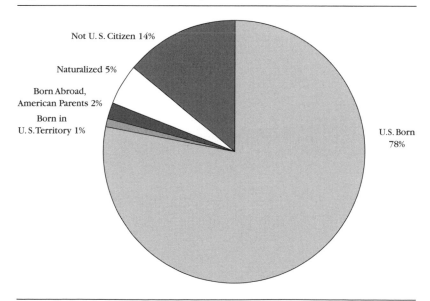

Not U. S. Citizen 14%

Naturalized 5%

Born Abroad,
American Parents 2%

Born in
U. S. Territory 1%

U.S. Born
78%

Source: U.S. Bureau of Census, 1990 Public Use Microdata Samples (5 percent) issued July 1993; Washington, D.C.

Figure 8.31   Citizenship of Hispanics in Nebraska, 1990

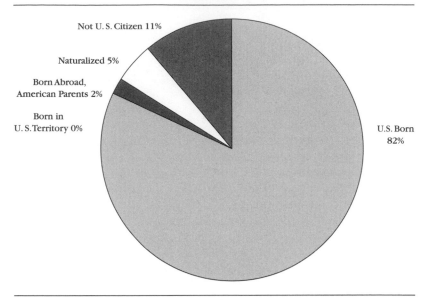

Not U. S. Citizen 11%

Naturalized 5%

Born Abroad,
American Parents 2%

Born in
U. S. Territory 0%

U.S. Born
82%

Source: U.S. Bureau of Census, 1990 Public Use Microdata Samples (5 percent) issued July 1993; Washington, D.C.

Figure 8.32   Citizenship of Hispanics in Arkansas, 1990

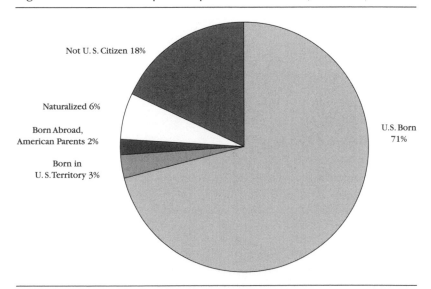

Not U. S. Citizen 18%

Naturalized 6%

Born Abroad,
American Parents 2%

Born in
U. S. Territory 3%

U.S. Born
71%

Source: U.S. Bureau of Census, 1990 Public Use Microdata Samples (5 percent) issued July 1993; Washington, D.C.

Figure 8.33   Citizenship of Hispanics in Nevada, 1990

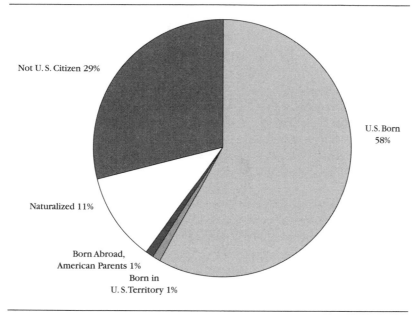

Not U. S. Citizen 29%

U.S. Born
58%

Naturalized 11%

Born Abroad,
American Parents 1%
Born in
U. S. Territory 1%

Source: U.S. Bureau of Census, 1990 Public Use Microdata Samples (5 percent) issued July 1993; Washington, D.C.

Figure 8.34   Citizenship of Hispanics in Tennessee, 1990

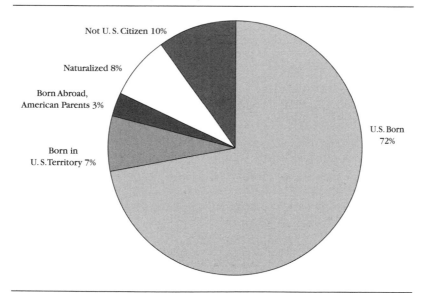

Not U. S. Citizen 10%

Naturalized 8%

Born Abroad,
American Parents 3%

U.S. Born
72%

Born in
U. S. Territory 7%

Source: U.S. Bureau of Census, 1990 Public Use Microdata Samples (5 percent) issued July 1993; Washington, D.C.

Figure 8.35   Citizenship of Hispanics in Georgia, 1990

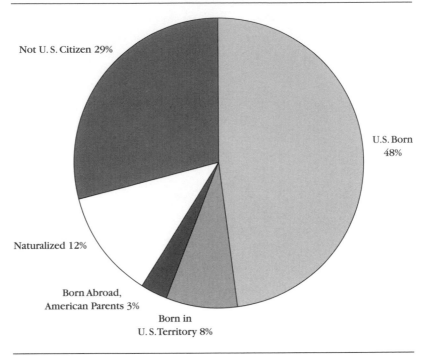

Not U. S. Citizen 29%

U.S. Born
48%

Naturalized 12%

Born Abroad,
American Parents 3%

Born in
U. S. Territory 8%

Source: U.S. Bureau of Census, 1990 Public Use Microdata Samples (5 percent) issued July 1993; Washington, D.C.

lations settling in Nevada, Georgia, and Maryland (figures 8.33, 8.35, and 8.36, respectively) between 1985 and 1990 were born in the United States or its territories. In each of these states, a greater proportion of the Hispanic newcomers were born abroad and thus were not U.S. citizens. In 1990, Maryland had the largest proportion of noncitizens among its Hispanic population (36 percent), followed by Nevada (29 percent) and Georgia (29 percent). In the remaining case-study states—Arkansas (18 percent), Iowa (14 percent), Minnesota (11 percent), Nebraska (11 percent), and Tennessee (10 percent)— less than 20 percent of the Hispanic newcomers during the late 1980s were not U.S. citizens.

Occupational Status

What roles do the Hispanic newcomers play in the restructured economies of our case-study communities? Are there significant or observ-

Figure 8.36   Citizenship of Hispanics in Maryland, 1990

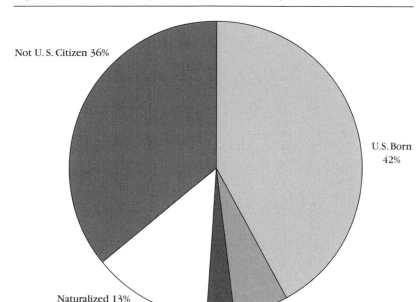

Not U. S. Citizen 36%

U.S. Born 42%

Naturalized 13%

Born in U. S. Territory 6%

Born Abroad, American Parents 3%

Source: U.S. Bureau of Census, 1990 Public Use Microdata Samples (5 percent) issued July 1993; Washington, D.C.

able differences based on community of origin—that is, are Hispanics moving from abroad playing a different role from those moving from another state in the United States? How do the labor-market experiences of the various Hispanic newcomer groups differ from those of black newcomers to these communities?

In an effort to provide preliminary answers to these questions, we extracted data from the 1990 census PUMS file on the occupations of all workers and of three groups of newcomers to the case-study communities between 1985 and 1990 (U.S. Bureau of the Census 1993): Hispanics moving from abroad, Hispanics moving from other U.S. states (that is, interstate movers), and blacks moving from other U.S. states. We then organized the occupations of these three groups into the following categories:

primary activities comprise agriculture, forestry, and fisheries

transformative activities comprise manufacturing and construction

distributive services comprise transportation, communication, wholesale, and retail trade

producer services comprise finance, insurance, real estate (FIRE), and
business services

personal services comprise entertainment, repairs, eating, and drinking

social services comprise medical, education, and government

active military comprises active status in a branch of the US military

For the purposes of this study, we present the resulting data in the
aggregate for all of the case-study communities, for those in the Midwest, for those in the South, and for those in the West.

In 1990, as we see from table 8.2, Hispanic newcomers, both interstate movers (48 percent) and movers from abroad (47 percent),
were concentrated in two industrial sectors—transformative activities
and distributive services—in roughly the same proportions as the total workforce (52 percent) across our eight case-study communities.
In contrast with the total workforce, however, Hispanics were overrepresented in what might be termed the low-wage sectors of the
economies of our case-study communities—primary activities and
personal services—especially those moving from abroad. Whereas
only 11 percent of the total workforce in our communities were employed in these two sectors in 1990, 17 percent of Hispanic interstate
movers and 27 percent of Hispanic movers from abroad were concentrated in these two sectors. At the other end of the occupational spectrum, the Hispanic newcomers were underrepresented in what might
be termed the relatively high-wage sectors of the communities' economies—producer services and social services. As table 8.2 shows, 36
percent of the total workforce were employed in these two sectors in
1990. However, only 27 percent and 21 percent, respectively, of Hispanic interstate movers and Hispanic movers from abroad were employed in these two sectors in 1990.

Previous research has suggested that employers prefer Hispanic and
immigrant labor over native-born and especially African American
labor in the restructured U.S. economy (Kirschenman and Neckerman 1991). However, there is no evidence that such preferences were
operating in our case-study communities during the late 1980s. The
data in table 8.2 reveal that the occupational profiles of the black
newcomers parallel those of the Hispanic newcomers to our case-
study communities. That is, in 1990, the black newcomers were basically at parity with the total workforce in transformative and distributive services (48 percent versus 52 percent), were overrepresented in
primary and personal services (19 percent versus 11 percent), and

Table 8.2   Distribution of Hispanic and Newcomer Workers in High-Growth States, by Occupation, 1990 (Percentage)

Occupational Category	All Workers	Hispanic Newcomers		Black Newcomers
		Interstate Movers	Movers from Abroad	
N (total workforce)	17,401,600	75,538	37,943	120,623
Primary Activities	4.1	4.0	7.8	5.1
Transformative activities	23.2	24.0	24.0	23.8
Distributive activities	28.8	23.9	23.3	24.1
Producer services	9.1	8.5	7.8	8.2
Personal services	6.6	12.6	18.9	14.1
Social services	26.8	18.0	13.6	17.0
Active military	1.1	8.6	4.3	7.5
Unemployed	0.2	0.3	0.4	0.3

Source: U.S. Bureau of the Census, 1990 Public Use Microdata Samples (5 percent) issued July 1993; Washington, D.C.

were underrepresented in producer and social services (25 percent versus 36 percent).

The role that active military duty plays in the resettlement patterns of the Hispanic (and black) newcomers is worthy of note here. Active military service does not appear to be a major source of employment for either Hispanics or blacks, but it should be noted that both groups are overrepresented in the active military across all eight case-study states. Although only 1 percent of the total workforce was engaged in active military duty in 1990, the comparable statistics for Hispanic interstate movers, Hispanic movers from abroad, and black newcomers to the case-study states were 8.6 percent, 4.3 percent, and 7.5 percent, respectively.

The occupational profiles for Hispanic (and black) newcomers to the South basically parallel those for all our case-study states (table 8.3). However, the profiles for the Midwest (table 8.4) and the West (table 8.5) differ in noteworthy ways from the pattern for all eight case-study states. In particular, as table 8.4 shows, the Hispanic newcomers were underrepresented in primary activities and personal services and overrepresented in transformative activities and distributive services in the Midwest, which is not surprising given the type of industries that dominated the restructuring of the Midwest economy over the previous two decades. In comparison with the rest of the case-study states, the degree to which the Hispanic newcomers were overrepresented in the primary activities and personal services occupa-

Table 8.3   Distribution of Hispanic and Black Newcomer Workers in Southern High-Growth States, by Occupation, 1990 (Percentage)

		Hispanic Newcomers		Black Newcomers
Occupational Category	All Workers	Interstate Movers	Movers from Abroad	
N (total workforce)	11,253	47,380	25,296	75,937
Primary Activities	2.8	3.6	8.8	5.3
Transformative activities	24.5	23.9	24.2	23.6
Distributive activities	28.8	24.0	26.1	24.6
Producer services	9.2	8.8	8.6	8.8
Personal services	5.9	6.8	11.3	8.2
Social services	27.1	19.7	15.1	18.8
Active military	1.5	12.9	5.8	10.6
Unemployed	0.2	0.2	0.2	0.2

Source: U.S. Bureau of the Census, 1990 Public Use Microdata Samples (5 percent) issued July 1993; Washington, D.C.

Table 8.4   Distribution of Hispanic and Black Newcomer Workers in Midwestern High-Growth States, by Occupation, 1990 (Percentage)

		Hispanic Newcomers		Black Newcomers
Occupational Category	All Workers	Interstate Movers	Movers from Abroad	
N (total workforce)	5,372,705	12,522	4,028	16,792
Primary Activities	6.8	3.3	3.6	3.5
Transformative activities	21.8	33.9	35.2	33.7
Distributive activities	29.1	28.3	23.2	27.2
Producer services	9.0	7.4	7.6	7.6
Personal services	5.7	4.2	5.8	4.5
Social services	27.0	19.0	22.4	20.1
Active military	0.4	3.9	2.1	3.4
Unemployed	0.1	0.0	0.0	0.0

Source: U.S. Bureau of the Census, 1990 Public Use Microdata Samples (5 percent) issued July 1993; Washington, D.C.

Table 8.5   Distribution of Hispanic and Black Newcomer Workers in Western High-Growth States, by Occupation, 1990 (Percentage)

| Occupational Category | All Workers | Hispanic Newcomers | | Black Newcomers |
		Interstate Movers	Movers from Abroad	
N (total workforce)	774,938	19,173	8,619	27,894
Primary activities	3.6	5.0	7.1	5.6
Transformative activities	15.0	18.9	18.0	18.5
Distributive activities	26.6	23.2	15.0	20.8
Producer services	9.3	7.6	5.5	6.9
Personal services	24.1	30.8	47.3	35.8
Social services	19.8	12.3	5.4	10.3
Active military	1.4	1.8	0.9	1.5
Unemployed	0.2	0.5	0.8	0.6

Source: U.S. Bureau of the Census, 1990 Public Use Microdata Samples (5 percent) issued July 1993; Washington, D.C.

tions was much higher in the West. This, too, is an expected finding, given that the occupational profile is based on data from one state, Nevada, whose economy is largely service oriented.

SOCIAL RECEPTIVITY

How were the newly arriving Hispanics received in these communities? Because the presence of Hispanics in the case-study communities is relatively recent, little systematic evidence exists on responses to their presence at the local level. Thus, we draw upon data from public opinion polls, media coverage, and anecdotal evidence in an effort to provide a preliminary answer to this question. The evidence that we have been able to assemble from these sources indicates that the public response in these newly emergent Hispanic communities has been mixed, not unlike the reactions Hispanic immigrants have received in Los Angeles and other port-of-entry communities (Oliver and Johnson 1984; Johnson and Oliver 1989; Johnson and Farrell 1993; Johnson, Farrell, and Guinn 1997).

On the one hand, local businesses in these emergent Hispanic communities appear to have embraced the Hispanic newcomers, extolling their work ethic (De La Cruz 1996; Branson 1997; Hamburg, Yates, and Becerra 1997a, 1997b; Molpus 1997) and their contributions to the local economy (Haga 1997; Ribadeneira 1996). In Iowa, for example, the influx of Hispanics and other people of color was credited with transforming the state from a net exporter to a net importer of population (Pins 1997). Recognizing the emerging market potential of their presence in these communities, new businesses have formed and existing businesses have made major adjustments in their business practices, in some of these communities, to address specific needs of the Hispanic newcomers. On the other hand, tensions and conflicts have arisen between the Hispanic newcomers and the locals over jobs, bilingual education, fair or equitable representation in social and political institutions, and other matters.

On the positive side, print media in these communities is replete with examples of the business community seeking to accommodate the needs of the Hispanic newcomers. Allina Health Systems, one of Minnesota's largest hospital and HMO systems, reportedly has begun to adopt alternative healing strategies, largely in response to the influx of Hispanic immigrants into the state (Slovut 1996), and a new business group has formed in St. Paul, Minnesota, to better address the insurance needs of Hispanics and other newly arriving groups (Gilbert 1996).

In several of these newly emergent Hispanic communities, media accounts indicate that banks and other financial institutions have begun to train their employees to deal with the growing immigrant population. In some cases, local businesses reportedly have expanded their workforce by hiring Spanish-speaking or bilingual workers in an effort to serve the Hispanic population more effectively.

To address the needs of the newly arrived Hispanics and to take advantage of this emerging market, English newspapers in these communities have increased advertising in Spanish, the circulation of Spanish-language newspapers has increased dramatically, and Spanish radio stations have proliferated (Plunkett 1997a; Casas 1997). In several of these communities, immigrant advocacy groups have formed to aid Hispanic newcomers in their efforts to secure various services and in obtaining documentation for employment and citizenship (Casas 1997; De La Cruz 1997).

In Nashville, Tennessee, a Mexican national was killed by police after brandishing a knife at a local hospital where he was seeking treatment. Many in the community felt this killing was unjust, and in response, community members from all walks of life came together to raise the funds needed to return his remains to his family in Mexico (Chavez 1997). In Maryland, as well, signs of community members' mobilizing in support of the growing population diversity occasioned by the influx of Hispanic newcomers were also apparent ("Newcomers Give Maryland a Boost" 1997). After President Bill Clinton signed the welfare reform bill, Maryland's governor vowed to use state funds to continue to provide Hispanics and other immigrants with welfare benefits (Dresser 1996). Several communities in Maryland also recently voted to allow noncitizens to vote in local elections, although one community rejected such a proposal (Scheets 1997). Many communities in the case-study states now sponsor ethnic festivals and cross-cultural events to acknowledge and celebrate the Hispanic or immigrant presence in their communities and to foster understanding and communication between newcomers and locals (Hughes 1997).

Unfortunately, there has also been considerable backlash against Hispanics (and other people of color) who have settled in these communities. Negative views about the impact of the Hispanic newcomers on the social fabric of these communities, which were formerly inhabited by a predominately non-Hispanic white population, appear to undergird the backlash (Pinney 1996; Howlett 1995).

A statewide Nebraska poll revealed, for example, that rural residents of the state felt that their quality of life was being adversely affected by the migration of Hispanics and other people of color into the state (Hendee 1997). Similarly, an Iowa poll that queried residents about the changing makeup of their towns revealed that those making less than twenty thousand dollars annually felt that a diverse population was a "disadvantage." Reflective of the depth of views of this type, a community group in Arkansas reportedly held public forums in an effort to garner support for a proposed five-year moratorium on foreign immigration to the United States (Harton 1997). In several communities, legislation has been introduced to establish English as the official language, in response to the linguistic diversity that accompanies the Hispanic influx (Scott 1997; Cain 1997).

Concerns about strains on public and social services also appear to undergird the negative attitudes toward the Hispanic newcomers uncovered in public opinion polls (Harold 1997; Molpus 1997; Pinney 1996; Howlett 1995). In both Nashville, Tennessee (Hadley 1997), and Howard County, Maryland ("New Challenge for Public Schools" 1997), local residents reportedly have registered concern about what they perceive to be an overtaxed education system as a consequence of the influx of lower-class Hispanic immigrants. In Iowa and Nebraska, concerns have been raised about the dramatic rise in crime rates, school enrollment and turnover rates, and pressures on existing infrastructure, social services, and housing—all of which are attributed to the influx of Hispanic newcomers (Gouveia and Stull 1995; Grey

1995). In Tennessee, media coverage suggests that the primary issue of concern among the locals appears to be alleged drug trafficking by newly arriving Hispanics (Bradford 1997). In Arkansas and Tennessee, according to media reports, the emergence of immigrant youth gangs, purported by law enforcement officials to be imported from the major metropolitan areas with a more established gang presence, is a pressing concern (Hamburg, Yates, and Becerra 1997a). Cultural conflicts and language barriers in schools, the health care industry, and grassroots organizations are also sources or areas of major concern (Plunkett 1977b).

In part as a result of these and other issues raised by long-term residents, ethnic tensions abound in many of these communities. The sources of the tension are varied. They range from the closure of a Hispanic dance club for alleged "racist" reasons and accusations of unfair jury selection in cases involving Hispanic defendants to white student opposition to the use of a multicultural curriculum in a high school undergoing ethnic transition and community votes to deny noncitizens the right to vote in local elections (see Ruggles 1997a, 1997b; King 1997; Hamburg, Yates, and Becerra 1997b; DeFrank 1997; Leahy 1997; Scheets 1997). Ethnic tensions over jobs also have arisen in these communities between blacks and Hispanics (Branson 1997). Such tensions and conflicts are likely to persist and escalate as we move into the next millennium unless there are proactive initiatives to counter these trends (Okazawa-Rey and Wong 1997).

CONCLUSION

In this chapter we have focused on a heretofore neglected dimension of the growing presence of Hispanics in the United States: the movement of Hispanics beyond the boundaries of port-of-entry communities into states and communities that historically have had little or no experience with Hispanic migration. More specifically, we have focused on eight states that experienced Hispanic population growth between 1990 and 1994 in excess of the national average. Our goals have been to highlight the areas in which the Hispanic newcomers are settling in these states and where they lived prior to moving into specific communities within these states; to provide insights into the ethnic, citizenship, and occupational status of the Hispanic newcomers to these communities; and to gauge the receptivity of the destination communities.

Hispanic population growth in excess of the national rate was widely dispersed throughout each of the eight case-study states—in both urban and rural counties. However, in each of the states, the Hispanic population is concentrated, for the most part, in metropolitan areas. Several states, most notably California, Texas, and Florida but also Illinois and several U.S. territories (especially Puerto Rico), are major redistributors of Hispanic population to the eight case-study states. Within these states and jurisdictions, large metropolitan areas, many of which were experiencing major economic woes during the late 1980s and early 1990s, constituted the in-migration fields or sending-source areas for the Hispanic newcomers to our eight case-study states. In addition, a substantial proportion of the Hispanic newcomers arrived in our case-study states directly from abroad.

Irrespective of whether they were moving from port-of-entry communities in the United States, from a U.S. territory like Puerto Rico, or from abroad, the economic and industrial transformation occurring in the Midwest and the Sun Belt appears to be responsible for Hispanic migration and settlement in specific destination communities within our study area. In each of these states, the Hispanic newcomers are employed primarily in transformative and distributive activities and secondarily in primary activities and personal services. Their concentration in transformative activities reflects the massive demand for labor in the construction industry in each of the eight case-study states and in the meat-packing industry in the midwestern states. Their concentration in distributive services and personal services reflects the emergence of the service sector, more generally, as a major employment growth area within the U.S. economy. Across all sectors, the growing presence of Hispanics reflects what is well documented in the research literature—employer preferences for Hispanic and immigrant workers in certain sectors of the U.S. economy (see Kirschenman and Neckerman 1991; Neckerman and Kirschenman 1990; Johnson, Farrell, and Stoloff, 1998), although we found no evidence of discrimination against either long-term residents or black newcomers in our case-study communities.

At the local level within the communities studied, reactions to the Hispanic newcomers have been mixed. Community business leaders appear to be excited about the role that the newly arriving Hispanics are playing in the local economy and about the emerging market opportunities afforded by their presence. However, local citizens have registered concerns about the impact of the Hispanic newcomers on the social fabric of their communities, and their concerns have led to ethnic tensions and conflicts over housing, jobs, schools, and other institutions and valuable resources.

Much of the evidence about emerging tensions and conflicts is, at best, anecdotal, but public attitudes toward the Hispanic newcomers uncovered in public opinion polls, and examples of specific incidences of tension and conflict covered in the news media, suggest that vigilant action on the part of state and local officials is needed to stem the tide of racial and ethnic antagonism in these communities. Lessons learned from Los Angeles, a port-of-entry community with a large Hispanic population, suggest that, if such steps are not taken, the prospects for racial and ethnic harmony with the newly emerging Hispanic communities will likely be bleak (Okazawa-Rey and Wong 1997).

REFERENCES

Barringer, Felicity. 1993. "Minorities on the Move, Often Unpredictably: Who Goes Where and Why." *New York Times*, June 6.

Bean, Frank D., and Maria Tienda. 1987. *Hispanics in the United States*. New York: Russell Sage Foundation.

Bradford, Michelle. 1997. "Hispanic Men Target of 'Meth' Crackdown in Fayetteville Area." *Arkansas Democrat-Gazette*, March 9.

Branson, Reed. 1997. "Immigrants Changing Dixie." *Commercial Appeal*, September 7, B5.

Cain, Andrew. 1997. "Tide of Illegals Surges into Washington Area; Cost to Taxpayers Defies Calculation." *Washington Times*, March 17.

Casas, Miguela. 1997. "Sign of the Times: Hispanic Influx Gives the Business Community an Exotic New Accent in Northwest Arkansas." *Arkansas Democrat-Gazette*, May 4.

Chavez, Tim. 1997. " 'Community' Aims to Help Those in Need." *Tennessean*, August 16.

Cole, Robert E., and Donald Deskins. 1998. "Racial Factors in Site Location and Employment Patterns of Japanese Auto Firms in America." *California Management Review* 31(1): 9–22.

Daniels, Michael. 1997. "Warm Areas Continue Hottest Job Growth." *Monthly Labor Review* 120: 43–44.

Davis, Daphne. 1997. "Hispanics May Get More Say on Northwest College Board." *Arkansas Democrat-Gazette*, January 5.

DeFrank, Sean. 1997. "Local Students Protest Multicultural Programs." *Las Vegas Review-Journal*, June 4, 3AA.

De La Cruz, Bonna. 1996. "Nashville's Lamp Draws Thousands; One-Third of Nashville's Growth Since 1990 Has Come from International Immigration." *Tennessean*, September 16.

———. 1997. "New Neighbors, New Ways." *Tennessean*, March 21.

Dresser, Michael. 1996. "Maryland to Pay Benefits to Immigrants; Governor Calls U.S. Ban on Aid 'Unacceptable'; State to Divert Savings; Reaction to Move by Glendening Is Generally Favorable." *Baltimore Sun*, September 17.

Foust, Dean, and Maria Mallory. 1993. "The Boom Belt: There's No Speed Limit on Growth Along the South's I-85." *Business Week*, September 27, 98–104.

Frey, William H., 1996. "Immigration, Domestic Migration, and Democratic Balkanization in America: New Evidence for the 1990s." *Population and Development Review* 22(4): 741–63.

Frey, William H., K-L. Liaw, Y. Xie, and M. J. Carlson. 1993a. "Interstate Migration and Immigration for Whites and Minorities, 1985–1990: The Emergence of Multiethnic States." Research Report 93-297. Ann Arbor: University of Michigan, Population Studies Center.

———. 1993b. "The New Urban Revival in the United States." *Urban Studies* 30(4–5): 741–75.

———. 1995a. "Interstate Migration of the U.S. Poverty Population: Immigration 'Pushes' and Welfare Magnet 'Pulls.' " Research Report 95-331. Ann Arbor: University of Michigan, Population Studies Center.

———. 1995b. "Immigration and Internal Migration: 'Flight' from U.S. Metropolitan Areas: Toward a New Demographic Balkanization." *Urban Studies* 32(4–5): 733–57.

Gilbert, Evelyn. 1996. "Changing Demographics Have Created New Market Opportunities and Prompted St. Paul Fire and Marine to Form a Multicultural Business Group." *National Underwriter-Property and Casualty*, April 15, 33.

Gouveia, Lourdes, and David Stull. 1995. "Dances with Cows: Beefpacking's Impact on Garden City, Kansas, and Lexington, Nebraska." In *Any Way You Cut It: Meat Processing and Small-Town America*, edited by David Stull, Michael Broadway, and David Griffith. Lawrence: University of Kansas Press.

Grey, Mark. 1995. "Port, Poultry, and Newcomers in Storm Lake, Iowa." In *Any Way You Cut It: Meat Processing and Small-Town America*, edited by David Stull, Michael Broadway, and David Griffith. Lawrence: University of Kansas Press.

Hadley, Ken. 1997. "Finding Health Care Is Hard for Latinos; Newcomers Face Language Barriers, Red Tape." *Nashville Banner*, July 15.

Haga, Chuck. 1997. "Twin Cities Journal." *Star Tribune*, January 11.

Hamburg, Jay, Jon Yates, and Hector Becerra. 1997a. "Murder Awakens Nashville to Emerging Hispanic Gangs; Latino Community Worries About Controlling Gangs, Now with an Estimated Six Hundred Members." *Tennessean*, July 20.

————. 1997b. "Some Say Immigration Raids Target Single Group." *Tennessean*, August 21.

Harold, Shareese. 1997. "Social Worker Seeking Volunteers to Help Hispanics Cope in Hope." *Arkansas Democrat-Gazette*, April 13.

Harton, Greg. 1997. "Shut Doors to Aliens, Rogers Group Say Influx Eroding Culture of Region, Member Claims." *Arkansas Democrat-Gazette*, July 8.

Havenmann, Judith. 1998. "Revival in the Heartland." *Washington Post National Weekly*, January 5.

Hendee, David. 1997. "Population Changes Worry Rural Residents: The Latest Rural Nebraska Poll Gauges Attitudes About Communities." *Omaha World-Herald*, September 4.

Holmes, Stephen A. 1998. "Immigration Fueling Cities' Strong Growth." *New York Times*, January 1.

Howlett, Debbie. 1995. "Midwest New Hub for Hispanics." *USA Today*, Dec. 15.

Hughes, Dave. 1997. "Festival to Exhibit Latin Food and Culture." *Arkansas Democrat-Gazette*, July 5.

Johnson, James H., Jr., Walter C. Farrell, and Jennifer A. Stoloff. 1998. "The Declining Social and Economic Fortunes of African American Males: A Critical Assessment of Four Perspectives." *Revue of Black Political Economy* 25(4): 17–40.

Johnson, James H., Jr., Walter C. Farrell Jr., and C. Guinn. 1997. "Immigration Reform and the Browning of America: Tensions, Conflicts, and Community Instability in Metropolitan Los Angeles." *International Migration Review* 31(4): 1055–95.

Johnson, J. H., Jr., David M. Grant, and Walter C. Farrell Jr. 1994. "The Myth of Welfare Magnets." *State Government News* 37: 21–24.

Johnson, James H., Jr., and Walter C. Farrell. 1993. "The Fire this Time: The Genesis of the Los Angeles Rebellion of 1992." *North Carolina Law Review* 71(5): 1403–20.

Johnson, James H., Jr., and David M. Grant. 1997. "Post–1980 Black Population Redistribution Trends in the U.S." *Southeastern Geographer* 37(1): 1–19.

Johnson, J. H., Jr., and Melvin Oliver. 1989. "Interethnic Minority Conflict in Urban America: The Effects of Economic and Social Dislocations." *Urban Geography* 10(5): 449–63.

Johnson, J. H., Jr., and Curtis C. Roseman. 1990. "Increasing Black Out-migration from Los Angeles: The Role of Household Dynamics and Kinship Systems." *Annals of the Association of American Geographers* 80(2): 205–22.

Johnson-Webb, Karen D., and James H. Johnson Jr. 1996. "North Carolina Communities in Transition: An Overview of Hispanic In-Migration." *North Carolina Geographer* 5: 21–40.

Kanter, Rosabeth M. 1995. *World Class: Thriving Locally in the Global Economy.* New York: Simon & Schuster.

Kaplan, David H., and Alex Schwartz. 1996. "Minneapolis–St. Paul in the Global Economy." *Urban Geography* 17(1): 44–59.

King, Laura. 1997. "Springdale Dance Club Allowed to Keep License." *Arkansas Democrat-Gazette*, March 23.

Kirschenman, Joleen, and Kathryn M. Neckerman. 1991. "'We'd Love to Hire Them, But . . .': The Meaning of Race for Employers." In *The Urban Underclass*, edited by Christopher Jencks and Paul Peterson. Washington, D.C.: Urban Institute Press.

Labich, Kenneth. 1994. "The Geography of an Emerging America." *Fortune* 129(13): 88–93.

Leahy, Michael. 1997. "You Can't Order People to Start Liking Each Other." *Arkansas Democrat-Gazette*, March 26.

Mair, Andrew, Richard Florida, and Martin Kennedy. 1988. "The New Geography of Automobile Production: Japanese Transplants in North America." *Economic Geography* 64(4): 352–73.

Melcher, Richard, and Kevin Kelly. 1994. "America's Heartland: The Midwest's New Role in the Global Economy." *Business Week*, July 11, 116–24.

———. 1996. "Ahead at Halftime: Minnesota at Mid-Decade." Minnesota Planning Worldwide Web Site http://www.mnplan.state.mn.US

Minnesota Planning. 1997. "Manufacturing Is Big Business in Minnesota." *Population Notes*, OSD 97-82. Minnesota Office of State Demographer. May.

Molpus, Jim. 1997. "Hispanic Community, City Showing Stresses of Growth; Economic Boom Draws Newcomers to 'Good Place.'" *Tennessean*, July 14.

National Research Council. 1997. *The New Americans: Economic, Demographic, and Fiscal Effects of Immigration.* Washington, D.C.: National Academy Press.

Neckerman, Kathryn, and Joleen Kirschenman. 1990. "Hiring Strategies, Racial Bias, and Inner City Workers." *Social Problems* 38(4): 433–47.

"New Challenge for Public Schools; Increase in Low-Income Students Will Test Educators Used to High Results." 1997. *Baltimore Sun*, May 20.

Newbold, K. Bruce. 1997. "Race and Primary, Return, and Onward Interstate Migration." *Professional Geographer*, 49(1): 1–14.

"Newcomers Give Maryland a Boost." 1997. *Washington Post*, Oct. 19.

Okazawa-Rey, Margo, and Marshall Wong. 1997. "Organizing Communities of Color: Addressing Interethnic Conflicts." *Social Justice* 24(1): 24–39.

Oliver, Melvin, and James H. Johnson Jr. 1984. "Interethnic Conflict in an Urban Ghetto: The Case of Blacks and Latinos in Los Angeles." *Research in Social Movements* 6: 57–94.

Oliver, Suzanne. 1996. "It's the Costs, Stupid." *Forbes* 158(10): 252–56.

Peterson, Paul E., and Mark C. Rom. 1990. *Welfare Magnets: A New Case for a National Standard.* Washington, D.C.: Brookings Institution.

Pinney, Gregor. 1996. "Minority Groups Resent Plan to Close General College." *Star Tribune*, April 4.

Pins, Kenneth. 1997. "From Distant Shores to Iowa; About Twenty-Two Thousand Immigrants Have Arrived in the State in the Last Decade, Changing—Slightly—the Demographic Profile of the State." *Des Moines Register*, January 20.

Plunkett, Chuck. 1997a. "Circulation Hits Three Thousand for Shopper in Spanish." *Arkansas Democrat-Gazette*, July 4.

———. 1997b. "Hispanic Relations Study, Group 'Lost in Shuffle.'" *Arkansas Democrat-Gazette*, July 13.

Ribadeneira, Diego. 1996. "Hispanics Find Warm Welcome in Cold Midwest." *Boston Globe*, January 8.

Roseman, Curtis. 1977. "Changing Migration Patterns Within the United States." Resource Paper 77-2. Washington, D.C.: Association of American Geographers.

Ruggles, R. A. 1997a. "Courts Weigh Changing How Jurors Selected." *Omaha World Herald*, February 21.

———. 1997b. "Jury Selection Is Contested by Hispanics." *Omaha World Herald*, February 5.

Saporito, Bill. 1994. "The World's Best Cities for Business." *Fortune*, 130(10): 112–42.

Scott, A. A. 1997. "English, Unofficially." *Des Moines Business Record*, February 24.

Scheets, Gary. 1997. "Garrett Park Rejects Immigrant Voting Right." *Washington Times*, June 18.

Slovut, Gordon. 1996. "Allina Looks at Herbal Diet and Ethnic Therapies." *Star Tribune*, October 24.

Stull, S., Michael Broadway, and David Griffith, eds. 1995. *Any Way You Cut It: Meat Processing and Small-Town America.* Lawrence: University of Kansas Press.

U.S. Bureau of the Census. 1993. *Census of Population and Housing, 1990: Public Use Microdata Samples, Technical Documention.* Washington, D.C.: U.S. Government Printing Office.

———. 1995. "The Nation's Hispanic Population, 1994." Statistical Brief 95-25. Washington, D.C.: U.S. Government Printing Office.

Valbrun, Marjorie. 1999. "A Wave of Refugees Lubricates the Economy of Rustic Utica, New York." *Wall Street Journal*, March 9.

Ward, Greg. 1997. "Hispanic Dreams Come True in Land of Labor Shortage; 'Nashville Is Growing and We Are Part of This.'" *Nashville Banner*, July 16.

CHAPTER 9

New Black Migration Patterns in the United States: Are They Affected by Recent Immigration?

William H. Frey

Since the end of World War II, migration trends among African Americans have followed patterns distinct from those of whites. Studies evaluating these trends up through the 1990 census (Johnson and Campbell 1981; Long 1988; Frey and Fielding 1995) have shown a turnaround in the historic black out-migration from the rural South to the urban North in the 1970s—a full decade after whites showed a wholesale shift toward the Sun Belt. This movement continued through the 1980s, when black destinations became far more concentrated in the rebounding southeast part of the country, increasing that region's already large historic share of the black population (Frey 1994; Johnson and Grant 1997; Frey 1998a).

Most discussions of this new movement have emphasized the economic "pushes" and "pulls" of declining Rust Belt and northeast metropolitan areas, coupled with the strong job-generating engines that have evolved in "New South" metropolitan areas like Atlanta, Dallas, and Charlotte. Somewhat less attention has been given to the impacts that immigration may impose upon the out-migration patterns of African Americans, especially those with low skills, from gateway areas outside of the South. This dynamic, when superimposed on other forces, will not only help to shape the redistribution patterns for blacks but may also hold important implications for the racial and ethnic makeup of immigrant gateway regions, which are becoming demographically distinct from other parts of the country (Frey 1995c, 1998b). The analyses in this chapter investigate the impact of immigration on the internal dynamics of black society, as contrasted with that of whites, and show what these and other new black migration patterns imply for the new "race-space" demographic profiles that are evolving across broad regions of the country.

311

THE DYNAMICS OF IMMIGRATION
AND INTERNAL MIGRATION

New dynamics of immigration and internal migration have become evident with recent analyses of the 1990 U.S. census and post-1990 estimates (Frey 1995c, 1996; Frey and Liaw 1998b). These studies show that those states and metropolitan areas that are most heavily impacted by recent immigration flows are witnessing a selective out-migration of internal migrants to other parts of the country where fewer immigrants reside. Although this phenomenon was already evident in the late 1970s (see 1980 census studies by Filer 1992; Walker, Ellis, and Barff 1992; and White and Imai 1993), its scope appears to have widened over time. Immigration flows to the United States remain highly focused on only a few port-of-entry areas. Yet over time, immigration has accelerated in absolute numbers and differed dramatically in its demographic composition (Borjas and Freeman 1992; Fix and Passel 1994). Current immigrants are predominantly from Latin American and Asian national origins and are, therefore, largely Hispanic and Asian minorities. Although migrant groups continue to be bimodal on social-class attributes, the newer immigrant waves are more heavily represented among the lower-skilled and low-income rungs of the socioeconomic ladder.

These larger magnitudes and changed demographic profiles of migration flows to a small number of port-of-entry destinations, it can be argued, will precipitate an out-migration of native-born Americans as a result of altered economic and social conditions (Tilove and Hallinan 1993). The increased number of immigrants with high-school educations or less compete with native workers for low-skill jobs and bid down their wages. The arrival of immigrant ethnic minorities, also in large numbers, changes the cultural milieu and perceptions of social costs for whites and more established minorities, which can lead to out-migration. My earlier analyses of migration patterns for the total population and for whites (non-Latino whites) are consistent with these views (Frey 1995b, 1996). However, these studies do not examine the impact of immigration on black internal-migration patterns.

The history of black long-distance migration in the United States is closely intertwined with the ebbs and flows of immigration into traditional port-of-entry areas (Reder 1963; Hamilton 1964). The recent waves of mostly Latin American and Asian immigrants[1] represent a renewed economic competition with blacks on the basis of skill substitution, informal networking, and even affirmative action regulations, which may serve to favor the new immigrant groups (Waldinger 1989, 1996; Tienda and Liang 1992; Hirschman 1988; Tilove 1993). The fact that national studies do not show blacks to be appreciably disadvantaged by the wave of immigrants on labor-force and income measures (see reviews in Fix and Passel 1994; and Espenshade 1993) might be explained by the out-migration of blacks away from high-immigration areas. Although such black out-migration was not evident in Randall Filer's (1992) study of 1980 census migration patterns, the magnitude and character of immigration to these areas has changed considerably since 1980. In thiss chapter we address two questions:

1. Has recent immigration exerted an impact on the internal out-migration of blacks similar to its impact on whites, in terms of its magnitude and selectivity?

2. Are the spatial patterns of immigration-influenced black out-migration similar to those for whites?

The data for this study draw primarily from a special migration matrix prepared from the 1990 census of population based on the question of residence "five years ago." These data permit an assessment of net internal migration, and migration from abroad from 1985 to 1990, for individual metropolitan areas. The data were compiled for all individuals age five and older in 1990 (who were alive in 1985) by race and ethnicity, poverty status, and, among persons age twenty-five and older, educational attainment. Because of the way the data were compiled, statistics for whites (non-Latino whites) had to be estimated (see Frey 1995b for details). The reader should also be aware that the data on migration from abroad, as reported in the census, substantially understates the population of illegal immigrants (Fix and Passel 1994; Center for Immigration Studies 1994).

THE IMPACTS OF IMMIGRATION ON WHITE MIGRATION

Before discussing our expectations regarding the relation between immigration and black internal migration, we review key findings of our analyses of immigration impacts on white internal movement. First, we found that immigration exerts a unique socioeconomic selectivity on white out-migration from metropolitan areas. Although typically long-distance migration disproportionately selects persons with higher educations and professional occupations (Lansing and Mueller 1967;

Long 1988), we have found that out-migration from high-immigration areas follows a unique pattern. It disproportionately selects less-educated and lower-income whites. This is consistent with the argument that it is the less-skilled native born who are in greatest competition with newly arrived immigrants.

A second significant aspect of immigration-influenced white out-migration is its unique spatial pattern. Here again, there is a contrast with more conventional long-distance migration. The latter tends to be more "pull-oriented," such that migrants around the country converge on a few metropolitan areas with high or rising incomes and good employment prospects. In contrast, out-migration from high-immigration areas follows a more "push-oriented" pattern in which destinations are more diffuse and, in the case of California, lead migrants to adjacent states (Frey 1995a).

Together, these unique attributes of white out-migration from high-immigration areas hold important implications for both local and national demographic structures. On the local level, the demographic displacement of out-migrating whites by immigrants and new minorities is exacerbated at the lower end of the socioeconomic spectrum, which can lead toward sharp disparities in an area's race and class structure. For example, California's 1990 census results show that whites make up 75 percent of the state's college-graduate population but only 29 percent of adults who did not graduate from high school. On a national scale, this selective out-migration from high-immigration metropolitan areas and states can lead to sharp demographic divides by race and class across broad regions of the country.

IMMIGRATION-DOMINANT METROPOLITAN AREAS

Much of this analysis focuses on a comparison of net migration in high-immigration areas with that in other areas where population changes were less strongly affected by immigration from abroad. We draw on an earlier study in which we identified metropolitan areas that are clearly high-immigration areas as compared with areas we consider to be strongly affected by internal migration streams (high-internal-migration areas) and those where there is significant internal out-migration but a relative absence of immigration from abroad (high-out-migration areas) (Frey 1995b, 1996). Our analysis at the metropolitan-area level is shown in table 9.1.

It is not surprising to learn that immigrants gravitate to only a small number of metropolitan areas, because these house the lion's share of the nation's existing immigrant minority enclaves (Bean and

Table 9.1 Net Internal Migration of Whites and Blacks, from 1985 to 1990

Metro Area[a]	Contribution to 1985–1990 Change		Rates of Net Migration[b]		
	Immigration from Abroad	Net Internal Migration	Total	Whites[c]	Black
High-immigration areas					
Los Angeles	899,007	−174,673	−1.3	−2.0	−1.1
New York	756,034	−1,065,580	−6.4	−6.8	−6.4
San Francisco	293,306	−103,498	−1.8	−2.2	−1.4
Miami	210,609	45,287	1.5	−1.0	2.0
Washington, D.C.	190,941	33,634	0.9	0.0	2.1
Chicago	179,524	−293,185	−3.9	−3.8	−5.0
Boston	119,646	−116,506	−3.0	−3.7	−0.3
San Diego	115,847	126,855	5.5	5.8	8.9
Houston	96,782	−142,227	−4.2	−6.0	−0.7
Philadelphia	79,975	−28,400	−0.5	−0.7	−0.3
Dallas	77,301	27,435	0.8	0.0	3.2
High-internal-migration areas					
Atlanta	42,878	192,065	7.3	5.5	11.3
Tampa–St. Petersburg	34,623	159,112	8.2	8.7	1.1
Seattle	63,870	146,026	6.2	6.4	4.1
Phoenix	43,861	139,678	7.2	7.6	11.5
Orlando	35,153	132,449	13.3	11.8	11.6
Las Vegas	20,551	128,680	18.8	19.2	13.2
Sacramento	36,380	117,732	8.6	8.3	12.0
West Palm Beach	21,485	107,940	13.3	14.7	2.6
Charlotte	8,926	66,961	6.2	6.7	3.6
Raleigh–Durham	12,451	66,088	9.6	9.3	10.4
Portland, Ore.	24,335	60,733	4.4	4.4	4.0
Norfolk	33,236	59,292	4.6	2.9	8.0
Nashville	7,569	57,639	6.3	6.6	4.7
Fort Myers, Fla.	3,469	57,613	18.3	19.0	3.8
Daytona Beach	5,137	55,074	15.8	16.5	5.7
High-out-migration areas					
Detroit	45,417	−136,352	−3.2	−3.5	−2.2
Pittsburgh	10,720	−89,759	−4.3	−4.4	−3.0
New Orleans	10,270	−88,356	−7.7	−8.9	−4.2
Cleveland	20,597	−79,925	−3.1	−3.2	−2.9
Denver	28,127	−61,360	−3.6	−4.3	0.2
St. Louis	19,132	−37,262	−1.6	−1.4	−2.7
Milwaukee	13,062	−34,801	−2.3	−3.1	2.3
Buffalo	10,717	−30,572	−2.8	−3.0	−0.8
Other areas					
Columbus, Ohio	13,933	44,622	3.5	3.1	6.0
Minneapolis–St. Paul	28,112	40,277	1.8	1.3	14.8
Baltimore	33,706	29,566	1.3	1.3	1.2

Table 9.1   *Continued*

Metro Area[a]	Contribution to 1985–1990 Change		Rates of Net Migration[b]		
	Immigration from Abroad	Net Internal Migration	Total	Whites[c]	Black
Indianapolis	8,141	15,278	1.3	1.1	2.1
Kansas City	13,962	13,269	0.9	1.2	−0.5
Providence	26,910	11,860	0.9	0.5	3.9
Cincinnati	9,517	9,259	0.6	0.5	0.4
Hartford	24,628	−5,143	−0.5	−1.0	1.6
San Antonio	29,372	−11,600	−1.0	−1.2	−0.4
Rochester, N.Y.	10,884	−14,691	−1.6	−1.8	−0.5
Salt Lake City	14,940	−20,525	−2.1	−2.3	4.9

Source: Author's analysis of special 1990 U.S. Census migration tabulations.
[a]Includes all metro areas with 1990 populations exceeding one million, in addition to six smaller areas which registered net internal migration from 1985 to 1990 exceeding fifty thousand. The metropolitan area definitions are consistent with Office of Management and Budget definitions of CMSAs, MSAs, and NECMA counterparts as of June 30, 1990.
[b]Rates per 100 population, 1990.
[c]Non-Hispanic whites comprise whites plus other races minus Hispanics.

Tienda 1987; Bartel 1989; Barringer, Gardner, and Levin 1993). What is noteworthy is that ten of the eleven high-immigration metropolitan areas showed either negative or negligible net internal migration over the same period. The only exception to this is San Diego, which is in the unique position of gaining large numbers from both sources. This consistent pattern raises the possibility that there is a link between immigration from 1985 to 1990 and the out-migration of internal migrants at levels as broad as the metropolitan-area level.

Comparisons of the data in table 9.1 also suggest that the internal migration in the other categories of metropolitan area are less affected by the nation's immigration dynamics than by their relative economic or social attractions for the nation's internal migrants. These other categories distinguish areas that either are dominated by internal-migration gains (fifteen high-internal-migration areas) or losses (eight high-out-migration areas) or constitute residual areas with relatively small gains or losses attributable to migration components (in the table, "other areas"). In addressing the questions for this analysis, we compare migration patterns of high-immigration areas with those of high-internal-migration and high-out-migration areas.

WHITE AND BLACK MIGRATION SELECTIVITY

To what extent do whites and blacks show similar net out-migration from high-immigration metropolitan areas? We can first examine the migration levels with the data presented in the right-hand columns of table 9.1. We focus here on rates of net migration, rather than actual numbers, because the relative sizes of the white and black resident populations differ across individual metropolitan areas.

The comparisons indicate that black net migration is negative in most of the same areas in which white net migration is negative. However, the magnitudes of the gains or losses tend to be smaller than those for whites. Among the high-immigration areas, both whites and blacks showed similar and high net out-migration from the New York metropolitan area, and in Chicago, where the late-1980s economy was particularly severe for blacks, the black out-migration rate exceeded that for whites. However, in Los Angeles, San Francisco, Boston, and especially in Houston, the white out-migration rate was noticeably larger. In Miami, Washington, D.C., and Dallas, the black population increased, whereas whites showed negligible gains or losses.

At first blush, it appears that blacks are likely to leave most high-immigration metropolitan areas but that their response is less pronounced than that of whites. This lower migration response tends also to typify black internal migration for other area categories. That is, blacks register gains in each of the high-internal-migration areas and declines in all but one (Milwaukee) of the high-out-migration areas. Yet in most instances, the magnitude of gains or declines was greater for whites than for blacks. Two notable exceptions to this were the higher rates of black gains for Atlanta and Norfolk—metropolitan areas that also registered the greatest numeric increases in blacks from 1985 to 1990.

The second aspect of our comparison focuses on the selectivity of migration for whites and blacks. White out-migration from high-immigration areas tends to disproportionately favor the lower end of the socioeconomic spectrum. This can be, in part, a result of increased labor-market pressure brought on by large immigration gains among populations with lower education levels. This is illustrated in figure 9.1, which displays average rates of immigration by educational attainment from 1985 to 1990 for the Los Angeles CMSA. It is clear from these rates that levels of immigration tend to be highest among

Figure 9.1   Educational Level of Immigrants to Los Angeles
Metropolitan Region, from 1985 to 1990

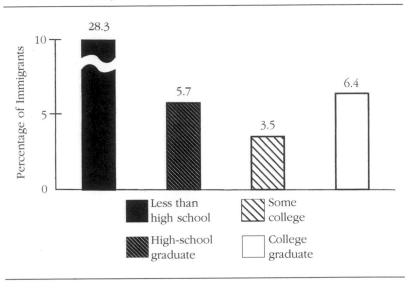

Source: Author's analysis of special 1990 U.S. Census migration tabulations.

adults with less than a high-school education. Among other high-immigration areas, these rates are particularly pronounced for San Francisco, Miami, and San Diego. However, it is also clear that immigration is bimodal with respect to educational distribution. In most areas, college graduation rates—although well below those of high-school dropouts—lie above those for high-school graduates and adults with only some college.

The data that permit us to evaluate the selectivity patterns of whites and blacks appear in tables 9.2 and 9.3. Here, we anticipate finding the "unique" selectivity patterns of out-migration for whites and blacks from high-immigration metropolitan areas. Yet, for redistribution across the other types of metropolitan areas we expect to find in- or out-migration to be highest among college graduates, consistent with traditional long-distance migration patterns (Long 1988).

Looking first at the high-immigration areas, we find overall conformity with expectations for both whites and blacks. That is, for the most part, greatest out-migration levels tend to be for adults with less than a high-school education or high-school graduates, rather than college graduates or those with some college. For example, among Los Angeles whites, high-school dropouts out-migrated at the rate of 5.3

percent, high-school graduates at 4.3 percent, and those who had completed some college at 3.2 percent; college graduates showed a net increase of 2.2 percent. In some cases (such as blacks in Houston) the pattern is not nearly as clear cut, but for the most part it is consistent with expectations.

One fairly common pattern among most of these areas for whites, and in some of these areas for blacks, is the net in-migration of college graduates along with the net out-migration of most of the less-educated adults. To some extent, this is consistent with the dual-labor-market model that has been applied to many of these high-immigration metropolitan areas with large advanced-service, corporate-headquarter components (Mollenkopf and Castells 1991). In these areas, it can be argued, low-skilled immigrants represent competition for low-skilled native-born whites and blacks. However, the former perform complementary activities that, in fact, increase the productivity of industries that employ high-skilled professionals. Not only are employees in these activities relatively immune from the competition of immigrants, but they may also benefit from their presence.

The more conventional patterns of migrant selectivity, expected for high-internal-migration areas and high-out-migration areas, are also borne out by the data on both whites and blacks. That is, in most high-internal-migration areas, migrant gains tend to be accentuated for college graduates and diminished for those with a high-school education or less. For high-out-migration areas, rates of out-migration tend to be most accentuated among the better educated. These areas are not affected nearly as much by the low-skilled immigrant gains that are present in the high-immigration areas.

Although these patterns tend to hold for most areas, there are exceptions. One notable exception for whites occurs in the case of Las Vegas. Here, there are uniformly high internal-migration gains at all education levels. This can be explained, in part, by the overflow of less-educated out-migrants Las Vegas receives from California, as well as the better-educated out-migrants from other parts of the country. Among black high-internal-migration areas, the South Atlantic regions of Raleigh-Durham, Norfolk, and Nashville show heightened internal-migration gains among less-educated categories. This may be because these areas are attracting black return migrants or out-migrants from some of the northern high-immigration-metropolitan areas. Finally, for both whites and blacks, not all high-out-migration metropolitan areas conform to the expected pattern. Here, the expected accentuated out-migration of college graduates is most evident

(*Text continues on p. 324.*)

Table 9.2   Rates of Net Internal Migration of Whites, from 1985 to 1990, by Social and Economic Characteristics

Metro Area	Below Poverty	Above Poverty	Less than High School	High School Graduate	Some College	College Graduate	Age over 65
High-immigration areas							
Los Angeles	−11.5	−1.4	−5.3	−4.3	−3.2	2.2	−4.7
New York	−17.1	−5.6	−5.4	−6.7	−7.9	−4.3	−7.0
San Francisco	−15.8	−1.6	−6.4	−6.0	−4.0	2.9	−3.9
Miami	−8.3	0.3	−2.4	−0.3	−1.4	3.3	0.4
Washington, D.C.	−20.9	1.2	−7.2	−5.5	−1.9	4.5	−5.6
Chicago	−19.4	−2.2	−4.7	−4.0	−3.6	0.4	−5.2
Boston	−5.9	−3.6	−3.8	−4.7	−5.9	−2.6	−3.3
San Diego	0.7	4.3	−0.4	−0.9	2.1	8.3	3.8
Houston	−20.7	−4.0	−6.6	−6.8	−5.6	−1.6	−1.1
Philadelphia	−5.7	−0.4	−1.5	−1.5	−0.6	1.4	−1.8
Dallas	−15.8	1.5	−5.1	−3.2	0.1	5.2	−0.1
High-internal-migration areas							
Atlanta	−10.1	7.2	−0.9	2.9	7.5	11.2	0.1
Tampa–St. Petersburg	5.5	9.5	6.8	9.9	9.7	10.8	7.7
Seattle	2.2	6.9	1.7	3.7	6.3	10.3	1.0
Phoenix	3.8	8.5	3.6	7.0	8.0	10.1	8.2
Orlando	5.5	11.9	4.7	9.2	12.0	14.2	4.9
Las Vegas	17.1	19.8	19.8	19.5	19.8	20.4	18.5
Sacramento	9.3	8.4	4.2	6.9	8.7	8.1	3.6
West Palm Beach	0.3	16.1	9.8	14.8	15.2	21.3	13.4
Charlotte	0.1	7.5	2.3	5.3	8.3	11.4	1.5
Raleigh–Durham	21.7	6.7	1.8	4.0	7.8	5.1	4.9
Portland, Ore.	2.7	5.5	1.5	4.1	5.9	7.8	2.7

Norfolk	−2.7	1.2	−1.5	−3.0	−2.3	2.9	2.1
Nashville	2.0	6.8	1.4	5.0	9.1	9.0	1.0
Fort Myers	13.0	20.4	14.6	18.7	23.3	24.6	13.5
Daytona Beach	15.0	16.7	14.7	18.5	16.3	11.3	11.7
High-out-migration areas							
Detroit	−9.8	−2.2	−3.9	−3.3	−2.4	−2.2	−5.0
Pittsburgh	−2.0	−3.9	−1.7	−2.3	−4.0	−6.1	−2.2
New Orleans	−12.3	−8.1	−5.7	−6.4	−9.8	−9.8	−2.5
Cleveland	−7.0	−2.2	−2.2	−1.9	−2.9	−2.9	−2.7
Denver	−7.8	−3.3	−5.0	−5.3	−3.9	−2.4	0.1
St. Louis	−7.9	0.0	−2.0	−1.0	0.3	1.4	−1.6
Milwaukee	−9.6	−2.1	−2.6	−3.0	−2.4	−1.3	−2.8
Buffalo	0.6	−2.9	−1.8	−1.9	−2.7	−5.8	−2.8
Other areas							
Columbus, Ohio	8.1	2.0	−0.3	1.0	3.3	−1.3	−0.5
Minneapolis–St. Paul	−3.7	2.2	−0.2	0.2	1.9	3.8	−0.1
Baltimore	−2.9	1.9	−1.6	−0.4	1.0	6.4	−1.7
Indianapolis	−7.1	2.5	−1.9	0.1	2.8	6.8	−1.5
Kansas City	−10.2	3.0	−1.6	0.1	2.9	5.8	−1.1
Providence	−0.1	0.0	−0.7	−0.5	0.5	0.8	−1.2
Cincinnati	−0.5	0.8	−1.5	−0.3	1.0	2.6	−0.9
Hartford	−13.8	−0.9	−2.1	−2.1	−1.5	0.7	−1.9
San Antonio	−6.0	−1.5	−2.8	−2.8	−2.6	1.3	2.5
Rochester, N.Y.	−3.3	−1.9	−1.2	−2.0	−1.8	−3.4	−2.1
Salt Lake City	−1.8	−2.0	0.5	−1.8	−2.5	−2.9	0.5

Source: Author's analysis of special 1990 U.S. Census migration tabulations.

Note: Rates per 100 population, 1990.

Table 9.3   Rates of Net Internal Migration of Blacks from 1985 to 1990, by Social and Economic Characteristics

Metro Area	Below Poverty	Above Poverty	Less than High School	High School Graduate	Some College	College Graduate	Age over 65
High-immigration areas							
Los Angeles	-4.6	0.5	-1.8	-2.0	-1.1	3.7	-0.7
New York	-6.9	-4.7	-5.0	-5.1	-7.0	-4.2	-4.6
San Francisco	-4.6	-0.4	-2.8	-2.3	-1.4	2.3	-1.4
Miami	-0.1	4.7	1.4	1.4	4.7	7.3	4.6
Washington, D.C.	-3.1	3.7	-0.6	1.1	3.4	7.2	0.9
Chicago	-7.0	-2.4	-3.8	-3.5	-3.8	-1.6	-1.6
Boston	0.0	-0.8	-0.8	-0.3	-1.0	-1.3	-2.6
San Diego	7.9	4.4	-3.5	0.0	1.1	7.5	2.3
Houston	-0.5	0.4	-1.0	0.2	-0.8	-1.0	0.6
Philadelphia	-1.7	0.3	0.1	-0.2	-0.3	1.7	-0.2
Dallas	0.2	6.0	-1.1	2.4	5.4	10.5	1.0
High-internal-migration areas							
Atlanta	5.8	13.9	3.4	8.4	17.4	19.8	4.0
Tampa–St. Petersburg	0.9	4.3	-0.4	2.0	4.3	8.7	4.1
Seattle	3.7	3.2	1.4	0.7	2.9	3.8	1.0
Phoenix	8.2	13.3	6.9	9.8	13.1	15.9	8.8
Orlando	5.6	14.1	7.7	13.4	17.4	19.2	8.8
Las Vegas	11.9	14.5	15.8	14.2	14.4	19.3	18.6
Sacramento	16.9	10.9	12.8	10.0	13.2	8.2	8.0
West Palm Beach	-1.6	5.4	1.1	5.4	11.2	12.1	4.2
Charlotte	3.1	4.5	1.0	3.7	5.2	7.7	0.8
Raleigh–Durham	8.2	9.0	5.8	7.2	11.9	4.8	4.2
Portland, Ore.	7.4	6.4	3.4	6.6	7.1	8.5	3.0

Norfolk	6.2	5.8	2.4	4.9	6.3	2.2	3.4
Nashville	2.1	3.7	2.3	2.7	4.8	0.2	0.6
Fort Myers	5.2	7.6	4.5	4.2	15.7	9.5	10.7
Daytona Beach	-2.7	5.2	-0.1	8.1	7.8	3.7	7.2
High-out-migration areas							
Detroit	-0.3	-0.8	-1.0	-1.1	-2.1	-0.1	-0.2
Pittsburgh	2.2	-4.4	0.3	-1.5	-2.7	-12.9	0.0
New Orleans	-2.0	-4.7	-1.6	-2.9	-6.0	-9.1	0.0
Cleveland	0.3	-1.3	-1.4	-1.5	-3.5	-3.2	0.1
Denver	2.3	1.6	-1.1	0.3	2.8	0.1	2.1
St. Louis	-2.8	-0.6	-2.1	-0.9	-1.4	-0.2	-0.5
Milwaukee	9.8	0.2	3.8	1.1	0.8	-5.2	1.7
Buffalo	2.0	-2.4	0.1	-0.9	-1.4	-6.5	-0.3
Other areas							
Columbus, Ohio	4.9	3.8	5.2	5.1	6.3	0.6	0.1
Minneapolis–St. Paul	26.4	9.6	17.4	15.8	13.3	7.0	3.7
Baltimore	1.5	1.8	-0.1	1.2	2.7	3.1	0.2
Indianapolis	2.3	3.5	0.7	3.0	4.5	4.4	1.2
Kansas City	1.3	0.7	-0.4	0.2	0.2	4.0	0.7
Providence	1.5	3.8	2.7	5.3	3.7	0.7	-2.5
Cincinnati	1.3	0.5	0.6	0.0	1.9	1.3	0.3
Hartford	1.2	1.8	0.6	3.9	1.7	3.7	-3.2
San Antonio	0.5	0.1	-2.7	-0.9	-1.1	-1.6	1.4
Rochester, N.Y.	0.7	-1.9	2.9	0.3	-3.3	-10.7	-4.5
Salt Lake City	22.7	-3.6	8.8	-4.1	-5.5	1.3	5.8

Source: Author's analysis of special 1990 U.S. Census migration tabulations.
Note: Rates per 100 population, 1990.

Table 9.4   Net Internal Migration Rates for Selected Social and Demographic Categories 1985 to 1990 and 1990 to 1996, Whites and Blacks

	California		New York		Texas	
Category	1985–1990	1990–1996	1985–1990	1990–1996	1985–1990	1990–1996
Whites[b]						
High school or less	−1.6	−7.6	−4	−5.6	−3.1	−1.1
Some college	1.2	−3.9	−5.6	−5.4	−2.5	1.2
Blacks[b]						
High school or less	−0.4	−1.7	−4.2	−9.3	−0.2	−6.8
Some college	1.2	2.7	−7.3	−9.5	0.4	0.5

Sources: Compiled by author from Special 1990 U.S. Census migration tabulations (1985–1990) and from single-year migration tabulations of public use tapes (1990–1991, 1991–1992, 1992–1993, 1993–1994, 1994–1995, 1995–1996) from the March supplement, U.S. Census Bureau Current Population Surveys.
[a]Non-Latino whites.
[b]Age 25 and older.

for the Rust Belt areas of Pittsburgh, Cleveland, and Buffalo and the "Oil Patch" New Orleans. For blacks, Milwaukee registers noticeable net migration gains among lower-education categories and for persons living below the poverty line. This may represent, in part, a spillover of the black out-migrants from nearby Chicago.

The foregoing analyses focus only on the period from 1985 to 1990, leaving the reader to wonder whether there may have been something unique to this period that caused the dynamic between immigration and internal migration. To partially answer this question, we have prepared net migration rates for the period from 1990 to 1996 from the Census Bureau's current population survey for California, New York, and Texas, shown in table 9.4. The selection of California and Texas is particularly noteworthy: California's economy went into a fairly dramatic slump in the early 1990s; in contrast, Texas's oil-depressed economy of the late 1980s rebounded strongly from 1990 to 1996. In both cases, however, the less-skilled segment of the population—both whites and blacks with at most a high-school education—exhibited net out-migration rates during both their good economic periods (from 1985 to 1990 in California, from 1990 to 1996 in Texas) and their bad ones. New York's economy did not shift as sharply over this period, but it also showed a net out-migration of whites and blacks with lesser skills.

In sum, this review of white and black migrant selectivity provides an affirmative answer to the first question raised in this analysis: There appears to be a general similarity in the out-migration responses of whites and blacks to immigration, as observed from these data for different categories of metropolitan area. Although the magnitude of the response to immigration is stronger for whites than it is for blacks, the socioeconomic selectivity patterns are quite similar. The unique out-migration patterns that select the least educated segments of the population are evident for both whites and blacks from high-immigration states.

SPATIAL PATTERNS OF WHITE AND BLACK OUT-MIGRATION

To what extent are the spatial patterns of out-migration from high-immigration-metropolitan areas similar for whites and blacks? We answer this question in two ways: first, indirectly, with some descriptive statistics that show the states that had the largest net gain and losses for white and black internal migrants as well as the most prominent white and black streams away from the high-immigration state of California. The second means for answering this question employs multivariate analysis to evaluate how closely the same metropolitan-area attributes—including an area's immigration level—influence white and black migration patterns.

Before discussing the descriptive portion of the analysis, I want to reiterate the significant finding from my previous study of white migration patterns (Frey 1995a): Out-migration from high-immigration-metropolitan areas registers the spatial imprint of a strong "push" effect—with the largest out-migration sharply focused from these states as origins but directed to many diffuse destinations. This contrasts with the more conventional "pull-oriented" migration pattern wherein well-educated or professional migrants are lured from diffuse origins to a more distinct set of destinations.

Both whites and blacks living in poverty display these spatial "push-oriented" out-migration patterns away from the high-immigration states and to fairly diffuse destinations. The four greatest out-migration regions for both impoverished whites and impoverished blacks are the high-immigration metropolitan areas of New York, Chicago, Los Angeles, and San Francisco (see table 9.5). Their destinations are fairly diffuse, consistent with historical differences in white and black migration patterns, which impose particular constraints on the destinations of blacks, who are reliant on strong friendship or kinship ties (Johnson and Roseman 1990; Cromartie and Stack 1989).

Figures 9.2 and 9.3 illustrate the distinction between the "push-

Table 9.5   Metro Areas with Greatest Net Internal-Migration Losses
in Poverty Populations, Whites and Blacks, 1990

Whites		Blacks	
New York	− 82,386	New York	− 43,451
Los Angeles	− 47,698	Chicago	− 26,912
Chicago	− 45,723	Los Angeles	− 9,466
San Francisco	− 29,543	San Francisco	− 4,010
Houston	− 28,219	Philadelphia	− 3,936
Dallas	− 24,858	Washington, D.C.	− 3,432
Detroit	− 21,945	St. Louis	− 3,044
Washington, D.C.	− 15,434	New Orleans	− 2,927
Philadelphia	− 12,099	Detroit	− 827
Boston	− 11,035	Houston	− 801

Source: Author's analysis of special 1990 U.S. Census migration tabulations.
Note: Population counts of persons age five and older in 1990.

oriented" out-migration spatial pattern for poverty blacks and the "pull-oriented" in-migration pattern of African American college graduates. The latter are much more focused than poverty migrants in their choice of destination (only nineteen states show net in-migration of the former, compared with thirty-one of the latter) and only three states—Georgia, Florida, and Virginia—appear among the top ten destinations for both. The diffuse destinations for poverty blacks not only include southern states, such as Kentucky, Mississippi, and South Carolina, but also northern states, such as Wisconsin, Michigan, and Ohio. Curtis Roseman and Seong Woo Lee's (1998) analysis of California out-migrants indicates that black "returnees" include significant streams of blacks who were born in the North as well as those born in the South. Their analysis shows that destination states in the Southeast include the lowest level of returnees, signaling the economic—rather than kinship—draw of this economically dynamic region.

For both races, domestic out-migration of low-skilled migrants from high-immigration states leads to a somewhat different set of destinations from the more conventional long-distance migration pattern. This becomes clear when we compare the destinations of poverty black out-migrants from California with college-graduate black out-migrants from California (lower panel of table 9.6). The former out-migrants are much more likely to go to traditional southern-origin and northern states, the states that originally sent black migrants to California. College graduate black out-migrants are more prone to

Figure 9.2   Spatial Pattern of Migration of Black College Graduates, from 1985 to 1990

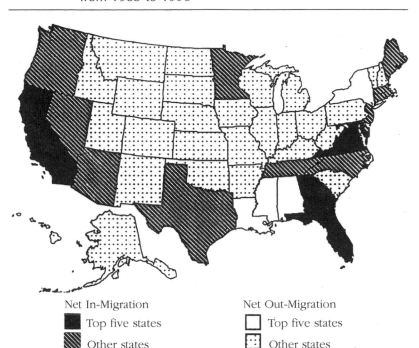

Net In-Migration
- ■ Top five states
- ▨ Other states

Net Out-Migration
- ☐ Top five states
- ▦ Other states

Source: Author's analysis of special 1990 U.S. Census migration tabulations.

locate in dynamic economic centers in Georgia (Atlanta), Virginia and Maryland (Washington, D.C.), and New York (New York City).

Another way to compare geographic linkages to the net migration patterns of whites and blacks is through the use of multivariate analyses that predict a metropolitan area's white or black net migration patterns. We present such analyses in tables 9.7 and 9.8 for whites and blacks, respectively. (Table footnotes indicate the criteria for including areas in this analysis.) The dependent variables in these equations pertain to the levels of internal migration for a specific demographic subgroup of a metropolitan area's white or black population.

Included in this analysis as independent variables are a geographic regional classification (dummy variables for the Northeast region, the Midwest region, the South Atlantic division, the Mountain division, and the Pacific division, where parts of the South, which are not

Figure 9.3   Spatial Pattern of Migration of Blacks Living Below the
Poverty Line, from 1985 to 1990

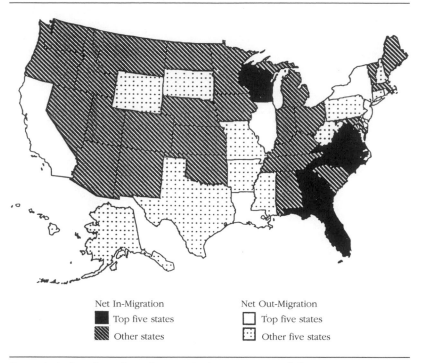

Net In-Migration

■ Top five states

▨ Other states

Net Out-Migration

☐ Top five states

⊡ Other five states

Source: Author's analysis of special 1990 U.S. Census migration tabulations.

included in the South Atlantic division, represent the omitted category); four variables reflecting the metropolitan area's economic structure (the unemployment rate of 1988, the per capita income in 1988,
the percentage of change in manufacturing employment from 1982 to
1987, and the percentage of males engaged in professional and managerial employment, based on the 1990 census); two variables pertaining to the area's minority structure (percentage of nonwhite and
percentage of blacks); the level of immigration from 1985 to 1990;
and the log of the metropolitan area's population size in 1985. All the
migration and population data were drawn from the 1980 and 1990
censuses. The economic characteristics were drawn from the *State and
Metropolitan Area Data Book, 1991*, compiled by the U.S. Bureau of
the Census.

As indicated, we wish to compare the similarities in the equations
for whites with those for blacks. In each we expected that immigra-

Table 9.6   Destination States of White and Black Out-Migrants from California, 1990, by Economic Status and Education

	All[a]		Below Poverty Line[b]		Above Poverty Line[b]		College Graduates[c]	
State		Size	State	Size	State	Size	State	Size
				Destinations of White Out-Migrants				
Washington		126,875	Oregon	15,330	Washington	107,295	Washington	26,637
Oregon		113,824	Washington	13,329	Oregon	93,506	Oregon	17,726
Arizona		104,818	Arizona	12,286	Arizona	84,631	Texas	17,658
Nevada		86,815	Nevada	9,104	Nevada	73,698	Arizona	17,148
Texas		79,545	Texas	7,320	Texas	66,865	New York	15,137
Florida		66,860	Florida	5,881	Florida	57,868	Virginia	14,262
Colorado		51,026	Utah	5,852	Colorado	41,247	Florida	12,986
Virginia		44,212	Colorado	5,184	Virginia	39,954	Colorado	11,832
New York		44,180	New York	4,652	Illinois	36,276	Illinois	11,481
Illinois		41,026	Missouri	4,516	New York	34,549	Nevada	9,670
				Destinations of Black Out-Migrants				
Texas		15,874	Texas	4,162	Texas	9,846	Texas	1,297
Georgia		7,974	Louisiana	2,801	Georgia	5,935	Georgia	1,006
Florida		7,354	Michigan	1,746	Florida	5,346	Virginia	969
Illinois		6,915	Illinois	1,701	Virginia	5,108	New York	947
Louisiana		6,719	Ohio	1,588	Nevada	4,960	Maryland	868
Nevada		6,646	Mississippi	1,477	Illinois	4,930	Illinois	781
Virginia		6,626	Washington	1,464	New York	4,414	Florida	767
New York		6,473	Florida	1,392	Washington	4,404	Nevada	572
Washington		6,451	New York	1,347	Arizona	3,746	Washington	541
Ohio		5,674	Georgia	1,339	Ohio	3,727	Arizona	519

Source: Author's analysis of special 1990 U.S. Census migration tabulations.

[a]Persons age five and older at the time of the 1990 census.

[b]Persons age five and older at the time of the 1990 census; poverty status determined in the 1990 census.

[c]Persons age twenty-five and older who reported having graduated from college in the 1990 census.

Table 9.7   Net Internal Migration of Whites from 1985 to 1990 in Selected Metropolitan Areas (Standardized Regression Coefficients)

		Income		Education			
Metro Attributes[a]	Total	Below Poverty	Above Poverty	Less Than High School	High School Graduate	College Graduate	Age 65+
REGION[b]							
Northeast	−.23[c]	−.05	−.27[c]	−.15[c]	−.20[c]	−.35[c]	−.27[c]
Midwest	−.18[c]	−.07	−.19[c]	−.16[c]	−.16[c]	−.20	−.22[c]
South At-lantic	.10	.04	.12	.10[c]	.10	.15	.08
Mountain	.18[c]	.14[c]	.15[c]	.10[c]	.09	.21[c]	.03
Pacific	−.01	.01	−.01	.03	.00	−.03	−.00
UNEMPLOY-MENT	−.17[c]	−.16[c]	−.13[c]	−.13[c]	−.11[c]	−.11	−.08
INCOME	.02	−.19[c]	.10	−.01	.04	.22[c]	.07
MFG GROWTH	.16[c]	.10[c]	.18[c]	.08[c]	.14[c]	.12	.07
% UPPER WHITE-COLLAR	−.10	.08	−.16[c]	−.14[c]	−.18[c]	−.13	−.10[c]
% NON-WHITE	−.03	−.06	−.05	−.02	−.04	−.04	.02
% BLACK	−.10	−.09[c]	−.09	−.11[c]	−.12[c]	−.06	−.18[c]
IMMIGRA-TION	−.72[c]	−.67[c]	−.73[c]	−.75[c]	−.76[c]	−.44[c]	−.81[c]
POP SIZE (LOG)	.07	−.22[c]	.19[c]	−.09[c]	.03	.31[c]	.03
R^2	.63	.80	.59	.81	.73	.36	.74

Source: Author's analysis of special 1990 U.S. Census migration tabulations.
Notes: Migration counts of 126 metropolitan areas with 1990 total population exceeding 250,000 and black populations exceeding 5,000, regressed on attributes of the metropolitan area.
[a]See text for attribute definitions.
[b]Omitted category includes the remainder of the South region (other than the South Atlantic states).
[c]Significant at .1 level.

tion would exert an independent effect on net out-migration and that this effect would be most pronounced for the the population living below the poverty line, for individuals with less than a college degree, and for the elderly. In fact, immigration is the only variable that exerts a significant effect on each equation for both races. However, for each race, the magnitude of the coefficient tends to be lower for college graduates than for any of the other demographic categories. It

Table 9.8   Net Internal Migration of Blacks from 1985 to 1990 in Selected Metropolitan Areas (Standardized Regression Coefficients)

Metro Attributes[a]	Total	Income		Education			Age 65+
		Below Poverty	Above Poverty	Less Than High School	High School Graduate	College Graduate	
REGION[b]							
Northeast	−.17	−.17[c]	−.19	−.13	−.16	−.18	−.20[c]
Midwest	−.13	−.09	−.13	−.08	−.11	−.12	−.09
South Atlantic	.13	.05	.19[c]	.07	.13	.22[c]	.10
Mountain	.14	.15[c]	.07	.16[c]	.11	.02	.13
Pacific	−.03	−.01	−.04	.00	−.02	−.07	.00
UNEMPLOYMENT	−.14	−.16[c]	−.07	−.15[c]	−.10	−.03	−.10
INCOME	−.01	−.06	.08	−.04	.03	.18	.01
MFG GROWTH	.05	.00	.09	.01	.04	.12	−.00
% UPPER WHITE-COLLAR	.04	.01	.02	−.01	−.00	−.07	−.04
% NON-WHITE	.03	−.03	.05	.02	.02	.03	.05
% BLACK	−.07	−.06	−.07	−.05	−.05	−.07	−.05
IMMIGRATION	−.68[c]	−.75[c]	−.60[c]	−.71[c]	−.76[c]	−.30[c]	−.72[c]
POP SIZE (LOG)	.09	.06	.23[c]	.02	.14	.24[c]	.12
R^2	.44	.54	.33	.50	.49	.21	.46

Source: Author's analysis of special 1990 U.S. Census migration tabulations.
Notes: Migration counts of 126 metropolitan areas with 1990 total population exceeding 250,000 and black populations exceeding 5,000, regressed on attributes of the metropolitan area.
[a] See text for attribute definitions.
[b] Omitted category includes the remainder of the South region (other than the South Atlantic states).
[c] Significant at .1 level.

is also noteworthy that, controlling for immigration, the metropolitan area's nonwhite percentage does not significantly affect migration for any category of either race. However, poverty whites and less-well-educated whites are more prone to out-migrate from areas with higher percentages of blacks. Beyond the immigration effect, the only similarities between the white and black equations are the negative effect of an area's unemployment on the migration of the poverty and less-educated population groups. High income levels exert a significant positive effect on white college-graduate migration and a close-to-significant effect on the comparable equation for blacks.

Although these equations do not show all the patterns that were anticipated, they do indicate that immigration bears a strong relationship with the net out-migration of whites and blacks on several demographic categories. Both these equations and the descriptive analyses given earlier indicate some broad similarities in the spatial patterns of low-skilled black and white out-migration and are consistent with the proposition that they are responding to immigration from abroad.[2]

RACE AND REGION

The dynamic between immigration and internal migration for low-skilled blacks represents one dimension of a broader return of blacks to the South for all demographic categories (Frey 1998b). This began in the 1970s (see figure 9.4), leading in the 1990s to a wholesale reversal of black southern out-migration, and the trend dominated the rest of the twentieth century (Hamilton 1964; Long 1988). Improved race relations, the "pull" of kinship ties for retirees and others, and the emergence of a strong black middle class all contributed to the turnaround. The gradual emergence of the southeastern states, especially Georgia, North Carolina and Florida, are apparent in looking at the maps of black net migration gains and losses for the late 1960s (figure 9.5), the late 1970s (figure 9.6), and the late 1980s (figure 9.7). States that once represented the prime destinations for South-to-North migrants—New York, Illinois, and Michigan—are now among the greatest "donor states" in the reverse regional flow of African Americans.

What is significant about the 1990s is the reversal of the black flow from the West to the South and the emergence of California as a net out-migration state for blacks. Although some of this may be attributable to the poor economy of the state from 1992 to 1995, our earlier results suggest that a dynamic relationship between immigration and internal migration is also operating. For the first time for any five-year period, the period from 1990 to 1995 saw a gain for the South from each of the three other major regions—the Northeast, the Midwest, and the West (see figure 9.8). In fact, current migration projections through the year 2025 show California to be the third-biggest net migration loser for African Americans following New York and

(*Text continues on p. 335.*)

Figure 9.4   Net Migration of Blacks in the South, from 1965 to 1995

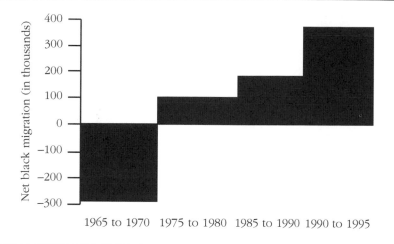

Sources: Compiled by the author from decennial U.S. censuses and from public use tape of the 1995 March Supplement, U.S. Census Bureau Current Population Survey.

Figure 9.5   Net Migration of Blacks, from 1965 to 1970

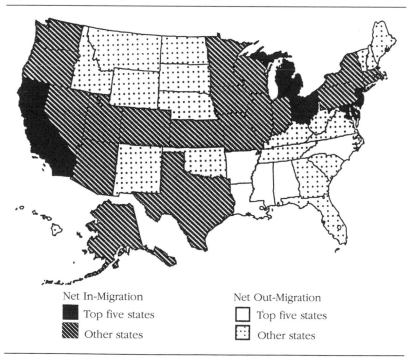

Source: Compiled by the author from 1970 U.S. Census.

Figure 9.6   Net Migration of Blacks, from 1975 to 1980

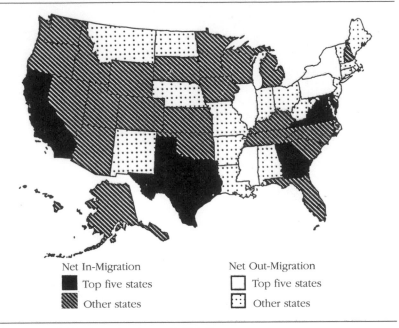

Net In-Migration
- ■ Top five states
- ▨ Other states

Net Out-Migration
- □ Top five states
- ⊡ Other states

Source: Compiled by the author from 1980 U.S. Census.

Figure 9.7   Net Migration of Blacks, from 1985 to 1990

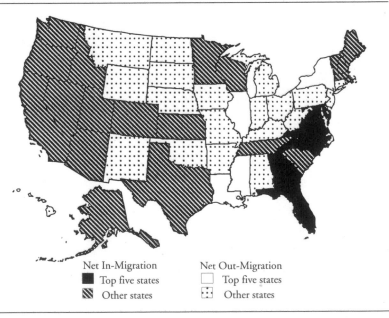

Net In-Migration
- ■ Top five states
- ▨ Other states

Net Out-Migration
- □ Top five states
- ⊡ Other states

Source: Compiled by the author from 1990 U.S. Census.

Figure 9.8 Net Migration of Blacks, by Region, from 1990 to 1995

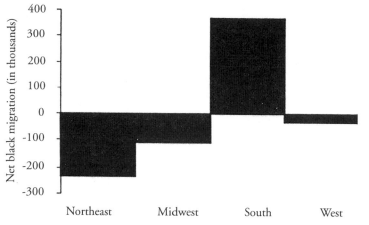

Sources: Compiled by the author from public use tape of the 1995 March Supplement, U.S. Bureau of the Census Current Population Survey.

Illinois. Texas, Georgia, Virginia, North Carolina, and Maryland are shown to be the largest gainers (see figure 9.9).

There appears to be a regional consolidation of African Americans toward the South appearing at the same time as focused immigration continues to cluster Hispanics and Asians primarily in high-immigration states. Again, a look at projections to the year 2025 are instructive (see table 9.9, which gives thirty-year projections for the combined immigration and internal-migration components). Over this period, black migration gains will accrue primarily to the South and states other than Florida and Texas. At the same time, northern and western high-immigration states, which will gain large numbers of Hispanics and Asians, are projected to lose blacks as well as whites through the migration process. Some of this out-migration, especially of low-skilled whites and blacks, derives from the immigration–internal migration dynamic reviewed in this chapter, although a large part of it is also attributable to economic attractions that exist in states other than immigrant gateway regions (Frey and Liaw 1998b). For blacks, and even more so for whites, these attractions occur in smaller metropolitan areas and nonmetropolitan areas outside of the high-immigration areas (Frey and Liaw 1998a). Yet, the existence of the dynamic, which focuses primarily on less skilled blacks and whites,

Figure 9.9   Projected Net Internal Migration of Blacks, from 1995
              to 2025

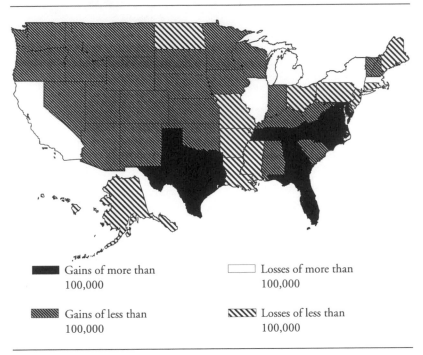

■ Gains of more than
  100,000

▨ Gains of less than
  100,000

☐ Losses of more than
  100,000

▧ Losses of less than
  100,000

Source: Compiled by the author from U.S. Census projection files.

holds important implications for the race and class structures of high-immigration regions.

RACE AND CLASS STRUCTURE

How do these migration processes influence the race and class structure of a metropolitan area's population? The answer to this question depends, in large part, on the existing race and class structure of the area, reflecting its history as a destination for different racial and ethnic groups. Although this chapter has attempted to determine the impact that immigration exerts on black internal migration, in most high-immigration areas blacks make up a smaller population than the other minorities combined. In the case of metropolitan Los Angeles, the data in table 9.10 show that the major migration dynamic, focusing on those living below the poverty line, the less-educated, and

Table 9.9   Projected Gains from Combined Immigration and
Internal Migration Among Blacks, Hispanics, Asians, and
Whites, from 1995 to 2005

| Region | Projected Gains from All Migration | | | |
	Blacks	Hispanics	Asians	Whites
North				
High-immigration states	− 564,192	1,220,004	1,316,120	− 3,422,328
Other states	15,626	844,553	552,958	− 1,554,576
South				
High-immigration states	843,835	3,503,372	412,240	3,701,562
Other states	1,640,343	793,086	629,898	4,879,988
West				
High-immigration states	− 219,031	2,502,434	3,134,948	− 1,468,578
Other states	156,942	1,635,471	893,036	3,172,832

Source: Compiled by the author from U.S. Census projection files.
Note: High-immigration states include New York, New Jersey, Massachusetts, Illinois (in North); Florida, Texas (in South); California (in West).

younger populations, involves migration from abroad of nonblack minorities (Latinos, Asians, and others) and the internal out-migration of whites. In this population, black out-migration exerts a relatively minor effect on the social structure. For example, from 1985 to 1990, the poverty population of Los Angeles was increased by 241,000 nonblack minority immigrants and was reduced by 47,700 whites moving to other parts of the country. The additional out-migration of 9,500 blacks made a relatively small dent in the poverty population. The impact of the two former contributions is reflected in the overall 1990 population statistics for Los Angeles (the last three columns of table 9.10). Not only is the poverty population made up of a "majority minority," but it is also a majority composed of only nonblack minorities. Similarly, nonblack minorities make up the majority of the metropolitan area's population who did not finish high school and children under age fifteen. Certainly, the out-migration of blacks makes a larger impact on the race and class structure of high-immigration areas with larger black shares, such as New York and Chicago.[3]

This chapter has focused mostly on the fairly pervasive pattern of low-skilled black migration away from high-immigration metropolitan areas. Yet, this is part of a larger pattern of black migration that is effecting something of a reconsolidation of the black population back to the South (Frey 1998a). The broader movement of blacks away from traditional northern, midwestern, and western

Table 9.10   Impact of 1985 to 1990 Migration on Los Angeles 1990 White, Black, and Other Minority Composition by Sociodemographic Category

	Whites			Blacks		
Category	Total Migration	Immigration from Abroad	Net Internal Migration	Total Migration	Immigration from Abroad	Net Internal Migration
Total	4.0	140.1	−136.2	5.2	16.9	−11.7
Poverty status						
Below poverty	−9.7	38.0	−47.7	−6.2	3.3	−9.5
Above poverty	16.4	101.8	−85.4	17.5	12.8	4.7
Educational attainment						
Less than high school	−17.8	20.3	−38.1	−0.9	2.3	−3.2
High-school graduate	−32.8	20.4	−53.2	−0.7	2.8	−3.5
Some college	−32.5	24.7	−57.2	0.9	3.7	−2.8
College graduate	63.1	31.6	31.6	5.6	1.6	4.0
Selected Ages						
Under 15	−9.7	21.8	−31.6	−0.3	2.8	−3.1
25 to 34	54.6	42.0	12.6	8.7	6.4	2.4
35 to 44	0.5	26.5	−26.0	−1.0	2.5	−3.5
65 and above	−42.2	8.0	−50.2	−0.3	0.3	−0.6

Source: Author's analysis of special 1990 U.S. Census migration tabulations.
Note: Population counts are given in 1,000s.

strongholds is related as much to economics, improved race relations, and familiar environments for retirement as to the "push" of immigration. Together, these broader black redistribution trends are contributing to a new regional-based clustering of racial and ethnic groups, which I have explored elsewhere (Frey 1998a, 1998c). This trend has emerged in the past twenty years as new immigrant minorities—Hispanics and Asians—continue to move primarily into gateway metropolitan areas. Despite the evidence of some spilling out into other regions of the country (chapter 8 in this volume), census

	Other Minorities			Percentage of Total Population		
Total Migration	Immigration from Abroad	Net Internal Migration		Whites	Blacks	Other Minorities
715.2	741.9	−26.8		50	8	41
223.3	241.0	−17.7		25	13	62
494.1	488.2	5.9		55	8	38
178.2	187.8	−9.5		30	7	62
49.8	54.0	−4.2		63	9	28
48.9	51.4	−2.6		67	10	23
76.9	65.4	11.5		72	5	23
100.0	110.1	−10.1		38	10	52
201.2	199.6	1.7		47	8	44
76.5	78.1	−1.7		54	8	38
18.0	19.1	−1.1		76	6	18

estimates indicate that 67 percent of the nation's immigrant growth from 1990 to 1998 occurred within the eleven high-immigration metropolitan areas that are the focus of this study. These areas are home to 57 percent of all U.S. Hispanics and 60 percent of all Asians, whereas only 26 percent of the Anglo-American population lives in these eleven areas. Over the 1990s, white gains have been more dispersed, although greatest in the West (excluding California) as well as in the southeast part of the United States.

When superimposed upon the expanded black return migration to the South, new racial and ethnic regional profiles are beginning to emerge. Instead of a single melting pot that spans the nation's landscapes, "multiple melting pots" are developing on the West Coast, in the Southwest, and in selected metropolitan areas on the eastern seaboard as well as in Chicago and Miami. Other large stretches of the country remain mostly white—in the mountain states, most of the Midwest, and New England. With the new migration patterns of African Americans, much of the nation's South, and especially its growing South Atlantic division, will remain mostly white and African American in its racial and ethnic profile. These new regional divisions will have social as well as political implications. Evidence already shows that most interracial marriages occur in California (Frey 1997) and that segregation between blacks and whites is most reduced in multiethnic high-immigration metropolitan areas (Frey and Farley 1996). At the same time, more conservative political views have swept into the less multiethnic mountain West states that have become the destinations of many whites who have left California in the 1990s (Barone 1997).

For blacks, the movement away from traditional northern, midwestern, and western strongholds toward the fast-growing Southeast is commensurate with improved levels of black southern socioeconomic status and increased residential integration (Farley and Frey 1994). The movement to the South of middle-class blacks along with more progressive whites from the suburbs of the Northeast is changing southern politics as well, according to recent elections, which show both Republican and Democratic candidates being pushed to be less socially conservative (Tilove 1999).

In sum, the new black and white movement patterns away from large metropolitan areas that also serve as high-immigration regions are changing the demographic profiles of local areas, as well as shaping new shifts in national social and political cleavages. These regional race-space dynamics deserve closer attention as our national population becomes more ethnically diverse.

NOTES

1. Among recent immigrants to the United States, African Americans constitute a decided minority. They make up 9.1 percent of those who immigrated to the eleven high-immigration metropolitan areas focused on in this study. Nonetheless, there is variation across these areas. No more than 4 percent of immigrants to Los Angeles, San Francisco, San Diego, and Chicago are African American. Blacks make up between 5 and 12 percent of immigrants to Houston, Dallas, Boston, and Philadelphia. At the high end of the spectrum are New York, Miami, and Washington,

D.C., where blacks constitute 18.5 percent, 17.2 percent, and 15.5 percent of recent immigrants, respectively. Yet the count includes a significant number of Caribbean immigrants, who are not likely to be incorporated readily into existing native-born African American communities and economic niches.

2. I make the case in these analyses, and others I have conducted (Frey 1995a; 1995b; 1996; Frey and Liaw 1998b; Liaw and Frey 1996), that low-skilled out-migration of native-born and long-term residents of high-immigration areas are associated with certain aspects of immigration, including competition from the import of low-skilled immigrants; social and economic costs perceived to be associated with immigrants; and a response to the increased race and and ethnic profile of the area. Frey and Liaw (1998b) indicate that immigration's impact on out-migration is especially strong for low-skilled and poverty-level whites and blacks.

   Some critics have suggested that the causality between immigration and low-skilled out-migration is not as straightforward as this (Wright, Ellis, and Reibel 1997, for example), and what may appear to be a causal relationship can be attributed to the effects of deindustrialization and other restructuring occurring within those high-immigration metropolitan areas, which also serve as global cities. It is argued that the emergence of global cities creates a demand for low-wage foreign immigrants without necessarily taking jobs away from longer-term residents. That is, observed out-migration of native workers may simply represent the demise of somewhat better-paying manufacturing jobs. This kind of argument rests heavily on the assumption that immigration responds somewhat freely to changes in the demand for low-wage labor. Although this is most certainly the case with much illegal immigration to the United States, legal immigration is constrained, to a large degree, by the presence and location of already resident family members (Martin and Midgley 1994). Therefore, it may not be possible to generalize this scenario beyond those global cities that also serve as traditional ports of entry. Even among these, the greatest decline in manufacturing jobs—which, the theory purports, explains the out-migration of low-wage native workers— occurred during the 1970s and early 1980s rather than the period (from 1985 to 1990) examined here.

3. New York and Chicago are examples of two high-immigration metropolitan areas with large black populations that evolved from the early movement from the South to the North over the course of the twentieth century. The current high levels of black out-migration in these cities are a result of a number of economic and social "pushes" and "pulls," only one of which is immigrant competition (Waldinger 1996). However, in

each of these areas there is also a demographic displacement occurring. In New York, for example, the black poverty population showed a net out-migration of 43,451 from 1985 to 1990, and at the same time immigrant populations of 78,850 poor Hispanics and 36,247 poor Asians moved into the metropolitan area. Chicago lost 26,912 to net domestic out-migration over the same period but gained 20,843 poor Hispanics and 8,540 poor Asians through immigration.

REFERENCES

Barone, Michael. 1997. "Divide and Rule." *National Journal* 29(28): 1408.

Barringer, Herbert R., Robert W. Gardner, and Michael J. Levin. 1993. *Asians and Pacific Islanders in the United States.* 1980 Census Monograph. New York: Russell Sage Foundation.

Bartel, Ann P. 1989. "Where Do the New Immigrants Live?" *Journal of Labor Economics* 7(4): 371–91.

Bean, Frank D., and Marta Tienda. 1987. *The Hispanic Population of the United States.* 1980 Census Monograph. New York: Russell Sage Foundation.

Borjas, George J., and Richard Freeman. 1992. *Immigration and the Work Force.* Chicago: University of Chicago Press.

Center for Immigration Studies. 1994. *Backgrounder.* Washington, D.C.: Center for Immigration Studies.

Cromartie, John, and Carol B. Stack. 1989. "Reinterpretation of Black Return and Nonreturn Migration to the South, 1975–1980." *Geographical Review* 79: 297–310.

Espenshade, Thomas J. 1993. "Immigrants, Puerto Ricans, and the Earnings of Native Black Males." Paper presented to the annual meeting of the Population Association of America. Cincinnati, Ohio (April 3, 1993).

Farley, Reynolds, and William H. Frey. 1994. "Changes in the Segregation of Whites from Blacks During the 1980s: Small Steps Toward a Racially Integrated Society." *American Sociological Review* 59(1): 23–45.

Filer, Randall K. 1992. "The Effect of Immigrant Arrivals on Migratory Patterns of Native Workers." In *Immigration and the Work Force*, edited by George J. Borjas and Richard B. Freeman. Chicago: University of Chicago Press.

Fix, Michael, and Jeffrey Passel. 1994. *Immigration and Immigrants' Setting the Record Straight.* Washington, D.C.: Urban Institute.

Frey, William H. 1994. "Black College Grads: Those in Poverty Take Different Migration Paths." *Population Today* 22(2): 1–2.

———. 1995a. "Immigration and Internal Migration 'Flight': A California Case Study." *Population and Environment* 16(4): 353–75.

————. 1995b. "Immigration and Internal Migration 'Flight' from U.S. Metro Areas: Toward New Demographic Balkanization." *Urban Studies* 32(4–5): 333–57.

————. 1995c. "The New Geography of Population Shifts: Trends Toward Balkanization." In *State of the Union: America in the 1990s*, edited by Reynolds Farley, vol. 2. New York: Russell Sage Foundation.

————. 1996. "Immigration, Domestic Migration, and Demographic Balkanization in America." *Population and Development Review* 22(4): 741–63.

————. 1997. "Emerging Demographic Balkanization: Toward One America or Two?" Research Report 97-410. Ann Arbor: University of Michigan, Population Studies Center.

————. 1998a. "Black Migration to the South Reaches Record Highs in the 1990s." *Population Today* 26(2): 1–3.

————. 1998b. "The Diversity Myth." *American Demographics* 20(6): 38–43.

————. 1998c. "New Demographic Divide in the United States: Immigrant and Domestic 'Migrant Magnets.'" *Public Policy Perspective* 9(4): 35–39.

Frey, William H., and Reynolds Farley. 1996. "Latino, Asian, and Black Segregation in Multiethnic Areas: Are Multiethnic Metros Different?" *Demography* 33(1): 35–50.

Frey, William H., and Elaine Fielding. 1995. "Changing Urban Populations: Regional Restructuring, Racial Polarization, and Poverty Concentration." *Cityscape* 1(2): 1–66.

Frey, William H., and Kao-Lee Liaw. 1998a. "Immigrant Concentration and Domestic Migrant Dispersal: Is Movement to Nonmetro Areas 'White Flight'?" *Professional Geographer* 50(2): 215–32.

————. 1998b. "The Impact of Recent Immigration on Population Redistribution Within the United States." In *The Immigration Debate: Studies of the Economic, Demographic, and Fiscal Effects of Immigration*, edited by 7James P. Smith and Barry Edmonston. Washington, D.C.: National Academy Press.

Hamilton, C. Horace. 1964. "The Negro Leaves the South." *Demography* 1(1): 273–95.

Hirschman, Charles. 1988. "Minorities in the Labor Market and Cyclical Patterns and Secular Trends in Joblessness." In *Divided Opportunities: Minorities, Poverty, and Social Policy*, edited by Gary D. Sandefur and Marta Tienda. New York: Plenum Press.

Johnson, Daniel M., and Rex R. Campbell. 1981. *Black Migration in America: A Social Demographic History*. Durham: Duke University Press.

Johnson, James H., Jr., and David M. Grant. 1997. "Post-1980 Black Population Redistribution Trends in the United States." *Southeastern Geographer* 37(1): 1–20.

Johnson, James H., Jr., and Curt C. Roseman. 1990. "Increasing Black Out-

Migration from Los Angeles: The Role of Household Dynamics and Kinship Systems." *Annals of the Association of American Geographers* 80: 205–22.

Lansing, John B., and Eva Mueller. 1967. *The Geographic Mobility of Labor.* Ann Arbor, Mich.: Survey Research Center, Institute for Social Research.

Liaw, Kao-Lee, and William H. Frey. 1996. "Interstate Migration of Young American Adults in 1985–1990: An Explanation Using a Nested Logit Model." *Geographical Systems* 3: 301–34.

Long, Larry. 1988. *Migration and Residential Mobility in the United States.* New York: Russell Sage Foundation.

Martin, Philip, and Elizabeth Midgley. 1994. "Immigration to the United States: Journey to an Uncertain Destination." *Population Bulletin* 49(2): 2–45.

Mollenkopf, John H., and Manuel Castells, eds. 1991. *Dual City: Restructuring New York.* New York: Russell Sage Foundation.

Reder, Melvin W. 1963. "The Economic Consequences of Increased Immigration." *Review of Economics and Statistics* 45(3): 221–30.

Roseman, Curtis C., and Seong Woo Lee. 1998. "Linked and Independent African American Migration from Los Angeles." *Professional Geographer* 50(2): 204–14.

Tienda, Marta, and Zai Liang. 1992. "Horatio Alger Fails: Poverty and Immigration in Policy Perspective." Paper presented to the Institute for Research on Poverty and the U.S Department of Health and Human Services, Conference on Poverty and Public Policy: What Do We Know? What Should We Do? Madison, Wis. (May 28–30).

Tilove, Jonathan. 1993. "Immigration Shifts Affirmative Action Fight." *Detroit Free Press*, December 20, 1993.

———. 1999. "The New Map of American Politics." *American Prospect*, 44(May–June): 34–42.

Tilove, Jonathan, and Joe Hallinan. 1993. "Whites Flee Immigrants: Flee White States." *Newark Star Ledger*, August 8.

Waldinger, Roger. 1989. "Immigration and Urban Change." *Annual Review of Sociology* 15: 211–32.

———. 1996. *Still the Promised City?: African Americans and New Immigrants in Postindustrial New York.* Cambridge: Harvard University Press.

Walker, Robert, Mark Ellis, and Richard Barff. 1992. "Linked Migration Systems: Immigration and Internal Labor Flows in the United States." *Economic Geography* 68(3): 234–48.

White, Michael J., and Yoshie Imai. 1993. "The Impact of Immigration upon Internal Migration." *Population and Environment* 15(3): 189–209.

Wright, Richard A., Mark Ellis, and Michael Reibel. 1997. "The Linkage Between Immigration and Internal Migration in Large Metropolitan Areas in the United States." *Economic Geography* 73(2): 234–54.

CHAPTER 10

The Impact of Immigration on Residential Segregation

Michael J. White and Jennifer E. Glick

Immigrant communities abound. It is common wisdom that immigrants arrive in a city and find themselves clustered—by choice or by discrimination—in selected urban neighborhoods. This is the model of American urban society that led Robert Park, and many who have followed, to see it as axiomatic that "spatial distance reflects social distance" (Park et al. 1925). We subscribe, at least in part, to this common wisdom, yet we reevaluate some of the ideas about urban residential patterns that have become so entrenched during the past few decades. To engage the discussion, we first give an overall picture of how ethnic congregation is fashioned in a pluralistic society and then determine how immigration might be changing the residential intermingling of blacks and whites. To this end, we offer two sets of empirical results: The first compares the segregation levels in 1990 of a wide array of ethnic groups, the second looks at the impact of immigration on the segregation of African Americans.

Segregation measurement provides key insights into urban residential patterns from readily available observational data, such as the decennial census. Theoretical and empirical studies of segregation remain a major window on ethnic and racial relations (Massey and Denton 1993; Farley and Frey 1994); yet our studies of segregation have become inadequate as the United States itself has become ever more variegated in its ethnic complexion. For decades the study of segregation focused on the separation of blacks from whites. This was in keeping with concerns raised by the Civil Rights movement. As Latinos and Asians came to be more visible and numerically important minority groups, segregation researchers brought these panethnic groups under the microscope. Data constraints also shaped the form of the analysis, with expansions of the ethnic categories taking place in successive censuses.

What insights can the study of residential segregation provide? Segregation indexes measure the cumulative impact of several related processes, including discrimination, self-selection, and population composition. From the point of view of policy, residential patterns are

345

both quite informative and a bit problematic. Housing patterns (and hence residential segregation) provide one of the most intimate domains in which public policy regarding civil rights intervenes. Furthermore, this involvement is asymmetrical: Although outright discrimination is forbidden, voluntary movement away from undesirable (or undesired) neighbors (white flight) receives no direct intervention. Similarly, self-segregation (absent denial of housing opportunities to others) enables ethnic enclaves without necessarily presenting the circumstances for public involvement. Residential patterns, therefore, become a key way in which to view the net results of policy, immigration patterns, and intergroup accommodation, especially in the urban environment (White and Omer 1997).

How the neighboring pattern manifests itself speaks volumes about the underlying social relationships in American society. It is unquestionable that the compositional differences among ethnic (and immigrant) groups—socioeconomic status, family size, age—all feed into residential outcomes. To the extent that they are merely correlated with ethnic group, we run the risk of measuring as ethnic segregation the clustering along these other dimensions. We know that these other traits do, in fact, figure notably in the residential outcomes of groups; (White, Biddlecom, and Guo 1993; White and Sassler 1995). But the accumulated evidence also indicates that ethnic differences matter greatly in their own right, and it is on these differences we concentrate.

This chapter reports on two empirical investigations. First, we examine basic segregation levels of a large number of ethnic groups, much larger than most studies have heretofore examined. Second, we place the analysis of segregation between blacks and whites in a dynamic metropolitan context. Specifically, we test competing hypotheses, one arguing that recent immigration to metropolitan areas polarizes black and white residential patterns, the other arguing that immigration diffuses residential patterns, resulting in more intermingling between the two groups. To the extent that immigration increases segregation between blacks and whites, calls for policy aimed at reducing immigration may be justified as a way to reduce or at least not exacerbate racial inequality. On the other hand, a finding that increased immigration decreases or has no effect on the residential separation of blacks and whites would suggest that our policy aims need be directed not at immigration per se but at other forces that perpetuate racial and ethnic discrimination.

The increasing diversity of American society calls upon us to rethink some of the standard models; our chapter takes a step in that direction. We hope that we provide insight into the evolving patterns of relationship between whites and African Americans in U.S. society, even as we call for a wider ethnic framework from which to analyze residential patterns. This analysis can also shed light on current debates about the very meaning of ethnicity, a concept that has itself evolved through U.S. history (Wright 1994; White and Sassler 1995).

BLACKS AND WHITES, IMMIGRANTS AND ETHNICS

Before we examine the relationship between recent immigration and segregation of blacks and whites, it is valuable to examine the relationship between immigration and segregation generally. Historical studies with aggregate census data have found that time in the host society produces greater residential intermingling, at least for European immigrants (Lieberson 1963). At the same time, scholars have repeatedly documented the persistent barriers that minority group members have faced in U.S. society. As our society continues to diversify, now adding immigrant streams from multiple origins in Asia, Latin America, the Caribbean, and still from parts of Europe, the question needs to be revisited. The task is to determine the relationship between ethnic-group vintage (time of arrival) and residential segregation from others in American society.

Immigration and ethnicity are closely intertwined. Immigration brings to the host society new members. Phenotypic or physiognomic distinctiveness helps differentiate them physically from the host society and forms the basis of distinction classified as racial. Immigrants' language, religion, kinship and family patterns, and occupational skills may further differentiate them. Does this "differentness" matter? Theoretical approaches loosely grouped under the rubric of the "melting pot" argue that the differences matter, though less and less over time. Immigrants themselves and successive generations assimilate, achieving socioeconomically and adopting the customs and norms of the host society. The contrary view, ethnic pluralism, holds that, despite the passage of time and considerable structural assimilation, ethnic groups remain distinct, even "unmeltable," to borrow Michael Novak's (1972) word.

A restatement of the distinction between assimilation and pluralism leads to testable hypotheses. The assimilation model argues that those groups with more time in the host country should be less segregated. The increased intermingling arises both from structural assimilation (educational attainment, jobs, income) on the part of the immigrants and their ethnic descendants and from accommodation of the host society to the new arrivals. Cultural assimilation, no doubt, plays a role, and the "new" group comes to adopt the practices of the host society in the first and succeeding generations. The model, guided by notions of inevitable assimilation, predicts that vintage—or group experience in the host country—will predict residential intermingling. It would argue, for example that Americans of German heritage (an "old" immigrant group) would be less segregated than Italian Americans, who arrived in more recent years. It would argue that Americans of Korean origin would be more segregated than those whose ancestors originated in Japan, because the latter have more time (generations) in the United States.

An alternative view, aligned more with the "pluralism" perspective, is the hypothesis of ethnic hierarchy. In this case, a group's reception and experience in the society rests not so much on time and adjustment as on position within a hierarchy in the host country. The dominant group (white Anglo-Saxon Protestants, in the conventional U.S. view) sits atop the hierarchy; racial minorities and immigrant groups fall into line below, according to the preference and prejudice system of the society. Such hierarchies can be identified through surveys in which the "social distance" of the ethnic group from the core or dominant group is measured directly. Position in the hierarchy, then, predicts residential intermingling for the various groups under review, and vintage or time has little to do with it.

By conventional standards, however, the segregation of the foreign born is modest. Direct calculation of segregation by nativity finds lower values than apply to large panethnic groups, such as Asians or Latinos. For instance, Hispanics, a group that contains many immigrants, are far more segregated than immigrants generally.[1] This more modest level of segregation is consistent with work done for 1980 on a national sample of cities (White 1986). In that study the foreign born were found to experience a moderate level of segregation in twenty-one U.S. metropolitan areas. In general, 1990 measures of segregation of the entire foreign-born population fell below levels experienced by racial and Spanish-origin groups.

The preceding addresses the expected residential patterns of new immigrants, but what of the effect of new arrivals on existing patterns? Recent immigration to the United States, bringing with it an array of new groups, might be expected to change the residential arrangement between blacks and whites—or perhaps not. Geographically and mathematically, nothing need inevitably happen. That is, the addition of the new groups does not necessarily change the segregation values that obtain between two preexisting groups. Social processes, however, may change this configuration, and the assimilation and ethnic-pluralism views predict very different outcomes.

One extension of the assimilation model would argue that segregation of blacks from whites should decline as other groups with less experience (that is, of a more recent vintage) arrive. Segregation would decline as it would have anyway, and the new arrivals offer no causal influence. Conversely, the ethnic-hierarchy model regards the classification of the new arrivals (and their physiognomic and cultural distinctiveness) as the crucial element. On one hand, if immigrants can act as a buffer between blacks and whites, we might see segregation increase, as the presence of a third group (or many more groups) enables further separation of blacks and whites in social space. On the other hand, immigrants, who are classified at the lower rungs of the ethnic hierarchy, might push blacks and whites into greater proximity. The null hypothesis has real relevance here, because the arrival of immigrants might *not* influence the segregation of blacks from whites.

Taking all this into account, we can define two models. The first model is one of polarization. With the arrival of immigrants (of differing ethnic background from the existing stock of whites and blacks), blacks and whites move (literally) further apart. New immigrants and ethnic groups allow whites and blacks to act on their discomfort or discriminatory tendencies and reduce their proximity. The new groups, such as those of Mexican or Chinese origin, become a buffer between blacks and whites in urban space. A polarization process is consistent with a pattern of ethnic relations driven by notions of ethnic (racial) hierarchy and intrinsic social distance. In this case, time and socioeconomic assimilation have very little to do with relationships among groups in space. Some ethnic groups are just preferred, while others are the objects of prejudice and discrimination. Because the age-old American racial hierarchy would put persons of African origin at the greatest distance from whites, the polarization model then leads to the hypothesis that as the immigrant presence in the city grows, segregation between blacks and whites will increase.

An alternative to the polarization hypothesis, the ethnic diffusion or polyethnic model, predicts that new arrivals will "stir the melting pot." In this scenario the arrival of immigrants from diverse origins breaks down the conventional patterns of race relations. What was once a two-group model (all whites versus all blacks) becomes culturally pluralistic. Although discrimination and prejudice persist, they can no longer be as concentrated as before. The spatial manifestation is that groups become more diffused—or confused—across space. There is a curious twist in the way in which cultural pluralism and assimilation models might work into this issue when more groups are added. In the case of pluralism, the maintenance of several somewhat distinct ethnic groups might add to this diffusion unless, of course, that distinctiveness goes so far as to maintain a racial hierarchy. On the other hand, the assimilation model weighs time heavily in outcomes. New groups are, virtually by definition, the least assimilated. Immigrants should be most likely to reside in enclaves and hence be less integrated with either blacks or whites. One extension of thinking along these lines would suggest that as some new arrivals appear at the bottom of the ladder, they push up others—and perhaps push them together.[2]

ETHNIC IDENTITY AND VINTAGE: DEFINITIONS

Ethnic identity is fluid, despite its concrete classification in surveys and censuses. The identity arises out of a dynamic interplay between hosts and new arrivals. Ethnic classification contains elements of both self-identification and "other-identification." By other-identification we mean identity recognized (and attributed) by the host society. These identities can be welcomed or forced. The process is particularly important for the way it manifests itself in measuring "ethnicity." We use "ethnicity" to subsume race and conventional ethnic differences. Just as one may actively articulate an Italian American heritage, the remaining society helps develop and reify that category. For many Americans of African descent, the experience of slavery and subsequent race relations in the United States serves to amalgamate various African origins and ethnicity. The net result of this on the residential plain is segregation. Although the U.S. census of 1890 included the categories of mulatto, quadroon, and octoroon (White and Sassler 1995), the system of racial apartheid in the United States clung to the "one-drop rule," holding that any African ancestry served to classify an individual as Negro or black. Experience in the host country can spur the evolution of ethnic identity, for instance, by encouraging regional origins (Sicily) to become subsumed under a wider geographic entity (Italy). Furthermore, residence in a plural society produces the opportunity for an individual to choose among several ethnic categories for his or her stated identity. Scholars working in the area of historical demography (again with census materials) struggle to work across country of birth, parentage, and language to classify persons (Watkins 1994).

Limited historical information about the spatial manifestation of these ethnic differences exists, but study of historical census materials suggests that the "new" groups of 1910 were quite highly isolated in urban space (Hershberg 1981; White, Dymowski, and Wang 1994). The different initial conditions and the subsequent experience of immigrant groups begs the question of how the assimilation process fared for each. Reynolds Farley looked in detail at selected 1980 census data for Chicago (Farley 1991). He found that white ethnic groups resident in the United States before the Civil War were least segregated from the English stock. Segregation of groups of Asian origin and Hispanics across Chicago neighborhoods was more substantial but still less than that of blacks. Descendants of late nineteenth- and early-twentieth-century immigrants fell into the middle range, at slightly more than half the dissimilarity of blacks. Farley notes of Asians and Hispanics that "many might be expected to settle in immigrant enclaves and thus be segregated from the English-origin population, perhaps at a level exceeding that of blacks. This is not the case" (283).

The census materials for 1990 with which we work in this chapter are a product of that process. The definition of race and ethnicity has evolved considerably in the United States (White and Sassler 1995). The 1980 and 1990 censuses elected to ask persons their self-identified "ancestry," and virtually no editing of the responses was done, save to remove responses in religious categories or to limit the number of classifications when many were given. Even these two recent censuses offer several routes to the measurement and identification of "ethnicity." Distinct questions (each with several response categories) are asked with reference to race, Spanish-origin, ancestry, place of birth, and language. Each one of these variables, then, offers a different dimension of ethnicity. In theory, a person could occupy any category on each of these variables. Classification as a Chinese (race)-Cuban (Spanish-origin)-Filipino (ancestry) individual is possible. (Particular options for language and place of birth could make the combination even more complex.) In everyday life, however, persons on the street, reporters, and the like do not think in census terms. We suggest, rather, that individuals think in the vernacular of ethnicity as a single dimension, but one in which a person may claim multiple heritages or responses. Our approach tries to incorporate this aspect of U.S. social life.

Intermarriage (or miscegenation) complicates the ethnicity picture even more. Even if people consistently identify a particular label for themselves, the intermingling of the population across ethnic lines creates further diversity and complications in measurement, even as it produces the very melting pot that America is purported to be.

Through intermarriage people gather multiple heritages. Two considerations are important. One is obvious: Rates of intermarriage vary significantly across ethnic groups (and sometimes by gender within an ethnic group). The second may be less obvious: As descent becomes complicated, there is a tendency toward selective reporting. This is aggravated by the fact that most social science survey instruments (including the census) allow for only one or a few responses to the question about ancestry. Thus, some ethnic heritages tend to be favored (or at least more frequently reported) than others. These responses vary with time. For example, the growth in the Native American population between 1980 and 1990 was too large to be attributed to natural increase and is attributable partly to increased self-identification (Eschbach 1993; Passel 1995).

In this chapter we also work with the concept of ethnic vintage, and we give it a quantitative representation. It has been common in the immigration and ethnicity literature to speak of "old" and "new" groups. More recently, observers speak of "new, new groups" or the "fourth wave" (Muller and Espenshade 1985). Despite the inevitable pitfalls of doing so, we attempt to calculate a measure that will indicate how "old" a group is. Besides the advantage of avoiding fumbling over terminology such as "new, new" the vintage concept can be introduced into quantitative studies of immigrant adaptation.

DATA AND METHODS

We use data from the 1990 census STF3A file and selected additional characteristics of the metropolitan area, many from the *State and Metropolitan Area Data Book*. The STF3A file includes tabulations for census tracts (neighborhoods) by race, Spanish origin, and ancestry, which categories we, in turn, use to develop segregation scores by ethnic group. Each of these tabulations taps a facet of ethnicity. Tracts are small, relatively compact areas into which urban areas are divided for statistical purposes. For all intents they are the closest demographic and statistical approximation to neighborhoods (White 1987). Tracts contain between three thousand and six thousand persons. They are quite useful for segregation statistics and have been used regularly by other researchers in the past. Our sample consists of 285 metropolitan areas in the United States.

We use the index of dissimilarity, or D, to measure segregation. This statistic, the most commonly used in segregation analyses, measures the fraction of one group that would have to relocate (in this case, to new neighborhoods) to produce an even, or unsegregated, distribution. Although many other indexes have been developed, and some may be superior (White 1986), the dissimilarity index is so broadly used that we continue to use it here. It is a chief indicator of "evenness" among competing measures of segregation (Massey, White, and Phua 1997).

The index of dissimilarity applies only to dichotomies. In our application we calculate the dissimilarity between the group of interest and all others. Thus, we calculate segregation between Koreans and non-Koreans or blacks and nonblacks. We do this because there is no consensus on distinct reference group. As a consequence the "others" in the application here include those of African, European, and even other Asian stock.

The index itself is calculated as:

$$D = \frac{1}{2} \sum_{i=1}^{N} \left| \frac{P_{i1}}{P_1} - \frac{P_{i2}}{P_2} \right|,$$

where P_1 and P_2 indicate the overall (metrowide or statewide) populations of groups 1 and 2. The values indexed by I in the numerator correspond to the group populations in the tracts. The sum is over all tracts in the metropolitan area.

The index of dissimilarity has one very attractive feature. Its value is intuitively meaningful: D is the proportion of one group that would have to relocate to produce an even (unsegregated) distribution. Values of D range from zero to one (100 percent). For example, in a region in which 10 percent of the population are immigrants, a value for D of 50 percent would mean that half the immigrants would have to relocate so that 10 percent of the inhabitants of every neighborhood would be immigrants. The calculation of D is limited to the comparison of two groups only. In many cases we calculate it for membership in a single group of interest versus all others. It should be remembered that although we attempt to define mutually exclusive ethnic groups by this procedure, the very format of the census—explicit response categories for questions pertaining to Asian and Spanish origin, open-ended responses for ancestries—may have influenced the relative frequency of responses.

In the present study we calculate the index of dissimilarity for one group as against all persons not in that group. Thus we look at the dissimilarities between Cubans and non-Cubans and between Italians and non-Italians. Such a calculation gives a summary of the residential experience of ethnic groups; for those with low levels of segregation (low values for *D*), the measure does not reveal the identities of other groups with which the particular group is residentially intermingled.

Ethnicity Analysis

To analyze ethnicity we combine information from questions on race, Spanish origin, and ancestry. From the detailed race tabulations in the STF3 file, we identify blacks and several Asian ethnicities as distinct groups. Detailed tabulations of Spanish origin yield several more Latino ethnic groups. Finally, we identify several additional, mostly European-origin, groups based on assignments from single and multiple ancestry. Those who report multiple ancestries are proportionately distributed across categories. For many very small groups we can (and do) make these calculations, but their very rarity makes the notion of national levels of segregation across U.S. metropolitan areas hard to define. For this reason we concentrate our discussion on the thirty-nine groups with populations greater than five hundred thousand as counted in the 1990 census.

A question about ancestry is asked of all persons who receive the long-form version of the census. A great deal of ink has been spilled in setting down the caveats for the analysis of ancestry questions on the U.S. census. Our earlier discussion gave some hint of some of the difficulties of definition, equally applicable to measures of race and Spanish origin. Ancestry appears to be a more malleable concept than nativity, race, or Spanish origin, and it is not as consistently reported by census or survey respondents. Moreover, the way that ancestry is coded and tabulated in the U.S. census allows for multiple ancestries to be recorded.

The confusion may be an authentic contrast to an artificially rigid and exclusive set of categories used for race. Of course, the introduction of the ancestry question itself was a response in part to a demand that "white ethnics," principally persons of European stock, be given a distinct recording mechanism in the census. Previous census-taking practice was one of "administrative assimilation," because the identification of ethnicity by a person's own and parents' nativity would fail by the third generation. Thus, ancestry, though somewhat problematic in its own right, provides the detail necessary to separate individuals into ethnic groups otherwise subsumed under the race and Spanish-origin items.

Vintage

Vintage is the new measure we introduce here. For each country of origin we can calculate the average year of arrival of immigrants. More precisely, we use U.S. Immigration and Naturalization Service statistics to calculate the median year of arrival (to the nearest five-year point) for each group. The median year is the date by which half of the immigrants recorded from that origin had arrived in the United States. Such a procedure has pitfalls, of course. It omits undocumented migrants, whether contemporary (such as Mexicans) or from an earlier point in time (from Canada, for example); it fixes national origins to a set of historical countries maintained by the Immigration and Naturalization Service.[3] Nevertheless, this measure serves as a reasonable proxy for immigrant or ethnic group vintage.

Change in Segregation Between Blacks and Whites

We use 1980 and 1990 dissimilarity statistics for a sample of about 168 major metropolitan areas for which comparable data are available to assess the change in segregation of blacks from whites. We employ straightforward multivariate models. First, we examine a cross-sectional (or level) model for 1980 and 1990, using OLS regression, to predict the level of segregation from contemporaneous characteristics of the metropolitan area. Then, we turn to a first-difference (or fixed-effects) model, in which change in the decade segregation level is regressed on change in the values of the covariates. This latter strategy is standard in many settings and is designed to remove the influence of unmeasured, unchanging traits. Because the key question is whether black and white residential patterns have been influenced by immigration, we look only at black and white outcomes in relation to one another.

We have elected not to transform the dissimilarity index. (A logit transformation might be suggested for a dependent variable bounded between 0 and 1.) This will ease interpretation of our results. We take several of our U.S. metropolitan-level variables from data used by Reynolds Farley and William Frey (1994), including functional specialization of the metropolitan area, age of metropolitan area, recent housing construction, and population size.[4] The covariate of particular interest is the proportion of foreign born in each metropolitan area. If the diffusion hypothesis is correct, then this coefficient will have a negative sign. That is, cities with greater growth in immigration will experience declines in segregation between blacks and whites. If, on the other hand, the ethnic-polarization hypothesis holds, then we would expect a positive coefficient, as cities with growing immigrant concentrations experience greater separation of the two groups.

SEGREGATION BY ETHNICITY AND VINTAGE

Table 10.1 presents average segregation levels exhibited by thirty-nine ethnic groups, each of which had a reported population of more than a half million in the 1990 U.S. census. For every one of these groups we can calculated the dissimilarity index for 285 metropolitan areas.[5] We choose the median to represent average segregation. Half of all U.S. metropolitan areas exhibit greater segregation than this value, and half less. The value of 0.536 for persons of Mexican origin therefore splits the U.S. metropolitan areas into two groups. By using the median, we can reduce sensitivity to some of the extreme values that would result from our using the mean (arithmetic average). Of the ethnic groups identified by the census ancestry question, most are of European origin. Segregation is modest for most of these groups, and it is especially low for the "old-stock" ethnic groups, such as those of German, Irish, French, and English ancestry. Despite the fact that the English stock are arguably the oldest vintage of the European-origin population, they are not the least segregated. That position is held by Americans of Irish ancestry.

Also falling into what might be classified as the middle range of segregation are persons of Russian descent,[6] persons of French Canadian descent, and persons whose origins are in Scandinavia or southern or eastern Europe. Many of these groups were prominently represented in the great immigrant wave at the turn of the twentieth century. Not all segregation of these ancestry groups is modest: Note that those of Portuguese ancestry (many more of whom arrived after some favorable changes in U.S. immigration policy around 1960) have an average dissimilarity index of near 70 percent. Several other European-origin groups have segregation values that skirt 50 percent. In this group is included "West Indian," mostly persons of African descent who trace their ancestry to the Caribbean and then further to Africa. Segregation for this group is about 75 percent. Notable, however, is the wide diversity of segregation values, even among the European-origin populations. Because the ancestry question (and our method) includes all persons of that origin (whether in the first or the

Table 10.1   Segregation Levels of Thirty-Nine Populous Ethnic
Groups in the United States, 1990

	Vintage	Size[a]	Index of Dissimilarity	Abbreviation
Census Group				
Arab	1983	716,391	57.1	ARA
Austrian	1907	545,856	52.0	AUS
Czech	1928	1,012,576	47.8	CZE
Danish	1899	980,868	50.2	DAN
Dutch	1914	3,475,410	31.2	DUT
English	1889	21,836,397	25.9	ENG
French	1900	6,204,184	28.4	FRE
French Canadian	1923	2,296,123	48.0	FRC
German	1884	45,583,932	31.2	GER
Greek	1920	921,782	50.7	GRE
Hungarian	1906	997,545	50.6	HUN
Irish	1870	22,721,252	20.2	IRI
Italian	1909	11,286,815	41.8	ITA
Lithuanian	1907	526,089	57.1	LIT
Norwegian	1902	2,517,760	54.1	NOR
Polish	1927	6,542,844	43.5	POL
Portuguese	1930	900,060	69.0	POR
Russian	1907	2,114,506	54.7	RUS
Scotch-Irish	1889	4,334,197	30.5	SCI
Scottish	1889	3,315,306	28.8	SCO
Slovak	1928	1,210,652	50.3	SLO
Swedish	1896	2,881,950	40.9	SWE
Swiss	1894	607,833	48.6	SWI
Ukrainian	1907	514,085	59.9	UKR
Welsh	1889	1,038,603	36.3	WEL
West Indian	1982	1,058,345	74.2	WIN
Spanish-origin groups				
Mexican	1976	13,495,938	53.6	MEX
Puerto Rican	1960	2,727,754	68.8	PUE
Cuban	1972	1,043,932	83.5	CUB
Dominican	1981	520,151	91.2	DOM
Salvadoran	1985	565,081	91.0	SAL
Racial groups				
Black	1865	29,986,060	59.9	BLA
American Indian	1865	1,659,234	51.1	AMI
Chinese	1972	1,645,472	74.9	CHI
Filipino	1982	1,406,770	74.0	FIL
Japanese	1920	847,562	78.0	JAP
Asian Indian	1982	815,447	79 4	ASI
Korean	1981	798,849	71.5	KOR
Vietnamese	1983	614,547	83.3	VIE

Sources: U.S. Immigration and Naturalization Service, *Statistical Yearbooks* (various years); 1990 U.S. Census.
[a]Population of the group in 1990.

seventh generation), the persistence of ethnic residential distinctiveness is noteworthy. The basic point here is that to assume all European groups are intermingled and thus equally segregated in American society—often implicit in studies of residential segregation—is fundamentally flawed.

The census allows us to identify several Latino groups each of which had more than half a million persons in 1990. Within the Latino subset, people of Mexican origin are the least segregated. Puerto Rican and Cuban persons are in the middle of the Latino group, but they are quite highly segregated compared with those of European ancestry. Finally, Dominican and Salvadoran persons are very highly segregated. Analysis of 1980 census data indicates that segregation by race *within* the Spanish-origin population was nearly as high as racial segregation overall (White 1986); this may still be the case, and it could serve to explain some of the high segregation levels observed for some Latino groups. We may be witnessing the self-segregation in the ethnic enclave, particularly in connection with Cuban patterns (Miami offering the paramount example), but direct empirical evidence on this point is harder to develop.

The segregation of most so-called racial groups is also appreciable. (We use "racial" only in pointing out the census classification; for this study, all "races" are subsets of ethnic groups.) African Americans, the most numerous and most regionally dispersed racial minority, exhibit a 1990 dissimilarity score around 60. Most European-origin groups are less segregated than this. By contrast, groups classified on the basis of race or Spanish origin in the census make up the ten most segregated groups. Note also that most of these (the Japanese are an exception) are recent arrivals. This begs the question, "How strong is the relationship between vintage and group segregation?"

The conventional vintage model of immigrant and ethnic settlement would predict that those groups with more residential experience in the United States would be the least segregated. We performed a simple, direct test of this, using information on ethnic vintage. For each of these groups we calculated from Immigration and Naturalization Service (INS) statistics the median year of arrival for the group. Thus, the vintage of the group is that year marking the point (between 1820 and 1990) at which half the total number of immigrants had arrived and half were yet to come. The value of the vintage for each group is also contained in table 10.1. Thus, we observe that the vintage of the Irish is 1870 and that of the Cubans 1972, reflecting their much more recent arrival to the United States in the wake of the Castro-era migration. We admit that this assignment is far from perfect. For Native Americans and African Americans, we assign the date of the end of the Civil War. In the eyes of a few this would mark unfettered access to the American system; on the other hand, these groups have been here as long as or longer than the oldest of the white Europeans, so a vintage date is not clear. Relatedly, for some of the "old-stock" groups—English, German, French—INS records make their average arrival more recent than it undoubtedly is. Nevertheless, this simple assignment sorts a wide array of groups along a 170-year time line.

Figure 10.1 plots the level of segregation against the duration of each group's presence in the United States (measured from the thirty-nine ethnic groups). (Data are taken from table 10.1.) The figure dramatically illustrates the relationship between group vintage and segregation. It is important to recall that the plotted line represents an approximate average time at which migrating members of each group, whether immigrants themselves or members of the second, third, fourth, or fourteenth generation, can expect to experience a certain amount of benefit or cost from group vintage. Thus, persons of Greek heritage in the United States today will face some impact from the fact that half of Greek immigration had taken place by 1920. For a Filipino on the other hand, the relevant vintage is 1982, and even a third-generation Filipino will be attached to that more recent vintage in the social structure. This is not to deny that individual traits—age, income, schooling—matter; in fact, the evidence indicates that they matter greatly. Rather, we argue that vintage is one element of group process and also a trait that attaches to an individual, both aspects of which may serve to influence observed patterns of ethnic segregation.

To be more precise about the relationship, we regressed dissimilarity on group duration (1990 minus vintage) for the thirty-nine census groups. The resulting equation is:

$$\text{DISSIMILARITY} = .7884 - .0037(\text{DURATION})$$
$$(R^2 = 0.59; \ p < 0.001).$$

Vintage (group duration) is a powerful predictor of segregation. For these thirty-nine groups, the R^2 statistic is 0.59, and we strongly reject the null hypothesis that there is no relationship between a group's time of arrival and the level of segregation the group experienced in 1990. As an illustration, consider a comparison between a group whose median immigrant entered in 1900 and another group whose vintage is 1980. The eighty-year span predicts a 0.31 decline in dis-

Figure 10.1   Segregation of Thirty-Nine Populous Ethnic Groups by
Vintage in the United States, 1990

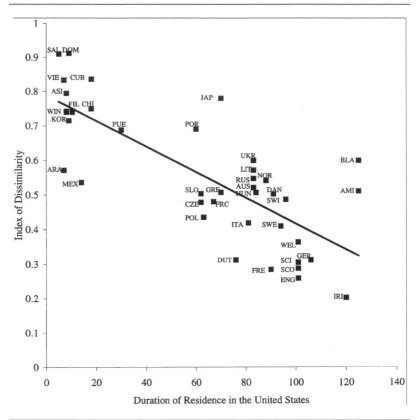

Source: Data from table 10.1

similarity, versus a range of about 0.70 among all the dissimilarity statistics.

Nevertheless, these results are only partly supportive of the vintage model. The points that fall far from the line in figure 10.1, points that are less well predicted by the regression equation, offer further instruction. Blacks and Native Americans are far more segregated than their "vintage" would indicate; indeed, if we offered a more realistic vintage, which might date to the founding of the nation, the results would be even more stark. Within the European-stock group it is true that some of the "old" immigrant groups (German, English) exhibit actual levels of segregation below the prediction, but the cause of this may be the assignment of a relatively recent vintage. Notable, however, is the low segregation level of the Irish, given the fact that the vintage concept probably does accurately capture the great waves of movement during and after the Great Famine. Notable for its place well above the line is the segregation of those of Japanese descent. These persons are far more residentially segregated than one would predict on the basis of their substantial (group) time in the United States. Persons of Mexican origin, although their index of dissimilarity falls in the middle range, are less segregated than vintage would predict. Despite the notable exceptions, the simple vintage calculation does show that for many groups of European, Latin, and Asian heritage this model offers some empirically verified description of the path of residential integration with time in the United States.

The analysis of vintage tells us that more-recent immigrants are appreciably more segregated. To the extent the relationship holds, it provides some evidence for the ethnic-diffusion model, in which time begins to wear away at ethnic divisions. These results also make it clear that the association between vintage and segregation is far from perfect. Most notably, African Americans are more segregated than predicted by any measure of vintage. It remains to be seen what the direct relationship is between new immigration (recent vintage) and the segregation of blacks from whites, the traditional pairing of interest to social scientists and policy makers.

CHANGE IN SEGREGATION BETWEEN BLACKS AND WHITES FROM 1980 TO 1990

One of the primary sources of increased ethnic diversity in the United States in the past several decades has been increased immigration, particularly the arrival of Asian and Hispanic immigrants. Previous research has attributed a decrease in black segregation from whites to this increased ethnic diversity in some metropolitan areas (Frey and Farley 1996). It is not clear, however, if the increase in the foreign-born population, per se, speeds the decreased separation of blacks and whites, as predicted by the ethnic-diffusion model, or slows the decrease that would be occurring by introducing a new buffer between blacks and whites, as predicted by the polarization models. We examine dissimilarity indexes (black versus white) for 168 metropolitan areas in the United States in 1980 and 1990. In particular, we ask to what extent changes in the proportion of the population that is foreign born contributes to changes in segregation between blacks and whites over this period.[7]

Table 10.2   Average Race or Ethnic and Nativity Composition of U.S. Metropolitan Areas by Segregation Between Black and White, 1980 and 1990

D-Values	Number of Metropolitan Areas	Percent Black	Percent Hispanic	Percent Asian	Percent Foreign Born	Percent Recent Arrivals
			1980			
50 or less	8	17.3	2.8	1.4	3.6	43.8
51 to 65	38	15.3	6.4	1.3	3.9	44.8
66 to 80	93	14.0	3.7	0.9	3.6	36.5
81 and up	29	13.5	4.9	0.8	6.7	28.9
			1990			
50 or less	13	15.1	5.0	2.3	6.2	41.8
51 to 65	57	15.0	7.6	2.5	6.5	38.5
66 to 80	85	14.7	2.8	1.2	5.6	32.2
81 and up	13	16.6	3.3	1.3	6.4	29.3

Sources: 1980 and 1990 IPUMS (http://www.ipums.umn.edu), *D*-values provided by Dr. William Frey.

Table 10.2 presents a summary of the racial or ethnic and nativity distribution of the metropolitan areas by the dissimilarity between blacks and whites. The number of areas with lower *D*-values increases between 1980 and 1990, reflecting the trend toward lower segregation levels overall. Those metropolitan areas with less segregation between blacks and whites (lower *D*-values) appear to be more likely to contain a more diverse population. That is, the metropolitan areas with lower levels of segregation tend to have higher percentages of the population made up of blacks, Hispanics, and Asians.

To test the effect of the racial or ethnic and nativity composition of the metropolitan area on black segregation from whites, we use cross-sectional OLS regressions for 1980 and 1990. The descriptive statistics of the measures employed are found in table 10.3. We include measures associated with segregation used in previous studies, such as region, age of city, functional specialization, and housing growth (Frey and Farley 1994). The regression results are presented in table 10.4. We find that smaller metropolitan areas and those experiencing recent housing growth exhibit lower levels of segregation. Areas characterized by government, university, and military activity show lower segregation levels; retirement areas are more segregated. These results are broadly consistent with previous research. As mirrored by the de-

Table 10.3   Descriptive Statistics for Variables Used in OLS and First-Difference Models of Residential Segregation Between Blacks and Whites

Variable	Percent
Population size	
1980	777,719
	(1,399,455)
1990	880,380
	(1,590,677)
Region	
South	48.4
North	10.2
Midwest	28.7
West	12.7
Age of City	
1900 or earlier	47.1
1910 to 1940	22.3
1950 to 1960	23.6
1970 or later	7.0
Functional specialization	
Durable goods manufacturing	18.5
Nondurable goods manufacturing	7.0
Government	7.0
University	7.0
Military	8.9
Retirement	6.4
Mixed functions	45.2
Housing built in previous decade	
1980	28.7
1990	18.6
Black	
1980	14.2
1990	14.9
Hispanic	
1980	4.6
1990	4.8
Asian	
1980	1.1
1990	1.8
Foreign born	
1980	4.3
1990	6.1
Foreign born arriving in previous decade (recent)	
1980	38.0
1990	35.0

Sources: 1980 and 1990 IPUMS (http://www.ipums.umn.edu), *D*-values provided by Dr. William Frey.
Note: Sample consists of 168 Metropolitan Areas. Standard Deviations in Parentheses.

Table 10.4   Measures of Dissimilarity Between Whites and Blacks According to OLS Regression Models, 1980 and 1990 (Percentage)

Variable	1980		1990	
	Model 1	Model 2	Model 1	Model 2
Population size (log)	3.34***	3.24***	3.17***	3.42***
Region (vs. South)				
North	−1.25	−1.94	4.42*	4.12
Midwest	0.48	0.11	3.70*	3.48*
West	0.76	0.23	2.81	3.01
Age of city (vs. 1970 or later)				
1900 or earlier	−0.22	0.03	0.48	0.79
1910 to 1940	−1.21	−1.00	−1.16	−0.65
1950 to 1960	−1.95	−1.83	−2.77	−2.69
Functional specialization				
Durable goods manufacturing	2.48	2.00	2.76	1.80
Nondurable goods manufacturing	−1.87	−1.75	−0.59	0.09
Government	−4.55*	−4.67*	−2.87	−2.65
University	−8.06**	−7.75**	−6.51**	−4.78*
Military	−12.39***	−12.65***	−13.02***	−12.76***
Retirement	15.07***	13.57***	13.29***	13.56***
Percent of housing units built in previous decade	−0.24**	−0.22**	−0.20***	−0.18***
Racial and ethnic composition				
Percent black	−0.07	0.02	0.16*	0.18
Percent Hispanic	−0.07	−0.08	−0.14*	−0.10
Percent Asian	−1.19*	−1.09	−0.66*	−0.44
Nativity Composition				
Percent foreign born	—	0.06	—	−0.05
Percent recent arrivals	—	−0.05	—	−0.14**
Constant	37.54***	40.25***	28.05***	28.37***
Adjusted R^2	58.8	58.3	64.5	65.8
Number of observations	157	157	157	157

Sources: 1980 and 1990 IPUMS (http://www.ipums.umn.edu), *D*-values provided by Dr. William Frey. Eleven observations have missing covariate data.
Notes: *p < .05; **p < .01; ***p .001.

scriptive results from table 10.2, we also find that segregation between blacks and whites in 1990 was significantly affected by the racial and ethnic composition of the area. Although the coefficients for race and ethnicity were not significant in 1980, they were in the same directions in both years, suggesting that increases in the percentage of Hispanics and Asians reduce segregation levels, whereas increases in the percentage of blacks tends to increase segregation, particularly in 1990.

Recall that our descriptive results (table 10.2) indicate higher levels of segregation in 1980 and 1990 in metropolitan areas with more foreign-born overall, and they indicate lower levels of segregation for areas with a greater influx of recent immigrants. In multivariate, results of table 10.4 (model 2), we find no effect of the proportion of foreign born on the overall level of segregation. We find that in 1990, areas with a higher fraction of recent arrivals are predicted to be less segregated, even while controlling for other metropolitan characteristics. Although the average percentage of foreign born was higher for all metropolitan areas in 1990 than in 1980, there is no significant effect of the percentage of foreign born in the metropolitan area and the segregation of blacks from whites at either point in time. There is, however, a clearer association between the timing of arrival of the foreign-born population, such that those metropolitan areas with lower segregation between blacks and whites tend to have a higher percentage of the foreign-born population arriving in the previous decade (from 1970 to 1979 for 1980 and from 1980 to 1989 for 1990). This would seem to discount the polarization model and lend support to the diffusion model, suggesting that new immigrants push or at least encourage closer residence between blacks and whites.

How might the changing composition of a metropolitan area affect the levels of segregation of blacks from whites over time? Table 10.5 presents the average increase or decrease in the proportion of the metropolitan area made up of racial and ethnic minorities by the change in the *D*-values of the area between 1980 and 1990. Those metropolitan areas that experienced the greatest declines in segregation over the decade also experienced increases in Hispanic and Asian as well as foreign-born residents. This is particularly the case for the addition of recent arrivals in the United States. Those metropolitan areas experiencing little change in segregation or actual increases in segregation had the fewest new arrivals between 1980 and 1990 as compared with the decade from 1970 to 1980.

The association between immigration and segregation in these 168 metropolitan areas is depicted in figure 10.2. This figure plots the

Table 10.5   Change in the Race or Ethnic and Nativity Composition of
168 U.S. Metropolitan Areas by the Change in Segregation
Between Blacks and Whites, 1980 to 1990

Change in *D* Value	Number of Metropolitan Areas	Average Increase or Decrease in Population Share (percent):				
		Black	Hispanic	Asian	Foreign Born	Recent Foreign Born
Decrease of 6 points or more	47	0.0	1.0	1.0	3.3	−0.4
Decrease of 3 to 5 points	50	0.7	0.1	0.7	1.4	−2.0
No change[a]	52	0.8	−0.4	0.6	1.3	−3.9
Increase of more then 1 point	19	1.6	−0.1	0.5	0.7	−5.7

Sources: 1980 and 1990 IPUMS (http://www.ipums.umn.edu), *D*-values provided by Dr. William Frey.
[a]Includes small decreases of 2 points or less, and small increases of less than 1 point.

change from 1980 to 1990 in segregation between blacks and whites against the change for the same period in the percentage of foreign born, along with the bivariate regression line for these variables (coefficient = −.588; $t = -4.790$; $R^2 = .12$). The greater the increase in the percentage of the population of a metropolitan area that is foreign born, the greater the decrease in segregation of blacks from whites.

To more fully test the effect of the arrival of new immigrants on segregation between blacks and whites net of other changes in the composition and growth of a metropolitan area, we run first-difference regression models. The dependent variable in these models is simply the difference between the dissimilarity scores of the metropolitan area in 1990 and in 1980. The fact that this variable includes Hispanic whites and Hispanic blacks both imposes constraints on our interpretations and lends strength to the results. All of the characteristics of the metropolitan area that do not change between 1980 and 1990 drop out of the model because we assume their effects remain constant over the decade. The independent variables, therefore, are all measures of change over the decade. We present three models with increasingly inclusive covariates: change in population size and housing growth (model 1), change in population size, housing growth, and racial or ethnic composition (model 2), and change in the per-

Figure 10.2 Change in Segregation of Blacks from Whites from 1980 to 1990 by the Change in the Percentage of the Population that Is Foreign Born U.S. Metropolitan Areas, 1980 to 1990

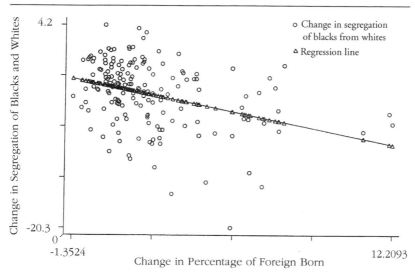

Source: Data from table 10.4.

centage of foreign-born persons in the metropolitan area and the change in the percentage of foreign-born residents who arrived in the United States in the previous decade (model 3). The results of these models are presented in table 10.6.

Model 1 confirms that overall population growth is negatively associated with segregation, although the addition of recent housing (net of population) tends to work in the opposite direction. Both of these growth effects are attenuated (but remain significant) upon the introduction of other metropolitan characteristics. Increasing racial and ethnic diversity (model 2), on the other hand, reduces black segregation from whites. The effect is strongest and remains significant for growth in the Hispanic population. It should be recalled, however, that some Hispanics are included in the dependent variable. Thus, the correct interpretation of the data is that the growth in the Hispanic population facilitates increased residential proximity of Hispanic and non-Hispanic blacks with Hispanic and non-Hispanic whites.

Nativity composition adds explanatory power, as model 3 indi-

Table 10.6   First Difference Models of Dissimilarity Between Whites and Blacks, 1980 to 1990

Variable	Model 1	Model 2	Model 3
Population size (log)	−14.13***	−11.72***	−8.24***
Percent of housing units built in previous decade	0.15***	0.11***	0.11***
Racial or ethnic composition			
Percentage black		−0.36	−0.12
Percentage Hispanic		−0.95***	−0.79***
Percentage Asian		−0.86**	0.60
Nativity composition			
Percentage foreign born			−0.95***
Percentage recent arrivals			0.00
Constant	248.44	229.05	182.79
R^2	38.5	51.5	58.6
Number of observations	168	168	168

Sources: 1980 and 1990 IPUMS (http://www.ipums.umn.edu), *D*-values courtesy of Dr. William Frey.
*p < .05; **p < .01; ***p < .001

cates. An increase from 1980 to 1990 in the proportion of the population that is foreign born further reduces black segregation from whites. It is important to note that this effect cannot be solely attributed to the increased ethnic mix of the population but is specific to nativity, because the changing racial and ethnic composition of the population is included in the model.

Overall, these empirical results lend credence to the diffusion model of segregation positing that blacks and whites will come into contact more frequently in areas with more diverse populations. Rather than serving as a buffer between blacks and whites, new immigrants appear to facilitate an integration of residential patterns among various groups.

CONCLUSION

Does immigration increase residential segregation? We have opened two windows to shed light on this question. A priori predictions are not clear. On one hand, according to the *polarization* model, immigration might increase segregation of existing groups, especially blacks and whites. On the other hand, according to our hypotheses from the *diffusion* model, immigration might stir the pot and make for more integration overall and specifically between blacks and whites.

Our examination of segregation patterns by vintage (average time since arrival) for thirty-nine major ethnic groups confirms that the longer a group has been in the United States, the less segregated are its immigrant members and their ethnic descendants. This work also shows, quite strikingly, that there are many exceptions. First, the deeper analysis of vintage indicates that the assumption, common in studies of residential segregation, that European groups are inter-mingled is erroneous. Second, African Americans, most notably, are far more segregated then their vintage (however counted) would indi-cate. Clearly, spatial separation based on a racial hierarchy persists in the United States.

The presence of ethnic groups of more recent vintage does not appear to have alleviated the segregation of African Americans, but we cannot determine whether the presence of immigrants per se has been the cause of continued segregation. We therefore also present a direct test of the relationship between immigration and segregation between blacks and whites, a key social indicator of race relations tracked for several decades. Our analysis of the segregation values for the period from 1980 to 1990 provides more evidence for the diffusion model. Metropolitan areas experiencing a growth in immigrants show lower levels of black segregation from whites. There is no evidence that immigration is driving the United States to become a more segregated society. Rather, the evidence we present here suggests that African Americans are less segregated in those areas receiving a larger number of immigrants. Thus, ethnicity and migration status influence resi-dential segregation such that dynamic communities with large num-bers of immigrants are more likely to experience decreases in the resi-dential segregation of African Americans. These insights into the evolving patterns of relationships between whites and African Ameri-cans in U.S. society are best understood in this context of a wider ethnic framework.

NOTES

1. Puerto Rican migrants are not counted as immigrants.

2. It is unquestionable that region, housing market dynamics, metropolitan functions, and other factors influence ethnic segregation. We do know, furthermore, that immigrants are differentially distributed across places along these dimensions. Hence, our models control for these other metro-politan traits.

3. Although based on documented migration, the vintage measure captures the approximate peaks of arrival to the extent that the time patterns of documented and undocumented migration is similar.

4. We include a measure of racial and ethnic heterogeneity by including the percentages of the area population that are black, Hispanic, and Asian. The increasing multiethnic composition of an area is expected to have a significant effect of the change in segregation over time (Frey and Farley 1996).

5. Vintage was calculated at 1960 for Puerto Ricans, a rough estimate from the migration described by Nathan Glazer and Daniel Patrick Moynihan in *Beyond the Melting Pot* (1963). Vintage for Arabs was assigned to be 1982 to match that of "other Asians," since that is the geographic classification used by the INS for Arabia. For both French and English Canadians the median arrival date was assigned to be 1923, which is the median for "Canada and Newfoundland" calculated from INS tables.

6. Some researchers take Russian ancestry to proxy the segregation pattern of the Jewish population.

7. We note that the dissimilarity index employed in these analyses (obtained through the courtesy of Professor William Frey) is calculated to include Hispanic whites as whites and Hispanic blacks as blacks. This means that the decreases in segregation between blacks and whites from 1980 to 1990 that we observe may include increased residential mixing between Hispanics and Blacks without necessarily implying the increased residential proximity of non-Hispanic whites to blacks. On the other hand, because Hispanic blacks are included as black in this measure, any reduction in segregation we measure will imply the reduced segregation of these groups, as well.

REFERENCES

Eschbach, Karl. 1993. "Changing Identification Among American Indians and Alaska Natives" *Demography* 30(4): 635–52.

Farley, Reynolds. 1991. "Residential Segregation of Social and Economic Groups Among Blacks, 1970–80." In *The Urban Underclass*, edited by Christopher Jencks and Paul Peterson. Washington D.C.: Brookings Institution.

Farley, Reynolds, and William Frey. 1994. "Changes in the Segregation of Whites from Blacks during the 1980s: Small Steps Toward a More Integrated Society." *American Sociological Review* 59(1): 23–45.

Frey, William, and Reynolds Farley. 1996. "Latino, Asian, and Black Segregation in U.S. Metropolitan Areas: Are Multiethnic Metros Different?" *Demography* 33(1): 35–50.

Glazer, Nathan, and Daniel Patrick Moynihan. 1963. *Beyond the Melting Pot.* Cambridge, Mass.: MIT Press.

Hershberg, Theodore, ed. 1981. *Philadelphia.* New York: Oxford Press.

Lieberson, Stanley. 1963. *Ethnic Patterns in American Cities.* New York: Free Press.

Massey, Douglas, and Nancy Denton. 1993. *American Apartheid: Segregation and the Making of the Underclass.* Cambridge, Mass.: Harvard University Press.

Massey, Douglas, Michael J. White, and Voon-Chin Phua. 1997. "The Dimensions of Segregation Revisited." *Sociological Methods and Research* 25(2): 172–206.

Muller, Thomas, and Thomas Espenshade. 1985. *The Fourth Wave: California's Newest Immigrants.* Washington, D.C.: Urban Institute Press.

Novak, Michael. 1972. *The Rise of the Unmeltable Ethnics.* New York: Macmillan Press.

Park, Robert, Errnest W. Burgess, and Roderik D. McKenzie. 1925. *The City.* Chicago: Chicago University Press.

Passel, Jeff. 1995. "The Growing American Indian Population, 1960–1990: Beyond Demography." Washington, D.C.: The Urban Institute.

Ruggles, Steven, and Matthew Sobek. 1997. *Integrated Public Use Microdata Series: Version 2.0.* Minneapolis: Historical Census Projects, University of Minnesota.

U.S. Department of Justice, Immigration and Naturalization Service. 1972. *Annual Report of the Immigration and Naturalization Service.* Washington, D.C.: U.S. Government Printing Office.

———. 1984. *Statistical Yearbook of the Immigration and Naturalization Service.* Washington, D.C., U.S. Government Printing Office.

———. 1995. *Statistical Yearbook of the Immigration and Naturalization Service.* Washington, D.C.: U.S. Government Printing Office.

Watkins, Susan Cotts, ed. 1994. *After Ellis Island.* New York: Russell Sage Foundation.

White, Michael J. 1986. "Segregation and Diversity Indexes in Population Distribution." *Population Index* 52: 198–212.

White, Michael J. 1987. *American Neighborhoods and Residential Differentiation.* New York: Russell Sage Foundation.

White, Michael J., Ann Biddlecom, and Shenyang Guo, 1993. "Immigration, Naturalization, and Residential Assimilation Among Asian Americans in 1980." *Social Forces* 72(1): 93–117.

White, Michael, Robert F. Dymowski, and Shilian Wang. 1994. "Ethnic

Neighbors and Ethnic Myths." In *After Ellis Island*, edited by Susan Cotts Watkins. New York: Russell Sage Foundation.

White, Michael, and A. Omer. 1997. "The Segregation of Immigrants in New Jersey." In *The Impacts of Immigration in New Jersey*, edited by Thomas Espenshade. Washington, D.C.: The Urban Institute Press.

White, Michael J., and Sharon Sassler. 1995. "Ethnic Definition, Social Mobility, and Residential Segregation in the United States." In *Population, Ethnicity, and Nation-Building*, edited by Calvin Goldscheider. Boulder, Colo.: Westview Press.

Wright, Lawrence. 1994. "One Drop of Blood." *The New Yorker* 25, July: 46–55.

CHAPTER 11

How Immigration and Intermarriage Affect the Racial and Ethnic Composition of the U.S. Population

Barry Edmonston and Jeffrey S. Passel

For four centuries, the ethnic composition of the U.S. population has shown a constantly changing picture because of varying sources of immigrants and different fertility and mortality levels of natives and new immigrants. The population also changed as the immigrants had children and grandchildren, thereby altering the generational composition of the country's population.

As the United States expanded to its present boundaries, its population changed from Native American to predominantly white and black, with some Spanish, Native Americans, and overlapping groups residing in the Southwest. By 1800, the U.S. population was about 80 percent white and 20 percent black. Significant immigration from Europe during the 1800s further altered the population's composition. By 1900, blacks accounted for only 10 percent of the population and resided mainly in the South.

The past thirty years have witnessed another massive shift in the countries of origin of U.S. immigrants (Passel and Edmonston 1994). What was a predominantly white society with a black minority is becoming more heterogeneous. The proportion of whites is falling as sizable numbers of Asian and Hispanic immigrants arrive. There is at least one significant new feature in the present situation. The fertility of the native-born population is so low—below the long-run replacement level, in fact—that any ethnic group not having significant immigration will decrease in size in the coming decades.

The United States is, therefore, once again on the eve of large ethnic transformations. In the past, major ethnic changes in the pattern of immigration have given rise to social disturbances, followed by periods of adaptation and integration of the immigrants (and adjustments by U.S. society). The current new phase has already involved social and political disturbances and raises new questions about who are "Americans." It is therefore important to examine changes in the ethnic composition of the population and identify the future directions of population growth. We employ new population projection techniques to do so here.

LIMITATIONS OF POPULATION PROJECTIONS

Projections of the type we present must be placed in a historical context. Early in the twentieth century, public interest focused on fertility differences between the "new" immigrants from southern and eastern Europe and the older "American" stock. Indeed, Theodore Roosevelt warned in his presidential inaugural address about immigration bringing on the "suicide of the race."

Had there been population projections during the peak of European immigration (from about 1880 to 1920) that tried to forecast what the U.S. population would look like by 2000, those predictions would probably have focused on European ethnic groups, not today's race groups. The projections would certainly have been wrong if they assumed that groups would not intermarry at all and that all future descendants would report the same ethnic identity as that of their mothers (or fathers). Such projections would have seriously overestimated the proportions of some European groups and underestimated others. Michael Hout and Joshua Goldstein (1994) remind us that the number of self-reported Irish Americans in the 1980 census could not possibly have come about purely as a result of immigration and the fertility of Irish immigrants; the number is simply too large. Rather, most of the growth of Irish Americans must have resulted from intermarriage and the choice of many children of intermarriage to claim Irish ancestry.

Projections made at the turn of the century would have been in error for two reasons. First, they would have had to deal with the vagaries of population projections about fertility, mortality, and immigration. Common to all projections is that the world changes and basic demographic parameters will vary in the future in ways that cannot be fully anticipated; thus, assumptions made about them may err. Second and more important, such projections would have missed the subsequent changes in the social meaning and functioning of the ethnic groups themselves.

There has always been variation in the experience of different ethnic groups with ethnic or racial identification. In the nineteenth century, the Irish were seen as a "race" apart from other European groups. They were stereotyped for their criminality, lack of education, and poor family values and were often portrayed in cartoons of the time as apes. If those debating immigration restriction in the early part of the twentieth century had done population projections to predict the "race suicide" they believed new immigrants were causing, they would have projected the numbers of southern and eastern Europeans and Irish and shown that these growing groups would have made white Protestants a minority by some date in the future. Yet we now know that such predictions would have been wrong.

Such projections would have failed to predict the decline in the relevance of boundaries separating European groups from one another. The children and grandchildren of immigrants from Ireland, Poland, and Italy—groups that were once seen as "unassimilable" and racially distinct—intermarry with others of different ethnic origins to such an extent that the descendants of most white European groups are virtually indistinguishable. Indeed, the descendants of all immigrant waves from eastern and southern Europe have reached equality with white Protestants in education, income, and occupational and residential distributions (Lieberson and Waters 1994).

At the turn of the twentieth century, marital "endogamy was castelike for new ethnics from eastern and southern Europe" (Paginini and Morgan 1990). Within the space of two generations, social, economic, and cultural changes led to levels of ethnic intermarriage that would have been unthinkable in the decades immediately following the major waves of immigration. As Richard Alba (1995b, 13) reports, "In 1990 Census data, more than half (56 percent) of whites have spouses whose ethnic backgrounds do not overlap with their own at all. . . . Only one-fifth have spouses with identical backgrounds." Under such conditions, ethnic identity is increasingly a matter of choice for whites in the United States. An American of Norwegian, Scottish, or Italian ancestry, for example, can "choose" to identify with one or more of his or her ethnic ancestries and discard or "forget" others (Alba, 1995a; Waters 1990).

The fluidity of white ethnic categories stands in contrast with the seeming essentiality of race in the United States. This fluidity is partially the result of the primacy of racial issues in American history, which necessitated unambiguous classifications, first for the purpose of racial discrimination and now to implement affirmative action. The social and legal forces of racial identity in the United States, however, are also idiosyncratic, the product of complex and contingent processes, and subject to change over the coming decades.

Those who believe that current immigrants from Asia, Latin America, and the Caribbean are less assimilable than those from European countries may be making important errors. First, they assume current racial categories to be fixed and essential; yet the rising rate of intermarriage means that the boundaries between groups may blur in the future. Ideas of what constitutes a race or a racial difference are likely to be very different in a few decades, just as they are now very different from what they were at the beginning of the twentieth century. In addition, they may assume that all the cultures of non-European groups will continue to be very different from what they think of as the core American culture. Yet that core American culture has absorbed a number of groups who were once defined as culturally different, and it will probably do so again in the future.

Both sides of the immigrant-assimilation equation are, in effect, moving targets. Groups that seem racially different now may not always seem so; and the core American culture into which groups are assimilating is itself constantly changing and evolving as it absorbs new influences. Immigrants contribute new customs of dress and cuisine, different national celebrations, and novel cultural expressions to the mosaic of American society. Some immigrants even discover their ethnic heritage in America as part of their socialization into the American ethnic community of earlier immigrant waves. As time passes and the descendants of earlier immigrant waves mingle through intermarriage, ethnic cultures have become defined as part of general American culture. The Americanization of St. Patrick's Day as a day of public celebration and the marketing of pizza, bagels, tacos, and egg rolls as American fast food suggest that immigrant culture is quickly incorporated into the broader American cultural framework.

THE IMPORTANCE OF INTERNATIONAL MIGRATION FOR POPULATION GROWTH

From a historical perspective, the territory now known as the United States has experienced several waves of immigrants, each distinguished by the migrants' ethnicity and places of origin. The first two waves of immigrants entered the North American continent tens of thousands of years ago, in apparently two separate movements, from Asia. These immigrants and their descendants eventually settled throughout the Americas. The third major movement of immigrants consisted of people moving north from Mexico into the area that is now the southwestern United States. This wave consisted of Spaniards and residents of the Spanish domain of Mexico. The colonization of the eastern seaboard of the United States by settlers from England and primarily western and northern Europe provided the fourth major wave of immigrants. Africans, forcibly brought in as slaves, accompanied the European settlement, locating mainly in the colonies of the southern states. These black arrivals made up the fifth immigrant wave. By the 1880s, the sources of European immigration shifted sharply, as another wave of immigrants—the sixth wave—arrived, originating principally from the southern and eastern parts of Europe. The United States is now experiencing a seventh wave of immigrants, which began roughly three decades ago and is dominated by Asia and Latin America, the sources for the three earliest flows of immigrants to the land now known as the United States.

Sources of recent immigration flows have been volatile. Many new immigrant populations have entered in large numbers within a relatively short period: Most of the Cuban-origin population entered during the period from 1960 to 1975; of the Vietnamese population in the United States in 1990, most arrived between 1975 and 1985. These two examples show that the movement of selected ethnic groups to the United States is somewhat unpredictable, depending to a great extent on conditions in other countries and U.S. response.

Several processes affect the future course of immigration to the United States. First, the federal government sets immigration quotas, and these quotas largely define limits on the number of immigrants from most countries. Second, the entrance of illegal aliens continues, in spite of enhanced Border Patrol activities and stronger employer sanctions associated with the 1986 Immigration Reform and Control Act (Bean, Edmonston, and Passel 1990; Passel 1996c). The future growth of the Hispanic population, especially the Mexican-origin population, derives to a considerable extent from illegal entrants. Finally, as shown in the examples of Cuban and Vietnamese immigrants, conditions in foreign countries can also quickly generate significant immigrant flows to the United States.

IMMIGRATION'S CONTRIBUTION TO ETHNIC POPULATION CHANGE

How will the racial and ethnic composition of the United States change over the next sixty years? How will immigration—current and future—contribute to that change? This chapter seeks to answer the second question, which in turn will help answer the first. It focuses on the characteristics of the immigrants and their descendants and explores how they will most likely change the ethnic demography of the United States over the next six decades.

Immigration is not the only force at work shaping the size and composition of racial and ethnic groups in the United States in coming years. It will interact with other demographic forces, already in place, that also play a large role in what the population will look like by the middle of the next century.

First, in the two decades following World War II, the baby boom greatly increased the annual rate of U.S. population growth and provided birth cohorts from about 1946 to about 1964 that were much larger than those of the decades before or after. The baby boom and the subsequent baby bust will have major ramifications over the next half century. The overwhelmingly white population born during the baby boom will become older; when they eventually enter the retirement years, the white population will experience increases in the observed death rate, contributing to a decline in the rate of natural increase.

Second, volatility in the volume and composition of immigration affects the U.S. population across many dimensions: its size and rate of growth, its age and sex composition, and its racial and ethnic makeup. In the future, a major source of variation in ethnic population change will lie in the volume and characteristics of immigration.

Immigration has consequences for key aspects of ethnic population change. In its relatively large flows and wide variety, immigration as the United States experiences it adds to the numbers of people in the nation and their diversity. Immigration works its longer-term effects through other dimensions, as well.

First, not every ethnic group of immigrants into the United States bears children at the same rate. Immigrant groups with persistently high fertility rates will grow over time, absolutely and in relation to other immigrant groups. Second, not every group of immigrants has the same life span—that is, their mortality rates differ; these, too, may change over time and thus shift in their relation to one another.

If immigrants have a higher fertility rate than the resident population, the nation will grow younger on average; and if immigrants have a higher mortality rate—that is, if they die at an earlier age—that trend will be reinforced. Again, the differences among groups of immigrants also matter, as do the shifts within groups and between groups as the generations unfold.[1]

Previewing the U.S. population in 2050, then, calls for making assumptions about the numbers of people entering and leaving the country, about the numbers from various racial and ethnic groups within the totals, and about fertility and mortality rates of individual groups. Moreover, it calls for assumptions about exogamy and ethnic affiliation—the degree to which groups intermarry and the way the descendants of intergroup marriages identify themselves.

This chapter offers a view of how future immigration will alter the racial and ethnic composition of the U.S. population. To paint that portrait, a framework is used to ensure consistency for alternative assumptions about the future course of immigration and emigration and their associated demographic implications.

POPULATION CHANGE FROM A GENERATIONAL PERSPECTIVE

The population projections reported in this chapter are obtained through the use of a modified cohort-component method. The initial population is characterized by age, sex, and ethnicity, as in a standard population projection. The modification used here, however, also distinguishes the population by generation. Each generation requires assumptions about the fertility, mortality, and migration flows for age and sex groups. The base population is then projected forward in five-year intervals, with successive application of the demographic dynamics. Births are added to the populations, deaths are subtracted, and net migration is added, depending on levels of immigration and emigration.

Demographic Dynamics and the Conceptual Bases for Projections

Population projections are determined by characteristics of the base population and assumptions made about the components of demographic dynamics. For our approach, the projection is also affected by assumptions made about generational and ancestry dynamics. Setting values for the demographic dynamics is therefore important for the results and interpretation of the population projection.

The population projections reported here are produced from a simulation perspective. The simulations are designed to generate output on the ethnic distribution of the U.S. population implied in assumed processes of fertility, mortality, and international migration. We would ordinarily prefer population projections that can be regarded as plausible outcomes for the future population. We use the term "plausible" to mean that the conditions for demographic dynamics could be regarded as likely for the future course of fertility, mortality, and international migration. Thus, we select demographic rates consistent with current observed levels for a narrow heuristic purpose: to examine the long-range demographic implications of the assumed conditions.

The population projections presented here derive from the assumptions made. Except for arithmetical errors, the projections must be "accurate" in a special sense because they derive logically from the assumptions of the demographic model. Hence, our concern here is to be explicit about the generational model used and the data assumptions made for the projections.

We stress that the projections for ethnic groups are not predictions for future population changes. Considerable uncertainty exists about the fertility and mortality dynamics for the future. We make reasonable assumptions about fertility and mortality, supported by the latest evidence, but considerable debate exists among researchers about the future course of these demographic processes. For future trends in immigration and emigration, a variety of plausible courses are examined. Later sections of this chapter review the assumptions made about fertility, mortality, and international migration.

The assumptions about future exogamy, births of multiple ancestry, and ethnic attribution rest on even less solid current data on levels and trends. Here again, we have incorporated in the projections a range of plausible values based on our analysis of the limited available data. In these areas especially, it should be stressed that an even wider range of assumptions could certainly be justified. Consequently, our projections should not be viewed as encompassing all possible futures.

Generational Dynamics

Standard cohort-component population projections move a population through time by assuming survival of the existing population under the conditions of mortality (survival of the living population at one period to the next period), fertility (survival of births to the living population during the projection period), and migration (survival of immigrants during the projection period and survival of the population until emigration). Such population projections consider the age and sex distribution of the population but do not give explicit treatment to immigration.

The new population projections presented here are distinguished by the consideration of the population by generation status. For each ethnic group, the population is categorized into four generational groups:

- first generation: the foreign-born population
- second generation: the sons and daughters of the first generation
- third generation: the sons and daughters of the second generation
- fourth and higher generations: the descendants of the third and higher generations

This characterization of the population by generation specifically recognizes the immigration perspective. The population projection model used in this chapter is described in greater detail by Barry Edmonston and Jeffrey Passel (1992, 1994).

A generational perspective in population projections has several advantages. First, there are important implications for research on the assimilation of immigrants and their descendants. The generations and their relative sizes are useful numbers and social indicators. For example, the first generation typically speaks the language and holds many of the cultural values of the country of origin. The second generation can be expected to grow up in households with the language of the parents' home country and many of its cultural values. By the third generation, however, routine exposure to a non-English-language and non-American culture may have disappeared. Knowing the generational distribution of an ethnic group, therefore, gives considerable insight into the group's retention of the immigrant culture or assimilation to English language and U.S. culture.

Second, a generational population projection has some methodological advantages. Generational characteristics present a more appropriate model of immigrants (who usually enter the United States as first generation, foreign-born individuals) and emigrants (the rate of emigration from the United States varies greatly with the number of foreign-born members of a racial and ethnic group). The model also offers the possibility for varying demographic assumptions by generation. For example, standard population projection models generally make the unreasonable assumption that childbearing patterns are the same for all generations. In other words, immigrants are assumed to acquire the fertility levels of the resident population instantly upon arrival in the United States.

For a generational population projection, the dynamics of population change must be incorporated on a generational basis, which requires more demographic mechanics and more assumptions than a standard cohort-component projection. For mortality, deaths in a generation reduce the numbers of that generation. However, each generation experiences mortality by age and sex that may differ across generations.

For fertility, births to a generation produce an addition to the next generation. Births to foreign-born immigrants are members of the second generation and would produce an addition to the youngest age group (from birth to four years) in the second generation in the next interval of the population projection. Because our model defines the highest generation as the fourth-and-higher generations, births to the fourth-and-higher generations would, by definition, become members of the same generation group.

For international migration, assumptions need to be made about the generational composition of migrants. Immigrants to a population are principally foreign born. However, a small proportion of immigrants to the United States are native-born persons who return to the United States after residence abroad. For example, a foreign-born couple residing in the United States might have children born in the United States and subsequently return to their country of birth. If their children later immigrate to the United States, they then constitute the immigration of second-generation individuals.

Emigrants from the United States are usually members of the first generation, people who immigrated to the United States and then decided to return to their country of birth. There are also a small number of native-born residents (that is, of the second or higher generation) who emigrate from the United States.

The Dynamics of Ancestry and the Role of Exogamy

Population projections of immigrant groups, characterized by ethnicity, also need to consider the persistence of ancestral membership. Members of an ethnic group who always marry and reproduce within the group would be practicing perfect endogamy and would maintain single-ancestry membership. Marriage to persons of other ethnic groups (that is, exogamy) and reproduction of a new generation would produce offspring of mixed ancestry. Mixed-ancestry individuals may identify themselves as any of their ethnic ancestries.

Standard population projection models of racial and ethnic groups (for example, U.S. Bureau of the Census 1996) make one crucial and debatable assumption: They assume perfect endogamy for the group for the projection period. Standard models assume that all members of a given group marry members of the same group and produce single-ancestry children; for example, all future descendants of the initial Hispanic population are assumed to be Hispanic. This assumption is clearly false for many groups. Thus, standard projections potentially present a misleading picture of future population composition. Our projections relax this strict assumption.

Recent research on ethnicity and marriage patterns offers two conclusions. First, considerable exogamy exists for many U.S. ethnic groups, and second, exogamy varies significantly by generation. Because current information on generational exogamy rates for specific ethnic groups is sketchy, we incorporate exogamy assumptions, based on the available data, into our projections. Thus, we later assess the effects of exogamy on the proportion of single-ancestry members, for varying levels of immigration. We then further assess the impact of alternative levels of ethnic attribution (or identification) of the size of ethnic populations.

RACE AND ETHNIC ORIGIN

Racial and ethnic classifications are best approached as social constructions (Davis 1991; Lee 1993; Waters 1990). There is no taxonomic basis, in biology and physiology, to support current U.S. classifications of groups into distinct races. Without a scientific basis, demographers working on race and ethnic population projections need to keep in mind that these categories may change as society revises accepted meanings of race and ethnicity and as people change their subjective identities. Given conceptual and measurement difficulties surrounding the concept of race, we prefer to use "ethnic group" and "ethnicity" to describe the population. Ethnicity is a more inclusive concept that does not rely on questionable distinctions of heredity or blood to separate people into races. However, we refer to race as needed because of current official usage and classification.

This chapter examines future population trends for the total population of the United States and five constituent ethnic groups: American Indian, Eskimo, and Aleut; Asian and Pacific Islander; Hispanic; black; and white. It should be noted that official federal classification for the U.S. population divides the population into white, black, Asian and Pacific Islander, American Indian and Alaskan Native, and "other" race groups.[2] Hispanic status is explicitly defined for purposes of creating a Hispanic population, which may be reported in any one of the "races." In practice, the Hispanic population mainly reports itself as either white or "other" (reports of "other" race include individuals who do not check a specific listed race but write in such responses as "Mexican"). The official current classification system is based on an arbitrary separation of race and ethnicity, defining American Indians, Asians, blacks, and whites as "races" and not ethnic groups. We prefer to use the conceptually broader concept of ethnic group for all five populations examined here.

The main implication of the official classification system is that population projections for the Hispanic population overlap with the overall projections for the main race groups. For the projections presented here, we calculate a base population in which the white, black, Asian, and American Indian and Alaskan Native populations do not include any Hispanic component, to avoid double counting Hispanic persons. We therefore offer projection results for five mutually exclusive and exhaustive ethnic groups: white,[3] black, Hispanic, Asian and Pacific Islander, and various native peoples (American Indian, Eskimo, and Aleut).[4]

Base Population

The base date for our projection is April 1, 1995, and we use the official population estimate of the U.S. Bureau of the Census (1997) by age, sex, and race or Hispanic origin for this date as our base population. We use such estimates for total population, including armed forces overseas, total resident population, resident civilian population, and civilian noninstitutional (CNI) population. These populations differ successively by the armed forces overseas, the resident military, and the institutional populations.[5] All populations are based on the 1990 census, corrected for undercount and carried forward in time to 1995; as such, they represent the total population and are not directly comparable to census counts.

Our projection model uses immigrant generations, but the population estimates are for the total population only. Thus, it is necessary to derive generational populations for all of the relevant populations (CNI, institutional, and military populations). We start with the CNI population from the March 1995 Current Population Survey (CPS), as reweighted to correct for weighting errors in the official Census Bureau figures (Passel 1996b; Passel and Clark 1998). The CPS data provide the necessary information to classify the CNI population into three generations by age, sex, and race or Hispanic origin. We next derive initial estimates of the institutional population by applying proportions of the institutional population by age, sex, and race or Hispanic origin for natives and immigrants from the 1990 census, assuming that the native proportions apply to both the second and third-and-higher generations. These initial estimates are scaled to agree by age, sex, and race or Hispanic origin with the official Census Bureau population estimates.

To derive the military population by generation, we use roughly the same procedure. From the 1990 census, we calculate for natives and immigrants the percentage of each age, sex, and race or Hispanic-origin group that is in the military. These percentages are applied initially to the 1995 CNI population to derive an initial estimate of the military population for each of three generations in 1995. We then scale these estimates to agree by age, sex, and race or Hispanic origin with the official population figures for the military. Each detailed demographic cell for each generation for the military is divided into resident and overseas with age, sex, and race or Hispanic-origin proportions from the official population estimates.

The result of these procedures is a fully detailed set of population estimates by age, sex, race or Hispanic origin, and three generations for the 1995 civilian noninstitutional, institutional, resident military, and armed forces overseas populations. The third-and-higher generation is split into the third generation and the fourth-and-higher generation, using information from historical "projections" fitted to U.S. populations by race for the period from 1880 to 1980 (Passel and Edmonston 1994), as carried forward to 1990 and 1995. The base population for the projections also makes use of single- and multiple-ancestry populations.

EXOGAMY AND ETHNIC IDENTIFICATION

We define exogamy to include both marital and nonmarital unions between people of different ethnic backgrounds that result in offspring. Although we use data on intermarriages and childbearing for our exogamy estimates, there are some noteworthy data problems in modeling the effects of exogamy. First, detailed intermarriage and childbearing data are not available for measuring the extent of interethnic unions for all ethnic groups. Adding the generational factor makes the problem of data availability even more serious. At present, census and survey data on intermarriages are the main source of reliable information that can be used, but they obviously exclude nonmarital unions. Second, fertility levels for interethnic unions are not necessarily the same as for intraethnic unions. Third, the available childbearing data are missing information on the race of father for a significant proportion of births. Nonetheless, enough is known to permit us to incorporate reasonable exogamy assumptions into our projections.

Factors Affecting Intermarriage

Research on endogamy has found some important associated factors, notably by focusing on Asian Americans (Lee and Yamanaka 1990; Lee and Fernandez 1998). Foreign birth is usually associated with a higher propensity to marry within the individual's ethnic community. This pattern is probably related to lower acculturation and fewer opportunities to meet potential partners outside the ethnic community.

In addition, many immigrants arrive as married adults (Hwang and Saenz 1990). Thus, all other factors being equal, prior research suggests that there will be lower levels of intermarriage among the foreign born. Second, ethnicity is important in explaining marital patterns. Research shows higher rates of endogamy for the black population and lower rates for American Indians, Asians, and Hispanics.

Third, for some ethnic groups, intermarriage also varies by sex. Intermarriage differentials by sex are affected by other factors, including the age and sex structure within an ethnic community, the conditions of intergroup contact, differences in socialization of males and females, and differential access to marital opportunities and rewards by gender. It is therefore not easy to explain observed sex differentials in intermarriage, even when they are consistent over time. For example, black males have higher rates of out-marriage than black females, whereas among Hispanics and Asians, the opposite is true. Fourth, age patterns are important for intermarriage rates of immigrants. Immigrant groups with younger age structures show higher levels of intermarriage, presumably reflecting increased assimilation with duration of residence in the United States. Fifth, group size has a substantial effect on intermarriage rates. Previous studies of intermarriage have shown that the probability of marrying someone with similar characteristics depends, in part, on the proportion of such persons in the population. In-group marriage is, therefore, positively correlated with the size of the group.

Measures of Exogamy

Most recent studies measuring levels of intermarriage have relied on census or survey data; these are prevalence measures, which include the entire adult population. Some studies also examine incidence data on marriages during a given year, although these data are not collected consistently for the entire country. Information on the black population indicates low levels of intermarriage (Kalmijn 1993). The rate of out-marriage is low, estimated at 7 percent using 1979 CPS data (Alba and Golden 1986), 2 percent using the 1980 census, and 6 percent using the 1990 census (Lee and Fernandez 1998). Intermarriage between blacks and whites is apparently increasing, however. There were 65,000 such unions reported in 1970, increasing to 231,000 in 1991 (Kalish 1992).

Hispanic data on intermarriage are meager because it is only recently that censuses started to record the Hispanic origin of respondents. Decennial census data indicate that 13 percent of all married Hispanic persons were married to non-Hispanics in 1980 (Lee and Yamanaka 1990) and 19 percent in 1990 (Lee and Fernandez 1998). Earlier survey data for New York state for the 1970s reported by D. T. Gurak and J. P. Fitzpatrick (1982) suggest that about 20 percent of Hispanic immigrants were married to non-Hispanics and that the out-marriage rate rose to 40 percent for second-generation Hispanics.

Asian Americans have moderate levels of intermarriage. Available research reports similar intermarriage rates for this population for the past fifteen years. Alba and R. M. Golden (1986) estimate an out-marriage rate of 23 percent using 1979 CPS data. Sharon Lee and Keiko Yamanaka (1990) estimate a rate of 25 percent using 1980 census data. Lee and Marilyn Fernandez (1998) estimate a rate of 15 percent from the 1990 census. National Center for Health Statistics marriage data reveal an intermarriage rate of 24 percent for 1980 and 21 percent for 1988. In sum, the intermarriage data for the 1980s are within the range of 15 to 25 percent for the Asian American population. Furthermore, it appears that the intermarriage rate declined during the 1980s, perhaps reflecting the large immigration from Asia during the decade.

Data on American Indian intermarriage are limited and are greatly affected by changes in self-identification over time (Sandefur and McKinnell 1985). Because a large proportion of the American Indian population has multiple ancestries, individuals may report different single ancestries over time and may report ancestries that are not necessarily consistent in population censuses and marriage registration. Lee and Fernandez (1998) report an intermarriage rate of 47 percent for American Indians in 1980 and 60 percent in 1990.

The white population shows very low intermarriage rates, which is to be expected given the large relative size of this population. Only 1 percent of all married whites in 1980 reported that they were married to a person of a different racial background (Lee and Fernandez 1998). Intermarriage rates, using NCHS data, are 1 percent for 1980 and 2 percent for 1988. Census data for 1990 reveal an intermarriage rate of 3 percent for the white population.

Exogamy Assumptions

Given the limited nature of the data available on exogamy and the almost total lack of information on intergroup nonmarital relationships, we approximate the exogamy coefficients needed for our projections in a three-step procedure. First, we rely on the available information about intermarriage to develop a set of 1990 intermarriage coefficients for the five main racial or ethnic groups by immigration generation. Second, we adjust the intermarriage coefficients to the observed pattern of interethnic births in 1994, using unpublished NCHS data by race or ethnicity of mother and father for foreign-born and native populations. Finally, because little further is known about generational patterns—information that is needed for our population projection model—we decide on reasonable intermarriage coefficients by generation, using available information.

The exogamy rates from the literature generally represent the entire adult population. As such, they are an average of the relatively higher rates in the younger adult population, somewhat lower rates in middle ages, and much lower exogamy rates among the elderly. Because exogamy enters into our projections through childbearing, it is important that the assumptions reflect the younger population. Calibration to recent data on births accomplishes the needed adjustment.

From 1994 NCHS data, we find that 92 percent of births to white mothers are also to white fathers. The implied exogamy rate of 8 percent for adults of childbearing age is much higher than the 1 to 3 percent intermarriage rates found in the census-based studies. For black mothers, 90 percent of births are also to black fathers, an exogamy level somewhat higher than the population-based measures. The other groups have much smaller proportions of births with fathers of the same group. Of births to Hispanic women, 68 percent have Hispanic fathers. The ratio is 66 percent for Asian mothers and only 58 percent for American Indian mothers.

To estimate intermarriage by generation, we note that earlier work with 1970 census and survey data, mostly analyzing Hispanics, reveals a roughly linear increase in intermarriage rates for the first, second, and third generations (Gurak and Fitzpatrick 1982). Data on natives, as an estimate for the combined second and higher generations, reflects the generational composition of racial and ethnic groups in 1990. Thus, the native-born estimates for the white and black population reflect primarily the third and later generations. Consequently, we use the native-born information for these groups as an estimate for both the third and fourth-and-higher generations and estimate the second generation by averaging estimates for the first and third generations.

For the Hispanic and Asian populations, we estimate the intermarriage rates for the second and third generations by assuming a linear change in intermarriage rates from the first generation to second and third generations, fitted to the observed intermarriage rates for the

Table 11.1   Exogamy Assumptions: Percent of Projected Marriages to Other Groups, 1995 to 2050, by Population Group and Generation

Population Group	Overall Total (1995)	Generation			
		1st	2nd	3rd	4th +
White	8	10	9	8	8
Black	10	14	12	10	10
Hispanic	30	8	32	57	57
Asian	20	13	34	54	54
American Indian	40	20	30	40	50

Sources: Authors' estimates using 1990 Census microdata, 1994 birth data from the National Center for Health Statistics, and from survey data cited in the text.

native-born population. We center the native-born estimate at the mean generation for the native-born population in 1995. From prior research (Passel and Edmonston 1994) we established the mean generational value of the native-born Asian population in 1995 as 2.6 and that of the Hispanic native-born population as 2.5. We assume that the fourth-plus generation has the same intermarriage level as the third generation.[6]

The final exogamy assumptions by generation and ethnicity are shown in table 11.1. The overall rates are a function of the generational composition of each population. For example, note that the overall exogamy rate for Asians is quite a bit lower than for Hispanics even though Asian immigrants have a higher exogamy rate than Hispanic immigrants and the rates for Asian natives are not very different from those for Hispanic natives. However, a much higher percentage of Asians are in the first generation in 1995 than for Hispanics, so that the overall Asian exogamy rate is lower.

We hold these generation-specific rates constant throughout the projection horizon. Thus, the overall rates by ethnicity change in response to generational changes. For Hispanics and Asians, especially, the exogamy rates increase over time, because these groups have a greater proportion of immigrants in the initial population than in subsequent years. To implement the exogamy model in our generational population projections, we make three key simplifying assumptions:

1. Exogamy varies by ethnic group and by generation. We assume, however, that exogamy rates are constant by age and that the exogamy rates do not vary over time. This assumption means that

exogamy rates change as the generational composition changes and as the ethnic composition changes.

2. Exogamy and fertility are independent. This key assumption means that women who marry (or are in sexual union with) men of a different ethnic group will have the same fertility as women married to men of the same ethnicity.

3. Male out-marriage rates are the same as female out-marriage rates. Thus, we assume that when females of a given ethnicity produce, say, ten thousand multiple-ancestry births, then males of the same ethnicity also produce ten thousand multiple-ancestry births.

Single- and Multiple-Ancestry Births and Assumptions of Ethnic Attribution

We consider two types of births: single-ancestry births, or births to parents who are of the same ethnic identification, and multiple-ancestry births, or births to parents of different ethnic identifications. The distinction between single- and multiple-ancestry births has no pejorative implications. We make no assumption that single-ancestry births are racially or ethnically "pure"; indeed, available evidence is that all commonly recognized racial or ethnic groups are of multiple descent in the evolutionary history of human populations. Single ancestry, in the context of this chapter, means only that both parents report themselves (in a population census or survey) as sharing a common ethnic origin.

There are challenges to modeling exogamy as single- or multiple-ancestry births. Our population modeling involves an exogamy coefficient that determines the proportion of births (to a group of women with common generation and ethnic characteristics) that are single ancestry. We assume that all other births to the group of women are multiple ancestry. Moreover, we assume that births to multiple-ancestry women are also multiple-ancestry births.

The meanings of racial and ethnic labels have changed in the past and will undoubtedly change in the future (Lee 1993). Such changes are further facilitated by the extensive use of self-reporting in collecting racial and ethnic data. Theoretically, one can consider two outcomes of racial and ethnic identification for persons of mixed ancestries. These are avoidance and affiliation. In the simplest case of persons who are of multiple ancestries, say P and Q, avoidance of one ancestry, let us say P, would mean that only people of single ancestry P would report P ancestry. On the other hand, if all persons of mixed

P and *Q* ancestries affiliate with *P*, then the reported number of people with *P* ancestry will include single- as well as mixed-ancestry persons.

The future size of a given ethnic group is not only a function of the demographic processes of fertility, mortality, and immigration but also of exogamy patterns and ethnic self-identification of multiple-ancestry persons. Thus, assumptions about racial and ethnic attribution are crucial for population projections (Chew, Eggebeen, and Uhlenberg 1989). Think of a child born to two parents, one of whom is Asian and the other is not. Now consider two possibilities for children born in this circumstance: in one, avoidance, the child never identifies as Asian; in the other, affiliation, the child always identifies as Asian. In the first case, no children born to a couple comprising one Asian and one non-Asian parent will identify as Asian; the only Asians in the next generation will be single-ancestry Asians (those with an Asian mother and father). In the second case, all multiple-ancestry Asians will report themselves as Asians. The Asian population will grow more slowly in the first case, because exogamous births will not be counted in it. In the second case, the Asian population will grow more quickly, because births to either Asian men or Asian women, regardless of the ethnicity of their partners, will add to the size of the next generation's Asian population.

Conventional population projections make a simple assumption that children will eventually report their ethnicity to be the same as their mothers. Our projections make a number of alternative assumptions. Our initial projections include no assertions about the ethnic identification of multiple-ancestry persons but merely distinguish single- and multiple-ancestry individuals of each ethnicity. One possibility is that no multiple-ancestry children identify with the racial or ethnic group of their mother. Another possibility is that all multiple-ancestry children identify with the racial or ethnic group of their mother.

Neither of these extreme assumptions is plausible. To provide more realistic bounds, we rely on actual data from the 1990 Census on racial and ethnic attribution. This information underlies our medium assumption about racial and ethnic attribution rates for multiple-ancestry persons, which ranges from 39 to 64 percent for the five ethnic groups. To illustrate variations for lower and higher ethnic attribution rates, other than the extremes of pure avoidance and pure affiliation, we assume identification rates that are 20 percentage points lower and 20 percentage points higher than observed rates. The full range of five alternative assumptions of ethnic attribution for each group is shown in table 11.2.

Table 11.2   Ethnic Attribution Assumptions: Percent of
Multiple-Ancestry Persons Choosing Own Group,
1995 to 2050, by Population Group

Population Group	Level of Attribution				
	Very Low	Low	Medium	High	Very High
White	0	22	42	62	100
Black	0	41	61	81	100
Hispanic	0	44	64	84	100
Asian	0	19	39	59	100
American Indian	0	35	55	75	100

Sources: Authors' estimates using 1990 Census microdata.

Single- and Multiple-Ancestry Base Population

For our population projections, the future size of a given ethnic group is the sum of the projected single-ancestry population plus multiple-ancestry persons who are assumed to identify with the group. Such projections require a base population configured in accordance with the assumptions. The simplest base population would assume that the entire population in 1995 (our base date) consists only of single-ancestry persons. This assumption is manifestly false, and projections based on it would understate the range of future possibilities for each ethnic population, given a set of demographic parameters. To reflect a more realistic range of futures, we derive estimates of single- and multiple-ancestry population for 1995 relying on information from the 1990 Census and 1995 population estimates.

Current government statistics in the United States maintain the notion of mutually exclusive groups commonly called races. Respondents to the 1990 census and recent Current Population Surveys, for example, are asked to select only one race from a list. A respondent reporting two or more racial groups is subsequently assigned to a single race. Post-1990 population estimates maintain this notion of single, mutually exclusive racial categories. Beginning with the 2000 census, however, respondents will be allowed to self-identify with two or more racial groups. Consequently, we expect that future censuses and surveys will increasingly observe respondents who report multiple races.

With current Census Bureau practice, information on whether a respondent is of Hispanic origin is collected with a separate question from the "race" item. Such census reporting complicates the analysis of racial and ethnic attribution becuase respondents could report both a racial and a Hispanic identity. This data collection methodology may overstate preferences for Hispanic identity and, conversely, understate preferences for other identities. If persons of Hispanic origin were asked to report only one primary ethnic identification, like non-Hispanic respondents, the number in the Hispanic category might decrease and the number in the white category might increase.[7]

To derive our base population, we start with data from the Public Use Microdata Sample (PUMS) of the 1990 census and tabulate the numbers of persons in major ethnic groups in three populations:

1. persons who are single ancestry

2. persons who are self-reported by race (that is, the baseline)

3. persons who report multiple ancestry

These groups are defined by three census items: the "race" question ("Fill ONE circle for the race that the person considers himself/herself to be"), the Hispanic-origin question ("Is this person of Spanish/Hispanic origin?"), and the ancestry question (the first two responses to "What is this person's ancestry or ethnic origin?"). For the self-reported definition, we tabulate persons by their self-identified race or Hispanic origin. This "baseline" definition is the same as that used by the Census Bureau for their population estimates and projections (and uses the five mutually exclusive and exhaustive groups discussed earlier). For the narrow definition of single ancestry, we include only persons who reported ancestries consistent with their baseline group. For the broad definition of a multiple-ancestry group, we include all persons who report a specific race or Hispanic group in either the race and Hispanic-origin items or as one of their ancestries, even if they do not self-report the same group as their primary racial or Hispanic-origin identification; note that under this multiple-ancestry definition, a person could be counted more than once—up to three times (a race group from the race question, Hispanic origin, and a different group from the ancestry question).

With these definitions, we can treat the difference between the broad multiple-ancestry population and the narrow single-ancestry population for a group as the number of persons in the population who have a multiple ancestry that includes the specified group. The difference between the baseline population and the single-ancestry population is the number of multiple-ancestry persons who have cho-

Table 11.3   Single- and Multiple-Ancestry Populations, by Race or Ethnic Group, 1990 Census (Population, in Thousands)

Population Group	Self-Reported			Total, with Multiple Ancestries
	Single Ancestry	Race (Baseline)	Multiple Ancestry	
All Groups	231,732	248,534	16,802	248,534
White	176,570	188,054	15,027	191,597
Black	27,739	29,762	2,476	30,215
Hispanic	19,299	21,266	3,823	23,122
Asian	6,624	7,211	1,292	7,916
American Indian	1,462	1,999	7,575	9,037

Sources: U.S. Bureau of the Census, 1990 Census Public-Use Microdata Sample.

sen the group as their principal ethnic affiliation or attribution. The ratio of this second, smaller number to the first number is the proportion of persons with a multiple ancestry including the specified group who choose the group as their principal attribution, that is, the propensity of multiple-ancestry persons to identify with a given group. As shown in table 11.3, there are a considerable number of multiple-ancestry persons within the self-reported race or Hispanic-origin groups (the baseline data).

The difference between the self-reported baseline number and the single-ancestry number is the number of persons counted in an ethnic group who are of multiple ancestry; thus, using whites as an example, 11,484,000 (188,054,000 minus 176,570,000) of the 188,054,000 persons who self-report as white are of multiple ancestry. In this way, we can calculate the proportion of multiple ancestry for each ethnic group for both the foreign and the native born (table 11.4).

Overall, almost 7 percent of the U.S. population identify a specific race or Hispanic-origin affiliation but report an ancestry that differs from their primary affiliation. For example, more than one-fourth of those reporting American Indian race report a non–American Indian ancestry. About 8 percent of Asian and 9 percent of Hispanic respondents report a non-Asian or non-Hispanic ancestry, respectively. These analyses support our belief that the future population will contain an increasingly larger proportion of the population with multiple ancestries.

To derive our 1995 base population, we project these 1990 census figures forward to 1995 and then scale them to the Census Bureau's 1995 estimates (U.S. Bureau of the Census 1997) for the population

Table 11.4   Percent Multiple Ancestry of Baseline Population, by
             Race or Ethnic Group, 1990 Census

Population Group	Total	Foreign Born	Native Born
All Groups	6.8	8.2	6.8
White	6.1	5.9	6.1
Black	6.8	17.8	6.2
Hispanic	9.2	3.7	12.5
Asian	8.1	5.3	13.7
American Indian	26.9	52.9	26.1

Sources: U.S. Bureau of the Census, 1990 Census Public-Use Microdata Sample.

by race and Hispanic origin. The 1995 scaled data are the baseline populations by race or Hispanic origin, for age, sex, and generation groups, that are used in our population projections.

DEMOGRAPHIC ASSUMPTIONS FOR THE PROJECTIONS

We project the five major ethnic groups from 1995 to 2050. For this chapter, we assume the fertility, mortality, and international migration information used in the most recent Census Bureau (1996) national population projections.

Fertility Assumptions

Fertility is the starting point for any demographic projection model. Higher fertility rates will make the future population larger, and subgroups with higher than average fertility will grow relative to other subgroups.

Age-specific fertility rates for the five major ethnic groups were estimated, using recent fertility data from the June 1994 CPS and tabulations for 1994 from NCHS. Separate estimates were made for the first, second, and third-and-higher immigrant generations from the CPS.[8] However, there is apparently some underreporting of births in the CPS, when compared with vital statistics for registered number of births. Consequently, we tabulated the number of births from vital statistics (for the 1994 calendar year) and from the CPS (for the period from July 1993 to June 1994) by race or ethnicity. We then scaled CPS-based rates to the known level of births by race of mother.

Table 11.5   Fertility Assumptions: Projected Total Fertility Rate, 1995 to 2050, by Population Group and Generation (Children per Woman)

Population Group	1995 Overall	Immigrant Generation		
		1st	2d	3d+
Total	1.98	—	—	—
White	1.81	1.82	1.82	1.81
Black	2.34	2.76	2.53	2.31
Hispanic	2.63	3.23	2.63	2.04
Asian	2.33	2.54	2.17	1.80
American Indian	2.11	2.11	2.11	2.11

Sources: Authors' estimates using June 1994 Current Population Survey data and tabulations from birth data collected by the National Center for Health Statistics.

Overall, the following total fertility rates were assumed for the projections for 1995 to 2050: 1.81 for the white population, 2.34 for blacks, 2.63 for Hispanics, 2.33 for Asians, and 2.11 for American Indians. Specifically, we assume the total fertility rates by generation shown in table 11.5. The generation-specific fertility rates were held constant for the entire projection period. However, fertility rates by ethnicity change as the generational composition of each group shifts. For example, the projection shows declining overall total fertility levels for groups that are heavily immigrant oriented at the beginning of the projection, notably Asians and Hispanics.

Mortality Assumptions

We assume that mortality follows the trends specified in the medium series of the national population projections for 1995 to 2050 by the Census Bureau. On that basis, overall life expectancy at birth increases from 75.9 years in 1995 to 82.0 years in 2050 (table 11.6). We make separate assumptions about mortality for males and females and for each of the five main ethnic groups; and we assume that mortality is the same for immigrant generations within each of the ethnic groups.

International Migration Assumptions

We make immigration assumptions about annual net immigration at five levels—termed zero, low, medium, high, and very high—in order: 0, 410,000, 820,000, 1,230,000, and 1,640,000. The medium

Table 11.6 Mortality Assumptions: Projections of Life Expectancy at Birth, for 1995 Baseline and 2050 Ultimate Year, by Population Group (Years)

Population Group	1995 Baseline			2050 Ultimate Year		
	Total	Male	Female	Total	Male	Female
Total	75.9	72.5	79.3	82.0	79.7	84.3
White	76.8	73.6	80.0	83.6	81.9	85.3
Black	69.4	64.5	74.3	74.2	69.5	78.8
Hispanic	78.6	74.9	82.2	87.0	84.4	89.6
Asian	82.3	79.6	85.0	86.0	83.9	88.1
American Indian	75.8	71.5	80.2	81.6	78.3	85.0

Sources: Mortality assumptions made in national population projections of the U.S. Bureau of the Census (1996).

assumption of 820,000 per year is close to the average for the period from 1990 to 1995 and includes about 225,000 net annual illegal immigrants. The zero assumption, as implemented, implies both zero immigrants and zero emigrants, providing a context for discussing the overall net impact of immigration on population change. The low assumption of 410,000 assumes a decline to immigration levels that are close to net legal immigration during the 1980s. The high assumption represents possible expanded legal immigration through modifications of immigration law. The very high immigration suggests greatly expanded immigration.

The immigration assumptions do not correspond to specific alternative immigration policies. For example, there could be changes in visa preference categories for types of family members; we do not model such policy changes in our projections. Rather, the immigration assumptions represent projection parameters that we allow to vary in order to understand how variations in the overall volume of immigration influence the racial and ethnic composition of the nation's population.

For the actual population projections, we make separate assumptions about immigration and emigration. For the five net immigration assumptions, we assume immigration levels of 0, 700,000, 1,040,000,[9] 1,360,000, and 1,720,000, in conjunction with emigration levels of 0, 290,000, 220,000, 130,000, and 80,000. We assume a racial or ethnic distribution, with an age and sex composition, that is the same as that made in the Census Bureau's 1995 projections. Our projections of annual immigration and emigration are presented in table 11.7. Our model also requires assumptions by immigrant generation.

Table 11.7   International Migration Assumptions: Projections of Annual Immigration and Emigration, for 1995 to 2050 by Population Group (Thousands)

Population Group	Net Immigration		Components	
	Amount	Percentage	In-Migration	Emigration
Total	820	100	1,040	220
White	186	23	259	73
Black	57	7	70	13
Hispanic	350	43	450	100
Asian	226	28	260	34
American Indian	1	0	1	0

Sources: Authors' assumptions based on current international migration.

We assume that all immigrants enter into the first generation (in other words, all immigrants into the United States are foreign-born persons) and emigrants are selected as follows: 95 percent are former immigrants, and 5 percent are children of immigrants. We assume no emigration from third-and-higher generations.[10]

RESULTS

Even without immigration and with the maintenance of currently low fertility levels, according to our model the U.S. population will continue to grow over the next twenty years. The current momentum of population growth—the result of a younger age distribution—provides a cushion of about 30 million more people in the next decades, even if immigration were to cease. A population projection with no immigration would indicate a U.S. population peaking at about 310 million and then slowly declining.

With an annual net immigration of 820,000 (that is, at medium assumption), the 1995 total U.S. population of 263 million will reach 327 million by 2020 and exceed 387 million by 2050 (table 11.8). Thus, the level of immigration and emigration assumed in these projections guarantees population increases in the next fifty years. Even with continued immigration, the rate of population growth of the United States will slacken slightly, however. The U.S. population will grow at an average annual rate of 0.8 percent from 1995 to 2000. This rate will gradually diminish, reaching a level of 0.6 percent within the next fifty years.

From this brief review, it is clear that continuation of current immigration levels would contribute to a larger population size. Al-

Table 11.8   Projected U.S. Population of Race or Ethnic Group, by
Level of Net Immigration, 1995, 2020, and 2050
(Populations in Millions)

Population Group and Year	Assumed Level of Net Migration				
	Zero	Low	Medium	High	Very High
	Projected Total Population				
Total population					
1995	262.8	262.8	262.8	262.8	262.8
2020	297.7	313.2	327.2	341.4	354.9
2050	307.1	349.0	387.3	425.9	463.5
White					
1995	193.6	193.6	193.6	193.6	193.6
2020	203.6	204.8	209.1	213.1	217.9
2050	187.6	190.7	201.4	211.2	222.9
Black					
1995	31.6	31.6	31.6	31.6	31.6
2020	39.9	41.1	41.9	42.9	43.4
2050	48.4	51.6	53.7	55.9	57.9
Hispanic					
1995	26.9	26.9	26.9	26.9	26.9
2020	40.3	48.1	53.7	59.5	64.6
2050	52.8	77.2	94.7	112.7	128.0
Asian					
1995	8.8	8.8	8.8	8.8	8.8
2020	11.3	16.5	19.6	22.9	25.9
2050	14.9	25.9	33.7	42.1	49.7
American Indian					
1995	1.9	1.9	1.9	1.9	1.9
2020	2.6	2.7	2.9	3.0	3.1
2050	3.4	3.6	3.8	4.0	4.2
	Projected Percentage of Total Population				
Total population					
1995	100.0	100.0	100.0	100.0	100.0
2020	100.0	100.0	100.0	100.0	100.0
2050	100.0	100.0	100.0	100.0	100.0
White					
1995	73.7	73.7	73.7	73.7	73.7
2020	68.3	65.3	63.9	62.4	61.4
2050	61.0	54.5	52.0	49.5	48.0
Black					
1995	12.0	12.0	12.0	12.0	12.0
2020	13.4	13.1	12.8	12.6	12.2
2050	15.7	14.8	13.9	13.1	12.5

Table 11.8   *Continued*

Population Group and Year	Assumed Level of Net Immigration				
	Zero	Low	Medium	High	Very High
	Projected Percentage of Total Population				
Hispanic					
1995	10.2	10.2	10.2	10.2	10.2
2020	13.5	15.3	16.4	17.4	18.2
2050	17.2	22.1	24.5	26.4	27.8
Asian					
1995	3.3	3.3	3.3	3.3	3.3
2020	3.8	5.3	6.0	6.7	7.3
2050	4.8	7.4	8.7	9.9	10.7
American Indian					
1995	0.7	0.7	0.7	0.7	0.7
2020	0.9	0.9	0.9	0.9	0.9
2050	1.1	1.0	1.0	0.9	0.9

Sources: Authors' population projections, under assumptions described in the text.
Notes: Assumed levels of immigration are as follows: zero, 0; low, 410,000; medium, 820,000; high, 1,230,000; and very high, 1,640,000 net annual immigrants.

though the population will continue to grow for several decades even without immigration, these results suggest the prospect for moderate growth for the next half century.

Growth of Ethnic Groups

The primary goal of this research is to observe the implications of population dynamics on the ethnic composition of the population. If immigration were zero, then the future ethnic composition would be determined solely by fertility and mortality differentials in the present population. This implies that, even with no immigration, the ethnic composition would change. It also indicates that the resident population composition provides the fixed component—the stock—for the effects of immigration.

The immigrant component plays the central role in determining the future size of ethnic groups in the U.S. population. There are two dimensions on which immigration affects ethnic population trends. First, the level of immigration matters. The number of immigrants has a direct effect on population growth, with each new immigrant adding one new person to an ethnic group. Second, the reproductive value of each immigrant affects the population by adding descendants. The immigrant's age and fertility level, in turn, determine his or her reproductive value. A young immigrant with high fertility will add the most descendants; an old immigrant or a low-fertility immigrant will add few, if any, descendants. Hence, the future growth of ethnic groups is the product of several interacting factors.

According to the 1995 base population, 74 percent of the U.S. population is white, with another 12 percent black, 10 percent Hispanic, 3 percent Asian, and about 1 percent American Indian (table 11.8). Future trends in immigration and differential fertility and mortality levels will lead to major changes in these proportions.

Looking first at the effects on the numbers of persons in ethnic groups (table 11.8), the white population group will increase its numbers from 194 million in 1995 to a peak of 211 million in 2030 and then decline slowly from that level, to about 201 million in 2050.[11] Within the first half of the next century, this group will become less numerous and drop from 74 percent of the total population to 64 percent in 2020 and slightly more than 50 percent in 2050, using the middle immigration assumption.

The black population will increase substantially from 32 million in 1995 to 54 million over the next half century (again assuming the current level and composition of immigration). The average annual growth rate for the black population is projected to be a moderate level of 1.0 percent. However, because other groups grow faster, the proportion of the total population that is black will experience only a slight increase, growing from 12 percent in 1995 to 14 percent in 2050.

The American Indian population is the nation's smallest major ethnic group, numbering 1.9 million in 1995, or 0.7 percent of the total population. There are relatively few immigrants into this population group. Moderate growth is expected, owing to continued identification of children of American Indian and non–American Indian couples. Accordingly, the American Indian population is projected to increase to 3 million in 2020 and 4 million in 2050, representing 1.0 percent of the total population.

Two groups are likely to experience substantial growth during the next century: Asians and Hispanics. The Asian population will grow at annual rates of about 2.4 percent for the next half century, under the conditions of this projection, increasing from 9 million in 1995 to 34 million in 2050. These gains will increase the Asian population's share of the population from 3 percent in 1990 to 6 percent in 2020 and 9 percent in 2050.

Hispanics—assumed to have a larger share of immigration, partially because of their predominant share of illegal-alien entry—will also grow substantially over the next fifty years. The projected average annual growth rate for the Hispanic population, 2.3 percent, is only slightly lower than that projected for Asians. The Hispanic population will increase from 27 million in 1995 to 54 million in 2020. If growth continues uninterrupted over the following fifty years, Hispanics will number 95 million and constitute 25 percent of the population. In this case, the Hispanic population will become the largest ethnic minority group in the nation well before 2010.

This description of the future ethnic composition of the U.S. population reflects the assumed continuation of high levels of immigration and the current ethnic composition of that immigration. There are serious questions about the reality of these projections over a fifty-year period, and we stress the use of these projections as a simulation representing the long-run implication of plausible current trends.

The Effect of Exogamy and Multiple-Ancestry Populations

Table 11.9 presents the results of including exogamy in a population projection by generations for ethnic groups under different assumptions. The single-ancestry population comprises persons who have only one major ethnic ancestry. The multiple-ancestry population comprises persons who have two or more ethnic ancestries. The total population of a group is the sum of the single- and multiple-ancestry persons.[12]

These projections imply substantial growth in the population of multiple-ancestry persons, regardless of the reported primary ethnic identification. About 7 percent of the population in 1995 reports one or more ancestries that differ from their primary race or Hispanic-origin identification. The percentage of the population reporting multiple ancestries is projected to more than triple, to 21 percent, in 2050, assuming that intermarriage continues at current rates. There is, however, substantial variation in the proportion of multiple-ancestry persons from one ethnic group to another. Trends for the white population are similar to those of the overall population, whereas the increase in the proportion of multiple-ancestry persons is somewhat lower for the black population. The relative gain in multiple-ancestry persons is especially high for the Asian and Hispanic population, reaching 36 and 45 percent, respectively, in 2050.

The major implication of these trends is to raise questions about the primary racial or Hispanic-origin identification of the large num-

Table 11.9   Projected U.S. Population of Race or Ethnic Groups, by
Single and Multiple Ancestry, 1995, 2020, and 2050
(Populations in Millions)

Population Group and Year	Total—All Ancestries	Single-Ancestry Population	Multiple-Ancestry Population	Multiple-Ancestry Population as Percentage of Total Ethnic Group
Total				
1995	262.8	245.0	17.8	6.8
2020	327.2	294.5	32.7	10.0
2050	387.3	306.7	80.6	20.8
White				
1995	197.2	181.7	15.5	7.9
2020	216.3	192.0	24.3	11.2
2050	212.7	167.9	44.8	21.1
Black				
1995	32.1	29.4	2.7	8.4
2020	43.9	39.6	4.3	9.8
2050	57.0	49.0	8.0	14.0
Hispanic				
1995	29.3	24.4	4.9	16.7
2020	58.1	43.9	14.2	24.4
2050	112.4	61.7	50.7	45.1
Asian				
1995	9.6	8.1	1.5	15.6
2020	21.5	17.4	4.1	19.1
2050	41.7	26.7	15.0	36.0
American Indian				
1995	9.0	1.5	7.5	83.3
2020	9.7	1.5	8.2	84.5
2050	11.0	1.4	9.8	89.1

Sources: Authors' population projections, under assumptions described in the text.
Note: Calculations are based on medium immigration assumption.

ber of persons of multiple ancestries. The ethnic affiliation of many Americans in the future must be considered uncertain from our current perspective. Today, virtually all Americans have parents and grandparents who are of the same ethnic origin, at least using the five broad racial and Hispanic groups as currently defined. However, a substantial and growing number have links to two or more ethnic ancestries, allowing wide latitude in how they may choose to identify themselves.

To display this blurring of single and multiple ethnic linkages, we show estimates for single and multiple ancestry of the current and future U.S. population in table 11.9. Of the 8.8 million persons in 1995 whose primary ethnic identification was Asian (table 11.8), the vast majority (8.1 million) had only Asian ancestry. In addition, there were another 1.5 million persons who reported some Asian ancestry—of whom we estimate that 700,000 would report themselves in the census as Asian. The net result is that we estimate 800,000 persons who had some Asian ancestry but would identify themselves as non-Asian. Overall, 16 percent of all persons with Asian ancestry have multiple ancestry.

Let us look now to the future and see what our model suggests about the multiple ancestry of Asians. If all persons of some Asian ancestry identified themselves as Asian, the reported population could be as high as 42 million in 2050. If only single-ancestry persons reported themselves as Asian in 2050, the population could be as low as 27 million. The projected Asian population of 34 million in 2050 in table 11.8 is between these two extremes because only a fraction of the multiple-ancestry Asian population will identify themselves as Asian. The salient secular trend is the increasing blurring of the lines of ethnic boundaries. By the middle of the next century, more than one-third of all of those with some Asian ancestry will have multiple ancestries, compared with only 16 percent today.

There is even greater latitude for variation in the future Hispanic population. In 1995, there were an estimated 4.9 million Hispanic persons with multiple ancestry, representing 17 percent of all persons with some Hispanic ancestry. By 2050, through continued high fertility and continued intermarriage, the multiple-ancestry Hispanic population will expand to 51 million persons, or 45 percent of all persons with some Hispanic ancestry. If only single-ancestry Hispanic persons report themselves as Hispanic in 2050, the Hispanic population will be 62 million (16 percent of the total U.S. population). If, instead, on the high side, all persons with any Hispanic ancestry report themselves as Hispanic, the population could be 50 million higher, at 112 million (29 percent of the total U.S. population).

The black population illustrates the other extreme of the plausible range, given the lower levels of exogamy assumed. Under the assumptions made here, there will be only small increases in the multiple-ancestry black population from 1995 to 2050. By 2050, we estimate a single-ancestry black population of 49 million and a multiple-ancestry population of 8 million. The overall black population could therefore be as large as 57 million in 2050, if all multiple-ancestry black persons were to identify themselves as black. Multiple-ancestry blacks would make up only 14 percent of the overall black population in 2050.

For American Indians, our projections are particularly problematic, given the high degree of volatility in self-identification. Our projections do not take into account the full potential range, as has been exhibited in the last three censuses; rather, we assume the current level of ethnic attribution and exogamy. The American Indian, Eskimo, and Aleut population contained a very substantial proportion of multiple-ancestry persons in 1995. The number of single-ancestry persons is predicted to change little over the next fifty years, the multiple-ancestry population to increase modestly, and the overall American Indian population—including single and multiple ancestries—to grow from 9 million in 1995 to 11 million in 2050. According to our projections, about 89 percent of the overall American Indian population in 2050 will be of multiple ancestry.

Taking all ethnic groups into account, including the white, black, and American Indian populations, the multiple-ancestry population is estimated to increase from 18 million in 1995 to 81 million in 2050, reaching 21 percent of the population that will have overlapping ancestries among the current classifications. This blurring of ethnic boundaries illustrates some of the ambiguity inherent in any ethnic projection. Today, three-quarters of the population identify themselves as members of the "majority" population (whites with no Hispanic ancestry). By the middle of the next century, the fraction will decline to a range of about 43 to 55 percent, depending upon the extent to which multiple-ancestry whites report their primary ethnic identification as white. The two groups that will expand significantly in relative terms are Hispanics and Asians. The relative size of the Hispanic population will more than double over this period, to a range of 16 to 29 percent in 2050, depending upon the self-identification of Hispanics of multiple ancestry. Similarly, the Asian population, which today constitutes 3 percent of the population, will rise to about 7 to 11 percent in 2050, depending upon the level at which multiple-ancestry Asians identify themselves as Asians.

The Effect of Ethnic Attribution

Table 11.10 presents possible future ethnic distributions of the medium immigration scenario based on alternative ethnic attribution assumptions. We start with some unrealistic extremes. Very low attribution assumes that no multiple-ancestry persons identify with a particular ethnic group, and very high attribution assumes that all multiple-ancestry persons identify with the ethnic group. We assume low and high attribution rates to provide a more realistic range. Low and high attribution levels reflect ranges around the medium attribu-

Table 11.10   Projected U.S. Population of Race or Ethnic Group, by
Level of Ethnic Attribution, 1995, 2020, and 2050
(Populations in Millions)

Population Group and Year	Assumed Level of Ethnic Attribution				
	Very Low	Low	Medium	High	Very High
	Projected Population				
Total population					
1995	262.8	262.8	262.8	262.8	262.8
2020	327.2	327.2	327.2	327.2	327.2
2050	387.3	387.3	387.3	387.3	387.3
White					
1995	193.6	193.6	193.6	193.6	193.6
2020	191.0	207.0	209.1	211.3	215.3
2050	175.5	195.2	201.4	207.8	220.3
Black					
1995	31.6	31.6	31.6	31.6	31.6
2020	37.5	41.6	41.9	43.0	43.7
2050	43.2	51.1	53.7	56.4	59.2
Hispanic					
1995	26.9	26.9	26.9	26.9	26.9
2020	43.7	51.5	53.7	56.0	57.9
2050	64.5	85.0	94.7	105.5	115.2
Asian					
1995	8.8	8.8	8.8	8.8	8.8
2020	17.3	19.1	19.6	20.2	21.4
2050	27.9	31.3	33.7	36.5	42.9
American Indian					
1995	2.3	2.3	2.3	2.3	2.3
2020	2.2	2.5	2.9	3.3	3.6
2050	2.8	3.2	3.8	4.4	4.6
	Projected Percentage of Total Population				
Total population					
1995	100.0	100.0	100.0	100.0	100.0
2020	100.0	100.0	100.0	100.0	100.0
2050	100.0	100.0	100.0	100.0	100.0
White					
1995	73.7	73.7	73.7	73.7	73.7
2020	58.7	63.2	63.9	64.6	66.1
2050	43.4	50.4	52.0	53.7	54.9
Black					
1995	12.0	12.0	12.0	12.0	12.0
2020	12.1	12.7	12.8	13.1	13.4
2050	12.7	13.2	13.9	14.6	14.7

Table 11.10   *Continued*

Population Group and Year	Assumed Level of Ethnic Attribution				
	Very Low	Low	Medium	High	Very High
	Projected Percentage of Total Population				
Hispanic					
1950	10.2	10.2	10.2	10.2	10.2
2020	13.4	15.7	16.4	17.1	17.8
2050	15.9	21.9	24.5	27.2	29.0
Asian					
1995	3.3	3.3	3.3	3.3	3.3
2020	5.2	5.8	6.0	6.2	6.6
2050	6.9	8.1	8.7	9.4	10.8
American Indian					
1995	0.7	0.7	0.7	0.7	0.7
2020	0.5	0.8	0.9	1.0	1.1
2050	0.4	0.9	1.0	1.1	1.2

Sources: Authors' population projections, under assumptions described in the text.
Note: Calculations are based on medium immigration assumption.

tion rates that are based on 1990 census data—the low is 20 percentage points less than reported 1990 levels, and the high is 20 percentage points greater.

The white population has low exogamy rates and attribution rates below 50 percent, resulting in population growth that is less than expected from conventional assumptions of no exogamy. It will reach a maximum of 210 million in about 2025 and then decline for all attribution assumptions except the extremely high one. For the plausible range of low to high attribution rates, the white population will range in size from about 195 million to about 208 million in 2050.

The black population also has relatively low exogamy rates but high attribution rates for multiple-ancestry persons. The medium attribution assumptions suggest that the growth of the black population will be slightly greater than conventional population projections. The results in 2050 under the low to high attribution assumptions are clustered within a narrow range, from 51 million to 56 million.

Although the Hispanic population is expected to expand rapidly, its growth will be magnified by moderate levels of exogamy and attribution rates above 50 percent, resulting in growth rates greater than those assuming no exogamy. Under the more reasonable low to high attribution assumptions, the Hispanic population is likely to increase in number from 85 million to 106 million by 2050.

The Asian population has moderate rates of exogamy and self-identification—less than 50 percent. As a greater proportion of the Asian population is accounted for by the second, third, and fourth-plus generations, the projection reflects the increasing level of exogamy. Overall, the size of the Asian population in 2050 for the spectrum of assumptions, from low to high attribution, is within a range of 31 million to 37 million.

The American Indian population has high exogamy and moderate attribution rates (more than 50 percent), resulting in population growth that is higher than under the assumption of no exogamy. In the range of low to high attribution rates, the American Indian population will increase in size to between 3.2 million and 4.4 million by 2050.

CONCLUSION

The U.S. population is ethnically diverse, with ethnic intermarriage increasingly common and with noticeable uncertainty about the future trends in ethnic self-identification of persons of multiple ethnic ancestries. All these facts call into question the wisdom of continuing conventional projections of ethnic population. The purpose of this chapter has been to explore the impact of ethnic exogamy on population projections for major ethnic groups in the United States.

The Effects of Persons of Multiple Ancestry

The assumption that the major ethnic groups in the United States are closed populations must be questioned. It seems clear that the multiple ancestry of ethnic groups, stemming from continued immigration and intermarriage, will substantially increase in coming decades. This increase will come on top of the present population, in which a significant proportion already reports multiple ethnic ancestries. Starting from a 1995 population with almost 7 percent multiple ancestry (based on analysis of 1990 census data), the proportion of U.S. population that is of multiple ancestry is likely to be, at a minimum, 7 to 8 percent in 2000, 8 to 9 percent in 2010, and approximately 9 to 11 percent in 2020. By the year 2020, assuming conservative trends and the estimates of multiple ancestry in 1995, the Asian population will be one-fifth multiple ancestry, and the Hispanic population will be one-fourth multiple ancestry. Such trends demand caution in interpreting the projected number of persons who may be reporting their primary ethnic affiliation in one of the current major ethnic groups.

Such shifts in the ethnic ancestry of the population have important implications. Ethnic identification within existing group boundaries will likely become "fuzzier," with the possibility of more-rapid changes in group definitions. Individuals with multiple ethnic backgrounds may choose to report a special, new identification (for example, Metis in Canada, Anglo-Indians in South Asia, and mestizos in Mexico) or to request that they be reported according to their multiple identifications. Multiple ethnic reporting is likely to continue to challenge official systems of classification for race and/or ethnicity in the United States.

Multiple ethnic identities will also challenge current official population projections, which assume that everyone has a unique, mutually exclusive identity (with the exception of Hispanics, who may report any "race" group). What demographic interpretation should be given to projections for the Asian population, for example, when the 2050 population might be 35 percent greater or lesser, under identical demographic assumptions, depending upon the self-identification of persons with multiple ancestries? What cautions should be exercised in forecasting the growth of the Hispanic population—and stressing that it would one day exceed the black population—when more than 50 million persons in 2050 might choose to identify themselves as Hispanic or opt for another ethnic identity?

Improvements in Projections of National Population

In the situation of exogamy with multiple-ancestry persons, future population projections might take different forms. One possibility is to discard present population projections by race or ethnicity, admitting that we know too little about intermarriage rates and self-identification for persons with multiple ancestries. Alternatively, ethnic projections might extend only five to ten years after a decennial census, after which time projections would be limited to the total population. A second approach, suggested by Leon Tabah (1993), is to produce population projections for major immigrant groups (Asian, Middle Eastern, Latin American, Caribbean, and African, for example) and estimate the future foreign-born population and their children. Such projections would recognize that there are significant and unknown levels of intermarriage after the second generation and that useful projections may best be restricted to immigrants and their children. Finally, a third option is to note explicitly the assumptions about intermarriage and acknowledge their impact on projections. This latter approach produces results similar to those shown in this chapter. Of course, in order to make point estimates, it would be necessary to make specific assumptions about the future self-identification of multiple-ancestry persons. Such a task seems formidable, mainly because of lack of data. However, in the final analysis, if population projections are seen as useful data, then an approach similar to the one reported in this research, which explicitly considers exogamy, is preferable.

Our work suggests three main areas for further research. First, our demographic modeling makes restrictive assumptions about exogamy for major ethnic groups by generation. The most serious problem is inadequate data. We need improved data for the baseline period and more work on likely trends.

Second, our projections make clear that there will be a substantial increase in the number of persons of multiple ancestry, particularly for the American Indian, Asian American, and Hispanic population. Two of these groups (Asian Americans and the Hispanic population) will be the fastest-growing ethnic groups in the United States during the next fifty years. We need more work on the self-reporting of ethnicity, especially for persons of multiple ancestry. We require more attention to revised race and ethnicity categories for the census and surveys and more research on ways to collect data from persons with two and more racial or ethnic origins.

Third, attention should be given to improving the modeling of exogamy in our population projection models. Our model makes strong assumptions about exogamy variations by age, sex, and over time. Improvements, based on better data and more research on self-identification of race or ethnicity, could be made in further work on an approach to population projection by generation.

This chapter builds on previous research and uses results from James P. Smith and Barry Edmonston, eds., 1997, *The New Americans*, National Academy Press, which in turn draws on previous work by Barry Edmonston and Jeffrey Passel.

NOTES

1. Even the apparently simple flow of immigrants into the country is not completely straightforward. The relevant concept is net immigration, the difference between the number of those entering the country and the number of those leaving it, whether foreign born or native born. These flows respond to various economic, political, social, and family

concerns, in the United States as well as in the sending countries, that themselves may be volatile.

2. There have been recent changes in the classification of race and ethnic groups for federal statistics (Edmonston, Goldstein, and Lott 1997 provide a background discussion to proposed changes). The major change that is relevant here is the creation of separate categories for Asian Americans and Pacific Islanders for the 2000 census. We include Pacific Islanders, numbering about 360,000, or 5 percent of the combined Asian American and Pacific Islander population in 1990, within the Asian American population for the projections in this chapter.

3. The white group is treated as a "residual" group in our analysis. It refers to people who identify as "white" on the census race question and also do not identify as "Hispanic." One might be tempted to label this group as European origin because most persons in this group claim ancestry from persons who originally came from Europe or came from other parts of the world but were originally of European descent. We say "tempted" because an increasingly significant proportion of "white" immigrants into the United States are from North Africa and the Middle East—in the late 1980s, about one-third of "white" immigrants into the United States. Most of these immigrants are Arab or Moslem, although some immigrants from this region are Christians and some, notably from Israel, are Jewish. It is unclear whether in the future a "racial" identity that has been principally associated with persons of European descent and Christian or Jewish religion will continue to be useful, even as a residual category.

4. Although the American Indian population has been greatly affected by shifts in self-definition (Passel 1996a), we include population projections for this group that rely on a simple demographic forecast, assuming a continuation of fertility and mortality trends.

5. The institutional population is treated as entirely civilian.

6. For American Indians, we apply the rate for the native population to the fourth-and-higher generation and interpolate for generations two and three.

7. In the 1990 census, both foreign-born and native-born Hispanics reported themselves in large numbers in the "white" or "other" racial categories. About 40 percent of Hispanic respondents reported themselves as "other" race in the 1990 census; most of the rest reported themselves as white. Overall, more than 97 percent of people reporting themselves in the "other" racial category were of Hispanic origin.

8. Fertility levels for the third and fourth-and-higher generations were assumed to be the same.

9. Following Census Bureau assumptions, we assume that medium immigration will be at a level of about 1,040,000 annually, including 685,000 legal immigrants, 115,000 refugees, 225,000 illegal aliens and a net gain of 15,000 from civilian and Puerto Rican movements.

10. These proportions for the generational composition of emigrants were derived from a historical reconstruction of the U.S. population (Passel and Edmonston 1994). Such a generational composition is consistent with the notion that most emigrants are foreign-born persons who return to their county of origin, taking their native-born children with them. In fact, some third-and-higher generation U.S. residents emigrate. However, the numbers are small enough to have little effect on the results reported here.

11. These projections use the medium immigration, exogamy, and ethnic attribution assumptions.

12. Note that the single-ancestry populations for each of the five ethnic groups sum to the total single-ancestry population. However, the sum of "all ancestries" and "multiple ancestries" for each of the five groups exceed the total because persons are counted more than once, in each of their ancestries.

REFERENCES

Alba, Richard D. 1995a. "Assimilation's Quiet Tide." *Public Interest* 119 (Spring): 3–18.

———. 1995b. *Ethnic Identity: The Transformation of White America*. New Haven: Yale University Press.

Alba, Richard D. and Reid M. Golden. 1986. "Patterns of Ethnic Marriage in the United States." *Social Forces* 65(1): 202–23.

Bean, Frank D., Barry Edmonston, and Jeffrey S. Passel. 1990. *Undocumented Migration to the United States: IRCA and the Experience of the 1980s*. Washington, D.C.: Urban Institute Press.

Chew, K. S., D. J. Eggebeen, and P. R. Uhlenberg. 1989. "American Children in Multiracial Households." *Sociological Perspectives* 32(1): 65–85.

Davis, F. James. 1991. *Who Is Black?: One Nation's Definition*. University Park: Pennsylvania State University Press.

Edmonston, Barry, Joshua Goldstein, and Juanita Tamayo Lott. 1997. *Spotlight on Heterogeneity: The Federal Standards for Racial and Ethnic Classification*. Washington, D.C.: National Academy Press.

Edmonston, Barry, and Jeffrey S. Passel. 1992. "Immigration and Immigrant Generations in Population Projections." *International Journal of Forecasting* 8(3): 459–76.

———. 1994. "The Future Immigrant Population of the United States." In *Immigration and Ethnicity: The Integration of America's Newest Immigrants*, edited by Barry Edmonston and Jeffrey S. Passel. Washington, D.C.: Urban Institute Press.

Gurak, D. T., and J. P. Fitzpatrick. 1982. "Intermarriage Among Hispanic Ethnic Groups in New York City." *American Journal of Sociology* 87(4): 921–34.

Hout, Michael, and Joshua Goldstein. 1994. "How 4.5 Million Irish Immigrants Became 40 Million Irish Americans: Demographic and Subjective Aspects of the Ethnic Composition of White Americans." *American Sociological Review* 59: 64–82.

Hwang, Sean-Shong, and Rogelio Saenz. 1990. "The Problem Posed by Immigrants Married Abroad on Intermarriage Research: The Case of Asian Americans." *International Migration Review* 24(3): 563–76.

Kalish, Susan. 1992. "Interracial Baby Boomlet in Progress?" *Population Today* 20(11): 1–2, 9.

Kalmijn, Matthijs. 1993. "Trends in Black/White Intermarriage." *Social Forces* 72(1):119–46.

Lee, Sharon M. 1993. "Racial Classifications in the U.S. Census, 1890 to 1990." *Ethnic and Racial Studies* 16(1): 75–94.

Lee, Sharon M., and Marilyn Fernandez. 1998. "Trends in Asian American Racial/Ethnic Intermarriage: A Comparison of 1980 and 1990 Census Data." *Sociological Perspectives* 41(1): 323–42.

Lee, Sharon M., and Keiko Yamanaka. 1990. "Patterns of Asian American Intermarriage and Marital Assimilation." *Journal of Comparative Family Studies* 21(4): 287–305.

Lieberson, Stanley, and Mary Waters. 1994. *From Many Strands: Ethnic and Racial Groups in Contemporary America*. New York: Russell Sage Foundation.

Paginini, D. L., and S. P. Morgan. 1990. "Intermarriage and Social Distance Among U.S. Immigrants at the Turn of the Century." *American Journal of Sociology* 96(2): 405–32.

Passel, Jeffrey S. 1996a. "The Growing American Indian Population, 1960–1990: Beyond Demography." In *Changing Numbers, Changing Needs: American Indian Demography and Public Health*. Washington, D.C.: National Academy Press.

———. 1996b. "Problem with March 1994 and 1995 CPS Weighting." Technical memorandum to CPS users. Population Studies Center, Urban Institute, Washington, D.C. Nov. 12.

————. 1996c. "Recent Efforts to Control Illegal Immigration to the United States." Report to the OECD Working Party on Migration. Washington, D.C.: Population Studies Center, Urban Institute.

Passel, Jeffrey S., and Rebecca L. Clark. 1998. *Immigrants in New York: Their Legal Status, Incomes, and Taxes*. Washington, D.C.: Urban Institute.

Passel, Jeffrey S., and Barry Edmonston. 1994. "Immigration and Race: Recent Trends in Immigration to the United States." In *Immigration and Ethnicity: The Integration of America's Newest Immigrants*, edited by Barry Edmonston and Jeffrey S. Passel. Washington, D.C.: Urban Institute Press.

Sandefur, G. D., and Thomas McKinnell. 1985. "Intermarriage between American Indians and White Americans: Patterns and Implications." Unpublished paper. Center for Demography and Ecology, University of Wisconsin.

Tabah, Leon. 1993. "Discussant's Remarks on Population Projections." Presentation to the meeting of the International Union for the Scientific Study of Population. Montreal (August 28).

U.S. Bureau of the Census. 1996. "Population Estimates and Projections." In *Projections of the Population of the United States by Ages, Sex, and Race: 1995 to 2050*. Series P-25, no. 1130. Washington, D.C.: U.S. Government Printing Office.

————. 1997. "Population Estimates for April 1997." Population Division Home Page. http://www.census.gov

Waters, Mary C. 1990. *Ethnic Options*. Berkeley: University of California Press.

INDEX

Page numbers in **boldface** refer to figures and tables.

West Indian workers: cultural stereotypes and economics, 19–20, 173,
195–200, 211–22; in ethnic niches,
110–11; occupational niche case
study, 200–211; segregation of, 356,
357, 358–61
White, Michael, 21–22, 358
white workers: entrepreneurship and
earnings, **146,** 147–53, **148, 154–
55,** 159; ethnic concentrations,
111–34, **120–22, 128, 130, 132,**
190–92; and European immigrant
workers, 3–7, 31, 356–61, 375–77;
internal migration patterns, 313–27,
315–16, 320–23, 329, 332–40; occupational niche case study, 72–95;
perceptions of West Indians vs.

American blacks, 210–15; population
projection and ethnicity, 7–9, 383–
410, **399–400, 406–7;** residential segregation, 355–56, 361–75, **363, 364**
Williams, Robin, 11
Wilson, Franklin, 17, 134
Wilson, Kenneth, 144, 174
Wisconsin: internal migration patterns,
315, 321, 323, 324; out-migration
patterns and, 326–28, **329**
women. *See* gender issues
work ethic, 198

Yamanaka, Keiko, 387

Zhou, Min, 18–19, 144, 145, 174,
176, 181

The
Revelations
of
Alvin
Tolliver

DAVID KHERDIAN

HAMPTON ROADS
PUBLISHING COMPANY, INC.

Cover design by Bookwrights Design
Cover art by Deborah Hayner

Hampton Roads Publishing Company, Inc.
1125 Stoney Ridge Road
Charlottesville, VA 22902

434-296-2772
fax: 434-296-5096
e-mail: hrpc@hrpub.com
www.hrpub.com

If you are unable to order this book from your local
bookseller, you may order directly from the publisher.
Call 1-800-766-8009, toll-free.
Library of Congress Catalog Card Number: 2001092124
ISBN 1-57174-255-7
10 9 8 7 6 5 4 3 2 1
Printed on acid-free paper in Canada

to gerald hausman

an introduction
to my story

I WANT TO TELL you about a brief period in my life when everything for me was changed forever. I guess you could say it was inevitable, given who I am and what I want from life. But then I might say the same about you, if I knew you as well as you are about to know me. Maybe, like me, all you've ever known about yourself is what you are doing or thinking or planning or dreaming at the time. But then, little by little, things happen—people come into our lives— and sometimes they change our lives—forever!

The mentors that came into my life, that I could just as easily call my heroes, were so unexpected . . . and yet, because of their influence, not unexpected at all.

You can say it all happened because I was an explorer, and an adventurer, and that that is the important thing. But what I found out was that we are not alone, but rather connected to others in mysterious ways that are sometimes hard to fathom and resolve with our ordinary minds. I guess that's why I needed all the different and peculiar experiences that belonged to me. Because if I hadn't started out on my journey—that I didn't even see as a journey at the time—I never would have found out what my life was about.

—*Alvin Tolliver*

crazy eli

— one —

I NEVER THOUGHT of Crazy Eli as being a part of my life. The fact that I saw him every week had nothing to do with it. I had to go by his house at least twice a day, on my way to and from school. Although he wasn't always visible, I couldn't help but look down from the sidewalk at the hovel in which he lived. It was really the basement of the house of someone whom I also didn't know.

By also, I mean I didn't know Crazy Eli either. I just knew where he lived. His house had an outside door, but no windows. No one had ever been inside his home—if you want to call it that—that I knew of, and I'm sure there wasn't anybody who wanted to enter his home, either.

The way we got to see Crazy Eli *intentionally* was if we stood on the sidewalk and taunted him, by saying things like "Kookoolala is kookoo, Kookoolala is kookoo," in a singsong voice. We called him Kookoolala until we grew old enough to switch to Crazy Eli, which was what the adults called him. I never did learn his real name.

It wouldn't be long before the door would fly open, and Crazy Eli would come charging out, waving a short-handled axe in his right hand, grunting and heaving and making strange gurgling sounds with his voice, because he either couldn't speak or had never learned how.

We always had enough of a head start, so we knew he could never catch us, but we didn't know if he might throw his axe and hit one of us. That was part of the excitement. Though we were never *really* scared until the moment when the chase began. But he never did. Nor did he ever really come close to catching us. At the first corner, we would split off into three different directions, even though he almost never chased us past that point.

If we saw him the next day, pulling his wagon with stuff he'd picked up along the street, we knew that whatever happened the day before was now forgotten. But that didn't mean we talked to him, because if we had there was no way of knowing *what* he might do. It meant you would have to go right up to him and speak up. And that called for more guts than any of us had.

Although we were afraid of Crazy Eli and thought he must be crazy, the way we looked at it was that he had as much right to be on the street as anyone else, and what he did with his wagon was his business. We just watched him out of the corners of our eyes and went about our *own* business. As far as I could tell he didn't see or notice any of us. It was his indifference that also made him seem different, and it was part of the reason we thought he was nuts.

If I thought about it, the only thing I had in common with Crazy Eli was that we lived in the same neighborhood. But we did have one other thing in common that, if you would have told me about it in advance, I would have said wasn't worth mentioning, or even worth trying to understand. What that was was that we were both loners.

But it was silly even to think about. Here I was, a sixth grader, a little over five feet tall, pretty heavy into style, and a good athlete with dreams about playing in the major leagues. Crazy Eli was over six feet tall *at least*, bony and gawky-looking, and always wore the same grey clothes. And he didn't know a baseball bat from an axe handle.

Although I never made the comparison myself, you might say that my knapsack was like Crazy Eli's wagon. That's where I put all the stuff I couldn't get into my pockets, just like he used his wagon for putting things in that he picked up on his travels around the city and in the neighboring woods. Of course, we didn't collect the same kinds of things. Crazy Eli was usually hauling pieces of wood, old bricks, jars, and branches, and stuff that looked to me like nothing but weeds. Also, there's a big difference between a knapsack and a wagon, just as there was a big difference in our routes.

My route was the river that came from somewhere in the north and wound its way down to the lake, which was the east side of our city. I mean, we didn't have an east side to our town; you either lived on the north side, the west side, or the south side; only the lake lived on the east side.

Some people thought the lake was the best thing about our town, but I preferred the river, which was mostly deserted and belonged to the animals, the tall grasses, the big oak trees, and other trees that grew along its banks. That's where I always went for my adventuring, and I always went alone.

Almost every day, once school was out, I would fill my knapsack, to which I tied my sectional cane pole, and then I would head out for the river.

I never made a plan because, when it comes to adventuring along the river, you can never tell what you are going to find, or where Nature's mysteries are apt to lead you next. I was always looking for edible plants, like the wild asparagus bed I found once, or herbs to take home to my mother. She liked to sneak a sandwich into my knapsack when I wasn't looking, even though she knew it made me mad because there was always more than enough food where I was heading.

Feeding myself was part of the adventure and fun. There were berries and nuts in season, and of course fish and crayfish to catch and cook. But mostly I liked to just observe everything around me. I knew where the dens of the different animals were, and some days I would camouflage myself and observe them without being noticed myself.

Other days I hunted for Indian flints and arrowheads while I searched for their caves and tried to imagine their presences long, long ago, when this land belonged to them alone. I liked to imagine myself an Indian because I envied their lives, which seemed both natural and true. I knew they had developed powers of observation, endurance, and survival skills, as well as tracking, hunting, and living from the land. The land was alive for them, and the land was alive for me.

— two —

I CAN REMEMBER the first time it occurred to me that Crazy Eli and I had something in common. It was the time I saw him in the woods, and without his usual wagon. He was holding a beat-up canvas bag and bending over what looked like a pile of weeds. I spotted him from the hill I was on. I sat down and watched him for over a half hour, until he left what he was doing and disappeared at the edge of a ravine.

What struck me as funny was that he didn't look crazy. I don't mean that he looked just like another person or anything, but only that he fit into the surroundings in a way he never seemed to fit himself into our neighborhood.

Once I was sure he wasn't coming back, I went down and examined the stuff I thought he had been picking. It could have been any one of two or three plain-looking plants, none of which looked out of the ordinary, so I picked the one with the largest leaf. The next day I looked it up in a book in the library. It was called comfrey, and it was supposed to be good for healing bones, also for making tea. It made me wonder about Crazy Eli.

I would have followed Crazy Eli on that day, to see where he was headed, but he was traveling in the direction of the one section of the woods I had been avoiding. There was a gang of older boys that had once built a shack in a wooded grove on the other side of the ravine. The shack was no longer there because the police had torn it down. That was after the gang was punished for capturing a boy about my age. They took him captive and made him take off all his clothes. That was all they did to him, except that he got so scared his parents kept him home from school for a week. He squealed, of course, and the gang got put on probation, but that didn't stop them from going back into the woods.

But now their hideout was a complete secret. I had seen them wielding axes and shovels—tools that seemed to me to be completely out of place in the wild. All I knew was that they were there, somewhere, and probably up to no good.

I didn't suppose they would mess with Crazy Eli. Nor did I think they could keep him out of "their" woods. Crazy Eli went wherever he liked in the city, and I was sure he could go anywhere he liked in the woods, also.

— three —

TWO WEEKS WENT by before I went to the river again. I sat down on the same boulder from where I had spied Crazy Eli, and then I went down again to the spot where he had been collecting plants to see if there were any other plants I might need to gather and do research on. Without knowing what I was doing, I started moseying over towards the ravine. I was getting curious about what else Crazy Eli was finding in the woods that might be unknown to me. Although it pleased me that I had secrets on my friends, it didn't please me that Crazy Eli had some secrets on me.

It didn't surprise me that the plant life along the ravine was different from everywhere else. What I did wonder about was if there were other herbs or medicinal plants here that Crazy Eli knew about and I didn't. It was really funny; in school, everybody wanted to teach you something or other, but none of it was interesting, whereas, in the woods, where you really could learn something useful, there were no teachers. It didn't seem right.

I must have been thinking these thoughts when I crossed over the ravine to the edge of the forbidden woods. The instant I realized what I was doing I started to turn back, but I caught sight of a worn path leading toward a wild blackberry bush just twenty yards in front of me.

I stood stock-still and listened. I was sure there wasn't anybody around. I decided to rush over and fill up on some berries before heading back to safe territory.

I was so intent on looking into the woods ahead that I didn't watch where my feet were taking me. The next thing I knew, the grass gave way under my feet, and I went crashing down into a dark hole. When I hit bottom, my leg buckled under me. I was covered with dirt and boards and clods of grass. I was choking and I was so frightened I didn't even feel the hurt in my leg at first. I knew at once that I had fallen into a trap, just as I knew who the culprits were who had dug the hole.

I looked up at the sky to see how deep the hole was. It was deeper than I was tall. I was aware that the boards that had fallen in with me would help me escape, but the minute I stood up my left leg gave out.

I felt the bump when I pulled my trouser leg up to have a look. There was a bulge, just above my ankle, the size of a baseball. It was beginning to throb, and for the first time, I was aware of my pain.

I looked up again, with my mind racing to find an answer. But there wasn't any answer. I was trapped, with no escape possible.

It was nearing evening now, which meant that the boys who set the trap would probably not be back until morning, at the very earliest.

I scuffled back and leaned against the wall. The pain was increasing, and so was the swelling. I wondered if my leg was broken, or just badly bruised. Either way, standing would only make it worse.

The temperature was beginning to drop, and before long, it would be dark. I was getting cold, and I was scared. I began to feel faint, whether from fear or pain I didn't know, but my mind was becoming fuzzy. . . .

The next thing I knew, everything was black. When I opened my eyes, it was dark outside. It took an instant before I realized that I had passed out. I heard a sound above my head, growing closer and closer.

The moon was staring down at me, but then, in an instant, everything became black again. Crazy Eli's face was blocking all but a fraction of the moon from my view. His silence frightened me until I realized that I had never heard him speak. I could feel him staring down at my leg.

Before I could say anything myself, he leaped into the hole, and grunting, he raised my arms as he tied a rope around my chest. He grunted again and I took hold of the rope above the knot. It was only then that I was aware that I had understood the meaning his grunts were conveying. I wanted to tell him that I understood, but he had already raised himself up, and placing a board at an angle against one of the walls, he dragged me backwards until my back was braced against the board.

The next thing I knew, Crazy Eli was out of the hole and grunting again—but this time not in speech. He was pulling me up, with my back sliding up the board, until he grabbed me under my arms and hoisted me up out of the pit.

I stood on one leg while he kneeled down and grunted for me to get up on his back. I wanted to say that I understood him, but this time I couldn't speak because I was crying. I felt safe, and because it had all happened so swiftly, I lost control of my feelings. I held tight to Crazy Eli's neck with my arms and leaned my head against his neck.

It was only then that I was aware of his smell, which was different from anything I had experienced before. It was a mixture of so many things: earth, plants, water, fabrics, and of course the body that held all these things together—Crazy Eli himself.

— four —

WHEN WE CAME OUT of the woods at the edge of town, Crazy Eli grunted for me not to move, while he slowly bent over and pulled his wagon out from under a bush. He eased me down off his back onto the wagon, placing my back at the handle end. He drew my good leg up to fit inside the wagon, and making a noose around my ankle he handed me the end of the rope so I could hold my bad leg up and keep it from bouncing. Then he began pushing me forward, instead of pulling me, so he could keep my back propped up with one hand while he pushed the wagon with the other.

The edge of the woods wasn't more than ten blocks from Crazy Eli's hovel, but even in the dark, I was afraid we would be stared at, and maybe even stopped by the police. Crazy Eli, I knew, had never been seen with another person before, and I didn't know what anybody would think if they saw us together. Maybe they would take me away from him, and arrest or insult him because they would think he was crazy, and therefore dangerous. I kept praying that this wouldn't happen. But I didn't have to worry, because we seemed to be invisible. Crazy Eli was taking me along secret pathways I had never known were there. By following alleyways, abandoned lots, and skinnying between garages and office and factory buildings, we managed to avoid the streets, except where we had to make a crossing.

It was thrilling because it was secret and dangerous and mysterious, and all of it new. We each had our secret pathways in the city and I was learning what his were.

When we got to his basement hovel, he slowly led me inside. I stayed in the wagon while he lit a fire in his fireplace. After he added three logs to the lit shavings, he helped me into the room's only chair, which I was sure he had made by hand. I didn't know that there was a shelf behind my head until Crazy Eli began to light a row of candles—nine in all, of which eight were held by flaring stems that came off a single base. The base held a single candle that was the tallest of the nine. Although it only partially lit the room, I was aware at once that this object was the only thing in Crazy Eli's hovel that had been made by someone other than himself. I also knew that it hadn't been purchased in an ordinary way because it had a feeling of holiness about it.

I wondered if he had lit it for me, and not for the light it was shedding. I was pretty sure that Crazy Eli, when alone, sat in the dark before his fireplace, which meant that these candles had a different purpose, though what that was I couldn't know.

I looked around the room. In the corner nearest the fireplace was a pallet, where Crazy Eli must have slept. There were a few utensils hanging from the wall of the fireplace, and from the beams, I could see rows of strung plants. There were two low benches, where Crazy Eli must have done his work, and perhaps have eaten as well. If there were any tools in the room, they must have been in the corners I couldn't see into.

To my surprise, I thought I could see the outline of a bicycle wheel in the corner farthest from me. I had never seen Crazy Eli on a bicycle, and so I couldn't help but wonder how often he used it, or where he went, or if he had a secret life none of us knew anything about.

I knew now that Crazy Eli was not crazy, as we had all believed. Something terrible must have happened to him once, which made something in him go slightly off. But that didn't mean that all of him was off. In fact, if he was worse off than any of us in one way, I was beginning to think that in still another way he was possibly better off than us. I wanted desperately to know what had happened to him, but I also knew that whatever it was it was none of my business. In fact, it wasn't anybody's business but his.

While I was busy with my thoughts, he began boiling some water in a kettle and sorting out some leaves of comfrey. I watched as he made a poultice that I knew was going to be for my leg. The first thing he had done when he had placed me in the chair was to give me some plant to chew on, and I began to notice now that the pain in my leg was beginning to ease because of it.

By the time the poultice was ready my eyes had become accustomed to the dark, and I began seeing things that were only a blur when we had first entered the room. Crazy Eli's room was like an inner sanctum, but not at all spooky. In fact, it was like what I dreamed my life would be like if I could live in a cave somewhere by myself. Everything in the room was handmade, and everything in the room was being used, or had been used, or would soon be used. Nothing was wasted, or extravagant, or unnecessary. And it was definitely a man's cave, a loner's cave, the cave of someone who was living his own life. No woman I knew would ever dare come into such a place.

While I sat there, with the poultice doing its work, and with my mind racing along with thoughts it had never had before, Crazy Eli was busy fashioning a crutch for me to walk with.

When he was done with his work he came over to me and grunted the way he had when he had first come to my rescue. I knew what he was saying, just as

I knew that he had stopped speaking because of some tragedy that must have happened a long time ago. It didn't mean that he didn't have words in him, or feelings, or thoughts. But did it mean that he no longer had any dreams?

I didn't think I could ever live without my dreams, but I knew now that whatever Crazy Eli had lost he had replaced with something better. Just as I knew that whatever that certain something was, it had begun when his ordinary dreams had ended.

When he began wheeling me back out of his cave, I knew that he was going to take me home. As he pushed me down the street, I guided the turns that had to be made, though I felt that he could have read my thoughts if he had wanted to.

When we got to the door of my house, he stood me up on my crutch, and once he knew I would be able to keep my balance, he knocked on the door. And then he was gone, disappearing into the same silence from which he had first appeared in the night.

the last muskie

SUMMER WAS ON its way again—at last. I had spent the winter boning up on my fishing books, and on Tom Brown's books on tracking. This was my year to catch a muskie. I was determined. No doubt about it. And one way or another it was going to happen.

I hadn't bothered to go out on opening day like everybody else. That was for amateurs. Besides, it's so cold at the start of the season that it's pure luck if you catch anything at all. I waited until everyone had their fill, so there wouldn't be anybody on the streams and lakes, before I got my line wet for the season.

Eagle Lake was deserted when I got there, just as I thought it would be. The water still hadn't warmed up. In another week or so the walleyes and pickerel would be running. The muskie were down deep, or hiding under shelves and fallen logs, and so they would be hard to find, and even harder to entice.

Muskie are the largest freshwater game fish in our part of the world. They're known to grow larger than ten feet, and one fish caught weighed over a hundred pounds. I wasn't figuring to catch a fish anything like that. A thirty-pounder would be a trophy fish, and not just for somebody my size, but for anyone. And anyhow, a thirty-pound muskie was about all I could handle with my tackle.

Eagle Lake was one of the more famous lakes in Wisconsin for catching muskie. We had fishermen coming up from Chicago, and lots of other places, to try their hand with Joe Kerensky as their guide. Old Joe, as he was called by us, lived in a shack on the lake. Eagle Lake was state-owned, but they let Old Joe take up quarters on the grounds because you couldn't think of Eagle Lake without thinking of Joe Kerensky.

They went together. And Old Joe wasn't just famous on Eagle Lake either, he was known far and wide, because he'd been written up in all the best sporting magazines as an expert on muskie fishing.

— two —

I DRAGGED MY CANOE out from where I kept it stashed in the undergrowth, and dragged it to the water's edge. Then I sat down on the bank. It was a ritual with me to sit on the bank and look out over the water before I began fishing. It was my way of fitting myself into the life of the water, and all the space surrounding Eagle Lake. I was asking permission of everything that existed to allow me to become a part of the world of this place while I was here. This was the only place were I felt I truly belonged.

I said aloud to the lake, "I'm going to catch a muskie today. I need to, and so I know I will. I've waited all winter for this day. Thank you!"

The water didn't answer. It shone green beneath

the towering trees and lay as still as a blanket of silk. Come summer, it would turn different shades of blue, but now it was the green of the surrounding fir trees that walled in its silence while casting their shadows over its unbroken surface.

I stepped into my canoe and took hold of the paddle. I paddled once and floated away from the bank. The canoe slowly turned its nose away from the shore, guided by a sudden gust of wind at my back.

Eagle Lake appeared to be shaped like a perfect bowl. But there were four coves, almost compass-exact. At Cove South, high in a Douglas fir stripped of its green needles, with its remaining branches broken and spindly, was an eagle's nest that the lake had been named after. I heard that the eagles had been here when man first discovered this lake.

Ordinarily, I would have headed for Cove South, especially if the eagles weren't visible over the lake, but not today—today there would be no time wasted. I had the rest of the afternoon to fish, but that was too little time for the catching of a muskie.

I passed Cove East, longingly, and headed for deeper water. A pair of blue-winged teal were swimming along the bank. They took no notice of me. As I approached the middle of the lake, an eagle flew high over my head. It made me feel alone and exposed, and in my mind, I could see myself as the eagle saw me. For a moment, I felt out of place, an intruder. I *do* belong here, I said to the eagle, though he was now gone from my sight.

I belong here because I feel more at home here than I do anywhere else. It isn't only the Indians, I continued, who can make of nature their home. But I knew I was lying. I wouldn't want to be here after dark, and I wouldn't want to live from the land the way Tom Brown, the famous tracker, was able to do— although that was my distant ambition.

I had reached the middle of the lake and began casting my spoon, retrieving it quickly. It was still day, and with the lake walled in by trees, I didn't have to worry about my canoe being blown into shore every fifteen minutes.

I kept casting and retrieving. I felt confident that I was going to catch a muskie, even though I knew the odds were all against me. I had never caught a muskie in my life, or even had one on my line. My dad had only caught two muskies in his whole life, and that was before he was married, when he could take a week or two off and go fishing in Canada with his buddies.

They'd fish night and day—because muskies also feed at night—and they weren't happy unless they brought home one or more trophy fish. My dad had one of his muskies mounted over the fireplace in his den.

Everyone who fished Eagle Lake fished for muskie. But not seriously. Not with the kind of devotion it takes to actually catch a muskie. All the local guys and kids that fished Eagle Lake were content to bring home a stringer of walleyes, pickerel, and perch, and, if they were lucky, an occasional northern pike.

After a good day's fishing, some guys would change rods and plugs and start casting for muskie, but it was a rare day when anyone actually hooked and landed a fish in this fashion.

— three —

I DIDN'T HEAR the boat until I heard the voice it belonged to. "Muskie fishing?" the voice said. I whirled around. It was Joe Kerensky, seated in his famous guide boat. I read the word *Lunge* painted in red on the side of his boat. Lunge was one of the less used names for muskies, the full name being muskellunge. I tried to catch my breath so I could speak, while I also tried to figure out how he could have come up on me unawares.

I had never spoken to Old Joe before, except for a couple of times when I was with my dad and had asked him a question about tackle and bait. Whenever Old Joe was on the lake with one of his fishing parties everyone knew to give him a wide berth. He was the king of the lake, that was for sure. And we showed him the proper respect.

I made a long, looping cast to demonstrate what I was doing, while I thought of an appropriate answer. "I'm going to catch a muskie today," I said, before I had thought out what I should say to Old Joe. I was surprised by my answer, and afraid of what he would think of me.

But if Old Joe thought I was crazy or something, he didn't let on. He seemed to be studying my line as it cut through the water on the retrieve. "Maybe," he said, at last, "you'll get one on, but if you do, that fish will take you to places from which you might never come back. I suggest you beach that craft and come aboard with me."

"Sure," I said, the word catching in my throat. I was too flabbergasted, thrilled, stunned, and disbelieving to say anything more. I finished reeling in my line and followed Old Joe to the landing.

I docked my canoe and got into his boat with my rod and gear in hand. I noticed at once that he had a rod with him, but for some reason, I didn't think he had come out to fish. Instead of heading for open water, Old Joe began rowing slowly along the bank toward Cove North. He was facing me as he rowed, but he wasn't looking at me. He wasn't looking at anything.

It took me awhile to figure out that he was listening. But listening to what? Was that his secret? Could he *hear* the muskies moving under water? Of course not! He caught muskies with skill and knowledge, not magic, not extrasensory perception! I wanted desperately to ask him what he was hearing—or listening to, or listening *for*—but I knew he wouldn't answer me because even if it could be explained with words. I was sure he wouldn't care to use the words it would take to tell it with.

He stopped rowing and dropped anchor. He was still facing me. He still hadn't turned or moved. He reached in his pocket and pulled out a pipe. He filled it, slowly. As he did, I studied his weather-beaten face. He had short grey hair that fell forward, naturally, and didn't look like it had ever been combed. His trimmed beard was white. He was square-built with short arms, broad, puffy hands, and stubby fingers. His face was lined and creased from age and weathering. But the thing I was really studying, as I looked at him, was how relaxed he was in his entire body. I had the feeling he never made a wasted move, or strained a muscle that didn't require straining. Maybe that was what the listening was about, or what I took the listening to be. Because everything he did was as effortless as it seemed his listening was.

He took the first puff from his pipe before he spoke. He was looking at me now. "See that submerged log behind me, at the edge of the cove?"

I nodded yes. A stem from the fallen tree ran out over the top of the water, and made casting over the invisible log that was beneath that branch impossible.

He went on, "It's resting on an underwater bar that's covered with weeds. That and the log make it the best muskie hole on this lake. But I never take people here. I tell them it's too hard to fish because of that limb that teases the water, and they believe me. I've gotten the locals to believe me, too.

"A lot of lures have fallen victim to that branch before they gave up," I said, giving him my agreement.

"I know," Joe said, "some of 'em are in my tackle box." He smiled for the first time.

I raised my rod, even though I knew enough not to cast until I'd been given instructions and permission. Old Joe puffed on his pipe and looked up at the trees. I looked up at the trees, after him, but there was nothing to be seen, as far as I could tell. I looked back at Old Joe. He was listening again. He slowly turned his head, and that was when I heard a small red squirrel chattering on the ground, running back and forth along the bank by the tree limb that extended over the water. I couldn't imagine what he was doing.

All at once he darted out on the limb, turned at midpoint, changed his mind again, and started back out again. The water beneath the squirrel began churning, sending a wave against the immediate bank. The squirrel lost his balance but was hanging onto the branch with his front legs, his back legs hanging free and his tail brushing the water's surface.

Suddenly I saw what looked like an alligator jaw open and close over the body of the squirrel, followed by a volcanic explosion that obliterated the sight of everything that had previously been there.

Old Joe turned back around, removed the pipe from his mouth and let out a cloud of smoke. "I've seen that happen before," he said. "I feel sorry for them squirrels, but that muskie deserves his feeding hole. He's been here longer than the eagles, and he'll probably be here after the eagles and us are gone.

"What beats me is why those critters go out on that limb, and why the message—since they do— never gets sent back to the others to stay away. You'd think they'd learn, but I guess critters have vices and weaknesses, just like humans do."

"Maybe they think that limb will take them out across the lake," I said.

"Maybe. Maybe not. I don't think it's up to us to find the answer."

I was dying to get my line in the water and over the head of that muskie that had just taken that squirrel for its lunch. When he broke water, I saw the configuration of the log Old Joe had mentioned. It wasn't directly below the limb, but extended out at an angle. It was obvious that the way to fish this hole was perpendicular to the log, and not out across it, as so many people had tried to do.

I mentioned this to Joe, for what it was worth. I was beginning to get the idea that this was a sacred spot with him, and that he wasn't going to let me fish here. But I was mistaken.

He smiled his approval when I made my observation. Then he slowly rowed out to a spot about fifteen yards from the bank, in line with the submerged log. He set anchor.

"That fish isn't small," he said, "but the rod and lure you are using are. That line of yours won't hold that fish, either."

He offered me his rod and took mine away. "Your rod is too limber. Muskies have tough, bony mouths and jaws. You wouldn't be able to strike hard enough with that rod to set the size hook you need to get the job done."

I tried to whip his rod but I couldn't. It was too heavy and stiff. I had tried out muskie rods at Mel's Sporting Goods Store, but I had never actually fished with one. My Dad's was packed away in the garage. He had promised it to me when I got older. On my sixteenth birthday. But that was nearly four years away.

I looked down at the plug. I wanted to ask what it was called, but I'd seen it before and should have known its name, so I kept my question to myself.

"You know where to place it," Joe said, "go ahead . . . wait!" he corrected himself, "let's see you cast out over open water first. You might make such a commotion over that fish he'll think you're bigger than he is—not that we want him to know the truth."

"What do you take his size to be?" I asked.

"Four feet, certain; maybe five or more. If that's the fish I think it is, he's been here maybe as long as I've been fishing this lake."

"Golly," I said. "Could be a record for this lake."

"You'd better hope not, your chances wouldn't be too good if he is."

"I'm catching a muskie today," I said.

"I know, you told me. Now take your time and cast out over there. Just relax. I want you to get the hang of it."

— four —

I HAD GOTTEN the hang of it quicker than I thought. And I had been casting for over an hour toward the bank and the fish that we both knew was there. But I couldn't raise him.

After a while, Joe had me switch to a wounded-minnow plug, and urged me to work it fast. "Persistence and repetition," he said. "If you get him angry he might strike. It takes five thousand casts on average to raise a muskie; did you know that? Just in case you're interested in percentages."

I wasn't interested in percentages or the law of averages, but I didn't bother to say so. I had already told him what I was going to do. I was concentrating with all my might on the muskie I knew was there, that I knew I could catch—if only I concentrated hard enough, and if I was determined in a way I had never been determined about anything before in my life.

I kept casting that plug beside the submerged log with such concentrated attention that nothing else existed for me. Time had stopped, and I was sure that I could and would will that muskie into taking my lure.

And then it happened. The water boiled over my plug, as if an underwater turbojet had come charging up from the depths. All I saw was white water charging over green, and then, as before, the alligator jaw of the muskie, and the flashing metallic shine of my plug, that was joined to the ferocious crater of the muskie's snout.

I heard, "Set the hook," and I did—without yet fully comprehending what had happened to me. "Again," came the call, and I set it again, "Again." And again I obeyed. And then I felt him on the line.

"Hold the rod high. The drag is set. Don't buck him. Up, up, hold it up! Let him take it, let him take it, let him take it. Good! He's going . . . good . . . good . . . good."

The muskie was gone, and with him the line that was singing out of the reel. Joe pulled anchor, and slowly our boat went the way of the fish, toward deeper water. "When he weakens, begin to reel in. Keep the line taut at all times. No slack, or he's lost. But don't pressure him."

I had come back to reality. But I was still trembling. I tried to keep my teeth from rattling, but it was no use. It made it impossible for me to talk. The shock of the strike had so dumbfounded me that if Joe hadn't hollered instructions I never would have been able to set the hook. But now he was on, and I was playing him. My determination, along with my will, was slowly returning.

"It's not going to be easy," I heard Joe say. "He should have broken water by now. It's only the biggest fish that never show themselves."

"Will the line hold him?"

"It's not the line or the rod I'm worried about."

"I'll hold him."

"You might have the strength, but it also takes savvy. This will be a long fight if it lasts. . . ."

I had let out a gasp. The line had gone dead in my hand. I was reeling in the slack, and there was nothing, absolutely nothing on the other end. "He's gone," I said. "Damn it, he's gone. I've lost him."

"Keep reeling, faster, faster," Joe shouted, watching my hands. Then he turned and looked beyond my rod. Just then I saw a flash of green passing under the boat, and in the next instant the muskie exploded on the other side, full length, coming completely out of the water, his red gills flashing, his snout extended, his teeth glistening in the sun.

Joe turned the boat instantly with his oar, freeing the action of my rod, which had nearly been pulled under the boat, and I quickly reeled in until my line was once again taut. This time he went deep, taking nearly all of my line before he weakened again and turned, allowing me to take control.

But before I could relax, he made another charge, and for the second time, the line went dead in my hand. This time he didn't crash to the surface. He came under the boat again, and stopped, rolling his serpentine body over, one eye showing, looking at us, while his ferocious mouth stayed closed.

"Now he knows who you are," Joe said.

— five —

THE SUN HAD BEGUN to set behind the trees before he tired. His runs had grown shorter, and little by little I was bringing him in. We had him to the boat once before, when he'd raised his snout and shaken his head, trying to loosen the plug. But this time, when I brought him in, he turned over on his side, as if the life had gone out of him.

Joe had been right; he was nearly my size in length.

"Tiger Muskie," Joe called out, when he saw his green striped sides. "The true fish of these waters, and the largest I've seen from this lake." He reached for his gaff, and when he did, he also picked up a lead pipe that I hadn't noticed before.

I reached over the side and touched the fish, that I thought of now as mine, and slowly slid my hand over the sleek body that was awesome even when still.

Joe looked from my hand to the fish's head and began to insert the gaff in his gills. "Don't!" I cried. "I don't want him. Remove the plug," I pleaded. "Please!"

Joe looked startled, but only for an instant. He quickly grabbed a pair of pliers from his open tackle box, and freed the plug from the muskie's mouth. He lay there for a moment, moving nothing but the tail that quivered and agitated the surface of the water.

He knew he was free—I was sure of that. But he waited, and then slowly—ever so slowly—he sank, turning into his upright position, until only his dark back was visible, and then he blended into the water, and only the remembered image of him remained.

— six —

WE ROWED BACK to the landing in silence. It was nearly dark when I leaped out of the boat onto the dock. I was holding onto the mooring ropes. Joe remained seated, holding the oars above water, our eyes now on each other.

I wanted to ask him what I didn't need to know. I already knew that the muskie had always been his secret. And that it was the one muskie he didn't want caught. Maybe by having let his muskie go free until now he was paying for all the muskies he had helped to take out of this lake.

Or maybe it was something else.

But he hadn't interfered with my need to catch the muskie—in fact, without him I couldn't have done it. Nor did he interfere when I asked him to let the muskie go.

No, none of this was important. The only really important thing was that we now shared a secret—and we knew it was the kind of secret we didn't need to discuss.

"I never learned your name," Joe said, breaking the silence between us.

"Alvin Tolliver," I said.

"You're Jake Tolliver's boy, then," Joe said. "I've seen you around."

"Yes," I said.

"I'm pleased to meet you, Alvin."

"I'm pleased to meet you, Mr. Joe."

"You come and see me sometime. I live up from

the West Cove. Park your canoe by my boat. You'll see the trail."

"I'll come soon," I said, and turned for the path that would take me home.

the owl and the lady

— one —

I WAS SITTING on the curb whittling a bird out of pear wood when Hannah Terchouni drove up in her jalopy pickup and came to a halt not ten feet from where I was working. I took out a piece of #2 sandpaper from my shirt pocket and began sanding one of the wings.

I'd never seen the Bird Lady this close up before, and so I wanted to have a good look. I heard her set the hand brake, open the door, and jump onto the macadam roadway. She was wearing her trademark bandanna and red-and-black checkered hunting shirt. It hung loose over a polka-dot skirt that fell over her L. L. Bean boots. The combination was about as appetizing as chocolate-covered anchovies served on a bed of thistles. But I guess it suited her. It certainly set her apart. If you were the town character, it was just as well not to pretend otherwise.

I don't know why she was called the Bird Lady except that we gave everyone nicknames whenever possible. Actually, I heard that she was as interested in four-legged creatures as she was winged creatures. Anything that was hurt, wounded, or sick, that she could nurse back to health.

"What's that you're whittlin' son?"

I couldn't believe she had just spoken to me. I tried not to sound alarmed or anxious. "A bird."

"I can see that! What kind?"

"No kind. It's just a bird."

"Uhm. Just a bird," she repeated, her voice indicating neither pleasure nor disappointment.

"My name's Alvin," I said, trying to lengthen the conversation. "Alvin Tolliver."

She stepped over the curb and walked behind me into Papa Foley's Market. "What kind of bird?" I asked myself, so I could make a new answer. "My kind of bird. If I wanted it to look like a real bird, I wouldn't be whittlin' would I? I'd take photographs. As soon as I earn enough for a pair of binoculars, I'm going to start saving up for a real good camera. The one I've got is okay, but it's not professional enough."

I was still deep in thought, but not exactly talking to myself, when she came out of Foley's with a sack of cornmeal, and another of beans, and threw them, one at a time, into the back of her pickup.

When she turned to go back inside for the rest of her supplies, I got up and walked into Mel's Sporting Good Store, whose door had just opened for the day. I wanted to have another look at Mel's binoculars.

— two —

TO TELL THE TRUTH, I had been fascinated by Hannah for some time. I figured we were both interested in the wilds, but probably very differently. My approach was tracking, sighting, and photographing. My trophies were strictly limited to what I could snap and have a souvenir of forever, and what I could see that I didn't shoot—because I wasn't a hunter—but that I would keep in my memory. It wasn't like one was better; they were just very different.

Tracking, of course, was my method—once I got to be good enough. My favorite books, my prize possessions, were Tom Brown's books on tracking.

Maybe I'd be a tracker myself someday and rescue people who got lost in the wilds; or a conservationist, who helped to preserve the vanishing wilderness; or else a guide in Canada, providing I was willing to leave my home in northern Wisconsin, which I actually wasn't planning to do. Not now or in the future, either.

— three —

ON THE FIRST CLEAR Saturday in May, after all the snow had melted, and the ground had thawed enough not to be too muddy to travel on with a bike, I took off on the trail bordering the McCann River and headed north of town.

I had been bicycling for nearly an hour before I realized I was heading toward Hannah's place. I had no intention of visiting her, or anything like that, but it occurred to me that I might explore the woods that bordered her land on the south. That was where the river trail ended. Her woods were posted, but since I didn't intend to fish or hunt, I didn't think the signs applied to me.

The squirrels would be busy now, as would the bears, both of them having ended their hibernation. Of course, I had never actually seen bears myself—only their tracks and droppings—but I'd heard them plenty, making their owl-like sounds, announcing that they were once more about and would be taking up where they left off from the winter before.

I was moving along, slow and easy, hoping to hear the drumming of the ruffed grouse, and also half-hoping to spot a bear in the distance.

I was in luck. I hadn't gone a hundred yards into the woods, when I heard the unmistakable drumming of a cock partridge in the distance. I moved forward as quietly as I could, and then, at once, I saw it perched on a fallen log in the distance, its neck puffed out, with its wings beating a staccato rhythm against the log on which it stood.

I dared not go closer, so I sat on the ground and tucked my legs under me. I was hoping to see the hen. I didn't know if she was close by, or if the cock was calling her from a distance.

I was so concentrated on seeing her that I began to notice every movement around me, and I could hear sounds I had never heard before. What puzzled me was that I couldn't make out what any of them were. All I knew was that each sound was natural and right, and that together they blended perfectly. It was like a woodland symphony but one that only a perfectly attuned ear could hear correctly.

I wished I knew which insect and creature belonged to each of the sounds I was hearing. Slowly, and then with increasing clarity, I began to hear a sound that I knew was unnatural because it didn't harmonize with the others, but stood out, the way a harsh sound does, separating itself from the noises around it.

Whatever it was, natural or unnatural, it was some distance away. I got up, forgetting the grouse for the moment, and began slowly and carefully to walk toward what sounded like a tiny broom being beaten against the surface of the earth.

Whenever the beating stopped, I stopped also. It wasn't long before I was in sight of whatever it was that was making the noise that I knew by now was a living creature, one that was engaged in an activity that was beyond my imagining.

The noise seemed to be coming from the tree just before me, but I could see no movement, until, cautiously circling, I saw a white feather beating on the ground inside the hollowed base of the tree.

I got down on my hands and knees and looked inside. I was amazed to see a great horned owl lying on its side, with one foot caught in a snag. The noise I had heard was that of its free wing beating against the side of the tree trunk. When it saw me peering in at it—our noses hardly six inches apart—it froze and stared at me, startled and probably as confused as I was. I doubt that it knew what I was, and I was glad it didn't, because that would have scared it even more.

I started talking softly to the owl and without thinking much about it, I reached in and freed its caught leg. As I did, it snapped at me hard with its beak, but to my surprise it didn't hurt. I think it knew that I didn't intend any harm. This didn't mean it wasn't frightened of me, because it was. I could see fear in its eyes. But I knew that it was as puzzled as it was frightened.

I tried talking to it in a soothing voice, before I reached in, carefully avoiding its talons. Gently cradling its body with one hand, I maneuvered its legs through the opening.

It was only when I had pulled it free that I saw that the wing it had been lying on was broken. I pressed its good wing down against its side with my other hand, and looked into its eyes, as it stared back into mine.

I was as puzzled as the owl, but differently. I knew if I let it go it would soon be food for some fox or bear. But what was I going to do with it? At the same time that I was worrying about its predicament, I was also admiring its beauty, which caused me to stroke its good wing. Although it was a large bird, I was surprised at how much smaller it was in my hands than I had imagined a great horned owl to be. I was also wondering how it had managed to break its wing.

I was thinking fast now. I had to, because the owl was becoming agitated. My first decision was to keep it. In that case, I told myself, you'd better get him out of here as quickly as you can.

When I got to the clearing, I was surprised to find myself at the edge of a barnyard. I knew at once that this was Hannah's land because it was different from any farmyard I had seen before. There were ducks and geese everywhere, squawking, honking, and running back and forth and all round, as if they were rehearsing for some delirious barnyard drama.

There were birdhouses hanging from every tree, and more bird feeders than I could count. There was a salt lick at the edge of the woods beyond the barn, and there were six cats stationed at the entrance of the barn. They were staring at me, letting me know that I was an outsider.

"What do you have there?"

I was so startled, I nearly jumped out of my shoes. That was when I saw Hannah, sitting on a tree stump in the midst of all the scurrying ducks and geese. She'd fit in so naturally that I hadn't even seen her.

"An owl with a broken wing." I answered, when I had regained my composure. "It got itself caught in a hollow log. Don't ask me how."

"Uhm," she said, and beckoned me forward to her perch. "Funny things happen, even to animals. Maybe it didn't know it was sharing that tree with another critter, and they ran into each other, one going in, the other coming out."

"Sounds reasonable," I said.

"Nothing's reasonable, everything's possible," Hannah laughed. "What are you going to do with it now?"

"I hadn't gone that far with my thinking. I was hoping, if you were here, that you could help out."

"Come inside," she said, getting to her feet. I followed her towards the ramshackle, unpainted house. The owl seemed lighter in my hand now, its wing damp from the sweat of my palm. I realized that I had begun to relax. Maybe, I thought, the owl had, too.

I hesitated at the door, while I took in the strong animal smells, the mixture consisting mostly of cats, with other smells unknown to me. Altogether, it smelled more like a barn than a house.

The door had hardly closed behind me when the parrots started screeching. "Don't be afraid," she said, and put her hand out to take the owl. With her gloved hand, she grasped it by the feet, gently but firmly. The owl took one peck at her hand and then looked up at her, its eye cocked to see better who she was.

She stroked its back and laid it gently on the kitchen table, and motioned me to hold it there while she gathered what she would need to make a splint.

I wondered how much the owl understood. Or if it understood anything of what was happening to it now. Until this moment, it had seemed a broken thing, only a replica of the great bird I had seen only a few times before in my life, when I'd been enthralled by its size and beauty and its fierce pride—if that's what it was. I wondered if she would be able to restore it again to its wondrous self.

— four —

"YOU SEE, IT'S FINISHED," the old lady said, pushing her tools aside. "Now we give it a temporary home. It's hungry and thirsty and it needs to rest. It's very young."

She smiled for the first time, giving her face an altogether new look—relaxed, warm, and happy. I was no longer afraid of her and smiled back; and then we both gave a little laugh of triumph—both for the owl, and for our combined effort to save its life.

"Let's go to the barn," she said, "and rig up a cage for this beautiful bird."

I hadn't thought about what was in the barn, so what happened next really knocked me for a loop. The stalls had all been turned into different-sized cages. We passed a raccoon, then a deer, a fox, a porcupine, followed by a series of small box-like cages stacked neatly from the floor up, each cage holding a different bird. In the very next stall; which had also been converted to a cage, was a coyote. It snarled at us as we approached.

"This one I can't befriend. Even when I feed him, all he shows me is his anger. It will be the first animal I've had that I will be completely happy to see leave."

I was staring at the coyote, who was slowly backing up while growling and showing his teeth.

"Of course I am happy to see *all* of them go back to their natural homes, but I miss them, too."

"It's only natural," I said.

She smiled down at me and walked to the corner cage that was as large as the one that held the coyote. It was matted with straw, like the others, but with a perch near the top. She opened the door and placed the owl inside. It stood up, in a perfectly frozen posture, looking both silly and cute in the stocking that had been fitted over its body, exposing only its head, good wing, and feet. It turned its head halfway around, surveying its surroundings.

— five —

IT WAS HARD to concentrate on my schoolwork or anything else during the next week. School seemed irrelevant, boring, and not at all real. I was waiting, very impatiently, for Saturday to arrive so I could visit the Bird Lady—and of course the owl that I thought of now as *our* bird.

Her place was like a free-running zoo. But it was a zoo for animals, not for animal-watching people. She was there to serve the animals; the animals were not there to serve her in some entertaining way, which is how I had always seen zoos before.

Zoos made me angry, but her place made me feel happy inside, and proud. At the same time, even though it seemed perfectly natural in one way, I had to ask myself why Hannah did what she did. And even how she thought up doing such a thing. As far as I knew, she was the only person in the whole world interested in doing the kind of work she did.

On Saturday, I told my mom I was going to go

scouting. I left right after breakfast. My father was still in bed, snoring away, when I walked down the hall, past his room, to get my jacket.

I went to the garage to fetch my bike. The lawn was wet with dew and there were dozens of spider webs that had been spun the night before scattered across the lawn. They glistened under the morning sun.

When I arrived, she was in her yard feeding her free-roaming chickens out of a bowl that was cupped under her left arm.

I waved at her, and felt foolish as soon as I did. She looked up at me but didn't respond. I got down from my bike, so as not to scare the chickens, and walked toward her.

"I was expecting you," she said, her back half turned, throwing sprays of seeds to her chickens. She cast the remaining seeds directly from the bowl with a sweeping motion of her right hand. She turned and walked toward the barn. I followed after her, knowing she expected me to. Once inside she opened the refrigerator door inside the barn door. I hadn't noticed the refrigerator the first time I was there. She pulled out a dead white rat. "Come," she said, "it's time to feed your owl."

The owl jumped down from its perch as soon as he saw us approaching. Holding the rat by the tail, she flipped it into the owl's cage. He leaped on it at once with his feet, making a swift twisting motion over the rat that made a popping sound.

"What was that?" I asked

"He was killing it."

"But the rat was already dead!"

"He didn't know that. But even if he had, he would have done it anyhow, out of instinct."

"I've never seen anything like that before," I said.

"Of course you haven't." She looked at me and smiled. "See that white, oblong ball over there?" She was pointing to an object inside the cage. "What do you think that is?"

When I didn't answer, she opened the cage, picked it up, and brought it out for me to hold in my hand. "I still don't know what it is," I said.

"That's yesterday's meal, digested and excreted."

"But it's white," I said. "Or rather, greyish-white."

"That wasn't excreted the way you think; it was upchucked." She began to slowly pull the fur ball apart, revealing the rat's crushed bones. "It's all here. If you knew how, you could reassemble that rat. Don't you think that would make a good 4-H project?"

I couldn't help but laugh. "That would be the day," I said.

"Come along; it's time to release the porcupine." We walked over to its pen. Before opening the cage door, she slipped on a pair of thick leather gloves. The porcupine didn't seem to object to being picked up. In the corner of his cage was a half-eaten old shoe. "Shouldn't we take that along?" I asked.

"He won't need that anymore. He'll go back to eating trees—now that he's strong enough to climb."

We walked out of the barn and headed for the woods. "Where will you release him?" I asked.

"Hereabouts, among the young cedar trees. His home wasn't that far from here. If he wants to go back he'll find the way." She placed him on the ground. When she brought her gloved hands away, I was amazed to see that they were covered with the porcupine's quills.

Hannah laughed good-naturedly at the puzzled expression on my face. "They don't shoot their quills, they simply release them to the touch. They stick because they're barbed."

"I didn't know that," I muttered, cautiously picking one of the quills from her glove and examining it. The porcupine had turned and was waddling off toward the woods. He was a funny sight.

"You look happy," I said. She was watching the porcupine and smiling to herself. We began walking back toward the barn. I didn't know what made me say that to her. It wasn't only that I felt completely relaxed with her, and at home within these surroundings, but I felt at home with myself. And with her. It was a new feeling, and one that I did not want to go away.

"Life *can* bring happiness," she said, answering the question I had nearly forgotten was in my mind.

"How?" I asked, thinking not about what she had said, but about what I was feeling.

"You saw the owl needed help, and so you found a way to help it. That is how it happens with me. Living in the woods, and watching the hunters come in the fall, disrupting the flow of life of this place and obliterating the tempo that I also belong to and live by, I realized one day—and then began to see in detail—all the suffering they were causing. Not just because of the animals they killed, but all those that were wounded, or confused and agitated and terrified. When that happens, when their lives become violated, the animals, in their confusion and terror, begin to have accidents. And so I help them to recover. Because I see their plight, I become responsible for their safety and their healing.

"Man is the most gifted animal on this planet, and that means he should be the steward of what is here. But he is not. He has not taken responsibility because he has not yet seen what he has done."

— six —

A FEW WEEKS PASSED before I had a chance to visit Hannah Terchouni again. When I rode up to her place, it was as if I had been there just the day before.

"Come," she said, as I walked with my bike to where she was standing. "Today the owl goes free. Maybe."

Once again, she removed a white rat from the refrigerator and carried it to the owl. He went through his ritual of killing the dead rat. Before eating it, he did something very strange. He looked up at Hannah and preened. She answered my puzzled look. "He thinks I'm his mother and is letting me know what a good hunter he is."

"Not only good," I laughed, "but proud."

After the owl had eaten its rat, Hannah entered his cage and undid the splint on his wing, and then, cupping his body in her gloved hands, she released her hold on him so he could fluff out. Then she carried him out of the barn and placed him on the ground.

We waited for him to spread his wing and test its strength to be sure he was ready to be released.

She picked him up by the feet with one hand, while holding him upright with her other hand. We walked to the first stand of poplars beyond the clearing. When she released him, he flew at once to the top of the nearest tree.

"He's strong enough to hunt," Hannah declared, "but it may be a couple of days before he'll be able to catch his own food. That rat he just ate is going to have to hold him."

"It's practically a miracle," I said.

She dropped her gaze and stared at me for a moment before speaking. "There isn't anything you can't say that about."

She turned then and went back into the barn to care for her other animals. I watched her disappear inside, and then I got on my bike and very slowly rode down the lane, listening to the crickets in the grass, while the wind whistled through the poplar grove, ruffling the feathers of the owl that by now was heading home.

the tracker

— one —

IT WAS SPRING AGAIN and the ducks and geese were flying north. Their flocks would soon be pouring into
Noricon Marsh. It was their calls in the air and their
quacking in the marsh grasses that meant to me that
spring was here. They thrilled me with their masterly
grace when in flight, and they amused me when they
came to ground and attempted to negotiate earthly
space, waddling on their webbed feet that their squat
heavy bodies threatened to crush. But when I pictured
them in my mind, it was always in flight, outfitted in
their magnificently colored uniforms, their wings and

heads and bodies differently colored and resplendently hued.

Noricon Marsh was the largest spread of federally protected land in all of Wisconsin. It was maintained as a breeding ground for waterfowl, and it was therefore a haven for bird watchers. But it wasn't ducks alone that made Noricon Marsh famous. At its center, there stood a dry piece of land that rose above it like a low-lying cloud. Because it was surrounded by the marsh, it was unreachable. Several people had tried and failed to pole through the thickly matted marsh grasses on a skiff. But they had all failed.

The mound was symmetrical, and according to aerial survey, it covered three acres of ground. I had once walked around the marsh on an overnight camping trip, just to prove to myself what I already knew to be true. There was something about the mound's unnatural perfection—or perhaps supernatural perfection—that made it both enchanting and eerie to behold.

I had, after years of exploration, found a passage that brought me to within two hundred yards of the mound. It lay through a large stand of alders, thick with underbrush. Beyond the alders, the land rose ever so slightly, making a razor-backed ridge that was invisible until you were there upon it and could feel the land falling away from you on both sides. It made me wonder if it hadn't once been a trail.

Every spring I cut a new zigzag path through the alders.

There was still another reason why I had always been attracted to Noricon Marsh. It was believed to be the domain of the famous Indian tracker, Philip Sunbear.

Few people knew him, and even fewer people had ever seen him, but he was as famous among us as the marsh itself.

Philip Sunbear did not have a known address. When the state police needed him to track down an escaped criminal, or to find some campers or hikers who had gotten lost in the woods, they would only be able to reach him through his sister, who lived in the hamlet of Belinda with others of her tribe.

— two —

IT WAS AT NOONDAY, late in April, that I cut my spring trail through the alders. I was sitting, facing the mound, with my back up against a large rock, eating a sandwich.

It was one of those hazy days of spring that kept threatening to turn in a definite direction—but whether what would follow would be rain, wind, sleet, or a glorious day of full sun and warmth was impossible to tell.

At the moment, the weather favored the ducks, who were, as always, very busy with their quacking and crazy zigzag flights through the tall marsh grasses. I had spotted mallards, black ducks, blue- and green-winged teal, pintails, and a lone canvasback—my favorite duck because it was becoming scarce.

I kept seeing little puffs of smoke that I couldn't distinguish or identify rising from the mound. At first I thought I was seeing things, but when it continued, and I discounted one by one the various things it might be—like cattail down floating up from the stream bed nearby—I decided that, whatever it was, it was the result of human doing.

I decided to have a closer look and began walking out on the razor-backed ridge that would take me within two hundred yards of the mound.

I was startled by a squirrel that jumped onto the path in front of me, and began running as fast as his three good legs would carry him. His left hind foot appeared to be broken.

I started running after him, without thinking why I was doing so. In a matter of minutes, we came to the tall grasses of the marsh. I slowed my step, but the squirrel never hesitated, leaping off the dry surface of the ridge, in a long, arching jump that landed him on a log that pointed straight into the marsh.

I almost couldn't believe my eyes. I stood stock-still and waited, and then I heard a light thud that sounded like the squirrel making another leap from one wooden surface onto another. Then everything went completely still. Even the ducks had stopped their flying. And with it their quacking.

There was only one thing to do. I leapt onto the narrow log and felt it sink under my weight. Slowly it rose, holding me precariously aloft. I cautiously went the way of the squirrel, and like him, I soon came to a plank that I suspected I would find.

It too was a log, but with one side sheared to make a flat running surface, that made walking as easy as the log had made it hard.

Parting the grasses as I went, I was soon in sight of the mound. And then, almost before I knew it, I was there, standing on its surface.

— three —

I NEVER SAW the squirrel again. The grasses on the mound were deceptively tall. They rose to my shoulders. I slowly worked my way to the top. When I reached the rounded cap of the hill, I was able, for the first time in my life, to see the entire marsh at once. The ducks, in varying flights, were visible everywhere. I could also see them puddling through the marsh grasses, in the slate grey waters.

I couldn't believe where I was. It felt like I was on the hub of this gigantic sphere of whirling activity that was sweeping over me and around me faster than I could think, almost faster than I could feel, or fully appreciate what had just taken place.

My eyes wandered down the base of the mound, where I could see the ducks had matted the grasses into bedding stations. This was their sleeping and resting ground, and also where they mated. All at once, I realized that I could be seen from where I was standing. The grasses in which I stood had been knocked down by the wind and scarcely reached my waist. If I was able to see around the circumference of the marsh, it meant that I, in turn, could be seen from every single point of the marsh's perimeter.

I quickly sat down, feeling vulnerable and scared, as if I hadn't the right to be where I was. Once I was seated, I felt secure and safe, and now the feeling of wonder swept over me again. I could just see over the waving grasses, and unless someone was looking through binoculars, I didn't think they would pick me up. My hair was nearly the same color as the dried yellow grasses that hadn't yet turned their summer green.

Now I was alone, as alone as I had ever been in my life. It felt wonderful. I knew what the mountain men must have experienced, guys like Jim Bridger, who saw sights never before seen by any white man.

The ducks must have had a similar feeling about their freedom, because here they were protected against hunters and other predators.

I watched those in the distance trailing across the sky like bands of ribbons, floating down and up, as if the wind were waving them into motion.

Closer in, the different pairings and groupings rose and fell throughout the marsh, seeking new places to feed, and perhaps other ducks they wished to become acquainted with.

I hadn't noticed the sun slipping in the sky, probably because I kept changing my position on the mound as different ducks caught my fancy.

I watched, entranced, as a flock of Canada geese rose from the marsh, fell into formation and headed north for the nesting ground they were named after. They reached the horizon and flew across the face of the sun, their moving bodies silhouetted by the flaming ball shimmering on the rim of the land. Far, far in the distance I could hear the hoot of the great horned owl.

The marsh was suddenly suffused with burning orange light, causing the water to shimmer and glow with its color.

I sat entranced until the sun was set, watching the light gradually fade, as the sun at my back sank beneath the horizon. The change in light caused me to realize what I hadn't thought of before that moment—that I was two hours from home, and that I would have to hurry if I wanted to get out of the marsh before nightfall.

I scrambled down the hill as fast as I could. I startled myself by jumping a family of mallards that had come on land to rest for the night. I stopped to catch my breath. Their frightened quacking had disturbed the tranquil calm of the marsh, which had suddenly gone dead silent. It sent an eerie chill up my spine.

I began searching for the log. I was certain I was in the right spot but the ridge was nowhere in sight.

I kept walking back and forth along the base of the mound, peering into the marsh, puzzled and frustrated by its mysterious disappearance. Then it occurred to me that, because I had taken so many different positions atop the mound, I may have lost my orientation. There was only one way to find out, and that was to climb back up to the top of the mound.

The minute I got to the summit and looked out, I knew I was lost. Everything looked the same. I tried to see if the trail I had first made was visible. But the only trail that was visible was the one I had made just now. The pressed grasses of my first trail had long since sprung back to their original shape. Then I remembered the alder grove I had come through on my way to the mound.

I searched the growing darkness, but what I saw was not one alder grove but three. But I knew that the alder grove I had come through was the one closest to the mound. I strained to see which of the three was the closest, but in the settling dark, I wasn't able to be sure. I quickly eliminated one of them and chose between the remaining two.

As I scurried down the hill, I remembered that the log I had come across on had stopped a good three feet short of the base of the mound. I remembered having to back up a step before leaping onto dry land.

If I had the right spot then it had to be there—somewhere within a radius of ten yards—but it had grown too dark to see, and I wasn't sure if I would have been able to distinguish it among the shadows.

I took off my shoes and socks and started to wade in. The water rushed up at once to my knees, and the tangled grasses attacked my feet, causing me to stumble and lose my balance. I pulled myself free and got back on land.

I knew, as I put on my shoes and socks, that it was now too late. I would not be able to find my way back before morning. I had begun to shake from the cold, and also from fear. Without the warming sun, the marsh had grown damp, chilling my bones. My only protection was the jacket I had thought to wear. I didn't know if it would be enough to get me through the night.

I sat down and tried to collect my thoughts. I wondered if there would be a search party. Even if there were, they would never think to look for me here. And of course, they couldn't reach me even if they tried. All I had on me was a book of matches. I suppose if they came, I could light my matches. It wouldn't get me any closer to home, but at least they would know where I was. And then it hit me, I hadn't told my parents where I was going. That was it then; I was trapped.

I was shivering from the cold when I took out my knife and began cutting grasses to lay over me against the increasing cold.

Twenty minutes or more had gone by. I lay on the ground and arranged the grasses over myself as best I could. It was only then that I noticed the vastness of the night sky above, with all the white stars perfectly jeweled into place.

Without my being aware of it, the day had changed. It was now clear and windless and dry. I could almost feel the temperature drop. I gave a shudder, not from the cold, but from the realization that it would be twelve hours or more before I would see daylight again.

Out of the corner of my eye, I saw something move at the edge of the sky. I couldn't tell if it was a light or the illusion of light because it came and went, rising and disappearing.

I tried to still my breathing. It increased in size, and I realized that it was very close to me. Then I caught a whiff of something, and I knew what it was—smoke. I hadn't yet made the connection between this and the smoke I had observed while I was eating my sandwich at the edge of the alder grove.

I got up and walked, slowly and silently, towards where the smoke was coming from, watching it rise, seemingly from the surface of the earth. I moved ahead with caution, as I came nearer and nearer its source.

Now I was before it, and watched it gently streaming up through the tall grasses. I was even more puzzled than before. I knelt carefully, attempting to still my fear, and slowly spread the grasses apart.

Curling up through the smoke, and the black hole it issued from, a voice said, "Do not be afraid."

I gave a jump backward and fell on my back.

"Hold your breath and enter through the smoke hole. I am in the cave. There is a small fire here inside."

I was tempted to run—and I would have if I hadn't been marooned on this island. I got back on my knees, wondering who the voice belonged to. I never expected to hear a voice coming from a hole in the ground, but the voice was both soothing and assuring.

I crept forward, very slowly, and once again parted the grasses above the smoke. Only then did I see a glint of light inside the hole that the smoke was issuing from.

"Do not be afraid," the voice said again. "The hole opens immediately into a cave."

I closed my eyes, stuck my head into the opening, and squirmed forward, twisting my body through the hole. When I opened my eyes, I saw a red glow from the fire and a dark figure beside it on the ground. I crawled toward the light and the human form, and as I did, everything came into focus.

"You are brave," the Indian said. "I was afraid you would run away."

"Who are you? How did you know I was here?"

"I saw you come across this afternoon, and I've been watching you ever since. I knew you were lost even before you did."

"You're Philip Sunbear, the tracker, aren't you? Those are your logs I came across on, aren't they? What are you doing here in this cave, anyhow, if you don't mind my asking?"

"Not so fast. Warm yourself. You are still shaking from the cold."

I let out a sigh of relief. The tracker laughed and handed me a strand of deer jerky. "I'm boiling water for tea. After you've warmed yourself we can talk."

"Can I ask you something?"

The tracker nodded his assent and fed a small stick to the fire.

"What kind of place is this we're on?"

"Before I answer that I would like to know how you found your way here."

"A three-legged squirrel led me here," I laughed. "No kidding. He only had three legs that worked, and he came out of nowhere and went darting down that razor-backed trail that's invisible until you are right on top of it—and I followed."

"I see," the tracker said. "There are no squirrels in this marsh. That was an omen. When certain animals behave in a peculiar way it means they are not of this world, but of the spirit world.

"Now I will answer your question. This place is sacred. By 'this place' I mean this spot. Because it is sacred, my forefathers built this mound here."

"Wait a minute! You mean to tell me this mound is manmade?"

"That's right, and you may be the first white man to have stepped foot on it."

"That explains its shape then. Of course! But what about this cave?"

"This cave was made when the mound was made. This is where I have fasted in the past, and where I received my vision quest."

"I want to know something," I said.

"You've been given enough to think on. Now you must drink some of this herbal tea, and rest. Tomorrow we will resume our talk."

— four —

I WAS AWAKENED by the honking of geese overhead. The cave was in semi-darkness, the fire was extinguished and its ashes removed, and the tracker was gone.

I sat up and looked around at the curved walls. I knew my parents would be very worried, but I also knew I was safe here. I got to my feet and worked my way back through the smoke hole and into the light of a new day that was just dawning.

The tracker was seated at the crest of the mound. He motioned me forward with his raised hand.

When I took my place beside him he asked me to repeat, as exactly as possible, all the thoughts that had gone through my head when I realized the night before that I was trapped on the mound.

When I finished, he said, "You did well under the circumstances. Now you may ask me your question before you go home so your parents will know you are still alive."

"Why did the squirrel lead me here? If he was an omen, like you say, then what was he an omen of?"

"He led you to me, because it was time. I have known of you for some time now. You have been seeking in the wilderness for most of your young life. Do you know what your search is for, or even what you seek?"

"Not really—not exactly. When I was younger, I thought I wanted to be a conservationist. Then I thought I wanted to be a fishing guide, and later someone who healed animals. Maybe a veterinarian. I don't know for sure. I only know that I'm alive when I'm in the woods in a way that I am not alive at any other time."

"What is your wish then?"

"To be a tracker, like you. I don't know if that's my final wish, but I don't think I can be happy until I can track and stalk, and be one with everything that lives in the wilds."

"Then I will teach you."

I didn't know what to say. I would never have had the nerve to ask Philip Sunbear to be my teacher and guide, though it was my greatest fantasy. "I never would have asked you," I said. "I didn't think I had the right. I can't believe you really mean it."

"These things are written. In time, you will know why it is written—a long, long time from now, perhaps. Even I do not know why I must teach you, I only know that I must. But we needn't think about any of this now. It is time now for you to go home. Soon we will begin."

sweat lodge
and vision

IT WAS SUNDAY. The summer had passed since my adventure on the sacred mound. I hadn't mentioned Philip Sunbear to my parents because they would not have understood. I had begun to wonder how much I understood from that day. When I had left him, I felt that a change had taken place in me, but in the days that followed the memory became dimmer and dimmer.

Because of my confusion, and a need I couldn't name, I suspended all my usual activities. I had even stopped seeing my friends, and my parents were beginning to look at me sideways. I knew they were whispering about me behind my back.

To be a tracker. Wasn't that what I wanted? But if

so, why had my moment of clarity with Philip turned into this mass of confusion and anxiety? He said he would teach me. Was this part of the teaching? If he knew who I was without knowing me, could he be teaching me without seeing me?

Whenever I felt lost in the past, I had gotten on my bike and ridden out to the country. Sometimes I would go down to the river and talk to the moving water. I knew somehow that I would be listened to, and this comforted me and gave me the feeling of belonging to something large enough to hold me in its thoughts without interfering with mine.

Lately, my thoughts were beginning to form pictures, and the one that repeated itself most often was the picture of the willow grove I passed on my rides into the country. There are certain sights in nature that I am so aligned with that I feel they imbue me with their beauty and sense of being.

The willow grove was such a place for me. It was framed by tall grasses, and sat in a depressed hollow that seemed to have arranged itself especially for this grove of willows. The willows' leaves, now in autumn, had turned from green to yellow that contrasted with their grey-green bark.

I rode out to it now, and stopped to admire the changing scene, made more brilliant by the sun, which had just broken through a heavy cloud. It was then I noticed for the first time that there was a trail from the road leading in the general direction of the grove. I wondered if it was a deer trail or one made by man. I could not tell. I had never entered the grove before because I was content to admire it from a distance, as a picture of something perfectly realized that didn't require participation or scrutiny on my part.

But something prompted me to follow. Something that knew what I did not, beckoning me silently and mysteriously into this region I had never explored. This time I didn't need an omen in the form of a three-legged squirrel—because it was more than curiosity that was calling me.

How I sensed all this in a single moment, I cannot say. It was as if the confusion I had been suffering all these weeks had shaped itself into one single instance of clarity, and I knew with some part of myself that understanding did not always come from my head but from a deeper part that I could only call my feelings.

I walked a short way forward before laying my bike down in the grasses at the side of the snakelike trail.

Slowly, I entered the willow grove, feeling its stillness, and the hushed silence that surrounded me. I moved hesitantly forward, and when I turned around, the world of a moment before completely disappeared. I moved forward again before stopping abruptly, enthralled by the trees' delicate branches moving upward toward what they could see but I could not.

It was then I felt their life as strongly as if they were a human body—but unlike people, they didn't require separate identities because they were clearly one. Is this what we were missing? I was shaken by the thought, but my insight went even deeper; I saw that it was only by giving to others that we could break this illusion that we are separate and therefore distinct.

I heard a voice chanting in the distance and I followed, knowing as certainly as I knew my name that it was Philip Sunbear. It was only when I had walked the length of the grove that I saw first the brilliant red band across Philip's forehead and then his deeply furrowed face, with a smile of welcome that I remembered from before.

He was standing at the edge of the willow grove beside the bent saplings of that year's growth, which he had apparently woven into a circular form. It reminded me of a honeycomb because of the small bee-hole opening. There was smoke issuing from the enclosure, and it rushed through the branches, in fingerlike strands rising and dispersing into the air.

"Another earth house," Philip said, answering my thoughts. "This one is for purification. Help me carry these stones inside; the burning logs have now turned to coals. Once these rocks have been heated we will be ready for the sweat."

"Okay," I said. I understood. But to myself I questioned both my readiness and my ability to enter this rite. Philip had promised to train me, but he had not stated the conditions required before he would accept me as his pupil.

I knew enough not to speak. Instead, I watched attentively while he readied the opening and spread blankets over the bent willow "roof" of the lodge.

My mind had turned from questions and doubts into an unfamiliar stillness that brought me to a deeper place of acceptance, but one in which my body was still in fear.

Philip was ready, and began to strip, motioning for me to do the same. We entered the lodge, crawling on all fours and sat across from one another on our haunches.

It was pitch black inside the claustrophobic space, and the heat was intense. Philip threw water on the rocks and it sizzled and steamed, sending vapors throughout the closed chamber. Again and again Philip poured water over the rocks, and now the heavy, moist air was burning my lungs and the heat had become unbearable.

I wanted to flee, but fought to stay, knowing I must not give up. It was only the presence of Philip that prevented the terror from the heat and claustrophobia from taking over my body. It was only then that I faced my fears, and it was only in controlling myself that I realized for the first time that I was not my body, but something else—what could that be but a hidden director or witness. It must be a guide for the body and for something else. . . .

"Now we go out," Philip said. Once again, I entered ordinary time. Sunbear poured water over my head. When I didn't react, he poured water over me again, and then again. "All right," he said, and I could see that for some reason, he was pleased. "Back inside now."

Philip continued to pour water over the rocks. I lost all sense of gravity, and then, although I felt I was in my normal waking state, I began to have dreams. And as I dreamed, Philip's chanting moved through my reveries.

But none of it, the chanting or the dreams, was understandable, belonging to regions unfamiliar and different from anything I had known before. The dreams slowly ended, but the chanting remained, moving deeper and deeper inside me, at first blending with the wind and the drizzling rain outside, then slowly turning deeper into a blessing that I knew included me.

When it was over and we were dressed, we looked at each other in silence, knowing that words and spirit cannot always join hands. I could see in Philip's eyes that he saw me differently now, and I had to believe that I *was* different, and that we were now bound together on the journey he had promised.

I was on my bike again and riding as before, without looking back at the willow grove that would never again be for me what it was before.

The wind moved over my face as I rode. I felt the immensity of everything around me, as well as my place in it—a small speck of movement, inside a wondrous order of life which had no name and which I could experience without the need for words.

Feeling the vastness of everything as it moved over me, I found myself staring up into clouds that were a moving mix of dark and light, the dark clouds threatening more rain or thunder, beside the white, wind-blown clouds. The sun was hidden from view, sometimes casting its light, and at other times not.

As I watched and wondered at the charged elements of life that move over us and around us, I began to see something in this interplay that was also in me, something so personal I felt possessed by the message it was sending me.

The dark clouds became all the unexamined parts of myself: my strange behavior, often dark and brooding, selfish, and cruel, but at other times, full of light and laughter and kindness—but never completely at peace—and I saw that only the sun could reconcile the two.

For the sun was light, and the light was truth, and the truth meant for me that I must face myself without fear, regret, or judgment, simply to see, as the sun would, my two natures, with a forgiveness that could reconcile the warring but necessary differences that need not divide me.

In that moment, the lessons of my life became

clear to me. I saw that it isn't enough just to have experiences, one has to understand their meaning, and that it is this understanding that makes growth possible. There is a reason for everything under the sun.

I had never known why I had released the muskie I had caught, I only knew that I had to—but now I understood that in releasing it to its destiny I was liberated to find the same possibility in myself.

And Hannah had taught me that it is not enough to respect animals, for it is only in kindness that we come to understand how we are related. More than anything, we were meant to be their guardians on this earth.

And that Crazy Eli had come to me to teach me that one must be oneself, even if persecuted, because that is a small price to pay to be true to one's life. This life, which is the gift we pay for by being all that we were meant to be.

about the author

David Kherdian is the award-winning author of more than fifty books that include poetry, novels, memoirs, and children's books, as well as critical studies, translations, and retellings. He is the winner of the Newbery Honor Award for *The Road from Home,* and other honors including the Jane Addams Peace Award, the Friends of American Writers Award, the Lewis Carroll Shelf Award, and the *Boston Globe/Horn Book* Award. He was the editor of *Ararat* magazine and the founding editor of *Forkroads: A Journal of Ethnic-American Literature.* Kherdian lives with his wife, Caldecott medal winner Nonny Hogrogian, near Portland, Oregon.